Maroon Cosmopolitics

Studies in Global Slavery

Series Editors

Damian Alan Pargas (*Leiden University*)
Jeff Fynn-Paul (*Leiden University*)

Editorial Board

Indrani Chatterjee (*University of Texas at Austin*)
William Clarence-Smith (*University College London*)
Pamela Crossley (*Dartmouth College*)
Seymour Drescher (*University of Pittsburgh*)
Stanley Engerman (*University of Rochester*)
Roquinaldo Ferreira (*Brown University*)
Luuk de Ligt (*Leiden University*)
Paul Lovejoy (*York University*)
Aurelia Martín Casares (*University of Granada*)
Ugo Nwokeji (*University of California, Berkeley*)
Stuart Schwartz (*Yale University*)
Ehud R. Toledano (*Tel Aviv University*)
Nigel Worden (*University of Cape Town*)

VOLUME 6

The titles published in this series are listed at *brill.com/sgs*

Maroon Cosmopolitics

Personhood, Creativity and Incorporation

Edited by

Olívia Maria Gomes da Cunha

BRILL

LEIDEN | BOSTON

Cover illustration: By mixing traditional and modern styles in their clothes and hairs, Maroon Ndyuka women and men carry their drums to celebrate Maroon's Day in the Wanhatti village (Cottica, Suriname), October 10th, 2016 (author: Olívia M. G. Cunha)

The Library of Congress Cataloging-in-Publication Data is available online at http://catalog.loc.gov
LC record available at http://lccn.loc.gov/2018964045

Typeface for the Latin, Greek, and Cyrillic scripts: "Brill". See and download: brill.com/brill-typeface.

ISSN 2405-4585
ISBN 978-90-04-35919-2 (hardback)
ISBN 978-90-04-38806-2 (e-book)

Copyright 2019 by Koninklijke Brill NV, Leiden, The Netherlands.
Koninklijke Brill NV incorporates the imprints Brill, Brill Hes & De Graaf, Brill Nijhoff, Brill Rodopi,
Brill Sense, Hotei Publishing, mentis Verlag, Verlag Ferdinand Schöningh and Wilhelm Fink Verlag.
All rights reserved. No part of this publication may be reproduced, translated, stored in a retrieval system,
or transmitted in any form or by any means, electronic, mechanical, photocopying, recording or otherwise,
without prior written permission from the publisher.
Authorization to photocopy items for internal or personal use is granted by Koninklijke Brill NV provided
that the appropriate fees are paid directly to The Copyright Clearance Center, 222 Rosewood Drive,
Suite 910, Danvers, MA 01923, USA. Fees are subject to change.

This book is printed on acid-free paper and produced in a sustainable manner.

Contents

Acknowledgements VII
List of Illustrations IX
Notes on Contributors XI

Introduction: Exploring Maroon Worlds on the Move 1
Olívia Maria Gomes da Cunha

PART 1
(Re) Encounters

1 A Half-Century of "Bush-Negro" Studies 35
Richard Price

2 Why the African Gods Failed the Aukan Maroons 54
H.U.E. Thoden van Velzen

PART 2
Effects

3 Research on Maroon Languages and Language Practices among
Matawai and Kwinti Maroons 83
Bettina Migge

4 Representations, Sexuality and Male-Female Relations among
the Boni of the Maroni Valley, French Guiana, at the Turn
of the Twentieth Century 117
Jean Moomou

5 New Lives for Ndyuka Women: "Everything's Changed but the Men" 147
Diane Vernon

6 Performing Ethnicity as a Way of Contesting Removals: Bureaucratic
Strategies and Affirmation of Busikonde Ways of Dwelling
in Soolan (French Guiana) 177
Clémence Léobal

PART 3
Incorporations

7   Spirits and Pain in the Making of Ndyuka Politics   203
     Stuart Strange

8   Funerals, Rhetorics, Rules and Rulers in Upper Suriname   234
     Rogério Brittes W. Pires

9   Self-Fashioning and Visualization among the Cottica Ndyuka   268
     Olívia Maria Gomes da Cunha

PART 4
Creations

10   Modeling Cultural Adaptability: Maroon Cosmopolitanism and the
      Banamba Dance Contest   307
      Corinna Campbell

11   "Real Bushinengué": Guianese Maroon Music in Transition   330
      Kenneth Bilby and Rivke Jaffe

12   An Anthropologist's Dilemma: Maroon Tembe in the
      Twenty-First Century   350
      Sally Price

Index   375

Acknowledgements

This book project would have been impossible had many of its contributors not accepted an unusual invitation, made by a beginner in Maroon studies, to participate in a two-day conference held in Rio de Janeiro on April 28–29, 2014. This event was a unique experiment in which pioneering scholars could meet up again, but also get to know those just starting their work in the field, sharing and exchanging ideas, ongoing research projects, and ethnographic material.

The conference at which most of the papers were presented, entitled 'Maroons and Businenges in the Guianas: persons, times and places,' was organized by the Laboratory of Anthropology and History (LAH), a research nucleus linked to the Graduate Program in Social Anthropology (PPGAS), and hosted by the Museu Nacional, and by the Casa da Ciência, Federal University of Rio de Janeiro (UFRJ). The Conference was generously funded by Brazilian national institutions supporting research on science and technology (in 2013-2014), namely CNPq (the National Council for Scientific and Technological Development) and CAPES (the Coordination for the Improvement of Higher Education Personnel). I thank all the PPGAS and UFRJ graduate students, also members of LAH, for their active participation in the event. I am grateful to Rogério B. W. Pires for his valuable support toward the executive organization of the meeting.

I am greatly indebted to all authors who presented and discussed their papers with students and scholars at the Museu Nacional, to those who, for various reasons, were unable to attend but sent their chapters to be part of this project, as well as others who have engaged in subsequent steps during the preparation of this volume. I thank professor Marjo de Theije for have introduced to Suriname. I would like to express my gratitude to my colleagues and friends Ine Apapoe and Thomas Polimé, respectively, scholars in political science and anthropology, both Maroon Ndyuka. Although for other reasons, their contributions could not be included in the book, their participation and continued dialogue throughout the process of its preparation have helped shape the final result of the project. My thanks to the Slavery Global Series' editors and Brill executive editors' support. Additional work toward writing and preparing the manuscript was supported by an intense and productive visiting professor fellowship at the University of Amsterdam (UvA), generously funded by the Royal Netherlands Academy of Arts and Sciences (KNAW), and I especially wish to thank Rivke Jaffe for her collegiality, academic partnership, and friendship during the Autumn of 2017 when I was working at UvA. Finally, my thanks to Rogério Viana, for his assistance in the preparation of the manuscript, Clémence Léobal, Richard Price and Alex van Stirpriaan for have granted me permission to use their maps, and to David Rodgers for the careful work of translation and editing some chapters of the volume.

Illustrations

Figures

2.1 Bigi Gadu Oraclel (H.U.E. Thoden van Velzen, 1962) 63

2.2 Gaan Tata's Oracle in Diitabiki (H.U.E. Thoden van Velzen, 2004) 64

2.3 Dance of the Papagadu mediums. Diitabiki, Tapanahoni (H.U.E. Thoden van Velzen, 1962) 68

3.1 The village of Bethel on the upper Saramacca River: view from the river (Bettina Migge, 2017) 92

3.2 Inside the village of Bethel on the upper Saramacca River (Bettina Migge, 2017) 93

4.1 Sawanie Pinas, painting 'A pasi fu lobi' (Jean Moomou, 2005) 126

5.1 House in an agricultural hamlet, Gaakaba (Diane Vernon, 1979) 154

5.2 House in the village of Malobi, constructed 1950s (Diane Vernon, n/d) 155

5.3 Young woman embroidering a pangi, Tabiki 1977 (Diane Vernon, 1977) 157

5.4 Lavishly decorated pangis (Diane Vernon, 2012) 158

5.5 Maroon market woman, SLM (Diane Vernon, 2013) 162

5.6 In a Catholic church in La Charbonière (Diane Vernon, 2013) 166

5.7 Cluster of spontaneous Maroon dwellings in SLM (Diane Vernon, 2011) 169

6.1 Lili's genealogical tree (Clémence Léobal, 2017) 186

6.2 The houses of Lili's family (Clémence Léobal, 2017) 187

6.3 "Awassa dead-end" in the final housing project (Clémence Léobal, 2017) 195

9.1 Mungotapu Village group at Poolo Boto in Moengo 2013 (Olívia M. G. Cunha, 2013) 292

9.2 A Poolo Boto being registered by Cottica Ndyuka's cameras in Wanhatti (Olívia M. G. Cunha, 2016) 295

9.3 Ovia Ollo's boto (Olívia M. G. Cunha, 2013) 297

11.1 Aluku Maroon women dancing Songe (Kenneth Bilby, 2007) 333

11.2 Drummer Miefii Moesé (Kenneth Bilby, 1987) 335

11.3 Local Song, a Ndyuka-Aluku Maroon dance band (Kenneth Bilby, 1987) 339

11.4 Rastafari youth in front of traditional Aluku Maroon house (Kenneth Bilby, 1985) 341

11.5 Paul Neman, member of Ndyuka-Aluku Maroon dance band (Kenneth Bilby, 1987) 342

11.6 CD by Aluku Maroon reggae band Positif Vibration (Kenneth Bilby, 2008) 343

11.7 Poster advertising Jamaican reggae artist Richie Spice's 2009 tour (Kenneth Bilby, 2009) 344

X ILLUSTRATIONS

12.1 Calabash bowl carved about 1960 by Anaaweli (Aluku) (Sally Price) 354
12.2 Table top carved by Marcel (Saamaka) (Sally Price) 356
12.3 Tourist art that combines painting with bas-relief (Sally Price) 358
12.4 Cover of Franky Amete, *Colorie tes tableaux tembe* (Sally Price) 364

Maps

0.1 Maroon territories in Suriname and French Guiana (from A.A. van Stipriaan Luiscius & Th. Polimé (eds.). 2009. Kunst van overleven: Marroncultuur uit Suriname. Amsterdam: KIT Publishers, p.7) 3
2.1 Vieira's map of Aukan Territory in 1761 (The National Archives (The Hague: V.B.K.L, nr.2131)) 57
2.2 The three divisions of the Aukan Maroons (1740-1780): Miáfiya, Lukubun and Ndyuka (Clémence Léobal, 2018) 58
2.3 Forest paths leading from the Suriname, Commewijne (Tempati) rivers and Sara Creek to Mama Ndyuka (Clémence Léobal, 2018) 65
3.1 The region of the Matawai villages (Kemper, 2018) 91
6.1 Old and new neighborhoods after removals (Clémence Léobal, 2018) 181
6.2 Lili's residential trajectory: a transborder life (Clémence Léobal, 2017) 182
6.3 The residential trajectory of Franz in Soolan (Clémence Léobal, 2018) 191
6.4 The residential trajectory of Gisela in Soolan (Clémence Léobal, 2018) 192

Notes on Contributors

Richard Price
is an American anthropologist who has taught at Yale, at Johns Hopkins, where he was founding chair of the Department of Anthropology, and at William & Mary, as well as at the Federal University of Bahia and several universities in Paris. He is the author, co-author, or editor of twenty-two books, many of which have won international prizes. A number have focused on Suriname and Guyane, such as The Guiana Maroons, First-Time, To Slay the Hydra, Alabi's World, Stedman's Surinam, Maroon Arts, Two Evenings in Saramaka, On the Mall, Les Marrons, Equatoria, The Root of Roots, and Travels with Tooy: History, Memory, and the African American Imagination. Several address other aspects of the African Diaspora, such as The Birth of African-American Culture, Maroon Societies: Rebel Slave Communities in the Americas and Romare Bearden: The Caribbean Dimension. Together with Sally Price, he has also written a novel about art forgery in Guyane, Enigma Variations. Recently, he has been involved in human rights work on behalf of the Saamaka People—see Rainforest Warriors: Human Rights on Trial and a just-published Saamakatongo version of First-Time called Fesiten. In addition to a book and several articles translated into Portuguese, he has had books translated into Dutch, French, German, and Spanish. With strong ties to the Netherlands, he serves as a book review editor for the New West Indian Guide (published in Leiden) and is an Honorary Member of the Royal Netherlands Institute of Southeast Asian and Caribbean Studies. For more details, see www.richandsally.net.

H.U.E. Thoden van Velzen
studied anthropology at the University of Amsterdam. In 1961-1962 he, and his wife Wilhelmina van Wetering, conducted fieldwork in Ndyuka Maroon villages along the Tapanahoni River. From 1966 to 1969 he was part of a research team of the Africa Studies Centre (Leyden) working in Tanzania. Between 1971 and 1991 he held the chair of cultural anthropology at the University of Utrecht. From 1991 to 1999 he was a professor of cultural anthropology at the Amsterdam School for Social Science Research. From 1991 to the present he is a member of the Royal Academy of Sciences of The Netherlands. Among his main works are The Great Father and the Danger (1988), In the Shadow of the Oracle (2004), Een Zwarte Vrijstaat in Suriname: De Okaanse Samenleving in de 19e en 20e Eeuw (2013) and Een Zwarte Vrijstaat in Suriname: De Okaanse Samenleving in de 18e Eeuw (2011), the first three of those with Wilhelmina van Wetering.

Bettina Migge

is Professor of Linguistics at University College Dublin, Dublin Ireland where she teaches modules on various aspects of language in its social context and language contact. She is also member of the Humanities Institute of Ireland and chercheur-enseignant of the French Research Group SeDyL/CELIA-CNRS (UMR8133). Her research focuses on issues of language variation and change and the role of language contact in language variation. Most recently she has been engaged in research projects and published on the role of contact-induced variation in language documentation and the negotiation of social identities through language in French Guiana and Suriname. Her other research interests are migration and language in Ireland, language and education and historical language contact. Empirically, her work focuses on the creole languages of Suriname and French Guiana, the Gbe languages (Benin, Togo) and varieties of English worldwide. Besides numerous publications on historical, descriptive and sociolinguistic aspects of Maroon languages, she published with Isabelle Léglise Exploring Language in a Multilingual Context (2013).

Jean Moomou

is a Ph.D. in history and civilization at the École des Hautes Études en Sciences. He is lecturer at the Université des Antilles (DPLSH de Saint-Claude en Guadeloupe). He is author of *Le monde des Marrons du Maroni en Guyane 1772-1860* (2004), *Les marrons Boni de Guyane* (2013), and *Le monde des Marrons du Maroni en Guyane* (editor, 2004), and editor (with APFOM) of *Sociétés marronnes des Amériques*, Actes du colloque, Saint-Laurent-du-Maroni, Guyane (2015).

Diane Vernon

has a PhD. in the École des Hautes Etudes en Sciences Sociales and has worked for decades in the Franck Joly Hospital Center of Western Guiana, where she combined medical work with anthropological research. She has published Money Magic in A Modernizing Maroon Society (1985) and La Représentation du Corps chez les Noirs Marrons Ndjuka (1992) and a number of articles. Currently she educates inter-cultural staffs in the same hospital twice a year, teaches cultural mediation courses in French Guiana and works on the material about the maroons gathered in the last thirty years.

Clémence Léobal

is a post-doctoral Fellow at the Ecole des Hautes Etudes en Sciences Sociales in Paris (Labex Tepsis). She defended her PhD thesis at the University Paris Descartes in 2017, entitled: 'Osu', 'shacks' and 'projects'. Redrawing the boundaries

NOTES ON CONTRIBUTORS

of the city in Soolan (Saint-Laurent-du-Maroni, French Guiana). She has recently published: "La blancheur bakaa, une majorité bien spécifique : race, classe et ethnicité dans les situations de démolition à Saint-Laurent-du-Maroni, Guyane", Asylon(s).Digitales 15.

Stuart Strange
has a Ph.D. in Anthropology at the University of Michigan. His research focuses on the semiotic comparison of Ndyuka and Indo-Surinamese Guyanese ritual, focusing particularly on divination, oratory and materiality. He engages interactional analysis to explore how forms of speech performance are generative of categories of sociality—particularly kinship, ethnicity, labor and gender. His work seeks to understand how spirit possession has been a key technology for elaborating alternative ethical/cosmological worlds in the post-slavery/indenture Guianas.

Rogério Brittes W. Pires
has a Ph.D in Social Anthropology at Museu Nacional, Federal University of Rio de Janeiro (UFRJ) and was a CAPES junior post-doctoral fellow at the Federal University of Minas Gerais (UFMG). His Ph.D dissertation is an ethnography about funerary rites among the Saamaka of Upper Suriname, and since 2015 he has done research on the topics of war and land rights among the Guiana Maroons. Before that, he has written a Master's thesis on the anthropological concept of fetish. He is the author of more than ten articles and book chapters on themes ranging from sexuality and religion to politics and economy.

Olívia Maria Gomes da Cunha
is Associate Professor of Anthropology, at the Museu Nacional, Federal University of Rio de Janeiro. Her Ph.D. dissertation on vagrancy and identification science in Rio de Janeiro in the early 20th century was awarded and published by Arquivo Nacional in 2002. In 2002 she received a John Simon Guggenheim Foundation fellowhip. She was a postdoctoral fellow at Harvard University (1999-2000), visiting-professor at the New York University (2006-2007), the University of Amsterdam (2017), and Tinker Visiting-Professor at the University of Chicago (2018). Her research for Guggenheim resulted in a forthcoming book on ethnography, archives, and artifacs of knowledge in Cuba, Brazil and US. She has published on postemancipation and social movements in Brazil and Cuba, and her current research is about art, creativity, and other cultural and political transformations among the maroon Cottica Ndyuka in Moengo, Eastern Suriname, after the late 1980s civil war.

Corinna Campbell

is Assistant Professor of Music at Williams College. Her research focuses on music and dance in the African Diaspora and West Africa, with a specialization in the traditional genres of the Suriname Maroons. Her primary interests include performance-educational strategies in bridging cultural divides, music/dance interconnections, and the uses of music, dance, and related social discourses in navigating broader systems of power. Campbell received her M.M. from Bowling Green State University and her Ph.D. from Harvard University. Her first manuscript, The Cultural Work: Maroon Performance in Paramaribo, Suriname is forthcoming.

Kenneth Bilby

is Research Associate in the Department of Anthropology at the Smithsonian Institution and Visiting Professor at the University of Colorado at Boulder. An anthropologist and ethnomusicologist, he has carried out fieldwork in various parts of the Caribbean and in West Africa. He has published widely on history, language, music, and the politics of culture in the Caribbean. One of his special interests is Maroon peoples of the Americas. He has carried out long-term fieldwork among two such peoples, the Moore Town Maroons of Jamaica and the Aluku (Boni) of French Guiana and Suriname, and has published numerous articles and book chapters based on this research. His book, True-Born Maroons (University Press of Florida, 2005)—a study of Jamaican Maroon oral narratives based on fieldwork spanning nearly three decades—won the American Historical Association's Wesley-Logan Prize. He is also co-author with Peter Manuel and Michael Largey of Caribbean Currents: Caribbean Music from Rumba to Reggae (Temple University Press, 1995, 2006). His most recent book (co-authored with Jerome Handler) is Enacting Power: The Criminalization of Obeah in the Anglophone Caribbean, 1760-2011 (University of the West Indies Press, 2012). He is currently at work on a book probing the complex cultural milieus from which the urban popular music of Jamaica (from ska through rocksteady, reggae, and dancehall) emerged. Centering on in-depth conversations with the music's creators, research for the book was supported in part by a Guggenheim Fellowship.

Rivke Jaffe

is an associate professor at the Centre for Urban Studies and the Department of Human Geography, Planning and International Development Studies at the University of Amsterdam. She previously held teaching and research positions at Leiden University, the University of the West Indies, and the Royal Netherlands Institute of Southeast Asian and Caribbean Studies (KITLV).

NOTES ON CONTRIBUTORS

Her anthropological research focuses primarily on intersections of the urban and the political, and includes an interest in topics such as popular culture, environmental pollution, and organized crime. She has conducted extensive anthropological fieldwork on these and other topics in Jamaica, Curaçao and Suriname. She is currently leading a major research program on public-private security assemblages in Kingston, Jerusalem, Miami, Nairobi and Recife, studying how urban governance changes through hybrid forms of security provision.

Sally Price
is an American anthropologist who has taught at several universities in the United States (e.g., Stanford, Princeton, and William & Mary), as well as the Federal University of Bahia (Brazil) and the Sorbonne in Paris. She is the author, co-author, or co-editor of fifteen books. A number of these have focused on Suriname and French Guiana, such as Co-Wives and Calabashes, Maroon Arts: Cultural Vitality in the African Diaspora, Two Evenings in Saramaka, On the Mall, Les Marrons, and Equatoria. Several address other aspects of the African Diaspora, such as Caribbean Contours and Romare Bearden: The Caribbean Dimension. Together with Richard Price, she has also written a novel about art forgery, Enigma Variations. But she is best known for her critical studies of the place of "primitive art" in the imaginaire of Western viewers: Paris Primitive: Jacques Chirac's Museum on the Quai Branly and Primitive Art in Civilized Places. In addition to the Brazilian edition of this last (Arte primitiva em centros civilizados, Editora UFRJ), she has had books translated into Dutch, French, German, Italian, and Spanish. With strong ties to the Netherlands, she serves as a book review editor for the New West Indian Guide (published in Leiden) and is an Honorary Member of the Royal Netherlands Institute of Southeast Asian and Caribbean Studies and a member of the Royal Dutch Academy of Arts and Sciences. For more details, see www.richandsally.net.

Introduction: Exploring Maroon Worlds on the Move

Olívia Maria Gomes da Cunha

The idea of 'transformation' not only expresses movement but also some kind of shift in the form or quality of someone or something. More intriguingly, it always contains a referential element that enables the thing or person transformed to be seen in relation to that which it no longer is. Anthropology has always seen transformation as a problem, a synonym of 'cultural shift,' a harbinger of cultural (and less frequently, demographic) loss and decay. Inevitably, when referring to the situation existing previously, the 'past' is depicted as the richest moment, the place and time of plenitude. Although these assumptions may have come under sustained critique over recent decades, the study of some subjects still seems to resist coming to terms with the epistemological orientation that invented them. Studies of Maroon populations settled in the forests and cities of Suriname and French Guiana is one such case in point. Various important themes involved in the creation of the 'Maroon peoples' or 'Maroon societies' as anthropological subjects call for more research. The uniqueness of the situation of the Guianese Maroon at the end of the twentieth century, still "the largest surviving population in America" (Price 1996[1976]: xxiv; 2015), has stimulated further historical and ethnographic analyses, and some minor interest in rethinking or challenging the existing theoretical and methodological orientations.[1] This book does not aim to answer this call per se, but rather to capture other effects of the ongoing process of transformation not just experienced and controlled by the Maroon, but also interpreted by them through their own concepts, categories, and cosmopolitical engagements.

---

1 Two important exceptions can be attributed to non-specialists on Maroon societies who have reflected on the role that knowledge of Maroon peoples – specifically the Saamaka – played in the epistemological model responsible for framing so-called Afro-American anthropology since the 1930s: Sidney W. Mintz (1964:50) and David Scott (1991). Curiously, examples of Maroon 'uniqueness,' as it was conceived in Melville and Frances Herskovits' ethnography on the Saamaka, fuelled further debates on 'retention' and 'creolization.' For a response to and engagement with Scott's criticism (1991), see R. Price & S. Price (2003), and R. Price (2001). For a comprehensive discussion of the career of 'creolization' in Afro-American and Caribbeanist anthropology, see Palmié (2007, 2013).

Paradoxically, this analytical orientation, shared in various ways by different authors, does not lead us to adopt a more theoretical engagement with the diverse ethnographic data discussed here. On the contrary, it allows us, via different paths, to pursue a kind of detour in which the ethnography itself comprises both the source and the conceptual toolkit with which we can understand the meanings of the worlds that the Maroon inhabit and transform. These worlds are made and recomposed by a multitude of relations in which Maroon personhood is continually composed and recreated. Below I identify some of the signs, traces and clues – in ethnographies that describe transformations of Maroon socialities and of the anthropology of Afro-American socialities – that precede the production of the present book, but which dialogue closely with it.

∙∙

The Maroon descend from people forcibly brought from the African continent by Dutch, English, Spanish and Portuguese Atlantic slave traders to work in the plantation systems of the Americas, and who resisted the violence of slavery by rebelling and escaping. Throughout the American continent, where social experiences have flourished based on human subjection, forced labour, and regimes of violence associated with the production of goods, hugely impacting Amerindian and African people and their descendants, forms of resistance, escape, alliance-building, and the establishing of new socialities based on kinship and affinity have equally multiplied. In the Guianas, the fugitives headed to the difficult-to-access rainforests, dispersing into different settlements in which linguistically and politically distinct groups were formed. From the eighteenth century, populations of fugitives calling themselves Saamaka, Matawai and Kwinti were located in villages close to the Suriname, Saramaka and Coppename Rivers and the central region of the Dutch colony, while the Ndyuka, Paamaka and Aluku were spread across territories along the shores of the Tapanahoni, Maroni and Lawa Rivers on the border with the French colony (Price 1973; 1990). The singularity of the settlements, the centrality of kinship in their social structure, the omnipresence of the ancestors, and the richness of Maroon cosmology, languages and arts, but also the rapid transformations that were already changing their ways of life, attracted the attention of travellers and explorers, historians and anthropologists who tried to analyse Maroon Societies over the twentieth century.[2]

---

2 For a comprehensive discussion of primary sources and the scholarly and non-scholarly bibliography on Guianese Maroon peoples, see Price (1996[1976] and this volume). For comparative analyses involving Jamaican Maroon and Brazilian Quilombola populations see, respectively, Bilby (1983, 1997) and Price (1998, 2007) and Gomes (2002).

INTRODUCTION: EXPLORING MAROON WORLDS ON THE MOVE

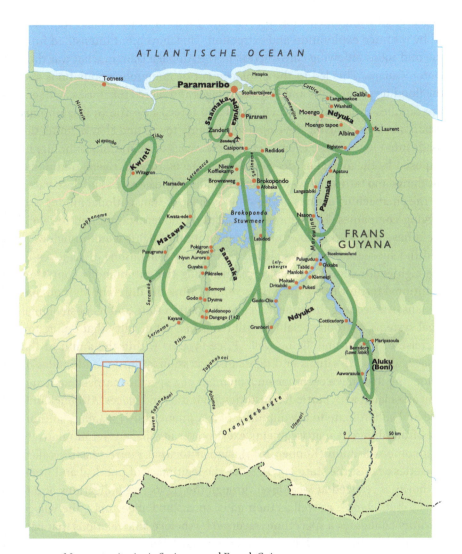

MAP 0.1 Maroon territories in Suriname and French Guiana
SOURCE: VAN STIRPRIAN AND POLIMÉ, 2009:7

Richard Price (1975, 1983), H.U.E. Thoden van Velzen & Wilhelmina Van Wetering (1988) Silvia de Groot (1969) and Kenneth Bilby (1990, 1994, 1997), among others, have described the transformation of Maroon societies as a result of territorial, clan and magical disputes between distinct groups of fugitives, as well as their contacts with slaves living under the control of the plantation systems and representatives of the colonial forces. Since the mid-nineteenth century, Maroon men have left their villages and crossed borders in search of work and access to consumer goods in frontier areas dominated by resource exploration and extraction. This movement intensified from the mid-1960s following construction of the Afobaka Dam in what was then Dutch Guiana. This led to the displacement of numerous populations and the flooding of Saamaka and Ndyuka villages and sacred territories, with entire families expelled from their lands and forced to settle in insalubrious urban outskirts, housing developments, shanty towns and shacks lining the roads into towns. These events set off new waves of migration, voluntary or imposed by the arrival of 'development' projects. Forests, rivers, traditional dwellings and territories were directly or indirectly destroyed and desecrated by the encroaching actions of the state or those of transnational mining and logging companies. The winding tentacles of modernization and development have also worked to erode the recognition of rights won through wars and the subsequent treaties signed by the first generations of fugitives in the eighteenth century (Bilby 1997), including the autonomous control of traditional territories by authorities representing the different Maroon matriclans. Anteceding the appearance of the nation state and its postcolonial legal systems, Maroon socialities still reaffirm a set of rules that define the exercise of power and 'living well' (Price 1975:32) within the ambit of the village, along with rituals and rights of succession, affinities and modes of belonging that make each person a member of a specific matrisegment and clan associated with particular histories, divinities and places. Although unified and subordinate to the authority of a supreme chief (gaaman), authorities from different matrisegments exert power at village level in relatively autonomous fashion (Köbben 1979), similar to what Pierre Clastres called 'societies against the state' (1971). Since the legitimacy of political and ritual authority is realized at local level through the rights and obligations of different matriclans – as well as their gods, spirits and ancestors – the village territory configures a spacetime traversed by sociocosmic relations that participate in the life of each person and their matriclan.

The impacts of these migrations in the nineteenth and twentieth centuries have been described by historians and anthropologists in a multitude of ways. Some have concentrated on exploring a process of approximation and assimilation. Terms like 'isolation' and 'social change' appear in descriptions of the confrontation between the actions of colonial governments and negotiations with traditional authorities. The premise of 'integration' not only informed the strategies used by state institutions and agents and Christian missionaries: Maroon responses to the growing desire to intervene in and control their ways of life were seen as resistance to 'integration' into national society (Kahn 1931; F. & M. Herskovits 1934; Lier 1919, 1940; Hurault 1958, 1961; de Groot 1969).

INTRODUCTION: EXPLORING MAROON WORLDS ON THE MOVE

At the same time, the 'social' effects of these processes mobilized more than just the migrants and traditional authorities: a profusion of beings, spirits and gods acted to define, in their own terms, not only the destinies of the villages, but also those of the Maroon person in a myriad of new relations with the non-Maroon universe. A new generation of anthropologists pursuing field research in Maroon villages from the 1960s onward made use of innovative theoretical approaches to reveal the relations maintained with other important beings and agencies in the social times and spaces of the villages and matriclans (R. Price 1983 [1976]; Elst 1971; Köbben 1979; Green 1974; Lenoir 1975; Beet & Sterman 1981; S. Price 1983; Thoden van Velzen & van Wetering 1988, 2004; Vernon 1985, 1992; Bilby 1990; Hoogbergen 1990, 2009; Price & Price 2003a, 1999). In these analyses, the relationships between people and their matriclans were carefully detailed, offering a rich ethnography of the ways in which the Maroon person and Maroon sociality are composed. They also revealed the effects produced by these entities and forces amid the migrations and transformations imposed by colonial projects designed to 'develop' and 'modernize' the interior (Thoden van Velzen & Van Wetering 2001).

Richard Price (1970, 1975), Andre Köbben (1979), Wilhelmina van Wetering (1973) and H.U.E. Thoden van Velzen (1966a, 1966b) were all quick to observe that the relations between villages, and between these settlements and the coast, encompassed a wide range of disputes, conflicts, witchcraft accusations and the flourishing of what they call 'messianic cults' in the regions drained by the Suriname, Sara, Tapanahoni and Cottica Rivers. Studying the migrational dynamic of Saamaka men from a village close to Pikílio, a description that appears in his first texts published at the start of the 1970s, Price (1975) observed a clear break in continuity with the previous generation: the dynamics by which Maroon men (and women) circulated through non-Maroon territories indicated a complex and intense relationship with the non-Maroon population. Reflecting on the changes occurring over more than 50 years of 'Bush Negro Studies,' Price (this collection) writes, "looking back over that same half-century in terms of scholarly publications about Maroons in Suriname and French Guiana, I am struck by how much of our understanding of these societies stems from that anthropological fieldwork carried out in the 1960s and 1970s."

These studies played a crucial role in stimulating wider academic interest in the histories and everyday experiences of Maroon peoples in the Guianas, as well as their implications for studies of multilingualism, gender, ethnobotany (Andel et al. 2009; Hoffman 2009; Jolivet & Vernon 2007; Groenendijk 2006), mining (Theije 2015, 2010; Theije & Heemskerk 2009; Hoogbergen & Kruijt 2004), logging and land rights (Heemskerk 2000, 2000a; Kambel & Mackay 1999), relations with Amerindian populations (Kambel & MacKay 1999; Collomb & Jolivet 2008;

Collomb 2008; Dupuy 2008; Hoffman 2009; Theije 2010; Guyon 2011; Bright & Grotti 2014), the explosion of 'traditional art' markets, and other themes central to the anthropology of Afro-American populations (Bilby 2000; S. Price 1982, 1993, 2001; S. Price & R. Price 2015; Jolivet 2008; Parris 2011; Sanderse & Jaffe 2009; Bilby & Jaffe, this volume). Notably, the specialist literature over the last few years has focused on the continual wandering of Maroon women and men in ethnographic contexts that have been increasingly exposed to a massive influx of technologies, roads, cars, motors, cameras, peace corps, prospectors, loggers and transnational mining companies (Price 2011; van Stirpriaan 2015, 2011, 2009; Jolivet 2007). Contexts in which, through ambiguous but nonetheless creative interactions with the bakaa, the 'past,' 'history,' 'tradition' and difference are produced. Musical and choreographic expressions, for example, generate corporal, rhythmic and thematic dialogues among Maroon youths who live or work in the cities, but still maintain connections with the villages (Bilby 2001; Campbell, this volume). In these displacements and intermittent sojourns in the cities (Léobal 2016, 2015, this volume), Maroon people have made increasing use of the different Maroon creole languages and, at the same time, valorised linguistic resources created in multilinguistic contexts – as Migge (2007, this volume) observes in her account of the Kwinti and Matawai settled in Bitagron and Bethel villages and in Paramaribo, and of the 'pan-Maroon' strategies of communication via radios in Saint Laurent du Maroni (Migge 2011). Aesthetic experimentations have incessantly incorporated new languages, knowledge and technologies in the production of landscapes and acoustic environments that are defined by Maroons themselves as businengue (Bilby & Jaffe; Campbell, both this volume), or that redesign other modes of visualization via gospel language and media (Cunha, this volume). Beyond all the demographic, migratory, environmental, socioeconomic and political factors – which include the Interior War (1986–1992) (Thoden van Velzen 1990; Kruijt & Hoogbergen 2005) and the emergence of political parties (Scholtens 1994) formed by Maroon members of the Surinamese parliament – and beyond the fact that young people with university degrees are now writing on different aspects of these social changes (Polimé 2007; Amoksi 2009; Moomou 2004; Apapoe 2017), the recent directions taken by the interest in 'Maroon culture' in Suriname and French Guiana (S. Price, Campbell, Cunha, both this volume) mostly reflect transformations occurring at village level and in the urban peripheries.

The present volume, Maroon Cosmopolitics: personhood, creativity and incorporation, provides a detailed examination of the contemporary configurations and cosmopolitical effects of these transformations by listening attentively to the new modes of Maroon circulation and presence in the Guianas – what some authors have called a population 'explosion' (Price 2013)

INTRODUCTION: EXPLORING MAROON WORLDS ON THE MOVE

and a proliferation of 'cultural forms' (Bilby 2000) over recent decades. Rather than searching for signs of a dilution of traditional Maroon life, the authors assembled in this volume look to describe, through their distinct styles and theoretical orientations, multidirectional displacements and forms of circulation, recognizing that the Maroons have never stopped returning, physically and spiritually, to the village of their matriclan at various or indeed numerous moments of their lives.

Creation and Cosmopolitics

On April 6th 2015, the death of an octogenarian Saamaka man was reported in Guianese newspapers and on the social networks that interconnect Maroon and non-Maroon users. However, the knowledge, travels and spiritual wanderings of the kapiten and óbiaman Alexander Tooy[3] had already reached an academic audience thanks to the publication of *Travels with Tooy: history, memory, and the African American imagination,* by Richard Price (2010). The description of the encounters between Tooy and the anthropologist provide a unique insight into the complex and often bewildering paths of what we could call Maroon ontology – a universe composed of multiple spatial and temporal planes inhabited by beings, ancestors, gods and agencies originating from distant rivers, forests and landscapes. At the same time, Tooy's misadventures with the French judicial system and non-Maroon interlocutors give a sample of the tribulations experienced by Maroon men and women living in the Guianese forests and urban peripheries at the start of the twenty-first century.[4]

Encounters such as the one between Tooy and Richard are not, of course, unique to the anthropology of Maroon societies. They are integral to what, since the end of the nineteenth century, the discipline's practitioners have referred to as 'anthropological knowledge,' but a knowledge always dependent on the existence of one or more interlocutors whose own knowhow is subsequently subject to some kind of interpretation or explanation by a scientific specialist. This in some ways asymmetrical relationship always encompasses diverse forms of interpersonal interaction, whether or not these directly

---

3 Kabiten is the village headmen and óbiaman a shaman, healer and spiritual practitioner. For an example of how Tooy's death was reported in the Guiana press, see "Un sage disparaît." France-Guyane, 2015. http://www.franceguyane.fr/actualite/faitsdivers/un-sage-disparait-238161.php

4 The Maroon population today is estimated at 210,000 people by Richard Price, making up "23% of Suriname's population and 26% of Guyana's" (this volume).

involve other institutional and political connections. Even before Melville and Frances Herskovits' brief summer fieldwork trips to Saamaka territory in 1928 and 1929, other travellers, missionaries, colonial staff, and explorers produced travelogues, reports, academic texts, photographs, and short films of Maroon women and men in their villages somewhere in the Guianas. These registers, 'artefacts of knowledge' (Strathern 1990) emphasizing 'primitiveness' and exoticism, were made out of interactions, encounters, mutual misunderstandings, and negotiations. Maroon people always took an active part in the making of these artefacts by establishing, through various means, the terms in which this knowledge should and could be created. They participated in its production, even when they had little or no idea about the eventual use and fate of their images, secrets, songs and objects. In a way, we could say that the almost three centuries of production of knowledge on Guianese Maroon peoples reflects continuous, as well as political and historically determined, attempts to capture, frame and understand Maroon transformations.

The travels undertaken by Tooy and 'his' anthropologist are, we could say, a magical cartography of many other places, inscriptions of encounters in which anthropologists and other non-Maroon people participate. Tooy's wanderings through spacetimes inhabited by non-human beings compose, side by side with Richard Price's field and archival notes, paths or 'doors' through which Maroon worlds can be accessed. The idea of a 'door' can be used as a metaphor that allows us to grasp how Maroon knowledge comprises a labyrinth of passages, planes, forbidden entrances and intricate pathways to some form of magical existence. At the same time, Tooy made use of this knowledge to live in the world of the *bakaa*. The latter made themselves available as both ontological and political resources. Tooy was able to access 'doors' that led him to the dwellings of spirits and ancestors though an engagement in magical negotiations that involved, among other practices, feeding, buying, taking care, honouring and keeping spiritual powers. But spirits and ancestors also protected him with tools and weapons that enabled him to confront persecution and poverty (Tooy made his living as a spiritual specialist and herbalist).

Tooy's shamanic travels find a myriad of recent and analogous examples in the anthropological literature on Guianese Maroons. This is the case, for instance, of the texts by anthropologist Stuart E. Strange (2016, 2016a), who carried out fieldwork in poor neighbourhoods and outskirts of Paramaribo, as well as the work of ethnobotanists such as Tinde Andel (2009) and Sara Groenendijk (2006), in their wanderings in *kampus*, backyards and *osu* where *bonuman* and *obiaman* live among magical objects, substances, plants and non-human creatures. Shamanism and possession are the main forms of contact with the latter. The recognition of these practices and body languages as

INTRODUCTION: EXPLORING MAROON WORLDS ON THE MOVE 9

the main vehicles for the actualization of the ancestors' presence in everyday life ranges from personal suffering and illness to the quarrels and conflicts involving individuals and their kin. Ancestors, gods and spirits to whom the first are historically associated – ever since the loweten (the first fugitives from captivity) – are often called on to reinstitute order, arbitrate over matriseg-mental disputes, and provide consultation on uses of witchcraft that result in unexpected deaths and sicknesses, or invoked to remind people of the duties and penalties imposed by vengeful spirits in the past. Through possession and divination, the ancestors and their auxiliary forces speak to the living. As Sally Price and Richard Price (2015, 2017), as well as, Migge and Strange (this volume, see also Borges 2013, 2014), have shown, language is a key element in mobili-zation of the body and the senses, signalling a shift of 'presences,' the partici-pation of human and non-human interlocutors in the conversation. 'Language practices' are not only an important aspect of the role of Maroon Creole lan-guages in internal and intra-group processes of differentiation, as Migge ob-serves, but a medium of access to other socionatures. Spiritual language thus reminds people not only of the power of the other-than-human beings in Ma-roon lives, it also instantiates the body and its relationships as the terrain for the production of Maroon ontology.

In 1962, another couple of young anthropologists – H.U.E. Thoden van Velzen and Ineke Wilhelmina van Wetering – met a Ndyuka woman and her songs, sung in an *ampuku* (bush spirit) language in Diitabiki village, situated in the Tapanahoni region. Recalling their encounter with Ma Kaabu, the me-dium of a powerful spirit, Thoden van Velzen turns to the same metaphor of the 'door' to describe a similar sense of revelation: "It was like a door opened onto another world" (Cunha & Thoden van Velzen 2016:266). The pioneer-ing ethnographies of the journeys between worlds made by figures like Ma Kaabu (Thoden van Velzen 1988) and Tooy (Price 2008) crystallized, each in its own way, a slow yet important change in orientation, already under way in the studies produced by anthropologists and other specialists in the Ma-roon societies of the Guianas. Attention has gradually shifted away from fo-cusing on specific groups of descendants of men and women who escaped from the slave plantations over more than three centuries of English, Dutch and French colonialism in the region. This earlier classic ethnographic mod-elling – framed by geopolitical borders and delimited institutions, generally in confrontation with the State, its own institutions and its colonial or na-tional representatives – idealized and reified the reference points of Maroon societies in the face of inexorable state and capitalist forces of 'integration.' However, the modes of Maroon territorialization (Deleuze and Guattari 1987) explored from diverse angles in this book indicate the exhaustion of this particular framing. Through the 'cultural' innovations (Wagner 1981) fabricated by ethnographers and their Maroon interlocutors, these studies allow us to learn about the worlds created by the anthropologies of Maroon and Afro-American societies, while remaining attentive to the conceptual modulations produced of anthropology more widely. One alternative to the excessively narrow approach that still appears to hold back other possibilities for analysis and comparison is, perhaps, to explore the recent contributions made by studies of populations in the Amazonian and Guianese regions with which Maroon peoples have historically engaged in all kinds of different relations (Rivière 1984; Gallois 2005, Brightman and Grotti 2014; Collomb and Jolivet 2008; Guyon 2011; Price 2010). The amplification of the anthropology of Guianese Maroon societies – or, seen from another angle, its reapproximation with Amerindian ethnology – allow us to, at the very least, abandon not only the earlier analytic frameworks imbued with the idea of irremediable 'cultural change,' but especially their 'local double,' namely the debate surrounding the theme of 'creolization' versus 'continuity' or 'retention' (Trouillot 2002; Palmié 2013; Scott 1991; Stewart 2016). This path can lead us through other 'doors' and offer, to paraphrase Eduardo Viveiros de Castro (2012) in his reflection on recent transformations in the study of Amazonian indigenous cosmologies, "more effective methods of transfusing the possibilities" opened up by Maroon worlds – as revealed by Ma Kaabu and Tooy, for example – "within the glocal cosmopolitical circulation, which finds itself in a clear state of acute intoxication" (2012:152).

An inquiry into these new modes of existence connecting the persons and families who circulate between towns and villages, and into how these modes link up with the production of the Maroon person, with the practices of creating artefacts and material forms that inhabit different cosmological universes and, finally, with the mechanisms used to incorporate knowledge, things and relations into Maroon socialities, will shed further light on a continuous process of composition, approximation and transformation. This process necessitates observing and participating in the designs of the beings that constitute 'nature' (Kohn 2013), not only the animals, plants, rivers and all kinds of entities that inhabit them, but the sets of relations that they establish among themselves and that infuse the spaces and times of the forest. As Descola (1992, 2005) and Viveiros de Castro (1998) have pointed out, it entails rejecting the centrality of the 'human' found in our conception of society, and, at the same time, opposing the dualism in which so-called 'Maroon culture' (S. Price, this volume) appears as the forefront of the creation of a unique and 'Creolized' society, distinct from the 'nature' in which it flourishes. As Tinde van Andel (2009, 2010) has observed, the effects of daylight on the forest canopy, tree trunks and the soil, the taboos related to diet and work activities, combined with hunting and fishing techniques, contribute to the production of the *busi* (bush, forest) as a sensory territory, controlled by rules, interdictions and dangers imposed by humans and non-humans. The *busi* is the ancestral territory of the Maroon peoples (and Amerindians) not only because their ancestors found refuge and shelter in it: the latter also brought knowledge and learning on how to participate in the same dynamic socionature made from the circulation of forces through the worlds of the living and the dead. As the Ndyuka shaman Akalali confided to Thoden van Velzen: "Everything has changed for us Aukans, we now live in a new world" (this volume: page 71). By 'new world,' Akalali was undoubtedly not referring to the modern mode that separates itself from (the supposed absence of historicity among) so-called primitive peoples, nor to the partition of colonial territories and governmentality. The old shaman knew and acted in the name of 'bush spirits' (*ampuku*) capable of responding angrily to the abuses of gods associated with the presence of the *bakaa* (Thoden van Velzen & Van Wetering 2004; Vernon 1985).

These encounters involve the composition of existential territories in which 'unknown' worlds and beings are summoned to intervene, act and participate in personal conflicts and political clashes. In dialogue with these entities, Maroon peoples experiment with different relations in which they participate in distinct 'socionatural worlds' (de la Cadena 2010:353), engaging, as Isabelle Stengers, Bruno Latour and others have recently claimed, in multiple cosmopolitics (Stengers 2005:995; Latour 2004; Jensen 2014). For our present purposes, it is important to recognize that although the concept has been intensely debated in diverse areas of the discipline, it has also been used to describe a variety of political engagements of traditional peoples against forms of subjection and capture promoted by states, nations, corporations and their enabling technologies. Paradoxically, there is no agreement either concerning the use of the other concepts and theoretical orientation that inform the ethnographical material explored by the contributors here. The book, though, exploits this multiplicity insofar as it works to reveal, rather than obliterate, differences in perspectives, generational choices and anthropological orientations, seeking above all to preserve the unique dimension of the ethnographic experiences involved. This element, explored by R. Price in the chapter opening the book, appears reaffirmed in this editorial project: though the authors do not share the same ideas about the subject of their study, the differences that emerge from their distinctive research approaches undoubtedly create bridges, connection points and dialogues. As for cosmopolitics, few of the authors make use of the concept. This fact may well initially prompt readers to question the adequacy of its appearance in the book's title. I shall justify its use, however, by exploring some of the motives that led me to organize a volume that combines diverse contributions to the anthropology of Guianese Maroon peoples, highlighting cosmopolitics as the concept that best illuminates the rich material discussed throughout book.

As I have argued elsewhere (Cunha 2016:272) with respect to the myriad situations of mediumship witnessed by the researchers, "[an] intense flow of spirits and unknown forces also assailed the ethnographers, inside and outside the field, albeit by dissimilar paths." What I want to recuperate here is precisely the ways in which other-than-human beings have made themselves present in a long tradition of ethnographic experience. This 'presence,' however, does not mean a special form of communication with the supernatural world, performed directly by the practitioners of the discipline. On the contrary, through divination and possession, these beings spoke with and told histories to the ethnologists, revealing past experiences that involved themselves and their mediums. The latter were asked to create forms of communication with these beings. However, a great deal of this knowledge was not only transferred to, and transformed into, ethnographies, co-authored in some form by the anthropologists: more to the point, much of what anthropology knows about Maroon cosmology and historicity (see, for instance, Thoden van Velzen, this volume) has primarily been spiritual work. So although, with a few exceptions, the role of other-than-human beings has not received much attention with regard to its theoretical implications, nor any real in-depth discussion concerning its methodological dimensions, the extensive literature on Maroon societies produced in the second half of the twenty-century has nonetheless consistently demonstrated the extent to which these beings have acted and participated in the production of the analysed knowledge. In a way we could say that Maroon ethnography has never been a modern and western narrative, but rather a native perspective on the ways in which events stand as 'non-reversible' situations, "yet-to-be-created myths articulated via divination'" (Price 1975:37). Experiences transformed into 'events' are, as Stephan Palmié ironically pointed out, "ghost stories" (2002:3). We therefore need to know how other-than-human beings participate in the anthropological explorations about Maroon modes of existence, but also, and above all, how we have been using the knowledge produced by them.

In this sense, what would an anthropology of Maroon socialities – of the ways in which the Maroon person is composed by layers and different interactions with the 'socionatural worlds' – be if not devoted to learning a way not only to understand but to describe these 'worlds'? Put otherwise, we can argue with Henare, Holbraad and Wastel, that "anthropologists may 'see different worlds' by creating them. On this view, anthropological analysis has little to do with trying to determine how other people think about the world. It has to do with how we must think in order to conceive a world the way they do" (2007:15). A starting point to a much needed shift in perspective would be to pay attention to Maroon personhood as a bundle of relationships in which not only diverse 'entities' may participate, but primarily 'worlds' in a constant flux of actualization. Following Latour (2004, 2004a) and Strathern (1992, 1995), we could say that maroon personhood is not encompassed in a 'subject': rather its subjectivity is distributed across ancestral interactions and spiritual links with the sociocosmos. These relationships are, as other authors have shown us, primarily constituted through kinship. Although Maroon villages are important, then, as instances in which relations between humans and other-than-humans are renewed and nourished, migration does not stop the production of Maroon personhood. Every Maroon person is ontologically and historically linked to a movement of rupture – from slavery, *bakaa* and colonial universes – irrespective of whether they are living in a village or in urban areas. This movement, historians have demonstrated, also implied negotiation, not only with the colonial forces left behind – the plantation world – but primarily with the 'owners' of the landscapes that harboured and protected the fugitives. As a consequence, the acceptance of these two important dimensions of the historical experiences of Guianese Maroons, and how they wield an enormous importance in the making of clans and all forms of segmentation based on alliances and kinship, sheds new light on the cosmopolitics of these distinct forms of sociality. It also, simultaneously, allows us to go beyond 'politics' – such as this term is generally understood in ethnicity-based approaches.

Contemporary Maroon experiences are formed through relationships constituted in the past by their forebears, who intervened in the worlds made by gods brought from Africa or 'found' in the forest (see Thoden van Velzen, this volume), below the rivers, above the skies, peopled by sacred animals, but also by their ancestors buried in the forest who continually return as nêsekis (namesakes), transforming newborn children's lives by imbuing them with qualities and spiritual duties. These relationships – or as Marisol de la Cadena puts it in her analysis of the Peruvian land reform movement, "world-making practices" (2015: 276) – cannot be limited to a 'cultural difference' that would distinguish the Maroons from other national groups with whom they share classrooms, workplaces, neighbourhoods, corporations, government positions, or even houses in Suriname and French Guiana. These differences cannot be accommodated within the nation state because they are made of another socionature. Whether in a village or in the city, each time a Maroon person is born or dies, whenever she suffers or is sick, she or her kin will be affected by the very same forces that actively shaped the history of her matriclan. The idea of a Maroon world (or worlds) that cannot be subsumed to an aggregate of 'cultural and linguistic elements' enables us to carefully reevaluate the use of concepts like 'ethnicity' to describe the emergence of new forms of Maroon or pan-Maroon identities, performed in urban contexts, as well as with the analysis of its complex relations with nationalist movements and policies in Suriname and French Guiana. To adopt this position also inevitably implies a critique of nation state-oriented debates on 'citizenship,' 'integration' or 'Francization' (see Price, Léobal, this volume) which fail to take into account how Maroon politics – performed, for instance, during the discussions in *kuutus* (palaver) (Migge 2004), on the ceremonial rules related to funerals, and the Saamaka concept of *politiki*, as a 'game of rhetorics' (Pires, this volume) – is the realm of unequal distributions of power and obligations among kin and non-kin. Always remembering that Maroon villages and matriclans are not isolated domains or spheres, in most cases *politiki* is connected to allegiances and interferences constituted in complex relationships with the *bakaa lanti* (Surinamese or French governments). If we look to the composition of the main Maroon political parties and their constituencies over the past few years in Suriname, it is not hard to identify the reproduction of the asymmetrical power of some matriclans, as well as their presence in certain villages, acting via the State's political machinations and its allegiances in the 'development politics' in the interior, including in relation to the distribution of resources.[5]

The interactions of Van Wetering & Thoden van Velzen with Ma Kaabu, along with the travels of Tooy described by Price (2010), provide interesting examples of what we could call a 'circulation between worlds'; transits through non-Maroon (*bakaa*) and Maroon (*businenge*) territories that harbour diverse spatiotemporal overlappings and interactions, involving a myriad of human and other-than-human beings. In Tooy's wanderings, these beings not only interact with him, they also compose him, forming part of the modes of incorporation and acquisition of knowledge and the ritual modalities performed by the shaman, turning him into a 'composite' person (Price 2010:290). As a consequence, someone who knows the names of secret forces, sacred languages

---

5 Although some Maroon people are involved in different positions of Surinamese politics, there are two parties whose members are almost exclusively Maroon: the ABOP (Algemene Bevrijdings-en Ontwikkeling Partij) and the BEP (Broederschap en Eenheid in de Politiek). On Maroon political institutions, see Pakosie (1996), on the relations between Maroons and political parties in Suriname during the twentieth century, see Schooltens (1994). Concerning the role of Ndyuka political parties, matriclans and gods during the War of Interior, see Thoden van Velzen (1990). For an exploration of the relations between Amerindians and Maroons (specially the Aluku) and the state and local politics in French Guiana, see Guyon (2010, 2011).

INTRODUCTION: EXPLORING MAROON WORLDS ON THE MOVE

and feared tongues is capable of traversing spacetimes that, in the *bakaa* apperception, oppose the forest and the cities. Tooy recomposes them and makes use of different forms of knowledge in his shamanic wanderings through the bodies of Maroon men and women. Not coincidentally, these journeys traverse ethnic and spatiotemporal boundaries, incorporating spirits and gods linked to the matrilineages of different groups, as well as mediumship and women's bodies. Over the last few decades, scholars of Maroon societies have explored the role of women, the relations between men and women, by looking at the making, exchange and ritual use of specific objects (S. Price 1982; Van Wetering 1966, 1992; Wetering & Thoden van Velzen 1982; Vernon 1985; Vernon this volume; Moomou this volume; Cunha 2018a). By considering native ideas of personhood and the way in which specific objects highlight particular aspects of persons and become intertwined with non-human agencies, these studies have shown that 'things' inhabit Maroon worlds as extensions of relations involving Maroon persons and their counterparts. Sally and Richard Price (2003:56) use the term 'individuation' to refer to the process through which, following the appropriation of a fabric (koosu and pangi), a relation is established between the person and the ancestors (see also S. Price 1983; Polimé & van Stirpriaan 2013).

What the spirit possessing Ma Kaabu and the shamanism of Tooy both conjure is a particular type of communication and specific kinds of relationships with the beings of the forest, the place that they inhabit and the abode of the ancestral spirits. Tooy, for example, not only communicates with beings in the form of spirits invisible to other humans, he dialogues with things that, for these other humans, apparently lack any capacity for communication. Neither can the notion of capture be reduced to a figure of speech. Tobacco, rum and the playing of the *apínti* (drums, drum language) are not just propitiatory objects and actions, they are tools used to search. Through them it is possible to engender a particular kind of capture in which the knowledge possessed by ancestors and spirits is appropriated by the *obiaman*. Both the *obias* and the ancestral spirits – the nêsekis – are owned by clans and persons. Capture implies making effective and manifest a relation that obeys the designs of the former and exposes the vulnerability and fragility of the Maroon body – a place of penetration, creation and metamorphosis.

In Maroon ontology, the person results from a combination of substances and knowledge inherited from the spirits who return, received by the ancestors of the maternal clan (*nêsekis*), and from the encounter with forces inhabiting the forest (*óbias* and *wentis*). The nêsekis are knowledges-agencies that accompany the living, lending certain qualities and characteristics to the latter. Among the Ndyuka like Ma Kaabu (Thoden van Velzen & Van Wetering

1988) – with whom Tooy lived, sharing gods and receiving a substantial portion of his divinatory powers from his wife Yaai through contact with their god Yontíni (Price 2008:166; Thoden van Velzen 2004) – the spirits participate in the gestation and creation of the body through dietary prescriptions imposed on the mother and unborn child. On the child's body are left the marks of the spirit of the deceased and the marks of death. Along with the akaa, the vital principle, part of the individuality created during the formation of the foetus, the nêseki (namesake) forms part of the body and cannot leave it. It is in the body and through the action of the nêseki that the ancestral principle – yooka (spirit of the dead) – reactualizes itself (Vernon 1992:28). There are no ritual boundaries defining the space of action of óbias and ancestors. As Price observes, "these powers participate in their individual capacities in their social world, in the same way as persons and the family. The detailed stories that Tooy tells about the historical origins of these powers are related to Africa, on one hand, and Suriname, on the other. Both form an integral part of their world" (p. 288). Perhaps we need to ask not only which stories participate in the worlds of Ma Kaabu and Tooy but also how, recognizing that the travels of medium and shaman through such diverse ontologies allude to a model of incorporation and, in Price's terms (2008:290), an 'additive,' 'composite' and 'agglomerative' singularity.

In order to explore the constant circulation of persons and knowledge, women and men, the incorporation of people, objects and beings, and their effects on the production of the person, the book's contributors move beyond an exclusive focus on life in the village and traditional practices and knowledge. Although not interpellated here from a unified and theoretically-oriented perspective, Maroon personhood is ethnographically explored in the chapters by Diane Vernon, Stuart Strange, Rogério B.W. Pires, and Olívia Gomes da Cunha. Indeed it emerges as an incidental theme throughout the book, a correlated aspect that reinforces the attention afforded to Maroon sociality, reflecting relations that each Maroon person establishes with her or his matrilineal kin and ancestors, as well as their protector gods and spirits. This multiplicity of relations makes up each person, but not a 'society,' the latter being fragmented through deadly conflicts, antagonisms and disputes. On the contrary, it is precisely at the level of personhood that a sociality made by distinct bodily and spiritual affections takes shape. A continually transformed body in which substance and ancestors contribute to the production of personal and matrilineal histories.

The intense relationship between body and ancestors among the Ndyuka, for instance, was described in detail by Diane Vernon (1992) in her inquiry into the role of sickness and malevolent forces in the making of the Ndyuka person,

INTRODUCTION: EXPLORING MAROON WORLDS ON THE MOVE

based on the description of the 'affections' or the ways in which conceptions of the person seem to be traversed by affects of different kinds (or natures). The affect produced in the body is manifested at two levels: on the skin and in the blood. In relation to the former, a series of precautions needs to be taken so as to maintain its integrity and temperature. Low temperatures, winds and rain can cause pathological variations capable of directly altering a person's blood or skin (see also Andel 2010). Cold interrupts the circulation, the pulse of life that keeps the body warm and prevents someone from ailing. As a consequence, diseases or affections have divine causes – associated with the life history of the sick person and his or her ancestors – and sociocosmic explanations. An important part of bodily care – especially the precautions taken by women during menstruation and after childbirth – is related to the avoidance of cold and falling body temperature, associated with the risk of death. Baths made from herbs with curative powers alter the porous capacity of the epidermis to absorb – and transfer to the blood – the beneficial properties available in the forest (1992:14). Upper parts of the body are responsible for sustaining life, lower parts for the reproduction of the matrilineage (bee) and the person. At the same time, they are more vulnerable to sicknesses and death. The heart (ati) is the location of human agency, the back (baka) the ancestors, while the belly localizes the reproduction of the bee. The body is thus in a constant state of vulnerability. Bodies can be invaded by, contain or conduct physical and spiritual forces.[6]

Studying body vulnerability and the person through forms of experiencing and conceptualizing suffering, Stuart Strange, for example, explores what he calls a 'poetics' in which: "Pain is poetic because it calls attention to the formal properties of Ndyuka persons that render them legible as combinations of relations, whether through descent or residential proximity" (this volume). The body is a space of intense metamorphosis sensitive to the penetration of different transformative agencies. Bodies are vulnerable not only to sickness and the malevolent harm produced by óbia and obiaman: modes of describing and identifying the sources of misfortune and suffering can lead to a (de) composition of the agencies inhabiting the body and responsible for making the person.

Non-human agencies participate directly in the fabrication of the body and person in the form of a sickness generated when someone enters prohibited areas of the forest, kills sacred animals, or consumes sacred foods/plants. Sexual

---

6   For similar body conceptions among the Choco Afrodescendientes communities in Colombia, see, for instance, Losonczy (1986).

and menstrual taboos among the Aluku women and men interviewed by Jean Moomou (this volume) involve maintaining disciplines of bodily care and attention. 'Genitor' spirits are activated by following certain dietary prescriptions during gestation and affect the mother-child (bee-person) relation. A 'pre-social' unit that, in Vernon's terms (1992:24), reactualized the paansu (generation) is responsible for the configuration of the new being's vital principle, its akaa (soul). The latter is released from the body of the deceased and continues to exist in the form of a nêseki – a physical extension of the ancestral principle – whose yooka will participate in the creation of a new akaa. The action of the nêseki must be controlled by observing dietary prohibitions since it can produce the marks of death and dead spirits on the child's body (Pires, this volume). As a legacy, the vital force of an ancestor, it is essential to ensure that the nêseki lives with and protects the living. The Maroon person results from the association between the actions of human and non-human agencies both in cosmic domains – busi, a powerful metaphor that signals the origin of these forms of existence – and in domestic life inside and outside the villages, since they participate in the indissociability of the paansu, the bee and the person. Not by accident, the space of the house and the careful observance of the division of ambients used for bodily care, sexual seclusion, cleaning and the separation of objects in contact with the body, childcare and food preparation together compose what Clémence Léobal describes as 'house configurations' (Léobal apud Marcelin, this volume), even in urban contexts subject to state control.

The circularity of these agencies and their work of producing relations at cosmic and physical levels do not annul the creation – or fabrication – of a new and distinct form of existence. These modes of reactualizing relations and powers converge in the ritual treatment of death, in bodily care, and in the control of the circulation of substances, words and intentions. Broadly speaking, the dead body is an array of open doors and thus an object of danger, as observed by Polimé (1998), Parris (2011) and Pires (2015). But it is also an artefact of memory. A liminality that places side-by-side the living, the dead, ancestors, kin and spirits in tense and feared relations (Cunha 2018, this volume). Differently from the trope that provides intelligibility to Amerindian thought and the configuration of relational universes – cosmological regions in which hunters/eaters versus prey/food (Viveiros de Castro 2002) comprise, first and foremost, different perspectives amid multiple forms of alterity – we could say that Maroon ontology inscribes the signs of difference in bodies. But if, according to Vernon, this body is a composite of multiple affections, liminal matter that articulates the human and non-human agencies that participate in its formation even prior to conception and are thus not always visible, the event of death – and with it the ritual treatment and ceremonial obligations to which the dead and the living are directly or indirectly involved – allows both to participate actively in the social constitution of the person.

Incorporations

Maroon people, óbiamen, spirits, forest gods and the ancestors that accompany them see different places. Ndyuka historians and interlocutors told Thoden van Velzen (this volume) how their 'African gods' were 'replaced' by others, encountered or revealed during the primordial era of flight. A significant part of the travels of anthropologists in Suriname and French Guiana involved accessing stories concerning the appearance of these beings and forces, as well as recognizing their presence in the world inhabited by their interlocutors. This recognition, nonetheless, seems to be indelibly marked by the distinct importance that the things seen and experienced by both have for the knowledge that Maroon and non-Maroon produce. Since, as Hoogbergen's informant remarked, "(...) if the bakras saw a tree as they were walking through the forest, it might not have been a tree at all, it might have been a Maroon from Broos and Kaliko's encampment!" (cited in Hoogbergen 2008: ix).

To these explorations of the cosmopolitics of Maroon experience and the ways in which they participate in multiple worlds, we can add a dichotomy always invoked by Maroon persons themselves when they need to delimit their own modes of existence: although they may interact, live and marry with *bakaa*, they never transform into one – a non-Maroon. In all the contributions to this volume, the Kwinti, Matawai, Saamaka, Aluku and Ndyuka peoples with whom the authors interacted drew a sharp distinction between the lives, things and people they call *bakaa* and those they identify as businenge. We could describe *bakaa* as an 'ethnographic concept' insofar as finding an applicable translation or equivalent is effectively impossible. The category primarily encompasses those not considered Maroon – the latter being a term used for the Ndyuka, Saamaka, Paamaka, Aluku, Matawai and Kwinti peoples (in Suriname, they also called Businenge, and in French Guiana, Bushinengue). This distinction establishes a profound ontological separation between kinds of person where skin colour or ethnicity are not of central importance. In Okanisi, for instance, it is possible to identify specific kinds of *bakaa*: there are *weti bakaa* (white people), and *bakaa nengue* or *baakaman* (black people). Amerindians (ingii) are excluded from this classification. Crucially, these differentiations are also directly linked to the oppositions that previously governed the colonial order, such as plantation areas/Maroon villages, slavery/freedom, city/forest, runaways/slaves, etc. Being *bakaa* is also to act as 'if,' to perform like, or to use things that are purportedly Other. *Bakaa* is also employed as a quality attributable to people or things. Its use for all non-Maroon people functions indexically sine it relates all Others to the position occupied by whites in the colonial past. As Köbben has pointed out, "the officials with whom the Bush Negroes have dealings are Surinamers and are all more or less coloured. Yet the Bush Negroes call them whites (bakra),[7] as they fulfil the same functions and behave in the same way as the whites did formerly" (1967: 13).

Using the concept can activate the memory and presence of the ancestors simultaneously, inscribing difference in the historicities that define clans, villages and forest landscapes, but also signalling, in the relations maintained in the present (Price 1983; Bilby 1994; Parris 2008), limits to the modes of being in the world. It is not a question, though, of an identity that may or may not be attributed to an outsider, but of a relationship constituted in the past that nonetheless remains relevant in the present – paraphrasing Da Col & Graeber (2011: vii), a concept that incessantly translates an 'event,' "unclassifiable remainder(s) that rearrange preconceived notions and categories by juxtaposing different cultural images and positions." This capacity to recall is precisely what entails that the name of a relation, and not a quality, is linked to a particular type of person. An exogenous item of knowledge, rule or practice, mobilized in the context of the traditional territories, is qualitatively *bakaa*.

Primarily displaying ethnographic approaches, the volume contains analyses of Maroon socialities in the twenty-first century, based on recent research undertaken in urban peripheries and capital cities like Paramaribo (Strange; Bilby & Jaffe; Campbell) and Cayenne (S. Price), small settlements like Moengo (Cunha), Para and Bitagron (Migge) and Saint Laurent du Maroni (Vernon; Léobal; Migge; S. Price), but also villages close to the Suriname River (Pires) and the Tapanahoni (Thoden van Velzen) in Suriname, and the Lawa River (Moomou) in French Guiana. By problematizing conceptions of the Maroon person linked to the use of bodies and artefacts, to their contact with the machines, money, technical staff and transnational corporations that circulate in the world of the non-Maroons, as well as to the gods and spirits that inhabit landscapes accessible through spiritual and linguistic skills, the authors participating in this volume provide richly textured descriptions of the worlds that the Maroon peoples of the Guianas create, inhabit and transform (see Vernon 1980).

Maroon Cosmopolitics: personhood, creativity, and incorporation contributes, then, to our understanding of Maroon ways of inhabiting, transforming

---

7 An outsider in Sranantongo.

and circulating through different localities in the Guianas, as well as their modes of creating and incorporating knowledge and artefacts into their social relations and spaces. In this sense, it diverges from the approach usually taken in the 'classic' literature on Maroon societies, focused on providing historical and documental depth and legitimacy to the lives of the descendants of those who fled from slavery in the mid-nineteenth century. Likewise, from the ethnographic viewpoint, its contributors eschew any emphasis on the symbolic, physical and cultural boundaries that have traditionally (especially from the viewpoint of outside observers) contrasted villages and towns, Maroon and non-Maroon. It does not constitute another edited collection of texts by researchers educated or working in Euro-American contexts on the sociocultural singularities of the Guianese Maroons. By bringing together authors from diverse generations, trained in distinct theoretical frameworks, and affiliated to a variety of academic institutions in France, the USA, Brazil, Holland, Ireland and French Guiana, the volume looks to decentre analytic perspectives that oscillate between a stress on the shared forms of 'resistance' of runaway slaves and their descendants, and the singularity of their material institutions and culture. Although the authors show themselves to be sensitive to the complexity of the experiences of Maroon people in diverse relations with non-Maroons, the signs of difference cease to be taken as 'ethnic' phenomena and are explored instead through the concepts and experiences mobilized by their Maroon interlocutors themselves. Consequently the emphasis is on the existential and personal dimensions implicated in kinship relations and in relations with ancestors and distinct spatiotemporal landscapes.

What makes Guianese Maroon socialities distinct are not the 'artefacts of culture' into which – as Sally Price explores in this volume – they and the things they produce have been transformed for the purposes of foreign consumption, but the way in which they have historically incorporated knowledge from different relations maintained with Maroon and non-Maroon humans, spirits and gods of the waterways, forests and times. This is how Maroon peoples have continuously created, populated and altered the landscapes in which they live. The theme of incorporation is not only of crucial importance to understanding the logics involved in the appropriation and creation of relations and things, it also allows comparisons to be made with other ethnographic contexts, such as Amerindian ethnology and the experiences of those Amazonian indigenous peoples with whom the Maroon still maintain close symbolic interactions, like the Trio and Saamaka on the border with Brazil, studied by Rivière (1984), or peoples with whom they share chiefdoms and traditional territories, like the Aluku and Wayana in French Guiana (Dupuy 2008; Collomb 2008; Collomb &

Jolivet 2008), or those with whom they are involved in territorial disputes, such as the Ndyuka and Kali'na on the Lower Maroni. The proximity to traditional indigenous territories and populations is rich in analytic possibilities for exploring themes seldom ventured in the Guianese case. Such possibilities also include the inventive approaches developed by ethnologists who have recently turned their attention to topics such as sharing substances, regimes of transformation and difference, conversion to Christianity, the relation between nature and culture, political alliances, and cosmological perspectivism in their studies of Amerindian and traditional populations in Amazonia. Nevertheless, the various thematic lines structuring the volume do not compose parts of a unified corpus of topics, data and analyses, nor do they approach the experiences of all six Guianese Maroon peoples with equal intensity. The foregrounded topics articulate questions common to various studied contexts, persons, collectives and situations, allowing the authors to compare and contrast the different methods and concepts employed in the treatment of these issues.

The collection as a whole does not aim to articulate analyses produced in different contexts and employing distinct theoretical approaches. Neither, as stated earlier, does it endeavour to include ethnographical material on all six Maroon groups living in the Guianas today. What the various contributions assembled here do produce is a singular and surprisingly harmonious composition on contemporary modes of Maroon existence. The book is organized in four parts in which the themes addressed by the authors are set out. There is no concern, therefore, with strict chronological order or with providing comprehensive geographic coverage of all the places with a Maroon presence in the region. Likewise, the themes reflect choices and interests manifested at different moments of the authors' professional careers. We could say that they reflect, each in its own way, questions that have affected not only their different Maroon interlocutors, but so too the researchers themselves, echoing their distinct experiences and varying forms of engagement.

As the following chapters will discuss, historical transformations, the increasing migration to the cities and even profound demographic changes are all just part of what many might call a 'context' of experiences that make Maroon persons and socialities present on multiple planes. Through meticulous ethnographic accounts of contemporary Maroon modes of existence, intensely related to the temporalities and histories of their ancestors, clans and villages, the authors united here explore the intricate relations between kin, affines, non-affines, spirits and ancestors who transit through and intervene in, to a greater or lesser extent, the fabrication and reproduction of the Maroon person, sometimes in situations involving deprivation, violence and the threatened loss of rights won more than three centuries ago. Just like Tooy, Ma Kaabu

INTRODUCTION: EXPLORING MAROON WORLDS ON THE MOVE 23

and their spirits of rivers and forests, the dead and the gods, the chapters making up the collection invest in intense dialogues, traversed by modulations of voices and presences, human and non-human, capable of creating and recomposing landscapes, making life in the concrete jungles possible.

References

Amoksi, Martina. 2009. De Marronvrouw in de Stad: een historische analyses van de gevolgen van de urbanisatie voor de marronvrouen in Suriname. Amsterdam, Ninsee/Amrit.

Andel, Tinde. R. v., Ruysschaert, Sophie, Van de Putte, K., & Van Damme, P. 2009. "Bathe the baby to make it strong and healthy: Plant use and child care among Saramaccan Maroons in Suriname." Journal of Ethnopharmacology 121(1): 148–170.

Andel, T. R. van. 2010. "How African-based Winti Belief Helps to Protect Forests in Suriname". In *Sacred Natural Sites: conserving nature & culture*, 139–145. Edited by Verschuren, B. et al.London: Earthscan.

Apapoe, Ine. 2017. "Governing Ndyuka Society Abroad: The Council of Kabiten and Basiya of Okanisi in the Netherlands." In Legacy of Slavery and Indentured Labour: Historical and Contemporary Issues in Suriname and the Caribbean, 213–230. Edited by Rassankhan, M. et al. Delhi: Manohar.

Beet, Chris de, ed. 1995 Skrekiboekoe, Boek der Verschrikkingen: Visioenen en historische overleveringen van Johannes King. Bronnen voor de Studie van Afro-Suriname 17. Utrecht: Vakgroep Culturele Antropologie, Universiteit Utrecht.

Beet, Chris de & Miriam Sterman. 1981. People in Between: The Matawai Maroons of Surinam. Utrecht: Krips Repro.

Bilby, Kenneth M. 1984. "The treacherous feast: a Jamaican Maroon historical myth." Bijdragen tot de Taal-, Land-en Volkenkunde 1: 1–31.

Bilby, Kenneth M. 1989. "Divided loyalties: local politics and the play of states among the Aluku." New West Indian Guide 63(3), 143–173.

Bilby, Kenneth M. 1990. "The Remaking of the Aluku: Culture, Politics, and Maroon Ethnicity in French South America." PhD diss., Johns Hopkins University.

Bilby, Kenneth M. 1994. "Time and History among a Maroon People: The Aluku." In Time in the Black Experience, 141–160. Edited by Joseph K. Adjaye. Westport: Greenwood Press.

Bilby, Kenneth M. 1996. "Ethnogenesis in the Guianas and Jamaica: two Maroon Cases" In History, Power, and Identity: Ethnogenesis in the Americas, 1492–1992, 19–142. Edited by Jonathan Hill. Iowa City: University of Iowa Press.

Bilby, Kenneth M. 1997. "Swearing by the Past, Swearing to the Future: Sacred Oaths, Alliances, and Treaties among the Guianese and Jamaican Maroons." Ethnohistory 44(4), 655–689.

Bilby, K. M. 2000. Making modernity in the hinterlands: new Maroon musics in the Black Atlantic. *Popular Music, 19*(03), 265–292.

Bilby, Kenneth M. 2001. "Aleke: New Music and New Identities in the Guianas." American Music Review 22 (1): 31–47.

Bilby, Kenneth M. 2001a. "New Sounds from a New Nation: processes of globalization and Indigenization in Surinamese Popular Music. Twentieth-Century Suriname: Continuities and discontinuities in a New World Society", 296–328. Edited by Rosemarijn Hoefte and Peter Meel. Leiden & Kingston, KITLV Press & Ian Randle Publisher.

Bilby, Kenneth & Jaffe, Rikve. this volume. " 'Real Bushinengué': Guianese Maroon music in transition." In Maroon Cosmopolitics: personhood, creativity and incorporation. Edited by Cunha, Olivia M. Gomes da. Leiden: Brill.

Borges, Robert. 2014. The life of language: Dynamics of language contact in Suriname. Utrecht: Netherlands Graduate School of Linguistics.

Borges, Robert. 2013. "The role of extralinguistic factors in linguistic variation and contact-induced language change among Suriname's Coppename Kwinti and Ndyuka Maroons." International Journal of Linguistics 45 (2):228–246.

Brightman, Marc, and Vanessa Grotti. 2014. "Securitization, alterity, and the state: Human (in) security on an Amazonian frontier." Regions and Cohesion 4.3: 17–38.

Campbell, Corinna. this volume. "Modeling Cultural Adaptability: Maroon Cosmopolitanism and the Banamba Dance Contest." In Maroon Cosmopolitics: personhood, creativity and incorporation. Edited by Cunha, Olivia M. Gomes da. Leiden: Brill.

Collomb, Gérard and Marie-José Jolivet, eds. 2008. Histoires, identités et logiques ethniques. Amerindiens, Creoles et Noirs marrons en Guyane. Paris: CTHS.

Collomb, Gérard. 2008. "Chroniques interculturelles en Guyane. Un point de vue Kali'na."In Histoires, identités et logiques ethniques. Amerindiens, Creoles et Noirs marrons en Guyane, p.45–75. Edited by Collomb, Gerard and Marie-José Jolivet. Paris: CTHS.

Cunha, Olívia Maria Gomes da, and Thoden van Velzen, H. U. E. 2016. "Through Maroon Worlds: a conversation with Bonno Thoden van Velzen." Canadian Journal of Latin American and Caribbean Studies 41.2: 254–278.

Cunha, Olívia Maria Gomes da. 2018a. "In Their Places: The Cottica Ndyuka in Moengo." In Ethnographies of U.S. Empire, 247–279. Edited by John Collins and Carole McGranahan. Durham: Duke University Press.

Cunha, Olívia Maria Gomes da. 2018b. "Making Things for Living, and Living a Life with Things". In Race and Rurality in the Global Economy. Edited by Michaeline Crichlow. Albany: SUNY University Press.

Cunha, Olívia M. Gomes da. this volume. "Self-fashioning and visualization among the Cottica Ndyuka." In Maroon Cosmopolitics: personhood, creativity and incorporation. Edited by Cunha, Olivia M. Gomes da. Leiden: Brill.

INTRODUCTION: EXPLORING MAROON WORLDS ON THE MOVE

Da Col, Giovanni, and David Graeber. 2011. "Foreword: The return of ethnographic theory." HAU: Journal of Ethnographic Theory 1.1: vi-xxxv.

de la Cadena, Marisol. 2010. "Indigenous cosmopolitics in the Andes: Conceptual reflections beyond 'politics'." Cultural anthropology 25.2: 334–370.

de la Cadena, Marisol. 2015. Earth Beings: Ecologies of practice across Andean worlds. Durham: Duke University Press.

Descola, Philippe. 1992. "Societies of nature and the nature of society." In Conceptualizing Society, 107–26. Edited by Adam Kuper. London and New York: Routledge.

Descola, Philippe. 2005. Par-delà Nature et Culture. Paris: Gallimard.

Deleuze, Gilles, and Guattari, Felix. 1987. A Thousand Plateaus: Capitalism and Schizophrenia. Minneapolis: University of Minnesota Press.

Dupuy, Francis. 2008. "Wayana et Aluku: Les jeux de l'altérité dans le Haut-Maroni." In Histoires, identités et logiques ethniques. Amerindiens, Creoles et Noirs marrons en Guyane, p.165–201. Edited by Collomb, Gerard and Marie-José Jolivet. Paris: CTHS.

Elst, Dirks van de. 1971. The Bush Negro Tribes of Surinam, South America: a synthesis. PhD diss., Northwestern University.

Gallois, Dominique. T. 2005. Redes de relações nas Guianas. São Paulo: Editora Humanitas.

Gomes, Flavio dos S. 2002. A" Safe Haven": Runway Slaves, Mocambos, and Borders in Colonial Amazonia, Brazil. Hispanic American Historical Review, 82(3), 469–498.

Groenendijk, Sara. 2006. "Winti Practices in Bigiston, Suriname. A Closer Lok at Bonuman Ruben Mawdo." PhD diss., Utrecht Universiteit.

Groot, S. W de. 1969. Djuka society and social change: History of an attempt to develop a Bush Negro community in Surinam 1917–1926. Amsterdam: Van Gorcum.

Guyon, Stéphanie. 2010. Du gouvernement colonial à la politique racialisée: Sociologie historique de la formation d'un espace politique local (1949–2008), St-Laurent Maroni, Guyane. PhD diss., Paris 1.

Guyon, Stéphanie. 2011. "Politisation et hiérarchies coloniales: Amérindiens et Noirs-marrons à St-Paul (Guyane française, 1946–2000)". Critique Internationale, 1(50), 21–37.

Green, E. C. 1974. The Matawai Maroon: An Acculturating Afro-American Society. PhD diss., The Catholic University of America.

Heemskerk, Marieke. 2000a. Gender and gold mining: the case of the Maroons of Suriname, Women in International Development, Michigan State University, Working Paper #269.

Heemskerk, Marieke. 2000. Driving forces of small-scale gold mining among the Ndjuka Maroons: a cross-scale socioeconomic analysis of participation in gold mining in Suriname. PhD diss., University of Florida.

Herskovits, Melville. J. and Herskovits, Frances. 1934. Rebel destiny: among the bush Negroes of Dutch Guiana. New York, Whittlesey House, McGraw-Hill Book Company Inc.

Hoffman, Bruce. 2009. Drums and Arrows: Ethnobotanical Classification and use of Tropical Forest Plants by a Maroon and Amerindian Community in Suriname, With Implications for Biocultural Conservation. PhD diss., University of Hawaii.

Hoogbergen, Wim. 1990. The Boni Maroon Wars in Suriname. Leiden: Brill.

Hoogbergen, Wim. 2008. "Frères et ennemis. Aluku et Ndjuka de 1710 à 1860." In Histoires, identités et logiques ethniques. Amerindiens, Creoles et Noirs marrons en Guyane, p.107–141. Edited by Collomb, Gerard and Marie-José Jolivet. Paris: CTHS.

Hoogbergen, Wim. 2009. Het kamp van Broos en Kaliko: de geschiedenis van een Afro-Surinaamse familie. Paramaribo: Vaco.

Hoogbergen, Wim and Dirk Kruijt. 2004. "Gold, garimpeiros and Maroons: Brazilian migrants and ethnic relationships in post-war Suriname". Caribbean Studies 32(2): 3–44.

Hurault, Jean. 1958. Étude sur la vie sociale et religieuse des noirs réfugiés Boni de la Guyane Française. Paris, Institut Géographique National.

Hurault, Jean. 1961. Les noirs refugies Boni de la Guyane Française. Dakar: Institut Français d'Afrique Noire.

Jensen, Casper Bruun. 2014. "Practical Ontologies." Theorizing the Contemporary, Cultural Anthropology website, January 13, 2014. https://culanth.org/fieldsights/466-practical-ontologies (1).

Jolivet, Marie-José. 2007. "Approche anthropologique du multiculturalisme guyanais: Marrons et créoles dans l'Ouest". Pratiques et représentations linguistiques en Guyane: Regards croisés, 87–106. Edited by Isabelle Léglise. Paris, IRD Éditions.

Jolivet, Marie-José. 2008. "Histoires du marronnage ou le difficile renoncement des Ndjuka." In Histoires, identités et logiques ethniques. Amerindiens, Creoles et Noirs marrons en Guyane, p.77–105. Edited by Collomb, Gerard and Marie-José Jolivet. Paris: CTHS.

Jolivet, Marie-José and Vernon, Diane. 2007. "Droits, polygamie et rapports de genre en Guyane." Cahiers des Études Africaines 187–188: 733–752.

Kahn, Morton. 1931. Djuka: the Bush Negroes of Dutch Guiana. New York, The Viking Press.

Kambel, Ellen-Rose and Fergus MacKay. 1999. The Rights of Indigenous Peoples and Maroons in Suriname. Copenhagen: IWGIA.

Kobben, Andre. J. F. 1979. In vrijheid en gebondenheid: samenleving en cultuur van de Djoeka aan de Cottica. Utrecht, Centrum voor Caraïbische Studies, Instituut voor Culturele Antropologie, Rijksuniversiteit Utrecht.

Kohn, Eduardo. 2013. How forests think: Toward an anthropology beyond the human. Berkeley: University of California Press.

INTRODUCTION: EXPLORING MAROON WORLDS ON THE MOVE

Kruijt, Dirk and Hoogbergen, Wim, 2005. "Peaceful Relations in a Stateless Region: The Post-War Maroni River Borders in the Guianas." Tijdschrift voor Economische en Sociale Geografie, 96 (2): 199–208.

Latour, Bruno. 2004a. The Politics of Nature. Cambridge: Harvard University Press.

Latour, Bruno. 2004. "Whose cosmos, which cosmopolitics? Comments on the peace terms of Ulrich Beck." Common Knowledge 10.3 (2004): 450–462.

Lenoir, J. 1975. "Surinam National Development and Maroon Cultural Autonomy". Social and Economic Studies, 24(3):308–319.

Léobal, Clémence. 2015. « Bidonvilles et camps de réfugiés: le tournant des années 1980 pour la catégorisation des marrons à Saint-Laurent-du-Maron.» In Sociétés marronnes des Amériques. Mémoires, patrimoines, identités et histoire du XVIIe au XXe siècle, 475–490. Edited by Jean Moomou. Matoury : Editions Ibis Rouge.

Léobal, Clémence. 2014. « Adapter le logement social à la « culture » des habitants en Outre-Mer. La résorption de l'habitat insalubre appliquée aux marrons de Saint-Laurent-du-Maroni (La Charbonnière, 1985). » In Logement et politique(s). Un couple encore d'actualité ?, 179–198. Edited by Fatiha Belmessous, Loïc Bonneval, Lydia Coudroy de Lille, and Nathalie Ortar. Paris, L'Harmattan.

Léobal, Clémence. 2016. "From Primitives to Refugees: French Guianese Categorizations of Maroons in the Aftermath of Surinamese Civil War." In Legacy of Slavery and Indentured Labour: Historical and Contemporary Issues in Suriname and the Caribbean, 213–230. Edited by Maurits S. Hassankhan et al. Dehli: Manohar.

Léobal, Clémence. this volume. "Performing Ethnicity as a Way of Contesting Removals: Bureaucratic Strategies and Affirmation of Busikonde Ways of Dwelling in Soolan (French Guiana)." In Maroon Cosmopolitics: personhood, creativity and incorporation. Edited by Cunha, Olivia M. Gomes da. Leiden: Brill.

Lier, Willem F. van. 1919 Iets over De Boschnegers in De Boven-Marowijne. Paramaribo: van Ommeren.

Lier, Willem F. van. 1940 "Aanteekeningen over het Geestelijk Leven en de Samenleving der Djoeka's (Aukaner Boschnegers) in Suriname." Bijdragen tot de Taal-, Land-en Volkenkunde 99.1: 130–294.

Losoncy, Anne-Marie. 1986. "La sagesse et le nombril. Rites de naissance et sages-femmes chez les Embera et les Afro-Colombiens du Haut-Choco (Colombie)". Civilisations, Vol. XXXVII: 259–287.

Migge, Bettina 2004. "The Speech Event Kuutu in the Eastern Maroon Community". In Creole, Contact and Language Change: Linguistic and Social Implications, 285–306. Edited by Escure, Geneviève, and Armin Schwegler. Amsterdam: John Benjamins.

Migge, Bettina. 2007. "Codeswitching and social identities in the Eastern Maroon community of Suriname and French Guiana." Journal of Sociolinguistics 11(1): 53–72.

Migge, B. 2011. "Negotiating social identities on an Eastern Maroon radio show". Journal of Pragmatics, 43(6), 1498–1511.

Migge, Bettina. this volume. "Research on Maroon Languages and Language Practices among Matawai and Kwinti Maroons." In Maroon Cosmopolitics: personhood, creativity and incorporation. Edited by Cunha, Olivia M. Gomes da. Leiden: Brill.

Mintz, Sidney W. 1964 "Melville Herskovits and Caribbean Studies: A Retrospective Tribute." Caribbean Studies 2.4: 42–51.

Moomou, Jean. 2004. Le monde des marrons du Maroni en Guyane (1772–1860): la naissance d'un peuple: les Boni. Matoury: Ibis Rouge Editions.

Pakosie, Andre R. 1996. "Maroon Leadership and the Surinamese State (1760–1990)." Journal of Legal Pluralism and Unofficial Law, 37/38: 263–277.

Palmié, Stephan. 2002. Wizards & Scientists: Explorations in Afro-Cuban modernity and Tradition. Durham: Duke University Press.

Palmié, Stephan. 2006. "Creolization and Its Discontents." Annual Review of Anthropology, 35: 433–56.

Palmié, Stephan. 2013. The Cooking of History. How not to study Afro-Cuban religion. Chicago: The University of Chicago Press.

Parris, Jean-Yves. 2011. Interroger les Morts: essai sur la dynamique politique des Noirs marrons ndjuka du Surinam et de la Guyane. Matoury, Ibis Rouge Editions.

Parris, Jean-Yves. 2008. "La mémoire des Premiers Temps: un enjeu politique ndjuka." In Histoires, identités et logiques ethniques. Amerindiens, Creoles et Noirs marrons en Guyane, p.143–163. Edited by Collomb, Gerard and Marie-José Jolivet. Paris: CTHS.

Pires, Rogério B. W. 2015. A Masa Gadu Konde: Morte, Espíritos e Rituais Funerários em uma Aldeia Saramaka Cristã. PhD diss., Museu Nacional, Federal University of Rio de Janeiro.

Pires, Rogério Brittes W. this volume. "Funerals, Rhetorics, Rules and Rulers in Upper Suriname." In Maroon Cosmopolitics: personhood, creativity and incorporation. Edited by Olivia M. Gomes da Cunha. Leiden: Brill.

Polimé, Thomas. 1998. "Dood en begrafenisrituelen bij de Ndjuka". OSO, 17, 71–73.

Polimé, Thomas. 2007. Het traditioneel gezag op een tweesprong: De Ndyuka-marrons'. In Ik ben een haan met een kroon op mijn hoofd. Pacificatie en verzet in koloniaal en postkoloniaal Suriname, 55–74. Edited by Win Hoogbergen and Peter Meel. Amsterdam, Uitgeverijn Bert Bakker.

Polimé, Thomas, and Alex van Stipriaan 2013. Zeg het met doeken: marrontextiel en de Tropenmuseum collectie. Amsterdan, KIT Publishers.

Polimé, Thomas and H.U.E. Thoden van Velzen. 1988. Vluchtelingen, opstandelingen en andere Bosnegers van Oost-Suriname, 1986–1988. Utrecht: Instituut voor Culturele Antropologie.

Price, Richard. 1970. "Saramaka Emigration and Marriage: A Case Study of Social Change." Southwestern Journal of Anthropology 26: 157–89.

Price, Richard. 1973. ed. Maroon Societies: Rebel Slave Communities in the Americas. New York: Doubleday/Anchor. [Third edition, revised, with a new preface, Baltimore, Johns Hopkins University Press, 1996].

INTRODUCTION: EXPLORING MAROON WORLDS ON THE MOVE 29

Price, Richard.1975. Saramaka social structure: analysis of a Maroon Society in Surinam. Puerto Rico: Institute of Caribbean Studies.

Price, Richard. 1983[1976]. First Time: the historical vision of an afro-american people. Baltimore and London, John Hopkins Universitry Press.

Price, R. 1990. *Alabi's World.* Baltimore: John Hopkins University Press.

Price, Richard. 1996[1976]. The Guiana Maroons: A historical and bibliographical introduction. Baltimore: Johns Hopkins Univ Press.

Price, R. 1998. "Scrapping Maroon history: Brazil's promise, Suriname's shame". New West Indian Guide 72(3), 233.

Price, Richard. 2001. "The miracle of creolization: a retrospective." New West Indian Guide 75.1–2: 35–64.

Price, Richard. 2007. "Liberdade, Fronteiras e Deuses: Saramakas no Oiapoque (c. 1900). In Quase-Cidadão: histórias antropologias da pós-emancipação no Brasil, 119–146. Edited by Olívia Gomes da Cunha and Flávio dos S. Gomes. Rio de Janeiro: Fundação Getulio Vargas.

Price, Richard. 2008. Travels with Tooy: History, memory, and the African American imagination. Chicago: University of Chicago Press.

Price, Richard. 2010. "Uneasy Neighbors: Maroons and Indians in Suriname". Tipiti: Journal of the Society for the Anthropology of Lowland South America, 8(2), 4.

Price, Richard. 2011. Rainforest warriors: human rights on trial. Philladelfia: University of Pennsylvania Press.

Price, Richard. 2013. "The Maroon Population Explosion: Suriname and Guyane." New West Indian Guide 87.3–4: 323–327.

Price, Richard. 2015. "Maroons in Anthropology". Wright, James. ed. International Encyclopedia of the Social & Behavioral Sciences, Vol. 14. Elsevier, pp.591–595.

Price, Richard and Sally Price, 2017. Saamaka Dreaming. Durhan: Duke University Press.

Price, Sally. 1982. "When is a calabash not a calabash?" New West Indian Guide, 56(1/2) 69–82.

Price, Sally. 1993. Co-wives and calabashes. Ann Arbor: University of Michigan Press.

Price, Sally 2001. "Patchwork history: tracing artworlds in the African diaspora." New West Indian Guide 75(1&2): 5–34.

Price, Sally. this volume. "An anthropologist's dilemma: Maroon tembe in the twenty-first century." In Maroon Cosmopolitics: personhood, creativity and incorporation. Edited by Olivia M. Gomes da Cunha. Leiden: Brill.

Price, Sally, and Richard Price. 1999. Maroon arts: cultural vitality in the African diaspora. Boston: Beacon Press.

Price, Sally, and Richard Price. 2003. The Roots of Roots or, How Afro-American Anthropology got its start. Chicago: Prickly Paradigm Press.

Price, Sally, and Richard Price. 2003a. Les Maroons. Châteauneuf-le-Rouge: Vents d'ailleurs.

Price, Sally, and Richard Price. 2015. "Epilogue: The Aesthetics and Politics of Multilingualism among the Saamaka". In In and out of Suriname: Language, Mobility and Identity, 242–260. Edited by Eithne B. Carlin, Isabelle Léglise, Bettina Migge, and Paul B. Tjon Sie. Leiden: Brill.

Rivière, Peter. 1984. Individual and society in Guiana: a comparative study of amerindian social organisation. Cambridge: Cambridge University Press.

Sanderse, J. and Jaffe, Rivke. 2007. "Jonge Marronmuzikanten: Muziek en Marginaliteit in Paramaribo." OSO 26(1): 43–60.

Sanderse & Jaffe, R., J. 2009. Surinamese Maroons as reggae artistes: music, marginality and urban space. Ethnic and Racial Studies, 9(1), 1–19.

Scott, David. 1991. "That event, this memory: notes on the anthropology of African diasporas in the New World." Diaspora: A Journal of Transnational Studies 1.3: 261–284.

Scholtens, Ben. 1994. Bosnegers en overheid in Suriname. De ontwikkeling van de politieke verhouding 1651–1992. Paramaribo: Afd. Cultuurstudies/Minov.

Stengers, Isabelle. 2005. "The cosmopolitical proposal." In Making things public: atmospheres of democracy, 994–1003. Edited by Latour, Bruno and Peter Weibel. Cambridge: MIT Press.

Stewart, Charles, ed. 2016. Creolization: history, ethnography, theory. London: Routledge.

Strange, Stuart E. 2016. Suspected Gods: Spirit Possession, Performance, and Social Relations in Multi-Ethnic Suriname. PhD diss., University of Michigan.

Strange, Stuart E. 2016a. "The dialogical collective: mediumship, pain, and the interactive creation of Ndyuka Maroon subjectivity." Journal of the Royal Anthropological Institute, 0, 1–18.

Strange, Stuart. this volume. "Spirits and pain in the making of Ndyuka politics." In Maroon Cosmopolitics: personhood, creativity and incorporation. Edited by Olivia M. Gomes da Cunha. Leiden: Brill.

Strathern, Marilyn. 1990. "Artifacts of History: events and interpretations of images". In Culture and history in the Pacific, 25–44. Edited by J. Siikala. Helsinki: Finnish Anthropological Society.

Strathern, Marilyn. 1991. Partial Connections. Lanham: Rowman & Littlefield Publishers.

Strathern, Marilyn. 1992. "Parts and Wholes: refiguring relationships in a post-plural world." In Conceptualizing Society, 75–106. Edited by Adam Kuper. London and New York: Routledge.

Strathern, Marilyn. 1995. The Relation – issues in complexity and scale. Cambridge: Prickly Pear Press.

Theije, Marjo de. 2010. "Transforming Land Tenure Systems in the Quest for Gold: Aluku, Wayana, and the State in the Suriname French Guiana Border Region." In L'acte de colloque Amaz'hommes, 353–365. Edited by Egle Baronne-Visigalli and Anna Roosevelt. Cayenne: Ibis Rouge.

Theije, Marjo. 2015. "Small-scale gold mining and trans-frontier Commerce on the Lawa River." In In and out of Suriname: Language, Mobility and Identity, 58–77. Edited by Eithne B. Carlin, Isabelle Léglise, Bettina Migge, and Paul B. Tjon Sie. Leiden: Brill.

Theije, Marjo de and Marieke Heemskerk. 2009. "Moving Frontiers in the Amazon Brazilian Small-scale Gold Miners in Suriname." European Review of Latin American and Caribbean Studies 87: 5–25.

Thoden van Velzen, H.U.E..1966a Politieke beheersing in de Ndyuka maatschappij: een studie van onvolledig machtsoverwicht. PhD diss., University of Amsterdam.

Thoden van Velzen, H.U.E.. 1966b "Het Geloof in Wraakgeesten: Bindmiddel en Splijtzwam van de Djuka Matri-Lineage." Nieuwe West-Indische Gids 45: 45–51.

Thoden van Velzen, H.U.E. 1990 "The Maroon Insurgency: Anthropological Reflections Civil on the War in Suriname." In Resistance and Rebellion in Suriname: Old and New, 159–88. Edited by Gary Brana-Shute. Department of Anthropology, William & Mary College.

Thoden van Velzen, H.U.E. 1995 "Dangerous Ancestors: Ambivalent Visions of Eighteenth and Nineteenth-Century Leaders of the Eastern Maroons of Suriname" In Slave Cultures and the Culture of Slavery, 112–44. Edited by Stephan Palmie. Knoxville: The University of Tennessee Press.

Thoden van Velzen, H.U.E. and Van Wetering, Wilhelmina. 1988. The Great Father and the Danger: religious cults, material forces, and collective fantasies in the world of the Surinamese Maroons. Dordrecht & Providence: Foris Publications.

Thoden van Velzen, H.U.E. and Van Wetering, Wilhelmina. 2001. "Dangerous Creatures and the Enchantment of Modern Life." In Powers of good and evil: moralities, commodities, and popular belief, edited by Peter Clough and J. P. Mitchell, 17–42. London: Berghahn Books.

Thoden van Velzen, H.U.E. and Van Wetering, Wilhelmina. 2004. In the shadow of the oracle: religion as politics in a Suriname Maroon society. Long Grove: Waveland Press.

Thoden van Velzen, H.U.E. and Van Wetering, Wilhelmina. 2013. Een zwarte vrijstaat in Suriname (deel 2): De Okaanse samenleving in de negentiende en twintigste eeuw Leiden: Brill.

Trouillot, Michel-Rolph. 2002. "Culture on the edges: Caribbean creolization in historical context." From the margins: historical anthropology and its futures, 189–210.

van Stipriaan, Alex. 2009. "Marrons in de stad; migratie in de twintigste eeuw." In Kunst van overleven: Marroncultuur uit Suriname, 146–155. Edited by Alex van Stipriaan and Thomas Polimé. Amsterdam: KIT.

van Stipriaan, Alex. 2011. "Contact! Marrons en de transport-en communictie revolutie in het Surinaams binnenland." OSO, 1, 28–46.

van Stipriaan, Alex. 2015. "Maroons and the Communications Revolution in Suriname's Interior". In In and out of Suriname: Language, Mobility and Identity, 139–163 Edited by Eithne B. Carlin, Isabelle Léglise, Bettina Migge, and Paul B. Tjon Sie. Leiden: Brill.

van Stipriaan, Alex; and Polimé, Thomas. eds. 2009. Kunst van overleven: Marroncultuur uit Suriname, 146–155. Amsterdam: KIT.

Van Wetering, Wilhelmina. 1966. "Conflicten tussen co-vrouwen bij de Djuka." New West Indian Guide 45 (1):52–59.

Van Wetering, Wilhelmina. 1973 Hekserij bij de Djuka: Een sociologische benadering. PhD diss., Universiteit van Amsterdam.

Van Wetering, W. 1992. A Demon in Every Transistor'. Etnofoor, 5(1/2), 109–127.

Van Wetering, Wilhelmina. 1995 "The Transformation of Slave Experience: self and Danger in the Rituals of Creole Migrant Women in the Netherlands". In Slave Cultures and the Culture of Slavery, 210–38. Edited by Stephan Palmié. Knoxville, The University of Tennessee Press.

Van Wetering, Wilhelmina, and H.U.E. Thoden van Velzen. 1982. "Female religious responses to male prosperity in turn-of-the-century Bush Negro societies." New West Indian Guide 56 (1/2):43–68.

Vernon, Diane.1980. "Bakuu: possesing spirits of witchcraft on the tapanahony." New West Indian Guide 54 (1):1–38.

Vernon, Diane. 1985. Money magic in a modernizing Maroon society. Institute for the study of languages and cultures of Asia and Africa (ILCAA) Tokyo University of Foreign Studies, Tokyo.

Vernon, Diane. 1992. Les representations du corps chez les noirs marrons Ndjuka du Surinam et de la Guyane française. Paris, Editions de l'ORSTOM.

Vernon, Diane. this volume. "New lives for Ndyuka women: "Everything's changed but the men." In Maroon Cosmopolitics: personhood, creativity and incorporation. Edited by Cunha, Olivia M. Gomes da. Leiden: Brill.

Viveiros de Castro, Eduardo Batalha. 1998. "Cosmological deixis and Amerindian perspectivism." Journal of the Royal Anthropological Institute: 469–488.

Viveiros de Castro, Eduardo Batalha. 2002. "O nativo relativo." Mana 8.1: 113–148.

Viveiros de Castro, Eduardo Batalha. 2004. "Perspectival Anthropology and the Method of Controlled Equivocation." Tipiti, 2(1), 3–22.

Viveiros de Castro, Eduardo Batalha. 2012. "Transformação" na antropologia, transformação da "antropologia." Mana 18.1: 151–171.

Wagner, R., 1981. The Invention of Culture, rev. ed. *Chicago: University of Chicago.*

PART 1

(Re) Encounters

CHAPTER 1

A Half-Century of "Bush-Negro" Studies

Richard Price

In the early pages of Fesiten, the recently published Saamakatongo version of First-Time, I tried to evoke, for younger Saamaka readers, some of the changes that their society had experienced since Sally Price and I began fieldwork in their territory a half-century ago. I described how, back then, no bakaa (outsider) could enter Saamaka territory without the explicit permission of the gaama (paramount chief), how in those days there wasn't a single tourist, how there was neither electricity nor running water in the villages, how latrines and telephones were unknown, how women were bare-breasted, adolescent girls bare behind, and men loincloth-clad. How most travel was by paddle canoe, how outboard motors were rare, and how the great majority of women had been to the capital for only one several-day visit in their whole life. And how all men carved canoes, paddles, stools and much else while all women sewed clothing and carved calabashes. Much else has changed too.[1] How often we wish we could go back and write an expansive account of what these fifty years of change have meant for Saamakas![2]

There have been major shifts in demography and residence. A half century ago, the total number of Maroons in Suriname and French Guiana was estimated to be 40,000, with almost all of them residing in the traditional Maroon territories of the interior (R. Price 1976:3–4). Today, these peoples number some 210,000 and fewer than half live where they (or their ancestors) once did, the others being spread among Paramaribo and other coastal Suriname locations, Saint-Laurent-du-Maroni, Kourou and elsewhere in Guyane, as well as the Netherlands, the United States, and other even more far-flung parts of the globe (R. Price 2013b). Maroons now make up 23% of the population of Suriname and 26% of the population of Guyane. Within 20 years they are likely

---

1   This paper is presented here largely as given as the opening address of the Colóquio "Maroons e Businenges nas Guianas: pessoas, tempos e lugares," Laboratório de Antropologia e História PPGAS | Museu Nacional | Universidade Federal do Rio de Janeiro, 28 April 2014.

2   For political reasons described in R. Price 2011, having to do with our role in defending Saamaka rights before the Inter-American Court for Human Rights, we are no longer welcome by the government of Suriname. More recently, we have addressed "the way it was back then" in R. & S. Price (2017). For the most recent demographic figures on Maroons in Suriname and French Guiana, see R. Price 2018.

© KONINKLIJKE BRILL NV, LEIDEN, 2019 | DOI:10.1163/9789004388062_003

to constitute the largest "ethnic group" in each of these territories (Ibid.) Women are now as likely as men to live outside of the traditional territories. The paved road to the Saamaka village of Atjoni, which provides a starting point for quick trips upriver, means that large numbers of Saamakas now have dual residence between the coast and the interior and much the same holds for other Maroons. Many traditional villages—along the Lawa, the Tapanahoni, and the Saramacca in particular—have few residents other than the elderly, and many Saamaka villages have sharply diminished populations as well.

The situation in Guyane has also changed dramatically. A half century ago, the Aluku (then some 2000 people) were living in their traditional villages along the Lawa in the "Inini Territory"—until 1969 a vast, separate, and largely unspoiled and unadministered forest world, with a few thousand Amerindians and Aluku Maroon residents. During the early 1970s, that territory began to be cut up by the French State into communes, arrondissements, and cantons (with all their attendant institutions: mairies, gendarmeries, écoles, cadastre). And as early as the mid-1980s, after only a decade and a half of forced françisation, only one-fifth of Alukus remained in those villages, another half living in one of the new administrative centers (Maripasoula or Papaïchton) and one-third of Alukus on the coast (Bilby 1990). Saamaka men, who had been coming over for several years at a time since the 1860s, continued to outnumber Alukus in Guyane at any one time, with Ndyukas and Pamakas as occasional visitors. Guyane had, including Ndyukas and Pamakas in garden camps on the French side of the Marowijne, a total of some 7500 Maroon residents or visitors in 1970. And then came the Civil War in Suriname, which changed Guyanais demography forever. My recent estimate, based on official figures, of 67,000 Maroons living in Guyane today is almost surely an underestimate (R. Price 2013a). Clémence Léobal predicts that by the end of the decade, the commune of Saint-Laurent will have a greater population than Cayenne (Léobal 2013:17). And right now, she estimates, the town's population stands at some 45,000 with Maroons representing at least 30,000 of these residents, making St-Laurent at once the largest Aluku-, Ndyuka-, Pamaka-, and Saamaka-speaking city in the world. Meanwhile, traditional Aluku territories, comprising Apatou and the villages and towns along the Lawa, are now thoroughly multi-ethnic, with Alukus now forming a minority within their own traditional territory. The social, economic, religious, educational, linguistic, medical, and political implications of these Maroon population movements over the past half century in Guyane simply boggle the mind.

In Suriname, Maroon sovereignty —which made it possible as late as the early 1980s to speak of "states within a state"—was vastly diminished by the Civil War, and this has created havoc in the traditional authority structure.

A HALF-CENTURY OF "BUSH-NEGRO" STUDIES

Government interference in Maroon affairs has markedly increased. All sorts of outsiders have moved into traditional Maroon territories—Chinese storekeepers, Brazilian garimpeiros, Creole tour operators, several generations of Peace Corps volunteers (all of whom had departed Suriname definitively by 2013), various evangelical and other religious leaders—and each has introduced new ideas, practices, and beliefs. A number of Saamakas are engaged in the tourism industry—for example, working at tourist camps, mounting a museum in Pikiseei, and to some extent "performing their culture" when outsiders request it, in exchange for money. Much of the Maroon economy now centers on illegal, artisanal gold mining. And with the recent introduction of cell phones and internet access, globalization is sweeping Suriname's interior, making it hard to imagine the time when its inhabitants lived relatively stable lives, running their own political and judicial affairs, engaging in complex and frequent communal rituals, and enjoying economic self-sufficiency through their hunting, fishing, and gardening, supplemented by the men's trips to the coast to provide manufactured items. That world—the one that Bonno [Thoden van Velzen] and Ineke [van Wetering] and Sally [Price] and I experienced as we began our anthropological engagements—is fast fading into a distant memory.

∴

Looking back over that same half-century in terms of scholarly publications about Maroons in Suriname and French Guiana, I am struck by how much of our basic understandings of these societies stems from that anthropological fieldwork carried out in the 1960s and 1970s. I am also struck by how many of those who carried out research during that period have moved on to other domains of study (or to completely different lives) and are no longer active in the field. André Köbben, who pioneered Ndyuka studies, retired long ago; John Lenoir, who conducted doctoral work with the Pamaka in the 1970s, became an attorney in the USA (though he maintains relations with the Pamaka through the children he fathered there); Ted Green, who wrote his doctoral dissertation on the Matawai, went on to build a career in public health as an Africanist, specializing in HIV/AIDS; Miriam Sterman seems to have left anthropology several years after completing a joint dissertation with Chris de Beet on the Matawai; Shelby Givens, whose doctoral thesis was on the Aluku, forged a career as university and Peace Corps administrator, directing the latter program in Suriname for many years; Thomas Price (no relation) retired from anthropology soon after conducting his brief Aluku fieldwork; and Dirk van der Elst now also lives in retirement. During the past several years, death has ended the careers of several veteran contributors to our understandings of Maroon life, notably Silvia de Groot, Chris de Beet, and Ineke van Wetering—we miss them as colleagues and as friends.

For purposes of economy, the half-century overview of Maroon studies that I present here includes only selected bibliographical references. I also acknowledge, at the outset, that its presentation places me in the awkward position of writing about my own (and Sally's) work as well as that of close friends, but there seems no way to ameliorate that discomfort but to acknowledge it and get on with the task. (For an overview of pre-1960s work by anthropologists and others among these peoples, with extensive bibliography, see R. Price 1976:43–69.)

There is little question that modern anthropological fieldwork among Suriname Maroons (then called "Bush Negroes") began only in the 1960s—for Dutch researchers when Indonesia ceased being a welcoming field site and for Americans, particularly in the 1970s, as part of the spurt in African American studies that followed the Civil Rights movement. In the 1960s and 1970s, Dutch and American anthropologists monopolized the scholarly territory, with the only French "participant" being Roger Bastide, who tended to envision "Bush Negroes" as essentially "African" (indeed, Fanti-Ashanti) but who never set foot in either Suriname or Guyane and worked solely on the basis of often-obsolete secondary sources (see Bastide 1961).

Anthropological studies of the Ndyuka began in 1961, when the Dutch Africanist anthropologist André Köbben spent a year among the Cottica Ndyuka while his students at the University of Amsterdam, Bonno Thoden van Velzen and Ineke van Wetering, began their long-term research in Diitabiki, on the Tapanahoni. Their common conceptual model was British social anthropology, Manchester style, and the resulting articles as well as the dissertations of both Bonno and Ineke were executed with full use of the case-study method. Köbben published a series of articles on kinship, social roles, sociocultural change, religion, the fieldwork experience, politics, and law (see, for example, Köbben 1967, 1968, 1969), and he later adapted some of these into a book (Köbben 1979). In their own publications stemming from this initial research, the Thodens focused on power, politics, religion, and witchcraft (see Thoden van Velzen 1966a and 1966b, van Wetering 1966, 1973, and 1975, and Thoden van Velzen & van Wetering 1975). During that same period, Silvia W. de Groot, another Köbben student, visited Suriname several times, never conducting fieldwork, but publishing archivally-based historical studies of the Ndyuka as well as an account of her 1970 trip accompanying the Maroon chiefs to West Africa (see de Groot 1963, 1969, 1974). During the early seventies, Ndyuka-born André Pakosie began his long career of publishing on aspects of Ndyuka society (see Pakosie 1972) and in the late seventies Diane Vernon, an American studying in

France, began fieldwork for a (never-completed) dissertation on the Tapana-honi Ndyuka. After she settled into her long-term work as cultural médiatrice at the hospital in Saint-Laurent-du-Maroni, she produced a series of publications on topics that ranged from ethno-medicine to money magic (see, for example, Vernon 1985, 1992).

As for the Saamaka, modern anthropology began in 1965, when the Prices, then studying at Harvard, initiated research on the Pikilio, as the waters behind the Afobaka dam were still rising. (Their only anthropological predecessors among the Saamaka, American anthropologists Melville and Frances Herskovits, had spent part of two summers there in the late 1920s—see Herskovits & Herskovits 1934 and Price & Price 2003b). The Prices' fieldwork model was thoroughly Malinowskian, with few areas of life left uninvestigated. Returning from their two-year stay on the upper river, they planned to write a general ethnography, but this soon gave way instead to a series of books (and articles) on a broad range of subjects, from social structure and gender to the visual and verbal arts, and from early history to ritual practices. Of particular note, RP's Maroon Societies (1973) placed Suriname Maroons firmly within the broader framework of African American Studies and his First-Time (1983a) and Alabi's World (1990) pioneered the use of oral history in conjunction with archival research, not only in Maroon studies but in anthropology and history more generally. SP's Co-Wives and Calabashes (1984) was the first book to focus on Maroon women's lives and led to a number of publications about women's, as well as men's, arts. During the mid-1980s and the 1990s, when fieldwork in Suriname became impossible for them, the Prices shifted their interests to Saamakas and other Maroons across the border in Guyane and published a number of works exploring the immigrant experience in that neo-colony. Finally, as Saamakas back in Suriname sought their help in dealing with the encroachments of the State on their traditional territory, they became more directly involved in activist work on behalf of Saamakas in Suriname, joining forces with human rights attorneys Fergus MacKay and Ellen-Rose Kambel to help Saamakas defend their rights (see, for example, Kambel & MacKay 1999, R. Price 2011). This activist role on behalf of Maroon peoples, which began in the final decade of the twentieth century, marked a break in the style of anthropology previously practiced among Maroons. (See, for bibliographic references covering all periods of the Prices' work, www.richandsally.net.).

The only substantive anthropology ever carried out among the Matawai and the Pamaka took place during the 1970s, with American John Lenoir writing about religious acculturation among the Pamaka (Lenoir 1973), and American Ted Green, soon to be followed by the Dutch couple Chris de Beet and Miriam Sterman, focusing on acculturation and in-betweenness among the Matawai (see Green 1974, de Beet & Sterman 1981). Dirk van der Elst, who as one of the last of Melville Herskovits' students had written an unpublished library thesis on "Bush Negroes" (Van der Elst 1970), spent part of a summer with the Kwintii, the only research ever carried out among this people (Van de Elst 1975a, b, and c). The de Beets went on to edit and translate a number of historical texts on Matawai and other nineteenth-century Maroons (see, for example, Albitrouw 1978, King 1981, and de Beet 1984, 1995), all published in the useful series Bronnen voor de Studie van Bosneger Samenleving, which continued, with three minor name changes, into the new millennium.

Field anthropology among the Aluku, following in the path of French geographer Jean Hurault's many 1940s-1950s expeditions and publications (see, for example, Hurault 1961, 1965, 1970), began with the brief visits of American anthropologist Thomas Price, who had been a Herskovits student, in the second half of the sixties (T. Price 1970) and African American Shelby Givens' dissertation research on social control (Givens 1984). Then, for three years in the mideighties (and during briefer visits later on), Kenneth Bilby, a doctoral student at Johns Hopkins University, conducted fieldwork among the Aluku on the Lawa and in Saint- Laurent, producing a dissertation about the changes taking place during the period of rapid, forced francisation (Bilby 1990) as well as numerous articles, particularly on Maroon (and other Suriname) musics (see for example, Bilby 1999, 2001) as well as comparisons between the cultural practices of Suriname Maroons and those of the Maroons of Jamaica, with whom he also conducted long-term fieldwork (Bilby 1996, 1997, and see also Bilby 2005).

Because of Suriname's Civil War (1986–1992), anthropological fieldwork in Suriname became difficult from the mid-eighties through the 1990s. (During the very early 1980s, the Belgian Joris Hoeree had conducted fieldwork among the Saamaka and wrote a dissertation [Hoeree 1983] but never followed up with publications.[3] And during the late 1970s and early 1980s, Surinamese ethnomusicologist Terry Agerkop also conducted some fieldwork in Saamaka, receiving a Ph.D. in cultural anthropology in 1991 from the University of Brasilia and now, apparently, living in Amsterdam (see Agerkop 1982). During this difficult period in Suriname, the Thodens made short visits to Ndyuka and continued a stream of publications, culminating in a study that for the first time brought psychoanalytic theory into Maroon studies (Thoden van Velzen & van Wetering 1988). Bonno's work during the war, in collaboration with Ndyuka-born Thomas Polimé, also led to publications that featured a unique Ndyuka

---

3 He apparently became an international consultant and, more recently, a consultant in the Belgian system of secondary education.

A HALF-CENTURY OF "BUSH-NEGRO" STUDIES   41

perspective on the conflict (see, for example, Thoden van Velzen & Polimé 1988). Ben Scholtens, from the Netherlands, completed his historical dissertation on relations between Maroons and the government (1994) as well as a jointly authored account of the rituals and other events surrounding the death of Saamaka gaama Agbago (Scholtens et al. 1992), paying with his life on the eve of his dissertation defense in a never-solved Paramaribo murder case that may have been mixed up with the Civil War. The Prices, meanwhile, continued publishing on the basis of both their earlier research in Suriname (plus archival research in the Netherlands) and new experiences with Maroons during their frequent visits to Guyane. During these turbulent years for Suriname, no further anthropological research was conducted among the Pamaka, Matawai, or Kwintii—an absence that has continued into the present, except for Bettina Migge's linguistic work among the Pamaka (2003).

Since the millennium, Ndyuka studies have continued to be dominated by the work of the Thodens, with their ambitious book on religious history (2004) and their magnum opus on more general 19th- and 20th- century Ndyuka history (2013), which culminated a half century of joint research. Meanwhile, Diane Vernon had been conducting work from her base in Saint-Laurent and Marie-José Jolivet had shifted her interests from Creoles to include urbanizing Maroons in that same area (see for example, Vernon & Jolivet 2014). Since 1990, and continuing until his recent incarceration in the Netherlands, André Pakosie has published (and written the bulk of) Siboga, a magazine devoted to Maroon issues, with an emphasis on Ndyuka affairs (see also Dubelaar & Pakosie 1999). Newcomers to the Ndyuka scene include French anthropologist Jean-Yves Parris, who conducted dissertation research on carry-oracle funerary divination on the Tapanahoni (Parris 2011); American Stuart Strange who recently carried out dissertation research on the Tapanahoni and with obiama in Paramaribo (Strange 2016); Ndyuka-born Ine Apapoe, who is working on her doctorate about Maroon leadership in a changing world, and another Ndyuka woman, Martina Amoksi, who wrote a brief book about Maroon women in Paramaribo (2009). Finally, Brazilian anthropologist Olivia Gomes da Cunha (2018, Forthcoming, in this volume) has been conducting fieldwork during the past several years with women in and around Moengo.

In Saamaka territory, American experimental filmmaker Ben Russell, who had spent two years in the Peace Corps in the village of Bendekonde, made a feature-length art film about modern Saamaka life (2009), inspired by a metaphor from First-Time, and Brazilian doctoral student Rogério Pires conducted fieldwork between 2011 and 2013 in the Christian Saamaka village of Botopasi, focusing on funeral rites—the first anthropological fieldwork in Saamaka since the onset of the Civil War (Pires 2015). Meanwhile, Richard

Price spent much of the early 2000s working with an elderly Saamaka friend in Cayenne, Tooy Alexander, resulting in a book that delves deeply into Maroon ritual and esoteric languages (R. Price 2008). During this same period, the Prices wrote a book in French aimed at educating people in Guyane about the Maroons they were encountering in their daily lives (Price & Price 2003a); several of their English-language works were also translated so that the rapidly-increasing number of French-speaking Maroons and others in Guyane could have access to them (Price & Price 2005, 2016b, R. Price 2010, 2012, 2013c—see also now a second Saamakatongo book, Price & Price 2016a).

During this same period, archaeological investigations were carried out for the first time among Maroons. Under the direction of U.S.-based Ghanaian archaeologist Kofi Agorsah, work on the eighteenth-century Saamaka site of Kumako, which extended over several summers, added—in my view—very little, if anything, to our collective knowledge and raised serious ethical questions about disturbing sites historically sacred to Maroons. Jamaican-born Cheryl White, now Cheryl Ngwenyama, wrote a PhD dissertation that presents the results of this work (2007, see also Ngwenyama 2009) and she is currently planning a new project on the historic Matawai site of Tuido. (Similar troubling ethical questions were raised by Saamakas regarding the Dutch underwater archaeological project under the Afobaka lake carried out in connection with the 2009–2010 Tropenmuseum exhibition "Kunst van Overleven" [see below, as well as Landveld 1989, Price & Price 2010].)

Post millennial work among the Aluku, all by French researchers, has included the continuing ethno-botanical research of Marie Fleury (Fleury 2014), investigations by anthropologist Francis Dupuy regarding Aluku-Amerindian relations along the Lawa (Dupuy 2014), Tristan Bellardie's continuing historical research, based on archival sources (Bellardie 2014), and the work of Aluku-born historian Jean Moomou, who incorporated some oral history into his recently published book on eighteenth- and nineteenth-century Aluku history (Moomou 2013). For some years now, two scholars have been carrying out fieldwork in the challenging context of goldmining camps in Suriname—Dutch anthropologists Marieke Heemskerk and Marjo de Theije (see for example Heemskerk 2000, de Theije 2007 and 2014, and de Theije & Heemskerk 2009). This important research has involved Ndyukas, Saamakas, and Alukus (as well as Brazilians, Chinese, and other denizens of the goldmining camps).

Finally, I should mention that since the 1980s, following in the wake of Silvia de Groot, several scholars have been publishing on Maroon history on the basis of Dutch and Suriname archives, notably Dutch anthropologist Wim

Hoogbergen (see, for example, Hoogbergen 1985, 1992, 1996, and Thoden van Velzen & Hoogbergen 2011) and Suriname-born historian Frank Dragtenstein (see, for example, Dragtenstein 2002, 2009). Several works by the Prices also fit into this category (R. Price 1983b, Price & Price 1988).

I should add at least a few words about linguistic studies among Maroons, which have gone on pretty much continuously during this half century. A review of linguistic work prior to the mid-1970s, with extensive bibliography, is available in R. Price 1975:60–62. Since that time, teams from the Summer Institute of Linguistics continued their work for some years in both Ndyuka and Saamaka, producing numerous articles as well as the first grammar of a Maroon language (Huttar & Huttar 1994). They have also produced an on-line dictionary of Saamakatongo (Rountree, Asodanoe & Glock 2000) and another of Aukans (Ndyuka) (SIL n.d.). Meanwhile, Maroon historical linguistics has flourished, particularly by the Amsterdam Creole Group (see, for example, Migge 2007). And sociolinguistic studies among Maroons, often by researchers based in Guyane, have similarly multiplied (see, for a summary, Migge & Léglise 2015). Saamaka linguist Vinije Haabo is currently putting the finishing touches on his impressive dictionary of Saamakatongo (Haabo 2015), Ken Bilby's long-awaited etymological dictionary of Aluku is nearing completion (Bilby n.d.), and a grammar of Saamakatongo has recently been published by John McWhorter and Jeff Good (2012).

Over the past half-century, there have been a number of exhibitions featuring Maroon art and life, and groups of Maroon performers have appeared, repeatedly, at festivals in Europe, the United States, the Caribbean, and South America. To mention only the largest such events: In 1980–81 an exhibition, "Afro-American Arts from the Suriname Rainforest," sponsored by the National Endowment for the Humanities and curated by the Prices, appeared in major museums in Los Angeles, Dallas, Baltimore, and New York (see Price & Price 1980). In 1992, Ken Bilby and Diana Baird N'Diaye curated "Creativity and Resistance: Maroon Culture in the Americas" for the Smithsonian Institution's Festival of American Folklife, which included performances and other participation by Ndyukas, Alukus, and Saamakas (see Bilby & N'Diaye 1992, Price & Price 1994). And in that same year, the Hamburgisches Museum für Völkerkunde organized an exhibition of their impressive Saamaka collection made by the Herskovitses in 1929 (see Price & Price 1992b). In 2003, the venerable Völkerkundemuseum Herrnhut, Germany, moved to a new building and asked the Prices to redesign and curate its permanent Maroon exhibit space (see Price & Price 2003c). In 2009, Amsterdam's Tropenmuseum organized the ambitious "Kunst van Overleven: Marroncultuur uit Suriname," curated by historian Alex van Stipriaan and artist Felix de Rooy (see van Stipriaan & Polimé

2009 and also Polimé & van Stipriaan 2013). Meanwhile in Cayenne, the Musée des Cultures Guyanaises has been organizing temporary exhibitions for the past twenty years, drawing on its Maroon holdings, and expanding cooperative projects with the Surinaams Museum in Paramaribo. In connection with many of these exhibitions, but also as part of independent cultural tours, scores of Maroons have traveled in groups to perform songs, dances, and ceremonies at venues around the world, considerably enriching their personal experiences. And, during the period, several collections of Maroon music were made available on CDs and on the internet (see, for example, Bilby 2010, Gillis 1981, Price & Price 1977).

Throughout this long period, as earlier in the twentieth century (see R. Price 1975:43–45), there has been an intermittent stream of popular (non-scientific) publications about Maroons, ranging from the identity- (and publicity-) seeking "expeditions" of the 1970s Harvard team who sought their "original brother" in the jungle (Counter & Evans 1981; see also R. Price 1982) to Canadian Andrew Westoll's five-month-long journey through "the most surreal country in South America," which includes eye-popping descriptions of Peace Corps volunteers in Saamaka villages who instruct the locals in lesbian practices, a rave party on an island in Alcoa's artificial lake, and much else of an eyebrow-raising nature (Westoll 2008), and on to Dutchman Menno Marrenga's accounts of his twenty-three years living in Saamaka territory as an outboard motor repairman, with mordant analysis of the changing scene from the Civil War to the present (Marrenga 2011). Although it might be fun to review these works, including the lurid accounts of Maroon quasi-cannibalism during the Civil War, that's a task for another day (which could include, as well, reviews of documentary films and T.V. programs about Maroons, novels—including two featuring Captain Anato, the only Ndyuka-born police inspector [Niel 2012, 2016]—, the many children's' books about Maroons, and so forth). It would seem that on the whole, recent journalistic publications have taken a less sensationalist turn than in the past, with authors increasingly calling on anthropologists to help them get their stories straight (see, for example, Delano 2014).

∴

To what extent have methods, theory, and approaches changed during this half-century for those studying Maroons? In some respects, surprisingly little. For example, Parris' 2011 book on carry-oracle divination follows (both stylistically and in terms of subject matter) very much in the line of things the Thodens were writing in the 1970s. On the other hand, certain long-term trends are discernable. The use of detailed oral history juxtaposed with archival materials, begun by R. Price in the seventies with Saamakas, has been followed in the recent work of the Thodens, sometimes in collaboration with Hoogbergen. Experiments in reflexivity and other forms of postmodern anthropology, also begun by the Prices in the early eighties, were continued by them in the 1990s (Price & Price 1992a, 1995) and have found their way into some of the Thodens more recent publications. Activist work on behalf of oppressed Maroons made its appearance in the 1990s and has grown in importance, coming full circle with the recent publication, at the behest of the Saamaka People, of Fesiten (R. Price 2013a; see also his 2011). And there seems to be at least some attempt more recently to challenge traditional categories of anthropological knowledge and discourse about Maroons and to begin asking new questions that arise both from changing circumstances on the ground in Suriname and Guyane and shifting theoretical perspectives in anthropology (see, for example, the chapters in this volume by Cunha, S. Price, Strange, and others).

Looking ahead, perhaps it would be a good time for some of us older hands to try to stand back and take a long, hard look at the past fifty years, since modern anthropology among Suriname Marrons began. That period, as we've seen, has witnessed wrenching changes in these societies themselves. Yet to date, none of us has fully described, much less really analyzed, what these changes mean to individuals and the broader societies in which they live.

If some of us old-timers don't feel quite ready to pass the baton definitively to the next generations, I think I can speak for us all in saying that there are few greater pleasures in this intellectual life than seeing one's work read and debated and used as a springboard for new discoveries and analyses. All of us stand ready—and email now makes it so much easier!—to help mentor, and to debate and discuss with, those younger researchers now investing themselves seriously in the field. We encourage them to be less shy about writing us and sharing their own discoveries, as they continue to think them through.

I would also encourage those younger colleagues who build on our work to always historicize it, to contextualize our findings within the specific circumstances of their production (both the regnant theories and practices within the discipline of anthropology at the time and the fieldwork context itself). Doing anthropological fieldwork among Maroons in the 1960s or seventies was a vastly different proposition from doing so today (as I hope Sally and I showed, analogously, in our analysis of our own predecessors in Saamaka, the Herskovitses, who were there forty years before us [Price & Price 2003b]). I join my fellow seniors in looking forward eagerly to reading the publications that emerge from the research being done by a new generation of anthropologists in the ever-changing and always fascinating world of the Suriname and Guyanais Maroons.

References

Agerkop, Terry. 1982. "Saramaka Music and Motion." Anales del Caribe 2:231–245.

Albitrouw, Isaak. 1978. Tori foe da bigin foe Anake: verslag van een messianistische beweging. Edited and introduced by Miriam Sterman. Utrecht: Bronnen voor de Studie van Bosneger Samenleving 2.

Amoksi, Martina. 2009. De Marronvrouw in de stad: Een historische analyse van de gevolgen van de urbanisatie voor de Marronvrouwen in Suriname. Amsterdam: NiNsee/Amrit.

Bastide, Roger. 1961. Les Amériques noires. Paris: Payot.

Beet, Chris de. 1984. De eerste Boni-oorlog, 1765–1778. Utrecht: Bronnen voor de Studie van Bosneger Samenleving 9.

Beet, Chris de, ed. 1995. Skrekiboekoe. Boek der verschrikkingen. Visioenen en historische overleveringen van Johannes King. Utrecht: Bronnen voor de Studie van Afro-Suriname 17.

Beet, Chris de & Miriam Sterman. 1981. People in Between: The Matawai Maroons of Surinam. Utrecht: Krips Repro.

Bellardie, Tristan. 2014. "Marronnage sur le Tampock en 1767 : des marrons guyanais ou des transfuges du Surinam," In Les marronnages et leurs productions sociales, culturelles dans les Guyanes et le bassin caribéen du XVIIème au XXème siècle. Edited by Jean Moomou. Matoury: Ibis Rouge.

Bilby, Kenneth M. 1990. "The Remaking of the Aluku: Culture, Politics, and Maroon Ethnicity in French South America." Unpublished PhD dissertation, Johns Hopkins University, Baltimore MD.

Bilby, Kenneth. 1996. "Ethnogenesis in the Guianas and Jamaica: two Maroon Cases" In History, Power, and Identity: Ethnogenesis in the Americas, 1492–1992, edited by Jonathan Hill, 119–142. Iowa City: University of Iowa Press.

Bilby, Kenneth M. 1997. "Swearing by the Past, Swearing to the Future: Sacred Oaths, Alliances, and Treaties among the Guianese and Jamaican Maroons." Ethnohistory 44 (4): 655–689.

Bilby, Kenneth M. 1999. " 'Roots Explosion': Indigenization and Cosmopolitanism in Contemporary Surinamese Popular Music." Ethnomusicology 43 (2):256–296.

Bilby, Kenneth M. 2001. "New Sounds from a New Nation: Processes of Globalisation and Indigenisation in Surinamese Popular Music." In Twentieth-Century Suriname: Continuities and Discontinuities in a New World Society, 296–328. Edited by Rosemarijn Hoefte and Peter Meel. Kingston, Jamaica: Ian Randle Press.

Bilby, Kenneth M. 2005. True-Born Maroons. Gainesville: University Press of Florida.

Bilby, Kenneth M. 2010. Music from Aluku: Maroon Sounds of Struggle, Solace, and Survival. Washington, DC: Smithsonian Folkways Recordings (SF 40512).

Bilby, Kenneth M. n.d. Dictionary of Aluku, a Guianese Maroon Radical Creole (with Comparative Data from other Creole Languages). [nearing completion]

Bilby, Kenneth M. & Diana Baird N'Diaye. 1992. "Creativity and Resistance: Maroon Culture in the Americas." In 1992 Festival of American Folklife, edited by Peter Seitel, 54–61.Washington, D.C.: Smithsonian Institution.

Counter, S. Allen & David L. Evans. 1981. I Sought my Brother: An Afro-American Reunion. Cambridge: MIT Press.

Cunha, Olívia Maria Gomes da. 2018. "In Their Places: The Cottica Ndyuka in Moengo." In Ethnographies of U.S. Empire, 247–279. Edited by John Collins and Carole McGranahan. Durham: Duke University Press.

Cunha, Olívia Maria Gomes da. Forthcoming. "Making Things for Living, and Living a Life with Things." In Race and Rurality in the Global Economy. Edited by Michaeline Crichlow. Albany: SUNY University Press.

Cunha, Olívia M. Gomes da. this volume. "Self-fashioning and visualization among the Cottica Ndyuka." In Maroon Cosmopolitics: personhood, creativity and incorporation. Edited by Olivia M. Gomes da Cunha. Leiden: Brill.

Delano, James Whitlow. 2014. "Mon voyage en terre marron"; "Une culture originale, entre Afrique et Amérique." GEO 419 (January), pp. 50–62.

Dragtenstein, Frank. 2002. "De Ondraaglijke Stoutheid der Wegloopers": Marronage en koloniaale belied in Suriname, 1667–1768. Utrecht: Bronnen voor de Studie van Suriname 22.

Dragtenstein, Frank. 2009. Alles voor de vrede: de brieven van Boston Band tussen 1757 en 1763. Amsterdam: NINsee/Amrit.

Dubelaar, C. N. & André R.M. Pakosie. 1999. Het Afakaschrift van de Tapanahoni in Suriname. Amsterdam: Thela Thesis.

Dupuy, Francis. 2014. "Noirs Marrons et Amérindiens des Guyanes : approche comparée des relations interethniques," In Les marronnages et leurs productions sociales, culturelles dans les Guyanes et le bassin caribéen du XVIIème au XXème siècle, edited by Jean Moomou. Matoury: Ibis Rouge.

Fleury, Marie. 2014. "Plantes médicinales chez les Aluku du haut Maroni : origine, symbolique, et usages," In Les marronnages et leurs productions sociales, culturelles dans les Guyanes et le bassin caribéen du XVIIème au XXème siècle, edited by Jean Moomou. Matoury: Ibis Rouge.

Gillis, Verna. 1981. From Slavery to Freedom—Music of the Saramaka Maroons of Suriname (Lyrichord—List 7354).

Givens, Shelby Matthew. 1984. "An Ethnographic Study of Social Control and Dispute Settlement among the Aluku Maroons of French Guiana and Surinam South America." Unpublished PhD dissertation, University of California, Berkeley.

Green, Edward. 1974. "The Matawai Maroons: An Acculturating Afro-American Society." Unpublished PhD dissertation, The Catholic University of America, Washington, D.C.

Groot, Silvia W. de. 1963. Van isolatie naar integratie: de Surinaamse Marrons en hun afstammelingen. Officiëlle documenten betreffended de Djoeka's (1845–1863). The Hague: Martinus Nijhoff.

Groot, Silvia W. de. 1969. Djuka Society and Social Change: History of an Attempt to Develop a Bush Negro Community in Surinam 1917–1926. Assen: Van Gorcum.

Groot, Silvia W. de. 1974. Surinam granmans in Afrika: vier groot-opperhoofden bezoeken het land van hun voorouders. Utrecht: Het Spectrum.

Haabo, Vinije. 2015. available at http://www.saamaka.com

Heemskerk, Marieke. 2000. "Driving Forces of Small-Scale Gold mining among the Ndjuka Maroons: A Cross-Scale Socioeconomic Analysis of Participation in Gold mining in Suriname." Unpublished PhD dissertation, University of Florida.

Herskovits, Melville J., and Frances S. Herskovits. 1934. Rebel Destiny: Among the Bush Negroes of Dutch Guiana. New York: McGraw-Hill.

Hoeree, Joris. 1983. "De Saramakaanse wereld: Formatie, stabilisatie, akkulturatie. Een antropologische studie vanuit een pragmatisch paradigma." Unpublished PhD dissertation, University of Ghent, Belgium.

Hoogbergen, Wim. 1985. De Boni-Oorlogen, 1757–1860: Marronage en guerilla in Oost-Suriname. Utrecht: Bronnen voor de Studie van AfroAmerikaanse Samenlevingen in de Guyana's.

Hoogbergen, Wim. 1992. "De Bosnegers zijn gekomen!": Slavernij en Rebellie in Suriname. Amsterdam: Prometheus.

Hoogbergen, Wim. 1996. Het Kamp van Broos en Kaliko. De geschiedenis van een Afro-Surinaamse familie. Amsterdam: Prometheus.

Hurault, Jean. 1961. Les Noirs Réfugiés Boni de la Guyane Française. Dakar: Institut Français d'Afrique Noire.

Hurault, Jean. 1965. La vie matérielle des Noirs Réfugiés Boni et des Indiens Wayana du Haut-Maroni (Guyane Française): Agriculture, économie et habitat. Paris: ORSTOM.

Hurault, Jean. 1970. Africains de Guyane: la vie matérielle et l'art des Noirs Réfugiés de Guyane. Paris-La Haye: Mouton.

Huttar, George L. & Mary L. Huttar. 1994. Ndyuka. London: Routledge.

Kambel, Ellen-Rose & Fergus MacKay. 1999. The Rights of Indigenous Peoples and Maroons in Suriname. Copenhagen: IWGIA.

King, Johannes. 1981. Berichten uit het Bosland (1864–1870). Introduced and translated by Chris de Beet. Utrecht: Bronnen voor de Studie van Bosneger Samenleving 7.

Köbben, Andre. J. F. 1967. "Unity and Disunity: Cottica Djuka Society as a Kinship System." Bijdragen tot de Taal-, Land- en Volkenkunde 123:10–52.

Köbben, Andre J. F. 1968. "Continuity in Change: Cottica Djuka Society as a Changing System." Bijdragen tot de Taal-, Land- en Volkenkunde 124:56–90.

Köbben, Andre J. F. 1969. "Law at the Village Level: The Cottica Djuka of Surinam," In Law in Culture and Society, edited by Laura Nader, 117–140. Chicago: Aldine.

Köbben, Andre J. F. 1979. In vrijheid en gebondenheid: samenleving en cultuur van de Djoeka aan de Cottica. Utrecht: Centrum voor Caraïbische Studies, Rijksuniversiteït Utrecht.

Landveld, Erney R.A.O. 1989. Ganzë: het dorp dat het meer verdronk. Utrecht: Drukkerij Nout.

Lenoir, John D. 1973. "The Paramaka Maroons: A Study in Religious Acculturation." Unpublished PhD dissertation, New School for Social Research, New York.

Léobal, Clémence. 2013. Saint-Laurent-du-Maroni: Une porte sur la fleuve. Matoury: Ibis Rouge.

McWhorter, John & Jeff Good, 2012. A Grammar of Saramaccan Creole. Berlin: De Gruyter Mouton.

Marrenga, Menno. 2011. Saamaka: hoe een paar dorpjes, diep in het oerwoud, opgenomen worden in Suriname. Paramaribo: Caribbean Media Group.

Migge, Bettina. 2003. Creole Formation as Language Contact: The Case of the Suriname Creoles. Amsterdam: John Benjamins.

Migge, Bettina. ed. 2007. Substrate Influence in the Creoles of Surinam. Special issue of Journal of Pidgin and Creole Languages 22(1).

Migge, Bettina & Isabelle Léglise. 2015. "Assessing the Sociolinguistic Situation of the Maroon Creoles." Journal of Pidgin and Creole Languages 30:63–115.

Moomou, Jean. 2013. Les Marrons Boni de Guyane: Luttes et survie en logique coloniale (1712–1889). Matoury: Ibis Rouge.

Ngwenyama, Cheryl (White). 2007. "Material Beginnings of Saramaka Maroons: An Archaeological Investigation." Unpublished PhD dissertation. University of Florida, Gainesville.

Ngwenyama, Cheryl (White). 2009. "Archaeological Investigation of Suriname Maroon Ancestral Communities." Caribbean Quarterly 55(1): 65–88.

Niel, Colin. 2012. Les hamacs de carton. Rodez: Rouergue.

Niel, Colin. 2016. Obia. Rodez: Rouergue.

Pakosie, André R.M. 1972. De Dood van Boni. Paramaribo.

Parris, Jean-Yves. 2011. Interroger les morts: Essai sur la dynamique politique des Noirs marrons ndjuka du Surinam et de la Guyane. Matoury: Ibis Rouge.

Pires, Rogério Brittes W. 2015. "A Mása Gádu Kóndë: Morte, Espíritos e Rituais Funerários em uma Aldeia Saamaka Cristã." Unpublished PhD dissertation, Museu Nacional, Universidade Federal do Rio de Janeiro, Brazil.

Polimé, Thomas & Alex van Stipriaan. 2013. Zeg het met doeken: Marrontextiel en de Tropenmuseum collectie. Amsterdam: KIT Publishers.

Price, Richard. 1973. ed. Maroon Societies: Rebel Slave Communities in the Americas. New York: Doubleday/Anchor. [third edition, revised, with a new preface, Baltimore, Johns Hopkins University Press, 1996]

Price, Richard. 1976. The Guiana Maroons: A Historical and Bibliographical Introduction. Baltimore: Johns Hopkins University Press.

Price, Richard. 1982. "Review of S. Allen Counter and David L. Evans, I sought my brother: an Afro-American reunion." American Ethnologist 9:608–609.

Price, Richard. 1983a. First-Time: The Historical Vision of an Afro-American People. Baltimore: Johns Hopkins University Press. [second edition, University of Chicago Press, 2002]

Price, Richard. 1983b. To Slay the Hydra: Dutch Colonial Perspectives on the Saramaka Wars. Ann Arbor: Karoma.

Price, Richard. 1990. Alabi's World. Baltimore: Johns Hopkins University Press.

Price, Richard. 2008. Travels with Tooy: History, Memory, and the African American Imagination. Chicago: University of Chicago Press.

Price, Richard. 2010. Voyages avec Tooy: Histoire, mémoire, imaginaire des Amériques noires. La Roque d'Anthéron: Vents d'ailleurs.

Price, Richard. 2011. Rainforest Warriors: Human Rights on Trial. Philadelphia: University of Pennsylvania Press.

Price, Richard. 2012. Peuple Saramaka contre État du Suriname: combat pour la forêt et les droits de l'homme. Paris: Karthala.

Price, Richard. 2013a. Fesiten. La Roque d'Anthéron: Vents d'ailleurs.

Price, Richard. 2013b. "The Maroon Population Explosion: Suriname and Guyane." New West Indian Guide 87: 323–327.

Price, Richard. 2013c. Les premiers temps: la conception de l'histoire des Marrons saramaka. Second French edition, with a new foreword by the author. La Roque d'Anthéron: Vents d'ailleurs.

Price, Richard. 2018. "Maroons in Guyane: Getting the Numbers Right." New West Indian Guide 92. http://booksandjournals.brillonline.com/content/journals/10.1163/22134360-09203001.

Price, Richard & Sally Price. 1977. Music from Saramaka: A Dynamic Afro-American Tradition. Washington, DC: Smithsonian Folkways Recordings (FE 4225).

Price, Richard & Sally Price. 1988. John Gabriel Stedman's Narrative of a Five Years Expedition Against the Revolted Negroes of Surinam. Newly Transcribed from the Original 1790 Manuscript, Edited, and with an Introduction and Notes, by Richard and Sally Price. Baltimore: Johns Hopkins University Press.

Price, Richard & Sally Price. 1992a. Equatoria. New York: Routledge.

Price, Richard & Sally Price. 1992b. "Widerstand, Rebellion und Freiheit: Maroon Societies in Amerika und ihre Kunst," In Afrika in Amerika, edited by Corinna Raddatz, 157–173. Hamburg, Hamburgisches Museum für Völkerkunde.

Price, Richard & Sally Price. 1994. On the Mall: Presenting Maroon Tradition-Bearers at the 1992 Festival of American Folklife. Bloomington: Indiana University Press.

Price, Richard & Sally Price. 1995. Enigma Variations. Cambridge: Harvard University Press.

Price, Richard & Sally Price. 2003a. Les Marrons. Châteauneuf-le-Rouge: Vents d'ailleurs.

Price, Richard & Sally Price. 2003b. The Root of Roots: Or, How Afro-American Anthropology Got Its Start. Chicago: Prickly Paradigm Press/University of Chicago Press. (Available gratis at www.richandsally.net)

Price, Richard & Sally Price. 2003c. "Suriname—Afroamerikanische Marron," in Ethnographie und Herrnhuter Mission: Völkerkundemuseum Herrnhut, Dresden, Staatliches Museum für Völkerkunde Dresden, pp. 138–149.

Price, Richard & Sally Price. 2010. "Review of Kunst van Overleven: Marroncultuur uit Suriname." American Anthropologist 112:655–656.

Price, Richard & Sally Price. 2016a. Boo go a Kontukonde. La Roque d'Anthéron: Vents d'ailleurs.

Price, Richard & Sally Price. 2016b. Soirées de contes saamaka. La Roque d'Anthéron: Vents d'ailleurs.

Price, Richard & Sally Price. 2017. Saamaka Dreaming. Durham NC: Duke University Press.

Price, Sally. Co-Wives and Calabashes. Ann Arbor: University of Michigan Press. [second edition 1993]

Price, Sally and Richard Price. 1980. Afro-American Arts of the Suriname Rain Forest. Berkeley: University of California Press.

Price, Sally and Richard Price. 2005. Les Arts des Marrons. La Roque d'Anthéron: Vents d'ailleurs.

Price, Thomas J. 1970. "Ethnohistory and Self-Image in Three New World Negro Societies," In Afro-American Anthropology, edited by Norman J. Whitten and John F. Szwed, 63–71. New York: The Free Press.

Rountree, S. Catherine, J. Asodanoe & Naomi Glock. 2000. Saramaccan-English Word List. Paramaribo: Summer Institute of Linguistics. http://www.sil.org/americas/suriname/Saramaccan/English/SaramEngDictIndexhtml.

Russell, Ben. 2009. Let Each One Go Where He May. [film:130 minutes]

Scholtens, Ben. 1994. Bosnegers en overheid in Suriname: De ontwikkeling van de politieke verhouding 1651–1992. Paramaribo: Afdeling Cultuurstudies/Minov.

Scholtens, Ben, Gloria Wekker, Laddy van Putten & Stanley Dieko. 1992. Gaama Duumi, Buta Gaama: Overlijden en Opvolging van Aboikoni, Grootopperhoofd van de Saramaka Bosnegers. Paramaribo: Cultuurstudies/Vaco.

SIL (Summer Institute of Linguistics). n.d. Aukan-English Interactive Dictionary. http://www-01.sil.org/americas/suriname/Aukan/English/AukanEngDictIndex.html

Stipriaan, Alex van & Thomas Polimé, eds. 2009. Kunst van overleven: Marroncultuur uit Suriname. Amsterdam: KIT Publishers.

Strange, Stuart Earle. 2016. "The Dialogical Collective: Mediumship, Pain, and the Interactive Creation of Ndyuka Maroon Subjectivity." Journal of the Royal Anthropological Institute 22: 516–533.

Strange, Stuart. this volume. "Spirits and pain in the making of Ndyuka politics." In Maroon Cosmopolitics: personhood, creativity and incorporation. Edited by Cunha, Olivia M. Gomes da. Leiden: Brill.

Theije, Marjo de. 2007. " 'De Brazilianen stelen al ons goud!' Braziliaanse migranten in stad en binnenland." OSO, Tijdschrift voor Surinamistiek en het Caraïbisch Gebied 26 (1): 81–99.

Theije, Marjo de. 2014. "Small-scale Gold mining and Trans-Frontier Commerce on the Lawa River," in In and Out of Suriname: Language, Mobility and Identity, 58–75. Edited by Eithne Carlin, Isabelle Léglise, Bettina Migge & Paul B. Tjon Sie Fat, Leiden, Brill.

Theije, Marjo de & Marieke Heemskerk. 2009. "Moving Frontiers in the Amazon: Brazilian Small-Scale Gold Miners in Suriname." European Review of Latin American and Caribbean Studies 87:5–25.

Thoden van Velzen, H. U. E. 1966a. "Het geloof in wraakgeesten: bindmiddel en splijtzwaam van de Djuka matri-lineage." Nieuwe West-Indische Gids 45:45–51.

Thoden van Velzen, H. U. E. 1966b. Politieke beheersing in de Djuka maatschappij: een studie van een onvolledig machtsoverwicht. Leiden: Afrika-Studiecentrum.

Thoden van Velzen, H. U. E. & Wim Hoogbergen. 2011. Een zwarte vrijstaat in Suriname: De Okaanse samenleving in de 18e eeuw. Leiden: KILTV.

Thoden van Velzen, H. U. E. & Thomas Polimé. 1988. Vluchtelingen, opstandelingen en andere Bosnegers van Oost-Suriname, 1986–1988. Utrecht: Insituut voor Culturele Antropologie.

Thoden van Velzen, H. U. E. and W. van Wetering. 1975. "On the Political Impact of a Prophetic Movement in Surinam," in W.E.A. van Beek & J.H. Scherer (eds.), Essays on the Anthropology of Religion: Essays in Honor of Jan van Baal, The Hague, Martinus Nijhoff.

Thoden van Velzen, H. U. E. and W. van Wetering. 1988. The Great Father and the Danger: Religious Cults, Material Forces, and Collective Fantasies in the World of the Suriname Maroons. Dordrecht: Foris.

Thoden van Velzen, H. U. E. and W. van Wetering. 2004. In the Shadow of the Oracle: Religion as Politics in a Suriname Maroon Society. Long Grove: Waveland.

Thoden van Velzen, H. U. E. and W. van Wetering. 2013. Een zwarte vrijstaat in Suriname: De Okaanse samenleving in de 19e en 20e eeuw. Leiden: Brill.

Van der Elst, Dirk. 1970. "The Bush Negro Tribes of Suriname, South America: A Synthesis." Unpublished PhD dissertation, Northwestern University, Evanston, Ill.

Van der Elst, Dirk. 1975a. "The Coppename Kwinti: Notes on an Afro-American Tribe in Surinam. Part I: History and Development." New West Indian Guide 50:7–17.

Van der Elst, Dirk. 1975b. "The Coppename Kwinti: Notes on an Afro-American Tribe in Surinam. Part II: Organization and Ideology." New West Indian Guide 50:107–122.

A HALF-CENTURY OF "BUSH-NEGRO" STUDIES

Van der Elst, Dirk. 1975c. "The Coppename Kwinti: Notes on an Afro-American Tribe in Surinam. Part III: Culture Change and Viability." New West Indian Guide 50:200–211.

Vernon, Diane. 1985. Money Magic in a Modernizing Maroon Society. Caribbean Study Series, no. 2. Tokyo: Institute for the Study of Languages and Cultures of Africa and Asia.

Vernon, Diane. 1992. Les représentations du corps chez les noirs marrons de Suriname et de la Guyane. ORSTOM Editions, collection Etudes et Thèses, Paris.

Vernon, Diane & Marie-José Jolivet. 2014. "La Coutume immigrée: une comparaison de deux systèmes légaux," In Les marronnages et leurs productions sociales, culturelles dans les Guyanes et le bassin caribéen du XVIIème au XXème siècle. Edited by Jean Moomou. Matoury : Ibis Rouge.

Westoll, Andrew. 2008. The Riverbones: Stumbling after Eden in the Jungles of Suriname. Toronto: Emblem Editions.

Wetering, Wilhelmina van. 1966. "Conflicten tussen co-vrouwen bij de Djuka." Nieuwe West-Indische Gids 45:52–59.

Wetering, Wilhelmina van. 1973. "Hekserij bij de Djuka: een sociologische benadering." Unpublished PhD dissertation, Amsterdam.

Wetering, Wilhelmina van. 1975. "The Sociological Relevance of a Distinction between Sorcery and Witchcraft," In Rule and Reality: Essays in Honor of André J.F. Köbben, 171–184. Edited by Peter Kloos & Klaas van der Veen. Amsterdam, Antropologische-Sociologische Centrum.

CHAPTER 2

Why the African Gods Failed the Aukan Maroons

H.U.E. Thoden van Velzen

The Suriname Maroons

Suriname was an English colony (1650–1667) before it passed into Dutch hands. Its agricultural regime was built on the labor of African slaves with sugar as its main cash crop. The colony became notorious for forcing these Africans to work long hours under inhumane conditions. Right from the beginning slaves planned and often managed to escape into the rain forest surrounding the plantation area. Maroons, as they are called in the anthropological and historical literature, or Runaways (Lowesama) as they name themselves, often received assistance from the Caribs and other native peoples. The Maroons themselves praise their gods for the help they got. Some of these gods had accompanied them in the slave ships on their way to South America. Other gods who had come to their rescue were native to the South American rain forest. Rivalry among the gods was considered a regular occurrence.[1] This paper deals with the way Aukan (Ndyuka, Okanisi) Maroons of eastern Suriname report about the divine assistance they received during their flight to safety and the subsequent building of a new society in the eighteenth century which was strong enough to negotiate a peace treaty with the planters in 1760. Who were these gods who had come to the rescue of the Aukans? And when and for what reason did disagreements among the divine beings erupt?

A Well-Regulated Cosmos

During the 1960s I was confident I knew the answer to the first question. The supreme supernatural being was Nana. This deity, however, would only intervene in human affairs when things got completely out of hand, a situation that occurred perhaps once in a generation. All other problems, no matter how serious, were the province of Gaan Tata (Great Father) or Sweli Gadu (God of the

---

1 Large parts of this paper rely on field work done by Wilhelmina (Ineke) van Wetering (1934–2011).

© KONINKLIJKE BRILL NV, LEIDEN, 2019 | DOI:10.1163/9789004388062_004

Oath), a deity seconded by an army of lesser spirits, the Kumanti. According to Aukan oral traditions Gaan Tata had escorted the Africans in the slave ships, shared their miserable fate on the plantations and helped them to freedom. The main places of Gaan Tata worship were situated in Diitabiki, an Aukan village on the Tapanahoni river.

Of equal stature with Gaan Tata was Agedeonsu. His temple was at Tabiki, an Aukan village not far from the confluence of Tapanahoni and Lawa rivers, this deity entertained strong ties with the Papagadu or Vodu spirits. In the 1960s Agedeonsu and Gaan Tata's priests cooperated in many areas. Mutual respect was shown during ceremonial visits by priests and followers to the shrines of the other deity.[2] During my fieldwork in the 1960s and 1970s quite a few complaints about the operations of Gaan Tata's priests were brought to my attention.[3] I didn't think much of it at the time. Aukan elders were never fully convinced that Gaan Tata's priests were strangers to corruption. But this didn't seem to detract from their supreme religious position. But, as we will see later, all this was to change drastically.

Most of my fieldwork was done in the Aukan village of Diitabiki, the residence of the Gaaman (Tribal Chief) and the seat of Gaan Tata.[4] Half a dozen priests were employed in the daily consultations of his oracle. The oracle's clients were usually patients seeking answers to questions about the causes of their illness and soliciting advise on proper treatment. The deity's opinion was also sought by village headmen on contentious political matters or when witchcraft accusations threatened the ordinary peaceful equilibrium of village life. During the 1960s Gaan Tata's priests were clearly in charge (Thoden van Velzen 1966).[5]

The fight against witchcraft was seen to be Gaan Tata's signal contribution to the welfare of his followers. People accused of such a crime (wisiman) were brought before the oracle. Nearly always the priests declared these persons innocent of such evil wrongdoings. But things proceeded differently during the post-mortem examination obligatory for all deceased. Nearly half of them were convicted of witchcraft. Extreme measures were then taken: the possessions

---

2 I filmed one such a visit by Agedeonsu's followers to the shrines of Gaan Tata. See my "Visiting Deities", on http://www.lah-ufrj.org/visiting-deities-pt.html.

3 The first phase of field work was conducted mostly in Diitabiki and neighboring villages in 1961–62, July 1965 and September to early November 1970.

4 The deity is also known under yet other names, for example Bigi Gadu, Gaan Gadu and Gwangwella.

5 Half-a-century earlier Van Lier (1919: 45) had come to the same conclusion: "(...) the (Gaan Tata) priests control everyday life and the people are kept on a rein."

of such people were confiscated and distributed publicly whereby the priests would normally confiscate more than half of the inheritances. This part was subsequently divided into two portions: one part was left at Santigoon, Gaan Tata's sanctum in the forest, the other was divided among his priests. The corpses of the wisiman, those accused of witchcraft, were brought to Santigoon to be left unburied.

For an outsider such as myself the post-mortem punishment was repulsive. Many months of fieldwork had to pass before I discovered that this was the case for most ordinary Aukans as well. Moreover, opposition against Gaan Tata's priests had always been fierce in clans beyond the purview of this anthropologist. It took years before I became acquainted with the core ideas of the religious creeds embraced by members of some other clans. First a few words about the clans (lo) Aukan society is composed of.

The Structure of Aukan Society

The traditional formula used by Aukans when they speak about their nation is: "There are twelve clans and Gaaman (the Paramount Chief) represents the thirteenth." In fact there are thirteen clans, not counting Gaaman (Parris 2011:99).[6] Many of those embrace a matrilineal ideology but some, such as the Dyu (clan), don't. They will say: "we hail from plantations owned by Jews." But these Dyu, like other clans, consist of a number of matrilineal groups (bee). And they continue to stress that little has changed since the beginning of their society.

Are Aukan historians right in claiming that clan names have remained the same for almost three centuries? Fortunately, their statements can be checked against the historical knowledge that became available when a peace treaty (1760) was negotiated between the representatives of the Surinamese planters and the leaders of the Aukan Maroons. These peace talks took place near the Mama Ndyuka region, bordering on the Lely Mountains, one of the areas where the Aukans had built their villages.

This is what the archival documents of those years tell us: at the time of the peace treaty of 1760 the Aukans were divided into three different groups: first

---

6 In 1805 a group of black soldiers fled their post and asked and received permission from the Aukans to settle in their land. They founded the village of Poligudu near the confluence of Tapanahoni and Lawa rivers (de Groot 2009: 107–117). They were considered a separate clan, the thirteenth. The classic formula when speaking about their society remained in place: "We, The Twelve."

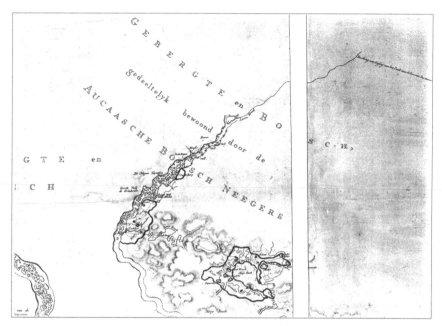

MAP 2.1 Vieira's map of Aukan Territory in 1761
SOURCE: NATIONAL ARCHIVES, 1761

an alliance under the leadership of the Dyu clan named Miáfiyabakaa (I don't trust the Whites), often shortened to Miáfiya. A second one was called Lukubun (Be Careful), it consisted mainly of the Otoo and Misidyan clans.[7] And thirdly the Ndyuka alliance under the leadership of the Dikan clan. This last federation remained in the Mama Ndyuka region until about 1780. The Otoo and Misidyan clans had moved southwards to the Tapanahoni River, and settled near the Gaan Olo falls around 1740. In about the same period the Dyu and their allies had built their villages some twenty miles further upstream.

Oral history insists that the Lukubun alliance clung to the veneration of Gaan Tata, their African god, while the Miáfiya federation had switched to an autochthonous god called Tata Ogii. The Dikan federation relied for the fight against witchcraft on the authority of Gaan Tata's priests. For all other spiritual problems, they clung to Agedeonsu, a deity that more than other gods

---

[7] In 1760 the Ansu clan was considered part of the Lukubun federation. This came to an end when the Ansu left for the Sara Creek region a few decades after the peace treaty. Around 1830 most of the Ansu had moved to the Cottica River in the coastal area. They remained loyal to the Gaan Tata creed.

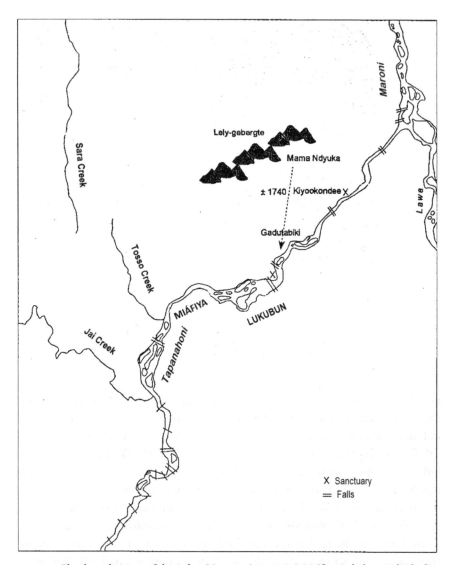

MAP 2.2 The three divisions of the Aukan Maroons (1740–1780): Miáfiya, Lukubun and Ndyuka
SOURCE: CLÉMENCE LÉOBAL, 2018

reminded the Aukans of the hell that life on the plantations had been and of the sins the Whites had committed against their ancestors. Under the umbrella of the Agedeonsu cult "tree worship" – the worship of spirits residing in certain trees – flourished. Certain reptiles were honored as well; they were considered "vehicles used by Papagadu spirits to move around" (boto fu Papagadu waka).

Later we will see that Gaan Tata entertained a close relation with Kumanti spirits while Tata Ogii often relied on Ampuku spirits. Before presenting three clusters of stories, viz. the Gaan Tata, Agedeonsu and Tata Ogii dossiers, a few cautionary words about terms such as history and historians are in order.

History and Historians

Aukan historians are those men and women who are known and admired for their knowledge of the past. Although much of that learning is specific to locality and kin group, a reputation as a historian can be gained only by those who have succeeded in collecting information about events considered crucial to the development of the Aukan nation as a whole. To offer one example: all historians are expected to have obtained some knowledge of the war with the Aluku Maroons (1792–1793), regardless of whether their own clans took part in the hostilities.[8] All historians need to know about other dramatic episodes of their history: the years of suffering (katiboten) on the plantations and the time of marronage, the escape and the following years of agony in an unknown environment (loweten). When dealing with loweten, the Aukan historians present different views of history. Most of them would fall in one of three categories: the Lukubun, Mama Ndyuka and Miáfiya version of history. As we will see those historical accounts are directly linked to the supernatural beings central to those federations.

It should be pointed out that the people I call historians seldom compare notes. No forum exists where diverging positions can be discussed and evaluated. When historians meet they often are at pains to discredit the knowledge of their colleagues. As a consequence, several accounts of important historical facts co-exist. A pertinent example is the exploratory march from the Mama Ndyuka creek to the Tapanahoni river which is said to have taken place well before the peace treaty of 1760 and which resulted in the founding of the village of Kiyookondee on the left bank of that river. Some historians hold that all twelve clans worked together when opening that footpath to the Tapanahoni. Others mention only three or four clans as having participated in the historical journey. However, the head captain (edekabiten) of the Dikan clan was quite resolute in declaring these positions untenable: "We Dikan opened up a path to the Tapanahoni river and no one else helped us!"[9] The Aukans have

---

8 On the war with the Aluku or Boni Maroons see Hoogbergen (1990).
9 I interviewed this head captain, da Baalawan, in May 1991.

no forum for discussing such widely diverging positions. The term "historian" is here used for all those Aukans who are known locally as surpassing others in knowledge of the past.

The Gaan Tata Files

Gaan Tata, an Alien Presence
Gaan Tata, the Great Father, is of African provenance. When Africans were enslaved and transported to Suriname He kept them company in the holds of the slave ship. Later, when they suffered on the plantations, He was their witness. Overcome by their misery He helped them to escape into the interior.[10]

Gaan Tata's Voyage
Gaan Tata was venerated by our ancestors in Africa (Afikaan Kondee). One day a number of Africans was invited to a White Man's ship. There was plenty of food and drink aboard, our African ancestors loved it. While this party was going on, the ship took to the ocean. None of our ancestors noticed this. The White captain was very clever. While the Africans were having a good time, he gave them bad things to drink, so that they would fall asleep. The next day, when they felt the swell of the ocean, they realized they had been kidnapped. Great was their consternation but there was nothing they could do about it. It was too late to swim back. Fortunately, one of our ancestors had taken the Gaan Tata Obiya with him.[11]

The Blood Oath (1)
To escape from the plantations was a risky business. You couldn't do that on your own. You needed companions. But were these companions to be trusted? If they betrayed you to the Whites torture and death would be your fate. That is why before fleeing from the plantations we took a

---

10   People from various clans told me this story.

11   Da Kofi Atyauwkili, Doisi Dyu (September 1970, Mainsi village).
Obiya: those parts of the supernatural forces that became available to mankind. At times Aukans have in mind objects charged with supernatural power, on other occasions the concept is used for invading spirits (Thoden van Velzen and Van Wetering 1988:17).
See for a similar story Aphra Behn's account (1668) of the royal slave Oronooko's misfortunes (Behn 2003:102). During her stay in Suriname (1663–1664) Behn collected a story of an African chief kidnapped by an English captain that was remarkably similar to the one that I collected in 1974.

sacred oath. A small incision was made in the arms of all participants to get a few drops of blood of each of them. This blood was collected in a calabash and mixed with a sacred potion. Each of us would then take a few sips from the liquid while swearing to the gods that if we betrayed our companions they should kill us. While doing so we asked Gaan Tata to punish those who broke the oath (sweli). That is why this god is also called Sweli Gadu.[12]

The Blood Oath (2)

While we were toiling on the plantations, Gaan Tata kept us company. We had to dig trenches, sometimes even canals where fishing boats could moor.[13] The work was too much! It killed us. No, we will never forget what your ancestors did to us. One day a number of us decided to escape. We swore a holy oath: "With God as witness I solemnly swear to run away. Thereupon we exchanged blood (kenki buulu). Each of us cut his arm to let a few drops fall in a liquid, and then we all drank from it. And then we spoke the oath: "Where you will die, I will die." Gaan Tata, hearing their oath, and seeing how miserable we were, came to our rescue. He showed us how to escape from the plantations and kept us company on their way to safety. Gaan Tata had been enraged when He witnessed the treatment of his people by the Whites (Bakaa). We killed many of them with a war Obiya Gaan Tata had given us.[14]

Grandmother's Obiya

From the sources of the Commewijne River we walked for seven days. Then one of the grandmothers folded her skirt into a small bundle which she tied to a rope. Through the movements of this bundle our ancestors learned where to go. Gaan Tata really took possession of this grand-mother of ours! And this is why our ancestors could find the river [the Tapanahoni]. Other people didn't have these skills; they had to accept our leadership.[15]

---

12   Da Asawooko, Misidyan, Diitabiki, 1962.

13   My guess is that his ancestor worked on a plantation on the right bank of the Commewijne River and close the confluence with the Suriname river. This was an area of sea clay in the tidal zone.

14   Da Kofi Atyauwkili, Mainsi village, Dyu clan, April 1977. The missionary Samuel Bauch described a similar ritual in 1893. [Bauch, 1893:320]

15   In Ndyukatongo this is expressed as "Sweli Gadu ben de logologo anga a mama." My source here is Da Bono Velantie, Otoo, April 1979.

Sweli Gadu's Taxing Laws

What we are telling you is not something we witnessed. We didn't see it, we heard about it (Ná si toli, na yee toli). My ancestress (mi afo) Kato and my ancestor (mi gaanta) Paangabooko were planning to escape from the plantation. Nobody forced them to do this. They just didn't want to be slaves any longer. Living the life of a slave was a horrible fate. We wished to live a proper life fit for humans (w'o suku libi). Sweli Gadu began to understand the suffering of his people. Like a dog who gradually learns what keeps his master's mind occupied.

Dikan (the people of the Dikan clan) solicited the help of ma Kato. "We would like to escape (lowe)" they told her. "Can you help us with your Obiya?" Ma Kato then allowed the Dikan to consult her Obiya. The Dikan explained to Sweli that the reason for their wish to escape from slavery was inhuman treatment on the plantations. In his answer Sweli showed his sympathy for the Dikan. But he pointed out that if they wanted him to support them they should obey all his rules and prohibitions (kina). These were his rules: Women in their menstrual period were to be kept apart from the main body of refugees.[16] And there were other rules as well: When angry with someone, don't send an evil spirit to that person (sende gadu). Never interrupt (koti mofu) someone when he is speaking in a palaver. All grievances have to be aired. The withholding of feelings of bitterness is a serious mistake; it will lead to problems in the future (fiyofiyo). Never harbor grievances (mandi fu sani). Dikan responded by saying that people would have no trouble honoring these divine dictates.

At first the Dikan clan was courageous enough to bring this demanding Obiya with them. But after a while, the Dikan were no longer happy about this. It was felt to be too pressing. They decided to take only Sweli Gadu's female side with them; that side is much softer. People tell me that the Otoo clan had no problem escaping with the male side of the Obiya. But they should tell you that themselves.[17]

A Carry Oracle Shows the Way

We were afraid of the great forest. We didn't know where to go. Fortunately, our ancestors were smart enough to ask Sweli Gadu for help. Two of us

---

16 Today women during their menses withdraw to a house at the outskirt of their village, the so-called *fagi* or *munu osu* (moon house). Contacts between these women and their family in the village is strictly regulated.

17 Da Kofi Atyauwkili, Dyu Mainsi village, 1978.

FIGURE 2.1 Bigi Gadu Oracle
SOURCE: H.U.E. THODEN VAN VELZEN, 1962

would carry a plank with the great Obiya tied to it. From then on it was immediately clear to us what direction to take. When Sweli Gadu came to a spot where dangers lurked he would stop his carriers. Stock-still they would stand! Then it was clear to us that we had reached a point where the enemy was hiding. Or where a difficult swamp had to be crossed. We followed Sweli Gadu's instructions to the letter. And that is how we ended up where we are today.[18]

The narrator here describes the pivotal role of the carry oracle in Aukan culture as he knew it. He himself often acted as one of the two carriers of Gaan Tata's oracle in the 1960s. There is little doubt that carry oracles were in use in preceding centuries as well. Whether the Runaways actually used the carry oracle on their march from the plantations to safety in the south is unlikely.

---

18   Da Sampake, Misidyan, Diitabiki, 1962.

FIGURE 2.2 Gaan Tata's Oracle in Diitabiki
SOURCE: H.U.E. THODEN VAN VELZEN, 2004

The Mama Ndyuka Clans

A Rift Opened Up

Very early in the eighteenth century, under military pressure, large groups of Maroons were forced to abandon the forest regions near the sources of the Cottica and Commewijne Rivers. They trekked first to the Gran Creek and from there to the Ndyuka Creek or the Mama Ndyuka, as the Aukans call it, a restricted area between two wings of hills radiating from Mount Lely. Many years before the peace treaty of 1760 the two dominant groups among them were the Dikan and Nyanfai clans. They were in close contact with the Otoo and Misidyan clans. A prominent leader of the Dikan (da Labi or Labi Labi Vod) was married to ma Kato, priestess of Gaan Tata.[19] As we have seen the Dikan gradually loosened their ties with the cult, orienting themselves to what they considered to be the realities of the new world they had come to inhabit. Much more serious disagreements arose when a Nyanfai chief called Agamun

---

19   This marriage was ended before the peace treaty of 1760 as the Dutch negotiators noted.

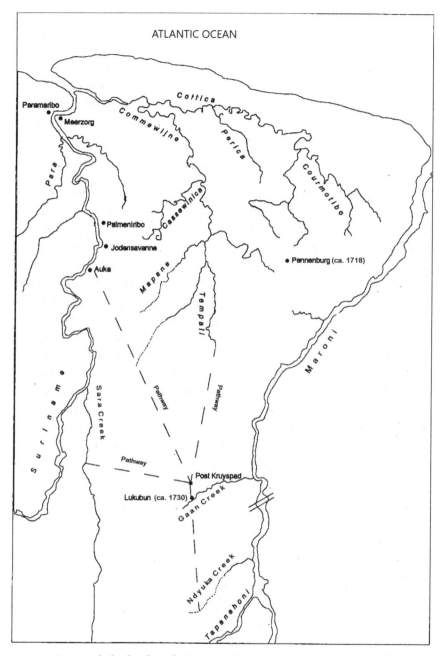

MAP 2.3 Forest paths leading from the Suriname, Commewijne (Tempati) rivers and Sara Creek to Mama Ndyuka
SOURCE: CLÉMENCE LÉOBAL, 2018

claimed to be entitled to the position of Gaaman, the chief of all Loweman in that part of Suriname. The Otoo argued that they had the oldest rights and therefore rejected the Nyanfai claims. The Nyanfai chief ordered a woman of the Otoo clan to be killed, the reason given was that she would have stolen maize from the common provision ground the Nyanfai had opened.[20] Whatever the truth of that complaint the result was total estrangement between the Otoo and Nyanfai clans. The Otoo and their allies left the Mama Ndyuka and trekked southwards.

A Cramped Place

With more Loweman coming in every day the departure of the Otoo and allies didn't mean the end of the problem of land scarcity. The system of slash-and-burn agriculture meant that vast areas needed to be at the disposal of the Maroons. Space to build houses was in short supply[21] When felling trees to make room for the growing population of the Mama Ndyuka region, some Maroons acted without distinguishing between types of trees and without the necessary ritual preparations. Certain trees are the abodes of spirits and are not to be felled unless after careful ritual preparation. Others, more versed in the knowledge of the Obiya, had to come to their rescue. In this way, relationships of guilt and ritual assistance developed between two main Aukan clans, the Nyanfai and the Dikan. Oral traditions reflect the close relationship between these two clans by giving either the Nyanfai or the Dikan clan a predominant place in tree worship. In one version it is a Dikan elder who had to accept the intervention of a prominent Obiyaman of the Nyanfai. In another version the Nyanfai needed the help of the Dikan. It is important to note that most of these historical accounts were presented to me by historians from clans that were not directly involved in the struggle for supremacy in that forest sanctuary.[22]

Next to tree worship, the snake cult is seen as one of the great assets of a cluster of clans comprising not only the Nyanfai and Dikan, but also the Pedi and Mbeei. Just as for the so-called tree worship, most Aukans insist that they

---

20   Maroon leaders were supposed to look after their people by opening up communal grounds. Much later in the 18th century the two famous leaders of the Aluku Maroons (Boni and Aluku) would do the same for their people. The murder of the Otoo "mother" by the Nyanfai is not forgotten. Even today the Aukan Gaaman doesn't stay the night in the village of Keementi, nowadays the Nyanfai village on the Tapanahoni. They put it this way: "Gaaman boto nai siibi a Keementi." (Gaaman's boat doesn't sleep in Keementi).

21   That the Mama Ndyuka region soon became a crowded area is also mentioned in the oral history account Morssink (1934) collected in the early 1920s.

22   When people refer to the area those four clans occupy today they call it Gaan Bilo (Great Downstream).

don't worship the tree itself but the spirit that houses in it. The same is true of snakes: Aukans don't worship snakes, but they do believe that certain snakes are vehicles for spirits, the Papagadu spirits (boto fu Papagadu waka).

The Agedeonsu Files

Why We Infuriated the Gods

Dikan, Pedi, Nyanfai and Mbeei, they were all assembled there [in Mama Ndyuka]. As it happens a huge tree, a kankantii, stood in the middle of their new village. To make room for more houses they had to cut down the tree. Everybody agreed that it had to be done. On top of the tree's enormous roots, the upper part above ground, a scaffold was erected. Only by doing so could they fell the tree at a point where it was not at its widest. Mi gaanta Sukati had built a scaffold consisting of planks and branches. It was getting dark by the time the scaffold was built. When mi gaanta Sukati returned to his work early next morning he found the scaffold in ruins. Mi gaanta Sukati rebuilt the scaffold and started the work of felling the tree. But what happened? At the very first stroke of the axe the tree started bleeding. Exactly at the spot where the axe had hit the tree. Mi gaanta Sukati's second strike didn't hit the tree, the axe had hit his foot. It seemed impossible to stop the bleeding. The wound couldn't be closed. Blood gushed out. The tree continued to bleed as well. Now finally they understood that this was not an ordinary tree. People realized that it was a sacred tree home to some deity. People realized what god-head housed in the tree. It was Agedeonsu, also known under the names Mamakiya, Tatakiya and ma Falu. The snake (Dyakasa) had also taken the tree for a home.

Mi gaanta Labi Vod [Labi Dikan] prepared a medicine (Obiya) for the tree and another one for mi gaanta Sukati. Both the tree and "that father of the Nyanfai (clan)" made a fast recovery. But serious trouble could no longer be avoided. The god Agedeonsu was infuriated. He considered both the Dikan and the Nyanfai sinners. And the Pedi and Beei clans were not without fault either. They had been watching when people tried to chop down the tree. And they hadn't lifted a finger. Till this very day Agedeonsu demands that all four clans serve him.[23]

---

23   Da Afuyee Menisaki, a Dikan from the village of Benanu, 1978.

FIGURE 2.3   Dance of the Papagadu mediums. Diitabiki, Tapanahoni
SOURCE: H.U.E. THODEN VAN VELZEN,1962

The Bleeding Tree (1)

One day one "father" (ancestor) went for a walk. There was this bird, a big one. Next to the place where they put a plank across the creek (probably used as a latrine). That was at the very end of the village. Where they had cut this path. There is no other way to tell this story. He prepared himself well (meaning: he took all ritual precautions in case he would encounter hostile magical forces). He took a rope. When he had taken this rope, he walked around this tree. He tied it firmly to the tree so that it wouldn't split or loosen. When he was ready he cut two branches. He pressed them into the ground next to the tree. On this side and again on the other. He cut a forked branch (hala). Two forked branches. Really pressed them into the ground. On their top he secured four sticks. He had constructed a scaffold (bakoto). When he had climbed on the scaffold, he took his axe and hacked. He hacked "poh, poh, poh!". A liquid gushed from the tree. Hey! What's happening? Hey, what's that? He said to himself: "look, a miracle happened!" The father said: "we shouldn't be afraid of this." He climbed down to call the others. Let all of them come!"

WHY THE AFRICAN GODS FAILED THE AUKAN MAROONS 69

The following day he cut another footpath to arrive at that tree. He took his axe again. Walked to the other side of the tree. Again, he was astounded by what he saw. Everybody came to watch him. They saw the blood of a human being. He told them: it doesn't matter. They asked him; "do you know what you are doing? Whose blood is this? Cut yourself, show us!" The father cut himself. Then it became clear to them that the blood on the tree was not his blood. Ohoo! [Expression of amazement], the father exclaimed. "Things have happened to me!"

A man called Agaamu had a message for him. Gaanta Agaamu said: "wait a minute!" He returned to the forest. When he came back he climbed the scaffold. He opened a bottle with Obiya in it. Kleen! (imitating the sound of a bottle opening) the bleeding of the tree stopped at once! He treated the father's wound. He opened the bottle: plop! Kleen!, the bleeding stopped. He arranged everything. He started tying the medicine to the tree till it was well secured. He dressed the father's wound. After three days the father was well again. The dressing could be removed. Ókolo (expression of surprise), he told them he had made a total recovery. He said: "nothing is wrong anymore." The father who had treated the wounds was called mi gaanta Agaamu from (the village of) Keementi, a Nyanfai (from the Nyanfai clan). The father who was responsible for this accident was mi gaanta Deesi from (the village) of Nikii, a Dikan.[24]

The Bleeding Tree (2)

The Loweman had made camp quite close to an enormous kankantii (silk cotton tree). When the wind blew one could hear this sound "Gumaaa. ..." In the top of the tree a door opened. This was heard by the Loweman. They heard someone walking over the planks of a tree house. Next to the kankantii there was yet another big tree. One man from the Nyanfai (clan) named Sukati planned to fell this tree. When his axe hit the tree it started bleeding immediately. Fortunately, there was this man from the Dikan. His name was mi gaanta Labi Dikan. He was well versed in Papagadu Obiya.[25] He took care of the tree's wound and cured it. From that moment on the Loweman and the "God of the Land and Creeks" became acquainted. The name of the God was Agedeonsu. But during those days we called him Tata Nesu. He helped us to hide ourselves from

---

24 Da Wayo, a Misidyan, kabiten of the village of Sangamansusa, 2006. Here is a Lukubun historian reciting the tales of the Mama Ndyuka clans.

25 Papagadu obiya, magical forces using reptiles as their vehicles.

the Bakaa with a special Obiya. The Obiya's name was kiibi pikin Obiya.[26] There is nothing more to tell.[27]

Here is yet another example of two clans helping one another to survive in the forest, only the roles are reversed. Now it is the Dikan clan coming to the rescue of the Nyanfai. These oral history accounts reveal the close cooperation of these two clans in the forest sanctuary.

The Man in the Tree

Our ancestors took seeds with them. They planted them. These seeds were sprouting. Then we knew the Obiya had manifested itself. A tree grew from the seeds. That tree still exists today. Go to (the village of) Nikii! You will see that tree. It is not an ordinary tree. Every morning at six o'clock you can hear someone who lives in that tree. You hear him opening the door; wèèè. Than you hear polón, polón. He is coming down a staircase. He is descending from the tree's top. Until he reaches its bottom. He climbs down till he reaches the ground. It is a stranger (Bakaa), a very white one. The name of that white man is Agedeonsu. But we also call him Ndyuka Gadu (God of the Ndyuka Maroons).[28]

Help from the Birds

A bird told us: "you have reached this place, but the river you have reached is not the right one, it is only a branch of the great river." We had arrived at Mama Ndyuka. That was what the bird could tell us. When the day had come to move further the bird guided us. When he was in charge he was called "toko." It is the bird "toko" who brought us where we are today.[29]

A New Earth

In 1973 by chance I encountered an Aukan friend who had settled in The Netherlands. He was the first to tell me about the great changes that had occurred since my last field work of 1970. His account could be summarized with one

---

26   Kiibi pikin obiya, the obiya that hides children (from the Bakaa). Here it means an obiya that would hide all Maroons from the Bakaa.

27   Da Kasiayeki, Dyu, Fisiti (Godo-olo) village, locally known as the best of Aukan historians, 1981. It is important to note that da Kasiayeki's clan is part of the Miáfiya cluster. Historians of his stature would not limit themselves to the tales of their own cluster of clans.

28   Kabiten Wayó, Misidyan, Sangamansusa, 2010.

29   Kabiten Wayó, Misidyan, Sangamansusa, 2010.

WHY THE AFRICAN GODS FAILED THE AUKAN MAROONS 71

of his first sentences: "Everything has changed for us Aukans, we now live in a new world." He told me of an Aukan man by the name of Akalali who had stepped forward with the claim that Tata Ogii, supreme divine ruler of the interior, had invaded him, charging him with the task to put an end to the evil corruption of Gaan Gadu's priests. Gaan Gadu's priests had broken the concordat with Tata Ogii when they left more and more corpses of witches unburied in the forest, thereby polluting the earth, creeks and rivers. It had also irked the godhead that the priests had been stealing from the people by confiscating the inheritances of the deceased, many of them falsely convicted of witchcraft.

At the end of 1973 I had returned to the Aukan villages of the Tapanahoni. Akalali had indeed broken all resistance of Gaan Gadu's priests. As a result, the oracle was no longer consulted and Tata Ogii had replaced Gaan Gadu as the chief deity of the Aukans. What surprised me most was the unanimity in people's negative judgement about Gaan Gadu. The enthusiasm about Akalali's destruction of the Gaan Gadu cult was equally astounding. People outdid themselves in remembering instances that supposedly showed the perfidiousness of his priests. Now, for the first time, people were willing to tell me about the key role Tata Ogii had played in the flight to safety of the Loweman and about their successful settlement in the interior.[30]

The Tata Ogii Files

A Giant as Trailblazer

When fleeing the plantations, we were entering a forest that seemed to go on forever. We were at loss where to go. It was hard work finding your way through the dark forest. But after three days of gruelling labor we received help. A giant came to our rescue. With his bare hands he had cleared a path for us through the forest. When we woke up in the morning, the path was there, leading us further away from the plantations. He walked ahead of us, we Loweman followed him. After three days we lost sight of him, but we could see a path he had prepared for us. Branches were broken; felled trees were lining the trail. In a straight line the forest path brought us to the Mama Ndyuka. We Loweman discussed this, and we came to the conclusion that we were now safe, far away from the plantations.

---

30   Had I done research in Dyu villages I would have heard about the role of Tata Ogii at a much earlier date.

We were very grateful for the deity's help. We would from now on have to make our own decisions. "This Thing" (a Sani, a euphemism for the god Tata Ogii) knew where the river was. That is how we could reach the river. We built a village there called Kiyookondee.[31] Nothing revealed which of the gods had helped us to get there. From Kiyookondee all clans went their own way.[32]

Commentary. This account attempts to demonstrate the significance of Tata Ogii for all Maroons, including the Otoo-Misidyan alliance. But it leaves unanswered the question when the followers of Sweli Gadu embraced the new faith. When we collected this narrative a prophet of Tata Ogii dominated Aukan religious life. But the feeling that in a foreign and strange territory one needs the help of the local gods will have been widely shared at a much earlier date. The notion that all Aukan clans first reached the Tapanahoni River at Kiyookondee is a key historical myth, not supported by facts.

Unexpected Meetings

One day the Aukan hunters saw a herd of bush pigs (pingo) cross the river. At the exact moment when the pigs are most vulnerable! When our people started firing their guns not a single pig was killed. But they soon understood why they had been so unsuccessful. Among the pigs they saw a creature of childlike proportions. The child's head betrayed the creature's abnormality. It was pitch-black! The child wore a black kamisa (loincloth). Now they knew they had seen an Ampuku (forest spirit). This spirit was protecting the pigs.[33]

Commentary. The Ampuku spirits are held to be Tata Ogii's soldiers. My source is a man from the Otoo clan devoted to the worship of Sweli Gadu. The belief in the powers of the autochthonous god had spread through all Aukan clans in the 1970s.

---

31 Aukans insist that Kiyookondee – village of Creoles, i.e. Maroons born in Suriname- was their first village on the Tapanahoni. The village was abandoned in the middle of the 19th century. Later it became a place of pilgrimage. In 1962, when I visited the pilgrimage site, it consisted of half a dozen houses and an ancestor pole (faakatiki). From Kiyookonde a well-cut path of about half-a-mile led straight into the forest. At the end was a tree in the middle of an area cleared off other vegetation. At the foot of the tree was a place for prayer.

32 Da Asawooko, Misidyan, Diitabiki, 1974.

33 Da Amadiyu, Otoo, Diitabiki, 1979.

A Ghost Guides the Loweman

The Loweman were visited at night by the ghost (yooka) of our ancestor Fiiman Kiyoo (Freeman Creole). He was born in the forest. He had never felt the yoke of slavery. During his life Fiiman was known for his knowledge of the Kumanti[34] Obiya. He was possessed by an Opete (Osoro) wenti. During our flight to safety we often heard the nasal sound of Fiiman's voice: "Why did you go to sleep so early? We haven't reached our goal yet."

Fiiman's spirit showed them places where they were safe. When we reached the river, we met Tata Ogii, God of the Interior. It was Tata Ogii who granted Fiiman's people permission to settle along the Tapanahoni. This prerogative wasn't easily won: a fight between Fiiman and Tata Ogii preceded it. Fiiman's ghost had found its final abode at Belenki Pali, in the Beeymancreek (a tributary of the Tapanahoni). The people of the Dikan clan inherited Fiiman's sacred Kumanti shrine. The tabernacle (pakáa) that housed Fiiman's spirit came in Dikan's possession as well. As all Aukans respect Fiiman Kiyoo it follows that they have to consult the Dikan first. No Gaaman can make an important decision without first consulting Fiiman's oracle.[35]

The story of Fiiman Kiyoo suggests that certain groups of Loweman later known as Aukans had gained their freedom quite early, perhaps during the closing decades of the 17th century. These Loweman, who would later be known as the Dikan clan, had settled in the Mama Ndyuka region long before 1760, the year Aukans and the planters concluded their peace treaty. The long trek of the Dikan from the plantations to the Mama Ndyuka probably started early in the 18th century. Fiiman Kiyoo (Freeman Creole) was born in the forest where he earned his reputation as a shaman well versed in Kumanti lore. Labi, the Dikan headman, described by the Dutch negotiators as of middle age, was also "born in the forest." Aukans say "He never felt the yoke of slavery." Fiiman Kiyoo belonged to an earlier generation of Maroons born in the forest. He could have been the child of one of the first groups of Loweman fleeing the plantations. The Otoo claim that Andiisi (Andries in Dutch accounts), was their first headman, and fled the plantation during the "War of the Indians" (1678–1684).

---

34 A religious organization venerating the spirits of healing and war, associated with the Sweli Gadu cult. See Borges (2014: 45–78).

35 Da Afuyee Menisaki, Dikan, Benanu, 1981.

Fiiman Kiyoo Fights with Tata Ogii

When the Dikan (clan) had reached the Tapanahoni it became clear to them that life there wouldn't be easy. Tata Ogii allowed them to build settlements along the river. But everything changed when our deceased ancestor Fiiman Kiyoo challenged Tata Ogii to fight him. It would later be known as a heroic battle. When no clear victor was in sight the battle was stopped, and both parties started to respect one another. Now the Dikan clan was convinced that they too should pay homage to Tata Ogii.[36]

Tata Ogii Denounces Abuses

Sweli Gadu's priests knew how to detect witches. They demanded that people suspected of witchcraft drink a sacred potion. We didn't object to that. Witches would fall ill and then we would feel safer. But gradually more and more people were ordered to drink this potion. When you died as a result of the ordeal all your possessions were confiscated. Your family would never get anything. To get their hands on even more goods, Sweli's priests began adding a poison to the sacred potion. People came to know about it when the Sweli priests accidentally dropped a bottle with the potion in the river. Aukans were used to drink river water but now they fell ill in great numbers. Their bellies would swell until they burst. This happened to some Bakaa as well who were visiting the Aukans. In great haste they fled to the city.[37]

Tata Ogii Calls on the Animals to Rescue the Aukan Nation

Around 1790 Boni, leader of the Aluku Maroons, started to distrust the Aukans. He decided to attack them before they came in cahoots with the Bakaa. Together with his Obiyaman Dyaki Atoonboti he travelled from his villages on the Lawa River, through the Gonini Creek, and then cut his way through the forest to reach the abandoned village of An-imbaw on the Tapanahoni, only a few hundred meters away from the newly founded village of Puketi. Tata Ogii decided to protect the Au-kans from this attack. The deity mobilized a herd of bush pigs to attack the Aluku.

Boni and Dyaki Atoonboti barely managed to repel the attack. From that moment on the Aluku leaders knew that the Aukans enjoyed powerful protection and that the war would be a life-and-death struggle.[38]

---

36 Da Afuyee Menisaki, Dikan, Benanu.
37 Da Pakosi, Misidyan, Puketi, this account was published by his son André Pakosie (1972:8).
38 Da Pakosie, Misidyan, Puketi, published by his son André Pakosie (1972:9)

First Encounter with the God of the Interior

It happened when our long journey through the forest came to an end. We, Fiiman (Maroons), were looking for a place deep in the interior where we could live in safety. After weeks of walking through the dark forest, we suddenly stumbled upon a wide river. A big, clear, space was in front of us. There was bright sunlight everywhere. But while we were enjoying this view all of a sudden a boat appeared. It was then that we first met with our God. He was lightly colored, like an Ingii (Amerindian). He was sitting in the middle of the boat. He was accompanied by two men, one was sitting in front of him, the other behind him. Nobody used a paddle and yet the boat moved forward, against the stream. And then, all of a sudden, the boat disappeared. Dissolved into thin air, as happens with spirits. The spirit in the middle must have been the most important one. After all, when a village captain or a Gaaman travels his place will be in the middle of the boat. All of us immediately realized that the spirit we had seen belonged there, he was in his own territory [genius loci]. It was also clear to us that he was in command of this new land. "We have seen Him for the first time on the river" we would later say. Many years later we came to know His name, it was Tata Ogii.[39]

The Dyu Have to Yield for the God of the River

We walked for a very long time. But on a morning, it was about ten o'clock we hit upon a wide river. We trusted that river. We didn't go upstream, we went downstream. Through the rapids downstream. Later we reached a point where another river joined ours. We called that place Poligudu. Now we were in a really big river [This must have been the Maroni River]. On the other side of the river was a mountain. We made camp there.

When we had been there for a while a creature (he says: "a Thing," wan Sani) emerged from the forest. [the narrator doesn't elaborate on the nature of this creature, but in all likelihood he was referring to Tata Ogii]. But the Thing didn't bring a message. One day we were attacked by other Maroons. They captured one of our women. Now we began to understand that something was wrong.

One of our leaders at that time was mi gaanta (my ancestor) Du. He had cleared a place and consecrated it to Sweli Gadu. By doing so, without being aware of it, he had committed a grave mistake. All that attention for Sweli Gadu, an African god, angered the God of the River [God of the

---

39   Da Akalali, prophet of Tata Ogii, Pataa, Nyunkondee, 1974.

Interior]. He considered Sweli Gadu a stranger, a guest at best, an African deity unfamiliar with the dangers of the forest. If the Aukans wanted His help, Sweli Gadu had to pay. And that's why the possessions of witches had to be brought to Santigoon, a place the Thing called his own.[40] For a long time, this arrangement brought peace to the River.[41]

The Use of Violence

The sharpest criticism of Tata Ogii's followers was directed at what they considered the hypocrisy of Gaan Tata's priests. They argued that these priests while advocating the ideals of harmonious and peaceful social relations (makandi libi) were stealing from the relatives of the deceased, were dumping corpses in the forest and polluting Tata Ogii's land and rivers. As an antidote Tata Ogii's prophets advocated the use of violence against witches when they were still alive. But they went yet a step farther. Acts of violence by Tata Ogii's mediums didn't need to be justified by depicting them as a form of defense against a corrupt regime. Gratuitous violence, more than anything else, would prove the authenticity of Tata Ogii's medium. Here are few examples starting from the most recent one and going back in time.

In 2006, Gangáa, an Aukan, donning the mantle of Tata Ogii, established a reign of terror in Tapanahoni villages.[42] Gangáa ordered his assistants to round up persons suspected of witchcraft. They were brought to the prophet's camp where they were beaten and tortured. One of the victims, a village headman, barely managed to escape being buried alive. The movement met with little or no opposition in Aukan villages of the Tapanahoni river. The crueller his acts, the more followers Gangáa appeared to attract. At the end of 2006 the prophet was arrested by the police when he visited the capital Paramaribo where a victim had identified him. The massive popular support Gangáa could count on revealed the great attraction the Tata Ogii cult enjoyed among the Aukan population. This is true for the Aukans of the interior as well as for the thousands of Aukans who have settled in the southern quarters of Paramaribo. In 2006, quite a few Aukans from the city returned to the Tapanahoni for short visits to witness the brutal and, in their eyes, liberating force of the new movement. People suspected of witchcraft were humiliated and beaten by a small group

---

40 A considerable part of the material possessions of persons posthumously accused of witchcraft were brought to Santigoon, a patch of forest near the Gaan Olo falls and site of an abandoned village. This ritual practice was discontinued after Akalali, Tata Ogii's propthet, ravaged the place in 1972 (Thoden van Velzen and van Wetering 1988: 337–339)

41 Da Telegi, ede-kabiten (head or first captain) of the Dyu, Kasiti subclan, Godo-olo.

42 Thoden van Velzen & Van Wetering, 2007.

WHY THE AFRICAN GODS FAILED THE AUKAN MAROONS

of women, all of them selected and trained for this work by the prophet. Later, after Gangáa's arrest, hundreds of Aukan city dwellers surrounded the court house where the prophet had to appear before his judges. Local newspapers described the scene as threatening.[43] After spending the better part of a year in jail Gangáa was released. Today he works as a gold miner and seems to have lost his aura of spiritual dominance.

During an earlier period of field work among Aukans another major religious upheaval had taken place (1972–1979). Its leader was the prophet Akalali who put an end to the daily public consultations of Gaan Tata. Akalali based his religious authority on a mandate he claimed to have received from Tata Ogii.[44] He destroyed Gaan Tata's places of worship and was successful in ending most forms of public worship of the deity. He reined the Maroon population of eastern Suriname with arbitrary dictates. A couple of married women were told to leave their husbands and settle in the prophet's village. No reason needed to be given: this was what Tata Ogii wanted. People considered this aggressive behavior proof that Akalali's claims to be Tata Ogii's medium were fully justified.

Similar religious upheavals accompanied by violence had occurred in the opening decades of last century, all involving prophets claiming to be the representatives of Tata Ogii.[45] Again, acts of gratuitous violence appeared to be the hallmark of genuine mediumship. In 1910, a shaman called Akule tyrannized the Cottica region, demanding total obedience. After a few months, the colonial authorities decided they couldn't accept these acts of violence in an area so close to the capital. They arrested Akule and imprisoned him in Paramaribo. When they released Akule after a few weeks a missionary had a chance to speak to him. He was surprised by the prophet's attitude: he appeared relaxed and almost cheerful. As it was suggested earlier[46] he may have felt relieved of a burden that had become too heavy. It underlines the obligatory nature of parts of the assignment: a religious duty that may have felt too onerous by those charged with it. I remember from conversations with Akalali when he, on quite a few occasions, complained about the burdens of mediumship.

Further in the past, in the first half of the 19th century, a man called Dikii, or Dicki Pambu, may have been the first to claim to be Tata Ogii's medium.

---

43   "Commotie bij rechtszitting Aucaanse 'spirituele' leider Gaanga." In: Dagblad Suriname, 14 February 2007.
44   Thoden van Velzen and Van Wetering, 1988:331–86.
45   Thoden van Velzen and Van Wetering, 1988: 194–252.
46   Thoden van Velzen and van Wetering (1988:221).

Countless stories refer to Dikii's iconoclastic and violent behavior or link him to important events that happened 200 years ago. Aukan historians stress that from a very early age Dikii was seen as embodying the powers of Tata Ogii. Dikii took it upon himself to hunt for new Runaways in the area between the plantations and Aukan territory. This violent and transgressive part of his career is not condemned by Aukans but seen as further proof that he was redoubtable (ogii), a necessary condition for life in the interior.[47]

Conclusion: Gods That Fail

All Aukan historians agree that Gaan Tata played an important role during the flight from slavery. But as the refugees penetrated deeper into the rain forest, the Loweman were facing challenges they had never encountered before. When they were opening parts of the forest to accommodate their growing population, trees started to bleed and accidents happened. Today this is seen as the beginning of what later would be known as the Agedeonsu cult. Other bands of Loweman met with phenomena that were even more unfamiliar and frightening. Gradually the refugees began to learn about the presence of an unfamiliar supreme power, an autochthonous deity by the name of Tata Ogii. The South American rain forest was his home. Later Aukans realized that this deity was in fact their host, Gaan Tata was merely a guest. The Africans fleeing slavery had to accept a simple fact as well: they could not expect to live in the interior in safety without honoring the local gods.

The Aukans soon learned that Tata Ogii jealously guarded his land, only people who respected him and his laws could hope to live in his domain without misfortune. Tata Ogii expected from the Aukans that they would behave as proper guests and live according to his rules. These maxims were enshrined in a concordat. Things came to a head when that sacred agreement was broken. When that happened, Gaan Tata was no longer a respected guest. Between 1972 and 1974 most of the sacred places of the cult were destroyed or violated by Tata Ogii's followers. Whereas in Gaan Tata's heydays aggression against one's relatives and neighbors was concealed, once Tata Ogii's prophets stepped forward it started to be accepted and respected.[48]

---

47   Thoden van Velzen and Van Wetering 1988: 176–190.
48   I would like to thank Olivia Gomes da Cunha for her leadership in the field of Suriname Maroon studies. I am grateful to Clémence Leobal for drawing the maps.

References

Bauch, Samuel. [Description]. Mitteilungen aus der Brüdergemeine, 54, p.320.

Behn, Aphra. 2003. "Oronooko or The Royal Slave, a True History." In Oroonoko, the Rover and Other Works, 73–141. Edited by Janet Todd. London: Penguin Books.

Böhm, J.G.R. 1761. Sketch of Vieira Map. V.B.K.L., nr. 2131 and 2.21205.09. National Archives. The Hague.

Borges, Robert. 2013. The Life of a Language: Dynamics of language contact in Suriname. Utrecht: Netherlands Graduate School of Linguistics.

Groot, Silvia W. de. 2009. "A corps of Black Chasseurs in Surinam: collaboration and rebellion." In Agents of their Own Emancipation: Topics in the History of Surinam Maroons, 101–133. Amsterdam: De Groot.

Hoogbergen, Wim. The Boni Maroon Wars in Suriname. Leiden: Brill, 1990.

Morssink, F. 1934. Boschnegeriana (misschien beter Silvae-nigritiana?) Eenige gegevens omtrent geschiedenis en missioneering onzer Surinaamsche Boschnegers. MS.

Parris, Jean-Yves. 2011. Interroger les morts: Essai sur la dynamique politique des Noirs marrons ndyuka du Surinam et de la Guyane. Matoury: Ibis Rouge, 2011.

Pakosie, André R.M. 1972. De dood van Boni. TS.

Thoden van Velzen, H.U.E. 1966. Politieke beheersing in de Djuka maatschappij. Een studie van een onvolledig machtsoverwicht. Ph.D. Dissertation, University of Amsterdam.

Thoden van Velzen, H.U.E, and W. van Wetering. 1988. The Great Father and the Danger: Religious Cults, Material Forces, and Collective Fantasies in the World of the Surinamese Maroons. Dordrecht: Foris.

Thoden van Velzen, H.U.E, and W. van Wetering.2004. In the Shadow of the Oracle: Religion as Politics in a Suriname Maroon Society. Long Grove: Waveland.

Thoden van Velzen, H.U.E, and W. van Wetering. 2007. "Violent Witch Finders and the Suspension of Social Order in a Suriname Maroon Society." In Wildness and Sensation: Anthropology of Sinister and Sensuous Realms, 157–176. Edited by Rob van Ginkel and Alex Strating. Apeldoorn/Amsterdam: Het Spinhuis.

Van Lier, Willem F. 1919. Iets over de Boschnegers in de Boven-Marowijne. Paramaribo: Van Ommeren.

Van Wetering, Wilhelmina, and H.U.E. Thoden van Velzen. 2013. Een Zwarte Vrijstaat in Suriname: De Okaanse Samenleving in de 19e en 20e. Eeuw. Leiden/Boston: Brill.

PART 2

Effects

CHAPTER 3

Research on Maroon Languages and Language Practices among Matawai and Kwinti Maroons

Bettina Migge

Introduction

The creole languages of Suriname and the Maroon Creoles in particular have been the subject of a fair amount of research spanning more than two centuries and figured prominently in research on creole genesis due to their rather conservative nature. Despite this, we know very little about the dynamics of their use, including the broad areas of language variation and pragmatics because most of the research has focused on structural linguistic aspects. This lack of attention to sociolinguistic issues is nevertheless surprising because Maroons' social and linguistic circumstances have been subject to a fair amount of change. Since the 1960s and particularly in the last two decades the social and spatial makeup of Maroon communities have been significantly transformed due to processes of migration, displacement, urbanization and greater contact with mainstream Surinamese, French Guianese, Dutch and more recently also French society (van Stipriaan 2015; Migge and Léglise 2015). However, research on the Maroon languages has, for the most part, continued to focus on relatively conservative language use among elders and village dwellers. This has led to a situation where research findings only represent Maroons' actual language practices in part and no dialogue can develop with anthropologists who have traditionally also shown a keen interest in Maroons (e.g. Thoden van Velzen, van Wettering; Richard and Sally Price).

This paper has three related goals. First, it gives a brief overview of the linguistic research that has been carried out on the Maroon Creoles of Suriname. Second, it explores data on those Maroon languages, Matawai and Kwinti, that have to date been mostly neglected by linguistic research. Third, it contributes to the kinds of research, namely sociolinguistic and linguistic anthropological research, that have to date received little systematic attention. The paper argues that the application of social approaches to language on the one hand allows us to obtain much needed insights into the (changing) social functions and nature of these languages and to open up a dialogue with the social

© KONINKLIJKE BRILL NV, LEIDEN, 2019 | DOI:10.1163/9789004388062_005

sciences; on the other hand, it also deepens our understanding of the makeup, emergence and development of these languages.

The paper is structured as follows. Part two provides an overview of the bulk of the linguistic research on Maroon languages to date, focusing on contact linguistic, historical and descriptive research. Part three discusses sociolinguistic research and compares language practices among speakers of Matawai and Kwinti, to those documented for the Eastern Maroon Creoles. The final section summarizes the findings and discusses their implications.

Early and Structural Research on the Maroon Creoles

It is generally agreed that records of the creole languages of Suriname have considerable time depth because the first speech samples started appearing at the end of the 17th and during the early part of 18th century, shortly after the emergence of these languages.[1] These samples appeared in a variety of written sources such as court records, novels, scientific/artistic studies of Suriname's flora and the colony itself (Arends 2002a: 184-87; van den Berg 2000). These earliest speech samples and much of the subsequent writings such as the different language primers (e.g. van Dyk 1765; Weygandt 1798) focused on the language use among the slave population and thus represent Sranantongo, rather than the Maroon languages. For a discussion of the sources, see Arends (2017).

Systematic documentation of the Surinamese Creoles started in the 1770s and went hand in hand with prosylizing activities of the Moravian missionaries in Suriname. Christian Ludwig Schumann, for instance, produced a number of religious texts in Sranantongo and Saamaka and also 'compiled two of the most valuable early creole dictionaries, one of Saramaccan (1778), the other of Sranan (1783).' (Arends 2002a: 192). Schumann's dictionary was subsequently revised and expanded by Johann Andreas Riemer (c. 1780) who also added a short grammatical description of the language.[2] The original Saamaka dictionary and its revised version were based on data from the village context where both Riemer and Schumann had spent time. Both versions of the dictionary provide rich insights into the lexical structure of the Saamaka language at that

---

1   In Migge (2003a) I argue that the plantation varieties emerged and stabilized roughly between the 1680s and 1720. This is also the period when some of the Maroon varieties (Ndyuka, Saamaka (and Matawai)) split off from the plantation varieties (Smith 2002), but see also Arends (2017) for a somewhat different view based on the analysis of primary documents.

2   It was reprinted in Arends and Perl (1995) along with English translations and information about its history.

time, the varied uses and semantic extensions of particular lexical items and the social context of use and patterns of variation. The illustrative examples and the metacomments (Arends 2002a: 203) of the compilers that accompany many of the lexical entries also provide valuable data for a morphosyntactic analysis of the early language and give rich insights into the socio-cultural context in which the language was/is embedded, see Arends (2017 for an analysis). Records on the other Maroon languages of Suriname are largely absent.[3]

Research on the Maroon languages intensified after the 1960s. The Summer Institute of Linguistics (SIL) started documenting the languages of Suriname for the ultimate purpose of producing bible translations for Ndyuka, Saamaka and Sranantongo. This work gave rise to translations of the New Testament, basic bilingual or trilingual dictionaries (http://www-01.sil.org/americas/suriname/Index.html) for Ndyuka, Saamaka and Sranantongo, a detailed grammar of Ndyuka (Huttar and Huttar 1994), a grammatical sketch of Saamaka (Rountree 1992) and a number of both academic papers (see also below) and language learning materials (http://www-01.sil.org/americas/suriname/bibliosuriname.pdf). More recently, a grammar of Saamaka (McWhorter and Good 2012) and a comparative grammar of Aluku, Ndyuka and Pamaka (Nenge(e)) (Goury and Migge 2003/2017) aimed at the French Guianese market appeared, and a trilingual dictionary (Nengee-French-English-Nengee) project is currently underway in French Guiana[4] and a comprehensive Saamaka-Dutch-Saamaka dictionary is currently being compiled by Vinije Haabo (Haabo ms). These various historical and modern resources for some of the Maroon languages are greatly enhancing our knowledge of these three languages, making them more accessible for research, but it is unclear if and how they are used by speakers of the language.

Much of the academic research on the Maroon languages has focused on shedding light on the genesis of creole languages and was aimed at refuting Bickerton (1981). He argued that creole languages provide privileged insights into the origin-of-language question because their putative creators – children growing up in the plantation setting – did not have access to viable languages

---

3 Although an important indigenous religious prophet of the time, the Matawai Maroon Johannes King, started writing in the 1860s, we have no records of Matawai from that time as he wrote in Sranantongo.

4 This project is run as part of the larger project DicoGuyane currently being carried out in French Guiana. It is based on a database put together by Kenneth Bilby in the 1980s and research carried out for the project. It involves collaboration between the author and speakers of Ndyuka, Aluku and Pamaka who work as mother tongue teachers (Intervenant en Langue Maternel) in French Guianese primary schools. It is funded by local French Guianese institutions.

and thus had to draw on their innate human blue print for language to create a common language. The resulting languages – the creole – presumably display strong parallels to structures found in first language (L1) interlanguage varieties. This view contrasts with the substrate view of creole genesis which maintains that creoles emerged from contact between varieties of European languages such as English or French on the one hand and the languages of the subordinated populations such as West African languages in the case of creoles spoken in the Caribbean, South American and Africa and Melanesian languages in the case of creoles spoken in the Pacific region on the other. Broadly speaking, the creators of creoles reanalyzed whatever they were able to learn of the dominant European language in terms of the structural rules and principles of their native languages (Migge 1998a, 2003a; Winford 2008).[5]

Proponents of the bioprogram theory (Byrne 1987; Veenstra 1996) have explored selected syntactic phenomena (e.g. movement phenomena, complementation and serial verbs constructions) in Saamaka and compared them to universals of language and to a lesser extent to equivalent structures in their input languages. They found that the Saamaka constructions closely resemble unmarked universal syntactic structures and do not match up well with those in African languages, suggesting that they emerged from independent processes of creation rather than from their (African) input languages. Researchers who advocated in favor of the important role of the African input languages typically focused on comparing morpho-syntactic phenomena in one or more Maroon creoles with equivalent ones in the main African input languages, namely varieties of Gbe and Kikongo and to a lesser extent Akan (Arends 1995). Based on increasingly more detailed comparative studies focusing on a range of different structural rather than lexical features – e.g. copular (Migge 2002; 2003a) and adjectival constructions (Migge 2000), complementation (Aboh 2006; Lefebvre and Loranger 2006; Migge and Winford 2013), locative constructions (Essegbey 2005; Yakpo and Bryun 2014), serial verb constructions (McWhorter 1992; Migge 1998a and b), tense, mood and aspect phenomena (Winford and Migge 2007; Migge and Winford 2009; Migge 2006, 2011; Migge

---

5 Lefebvre (1998) conceptualizes the main process of contact (referred to as relexification) somewhat differently but comes to the same conclusion that African languages played a major role in creole formation. See also the following edited works that deal specifically with the genesis of the creoles of Suriname (Migge and Smith 2007; Essegby, Migge and Winford (2013); Muysken and Smith 2014).

There is another, minor, theoretical strand, namely the Afro-genesis theory. It argues that a basic pidgin variety had formed on the West African Coast and was then transported across the Atlantic and further developed there in the different territories (Hancock 1969; McWhorter 1995; Parkvall 2000; Devonish 2002; Smith 2014a).

and Goury 2008; Winford 2006; Essegbey et al. 2013; van den Berg and Aboh 2013), morphological processes (Migge 2003a and b), word level semantic structure (Essegbey and Ameka 2007; Huttar et al. 2007; Huttar et al. 2013) – these investigations showed that there are important similarities between certain African languages and particularly the varieties of Gbe and the Maroon languages. Maroon features are typically not exact copies of features in African languages but the similarities suggest that they arose from contact between the African languages and between African and European input languages; in addition, they have also undergone change over the last 200 years. On the one end of the continuum, there are content and function morphemes, including their etymology, that were retained from African languages (e.g. Smith 2006, 2014). On the other end of the continuum, there are constructions that retain their basic structure or the main features from an African source, but the actual morphemes and some of their functions derive from a different source, often a European language (e.g. Migge and Goury 2008; Essegbey 2005). Most of their properties appear to involve lexical items derived from European languages whose structural features (including their semantics, syntax and phonotactic structure) derive in large part, but generally not exclusively, from African source languages.[6] This suggests that the African source languages played an important role in the emergence of the Surinamese (Maroon) creole languages, however, substrate influence was by no means the only influence. While the African languages often set the overall or broad frame for an area of grammar and the types of constructions they involve, other sources such as the European languages, particularly English and to a lesser extent Portuguese, contributed important aspects of grammar that went well beyond the etymological shapes of words in most cases. Once such hybrid structures had emerged, other processes such as grammaticalisation, pragmatic reinterpretation, semantic extension and narrowing driven by language contact or non-contact based factors further affected the Maroon languages, giving rise to the emergence of this unique family of languages.

There are two other lines of research that have had a major impact. One focuses on understanding the socio-cultural context in which these languages emerged and exist. Examining a range of historical documentation such as records pertaining to slavery (e.g. Postman 1990), population movements in West Africa, popular and official descriptions and records pertaining to various aspects of plantation life, researchers attempt to reconstruct the different socio-cultural factors that conditioned the contact settings in which creoles

---

6   Of course, there is also some overlap between features in European and African sources.

emerged and developed. They contain valuable information on issues such as the types of populations that were present, their relative sizes, their social and linguistic background, the patterns of inter- and intra-group contacts and the broad norms of interaction. In the case of Suriname, publications by Jacques Arends (1995, 2002b; 2017) have been instrumental in revealing the sociocultural matrix of creole genesis and in furthering our understanding about the social context of language contact. In relation to the history of the Maroon populations and the process of maronage, a number of publications are now available that examine the history of individual Maroon groups. These publications are based on both archival material and/or oral history narratives (see e.g. Hoogbergen 1983, 1990; Price 1983, 1996; Moomou 2004, 2013; Thoden van Velzen and Hoogbergen 2011; van Wettering and Thoden van Velzen 2014). When combined with careful linguistic analysis, this information allows for a detailed reconstruction of the processes of change involved in the emergence of Maroon languages.

A fourth line of research analyses early documents written in a creole language. Since the first documents for Suriname date from the beginning of the 18th century, they provide valuable insights into how the languages have changed over time. For Suriname this research focuses predominantly on Sranantongo (e.g. Arends 1989; Bruyn 1995; van den Berg 2007) and to a lesser extent on Saamaka due to the scarcity of documents for the other languages. Analysis suggests that the Creoles of Suriname developed gradually rather than abruptly and that some areas of grammar underwent significant change and/or displayed variation over time while others were relatively static over time. Contemporary varieties are the result of complex processes of change that were in part driven by contact-induced language change between Sranantongo and European languages, but also by processes of koinization involving contact, competition and selection between the different creole varieties such as between Maroon creoles and Sranantongo on the one hand and different varieties of Sranantongo (and different Maroon languages) on the other. However, this latter aspect has hardly been explored in detail as research has mostly focused on structural linguistic rather than on sociolinguistic (Migge and Mühleisen 2010) concerns.

While research on creole genesis has significantly improved our knowledge about the grammatical makeup of the Creoles of Suriname and the social and linguistic processes that were involved in their formation, it has also led to a situation where Maroon languages are viewed as static or frozen in time, and as unidimensional linguistic objects. Since research has predominantly focused on the syntax and structural functions of single linguistic forms and constructions we know very little about language practices, pragmatics and the overall speech economy. For instance, we do not know what varieties are recognized by members of the community, how they differ from each other, what their linkages are with social and pragmatic dimensions and how they are distributed across social groupings and social contexts. Equally lacking is knowledge about ideologies of language use and patterns of variation including contact with other languages. These issues are of interest from the point of view of sociolinguistics and for applied purposes but are also likely to provide important insights into processes of language change (e.g. the precise nature of the relationships between the different Maroon languages and Sranantongo, the processes of change that have been affecting Maroon languages throughout their history).[7]

Research on Language Practices

To date sociolinguistic research on Suriname and its diaspora communities in the Netherlands and French Guiana is relatively rare (but see Migge and Léglise 2005, 2011, 2013 for French Guiana). We also still lack work on diaspora communities in France that have been emerging over the last decade or so. There is some research on ideologies relating to Sranantongo (Gleason Carew 1982; St-Hilaire 1999, 2001) and to some of the other major languages spoken in Suriname, including Maroon languages, dating from the 1970s and 1980s (Charry et al. 1983). These were generally based on an analysis of census data, an analysis of regulations and a few guided interviews. They argue that while languages other than Dutch have covert prestige among their speakers in Suriname, they are not highly valued in the public domain and among non-speakers. Its (monolingual) speakers were often also found to be subject to various kinds of language-based discrimination. Recent survey-based research in both Suriname (Léglise and Migge 2015; Migge and Léglise 2015; Kroon and Yagmur 2010) and French Guiana (Léglise 2007; Migge and Léglise 2015) still registered traces of these overt negative perspectives, but found that overall society-wide and speakers' overt evaluations of Maroon languages have definitely improved especially in Suriname but also in French Guiana and that processes of rural-urban and transnational migration have not negatively affected speakers' alignment with

---

7 A first attempt at comparing modern L2 practices in the Maroon Creoles and historical data written by Europeans (Migge and van den Berg 2009), for instance, suggested that some of the patterns of variation found in the historical data might have equally been simply second language (L2) practices of Europeans rather than being indicative of change in progress within the language as a whole.

Maroon languages. In fact, Migge and Léglise (2015) found that positive identification with Maroon languages is higher in western French Guiana than in Suriname. This is most likely due to both Maroon's growing demographic importance in both contexts and their greater participation in the local urban mainstream or official contexts. In the remainder of this section I will look in more detail at what we know about Maroon's language ideologies and actual language practices in both intra- and inter community contexts with particular reference to Matawai and Kwinti as these communities have to date received very little attention in research (but see Migge 2017).

The data for the discussion come from observations, discussions and recordings of interactions among Maroons in the village context and in the urban context in Suriname and in western French Guiana since 1995. The initial research focused predominantly on the Pamaka community and the rural context. Since 2000 my research has focused increasingly on the urban context. It mostly follows a participant observation approach and recordings were carried out by myself and by community members or with both present.

The data on Matawai and Kwinti were collected in 2013 with financial support from CNRS-SedyL, the Ohio State University and sabbatical leave from University College Dublin. I visited the Matawai villages for about ten days in August 2013, see Map 3.1;

I stayed in the upriver village of Bethel and visited other villages together with a Matawai elder and sometimes other relations of his. During these visits I was given the opportunity to record interactions that occurred. I spend about a week in September 2013 in the remaining Kwinti village Bitagron on the Coppename River where I was given the opportunity to observe everyday life and to record a few interactions.[8] The interactions in the village setting occurred organically as a result of our visits. In addition, I also made recordings with speakers of Matawai and Kwinti in Paramaribo. Recordings consisted either of naturalistic interactions where the author was mostly a by-stander, typically in the village context, and semi-guided discussions that mostly occurred in town. The older recordings were made available to me by Miriam Sterman and come from anthropological research carried out by Miriam Sterman and Chris de Beet in the 1970s in the upriver region (Boslanti) (de Beet and Sterman 1981). I would like to thank Miriam Sterman for patiently checking the transcriptions for me.

---

8 On previous occasions I had visited the Kwinti villages of Bitagron (2010) and Kaimansiton (1996) for a few days each time and the Matawai villages of Kawkugron and Nieuw Jakobskondre (2010).

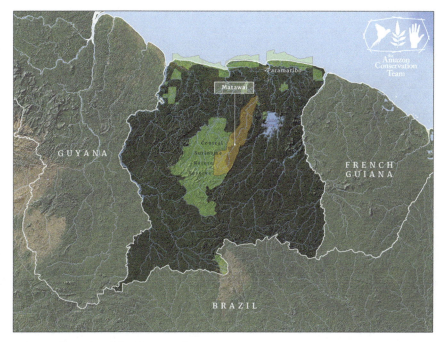

MAP 3.1 The region of the Matawai villages
SOURCE: KEMPER, 2018

The Sociolinguistic Makeup of the Maroon Communities

The common assumption is that members of Maroon communities are monolingual and that Maroon languages are essentially mono-stylistic. However, analysis of members' discourse about language suggests that Maroons perceive both their linguistic environment and their own language to be linguistically complex (Migge and Léglise 2013: 262). Most basically, all Maroon communities distinguish between good or respectful speech, common speech and also disrespectful speech. It is the two extremes, respectful and disrespectful speech, that are the focus of people's attention. Matawai speakers often refer to the former as *fan ku lesipeki* while Kwinti speakers refer to it as *lesikepi taki*, like their Eastern Maroon (EM) counterparts. Common speech is often not overtly referred to, but essentially covers everything that is not considered markedly respectful or disrespectful. Disrespectful speech is referred to as *goofu taki* 'rough speech.' They are distinguished in terms of both content and form or manner of delivery. Respectful speech is ideologically strongly associated with male elders or an aura of importance and tends to involve negative politeness practices such as polite variants of lexical forms and a certain presentational style. Traditionally, this involves an overtly dialogical style called *piki taki* 'ritual

FIGURE 3.1 The village of Bethel on the upper Saramacca River: view from the river
SOURCE: BETTINA MIGGE, 2017

responding' where the speaker (*takiman*) leaves frequent intervals during his speech into which the designated responder (*pikiman*) inserts short responses that support the speech of the speaker. A next speaker has to wait until the current speaker has overtly signaled the end of their contribution. Extract (1) exemplifies the typical features of such a very formal style. It comes from an official meeting (*kuutu*) held in an upriver Matawai village in the 1970s.

Extract (1)
1. Takiman: M., di a dɛ taki u o kon miti a kuutu tide
   'M, when it was announced that we'll meet at the meeting today.'
2. Pikiman: Eya 'Yes.'
3. Takiman: Wɛ di mi dɛ u Boslanti fa mi du?
   'Well, since I am from Boslanti, what can I do?'
4. Pikiman: Mh 'Yes.'
5. Takiman: Wɛ di i seepi dɛ u Boslanti, i musu kon
   'Well, since you yourself are from Boslanti, you have to come.'
6. Pikiman: I musu kon 'I have to come.'
7. Takiman: Fu kon seeka libi, na so nɔ?

FIGURE 3.2 Inside the village of Bethel on the upper Saramacca River
SOURCE: BETTINA MIGGE, 2017

'To deal with (pending) issues, right?'
8   Pikiman: So a dɛ 'That's right.'
9   Takiman: Nɔɔ i sa fa gadu da mi ye?
    'You know what god told me?'
10 Pikiman: Ya 'Yes.'
11 Takiman: Bo takii. 'Let's say'
12 Pikiman: Ya 'Yes.'
13 Takiman: U bi abi wan fesiman, masa teki en.
    'We had a leader, but he died.'
14 Pikiman: So a dɛ 'That's right.'
    ...

Only one person speaks at a time. The responses of the pikiman, which come from a restricted lexical set, function as a kind of feedback. They either signal to the current speaker that he is being listened to (continuation tokens, lines 2, 4, 10, 12, 14) or provide feedback (assessment tokens, lines, 6, 8) of the content in order to encourage him to carry on with his speech (Migge 2011). The current speakers' expression is euphemistic. The speaker does not directly name the matter at hand but uses metaphoric and euphemistic expressions to avoid open face threats (Migge 2004; Migge and Léglise 2013). In less formal contexts, the overall setup is the same but the rules are relaxed in various ways. Expression tends to be more direct and less veiled and no one in particular might perform the role of ritual responder. Either the speaker emulates the overall rhythm of the *piki-taki* style but no one provides the responses or the responses are less 'formal' and less frequent. Extract (2) is a case in point. In this extract, a village head (kapiten) from another village is telling an elder (P) and his wife (M) (and a few others who happened to be around) about something that happened during a recent burial ceremony in another village. This was a spontaneous event as it was prompted by our arrival at the elders' house, but it was more formal than a regular chat because the speaker is informing the couple about a serious matter, in this case someone's admission of an attempt at making use of supernatural power.

Extract (2)

1. K: (...) hen a balaki kon – da di a balaki kon, nɔɔ hen den famii tei faya – M go a
2. – a Paakiiki – M go a Paakiiki –
   'Then he poured everything out – when he had poured everything out, then the members of the family started speaking – M went to Paakiiki – M went to Paakiiki.'
3. M: ehe 'Yes.'
4. K: nɔɔ di mi ku i go a Paakiiki – 'When I and you (the person) went to Paakiiki.'
5. M: ehe 'Yes.'
6. K: di sondi di u go du a Paakiiki ala – 'The matter that we went to Paakiiki to do'
7. M : eya 'Yes.'
8. K : di u kon dolu – nɔɔ di muyɛɛ aki an de moo – a waka, a guwe, a go a booko
9. matu –
   'When we arrived – this woman was not there anymore – she had left, she had gone to the burial ground.'
10. M: aha 'Okay.'
11. K: nɔɔ di a go a booko matu, go bei – nɔɔ a di bakadina f'en – nɔɔ i ta kon
12. piki – nɔɔ yu kon fu piki taki – nono, basia, kapten – di soni di ta tyuma mi

RESEARCH ON MAROON LANGUAGES 95

13 ati aki – di mi ku kapten M go du eee – ee mi an taki mi an sa booko di dia –

14 i fustan?–

'After the burial – the same evening – you come and tell me – you come to tell me – no, no village leaders – the matter that is bothering me – when I and the village leader set out to do the burial ceremony – if I don't say (what bothers me), I won't make it through the night – you understand?'

15 M: a yei i! 'He heard and understood what you said.'

16 K: ee mi an taki di soni aki, didia ná o limbo mi. –

'If I don't talk about the matter, I will not make it to the next day.'

17 M: ee mi taki en puu 'If I talk about it,'

18 K: – di didia o limbo – The next day will rise.

In Extract (2) the kapiten is marking the topic of his speech as important by using punctured speech (–). However, since he did not designate anyone as a *pikiman* at the beginning, there are parts of his narrative (lines 1, 8-14) where no one provides assessment or continuation tokens in the intervals that he leaves throughout his speech. His main interlocutors, M and P, however, provide responses in some parts of the narrative to help him to develop his speech (lines 3, 5, 7, 10, 17). Note, however, that the types of responses, especially (lines 3, 5, 7, 10), are of a more informal nature in that they are more commonly associated with everyday speech. In addition to only approximating the *piki-taki* style, the speaker in Extract (2) also uses a much more direct manner of expression – he overtly names the fact that wrong-doing has occurred – and makes use of more colloquial language – balaki, i fustan?, anga – than would be acceptable in a formal meeting.

Goofu speech is typically associated with positive politeness practices, including highly informal language involving swearing, loud shouting or explicit talk about people's problems and defects, such as gossiping. It is felt to be hurtful and thus endangers social relationships. It is often ideologically linked to talk between middle-aged women or male youngsters. Common speech is most closely associated with 'good' women as they are ideally supposed to neither be particularly verbally skilled or 'bad,' both of which are the domain of men.

Apart from these stylistic varieties which play a very important role within the community and function as important gate-keepers of access to power, people also recognize regional varieties. Speakers of Matawai, like speakers of other Maroon varieties, usually identify people from the upriver community as speaking the most prestigious or true variety of Matawai. People from the lower Saramacca River were often said to speak a less pure form because historically there was a lot more contact with members of other Maroon communities such as Saamaka, Ndyuka and Kwinti as well as people from the Para region. In addition, people often pointed out that the speech of the people in the traditional downriver villages such as Bilawata, Nuiew Jacobskonde, Balen is more conservative (i.e. more typically Matawai) than that of the people associated with Kwakugron, Makakiiki, Commisaisikonde which are all located about three hours downriver from the traditional downriver villages. The latter's speech is frequently designated as *moksi* 'mixed'; it is felt to be a mix between Matawai and a Ndyuka-style speech. Little is overtly said about the speech of Matawai people who live in Paramaribo and along the Zanderij road who are currently more numerous than the people who live in the traditional villages. Members of the Kwinti community argued that the people from the other, currently uninhabited village of Kaimansiton which is upstream from Bitagron speak in a more conservative manner than people in Bitagron.

In terms of the languages recognized within the community, people point to three distinct entities: Matawai, Sranantongo and Dutch among the Matawai and to Kwinti, Sranantongo and Dutch among people in the village of Bitagron. Other Maroon languages (Saamaka and Ndyuka most particularly) are also recognized as separate entities, but they are typically linked to visitors rather than seen as an integral part of these communities. In the Matawai village context, it is Matawai that is most widely spoken and Sranantongo mostly appears in certain contexts such as in interactions with outsiders and in contexts involving status negotiation (see below). In the Kwinti community, traditional Kwinti is rarely used as people regularly use a generalized Maroon code involving features from traditional Kwinti (see below) and Sranantongo. Dutch is very much restricted to the school context in both communities. Among urban dwellers, who nowadays make up the majority of both communities, Sranantongo and Dutch, depending on people's social backgrounds play a very important role as people frequently interact with non-Maroons and Dutch enjoys high status. Both Kwinti and Matawai are mostly restricted to home and community events such as burials etc, but even in these contexts, they co-exist with both Dutch and Sranantongo. Both languages are not widely transmitted to younger generations in the urban context as many families of both communities also do not appear to have strong family language maintenance policies, especially in the case of parents who have professional jobs. In fact, it seems that many urban young people are learning Kwinti and Matawai as second or rather third languages and often have a highly reduced speaking competence as they often only start speaking them in their teens.

The Kwinti and Matawai situation squarely contrasts with what is happening in the Eastern Maroon communities where language maintenance in both

RESEARCH ON MAROON LANGUAGES

urban and rural contexts is very strong and possibly expanding due to favourable demographic developments and improvements in terms of wider societal perceptions of these languages and their speakers (see Migge and Léglise 2013, 2015). In the following section, I will look in more detail at linguistic practices.

Linguistic Practices

As in all communities, language use among and by Maroons is not static but subject to variation and change. Variation is productively used to negotiate social identities and relationships (Buchholtz and Hall 2010). Over time certain patterns of variation might become conventionalized and thus give rise to language change. In the Maroon communities, the main agents of language change are men, and particularly younger men, as they traditionally have the greatest number of social ties to the world beyond the local community and family networks. Display of linguistic versatility also carries social importance for men because it displays their engagement with the world beyond the local community, an integral part of local notions of young manhood. Women, in contrast, have to use external linguistic practices with care as they do not match up well with ideologies that locate women in the domestic sphere. Sustained use of European languages might give rise to charges of arrogance and use of Sranantongo carries overtones of a questionable sexuality; the latter practices are thus more difficult to sustain for women than those linked to Dutch. The recordings from the Matawai community suggest that, as in the case of Eastern Maroons (Migge 2007; Migge and Léglise 2013), interactions with outsiders or discussion of topics that are linked to non-community-based issues, such as the world of male cash labour, make use of Sranantongo. Extract (3) is a case in point. It comes from a longer narrative about the charismatic leader of the Matawai, Johannes King, who brought Christianity to them, which it was recorded by the anthropologists Miriam Sterman and Chris de Beet in the 1970s. The narrative was told to them by one of the village elders who was also involved in local church matters.

Extract (3)

1 W: _da_ a _futeri_ mi, en en ku, en _mɛki_ mi
   'Then he told me, he and, he is my father (lit. He gave birth to me).'
2 M: Aay 'Yes.'
3 L: En pali mi. 'He is my father (lit. He gave birth to me).'

4 William: En pali mi. _Da_ a <u>taigi</u> mi, a konda da mi takii de bi dɛ a _Mali-paston_

5 yaika mi nango a di bakaa tongo – na Kwakugɔɔn bause ala di _konde_ bi dɛ, a

6 Kwakugron bilose _anda_, ala di _konde_ fu den bi dɛ, de kai Maipaston. _Da_ wan _dei_

7 Johannes King, Johannesi King, di tata de kai Johannes King, da a siki. _Kerki no_

8 _ben_ dɛ a _Maripaston_. Keiki aan bi dɛ a Maipaston. Wɛ di a siki, _da_ wan <u>dei</u>, a

9 siki <u>tru-tru</u>, _da_ hen sisa Muui, a abi wan _ssa_ de kai Muui, Muui, so, a abi wan <u>taa</u> 10 baala de baka ma dati mi _figiti_ en nen f'en, a dɛ a buku
'He gave birth to me. He told me, he told me that they were at Mali-paston – listen I changed to European's speech – the village was downriver there from Kwakugron, downriver from Kwakugron, there their village was, they called it Maipaston. One day, Johannes King, Johannesi King, the elder called Johannes King, he got sick. There wasn't a church at Maripaston, there wasn't a church at Maipasiton. When he was sick, one day, he was really sick, thus his sister Muui – he had a sister by the name of Muui – Muui, so there was another brother born after her, but I've forgotten his name, it is written in the book.'

In Extract (3) the elder W, who is a fluent speaker of traditional Matawai, keeps alternating between Matawai (regular type set) and features that are clearly Sranantongo (italics) and those that are not considered Matawai but are not Sranantongo either, but appear to belong to a generalized Maroon code that in several ways resembles Eastern Maroon varieties (underlined and italics). Throughout the narrative, which goes on for a considerable amount of time, another Matawai elder who is present (L) keeps reminding him to speak Matawai either by telling him to do so or by reformulating the same content in Matawai (e.g. line 3). In response to such reminders, he reformulates parts of his non-Matawai speech into Matawai (line 4, 5-6, 7, 8), but eventually keeps lapsing back into this mixed speech. W's code alternation can be attributed to two factors, namely the fact that he is addressing two Europeans who speak L2 varieties of Matawai and that he is explaining in front of a microphone a matter – the story of a local Christian prophet – that is not typically linked to local everyday life. Note that this kind of code switching does not involve a complete switch from one language to another. Instead, speakers essentially adopt a grammatical frame that is shared among the Surinamese Creoles or

RESEARCH ON MAROON LANGUAGES

is even linked to one particular Maroon Creole and variably insert single elements from the different lexical sources into it, thus creating what could be called a mixed variety. This mixed code has different indexicalities from the monolingual varieties. In this context, it is essentially used to signal otherness or non-localness. In this function even women tend to make greater use of Sranantongo though note that women much more rarely engage in these kinds of interactions.

Another reason for code alternation is identity construction. Elders, who tend to have strongly distance-based relationships, employ code alternation to negotiate solidarity type relationships (Migge 2007). An example of this positive politeness strategy is extract (4) where KB is asking E to help him with a faulty rice mill. They are both roughly similar in age, in their 60s, and have a cordial relationship. However, KB is an important upriver village leader while E works in transport for the government. He has good connections to the ministry of regional affairs but from a local perspective, he is simply one of KB's 'subjects.'

Extract (4)

1 KB: ya da mi kɛ, m' begi *basi* aki so
  'Yes, thus I want, I'm asking the boss here'
2 E: mhmm 'Yes'
3 KB: fi i ko daai en bika i sa soni fi en.
  'For you to come and try it out because you know things about it'
4 E: eyee 'Yes'
5 KB: *drai* en da u, mɛ a sa wooko, te di *man* ko a mu si   <
  'try it out for us and make it work, when the man/guy comes, he must
    see (it working)'
6 E: ya 'Yes'
7 KB: ma efu a ko de, ma efu a ko si en so, da a, a, a to *fokop*   <
  'but if he comes and sees it in this state, that'll be bad'
8 E: mhmm 'Yes'
9 KB: da a mu si taaki di alisi *mili* ta wooko   <
  'he has to see that the rice mill is working'
10 E: ya 'Yes'
11 KB: bika a *aksi* mi taki 'we luku di alisi *miri*, fa di alisi *mili* de ?'   <
12 mi taki di alisi *mili* de bunu   <
  'Because he asked me 'well, how about that rice mill? I said that it
    is fine.'
13 E: ooh 'Oh'
14 KB: we di a to ko dolu, *da* di alisi *mili* an ta *drai*, *da* a soso problem *tok.*<

'well, when he'll come here and the rice mill won't work, now that'll create problems, right'
15 E: mhmm 'Yes'
16 KB: *a* mi beg' *unu* basi, mε a ko yeepi mi *drai* en ...   <
   'I'm begging you, boss, come and help me to make it work.'

KB makes his request for help (lines 1, 3, 5) in Matawai, by flattering E – he addresses him with the term *basi* 'boss' (line 1) linked to urban power relationships playfully implying that E is (more) powerful – and highlighting reasons for his request: E's special knowledge (line 3) and the fact that he would end up in an embarrassing situation if the important coastal Maroon leader who got him the machine would find out that it does not work (line 7, 14). Finally, he reasserts his request for help (line 16) – note that he uses the Sranantongo second person plural pronoun *unu* which is also used as a respect form to address E. It underscores the sincerity and urgency of the request.

In this Excerpt (4) KB makes use of a Maroon style that is interspersed with features from Sranantongo which is typical of male peer-group interactions. However, he switches to a style heavily influenced by Sranantongo in lines 11-12 when depicting his interaction with the Maroon leader. The latter is an urbanized non-traditional Ndyuka Maroon and thus most likely to employ a code-mixed style – it also voices and underlines the leader's lack of refinedness from the perspective of Maroons. The density of non-Matawai forms is also high in lines 14 and 16 where he restates his calamity and request for help, a highly face-threatening activity. This density of Sranantongo forms functions at the same time to underline the urgency of his request and to mitigate the possible threat to E's negative face (the imposition on E's time) and his own negative face (lack of power). By voicing it in a code-mixed style, he is making it into a friend-to-friend or brother-to-brother request rather than a formal kabiten request. He is thus appealing to the notion of mutual help relationships that exist among age-mates. This usage of code-switching is generally not used among women who alternate between respect type speech and regular everyday speech.

Younger men make different uses of code alternation. Since they have low social status in the traditional system due to their dependence on the goodwill of elders and usually maintain friendship-type rather than hierarchical relationships among each other, they are usually at pains to raise their social status through foregrounding of their knowledgeability and sophistication. They thus employ code-switching with Sranantongo and Dutch to foreground their knowledgeability and thus raise their status because they are linked to a certain prestige that is attainable for young men. A case in

RESEARCH ON MAROON LANGUAGES 101

point is Extract (5). Just before Extract (5), M, a Matawai man in his early 30s, had told a group of men who were chatting informally that they have to redevelop tourism and some of the issues such a project faces. At some point in the discussion, the author (B) enters into the conversation suggesting that the main thing they need are a few small houses and decent toilets (line 1). M then launches into a speech about what is needed and how he knows that. His talk is mostly addressed at the other men present. In his turn, he is clearly at pains to display his involvement with and knowledge of the tourism industry. His heavy use of Sranantongo (italics) or elements from a more generalized Maroon code (italics & underlined) clearly underscores his identity construction as a man of urban sophistication in that it actively invokes the non-local voices of the urban area.

Extract (5)

1 B: dii piki wosu, anga, eh, ku toilet, a sali kaba.'Three small houses with, eh with toilest, that's sufficient.'

2 M: mi sabi, ya _den man_ piki mi, mi go a foto ala, a _touris orga_, den taki meki tu _oso nanga_ wan bun _toilet_, a _toilet nomo_ mu _bun. ala_ den tra _sani, moy oso_ mu meki _nanga_ tasi no go, eh wasi dan dendu, de mu kisi kumalu, _ala sani_, lawai i mu _tyari_ den _kon_ da den man taki _sori a nymara_ da wo _tyari a_ aga go _poti_ ne en gogo kisi _ala sani_ de _man_.

'yes, I know, they (tourist operators) told me, I went to Paramaribo, a tourist operator, they said make two houses and a good toilet, the toilet has to be good. All the other things, nice houses have to have a traditional leaf roof, swim in the rapid, they have to catch fish, all these things, you have to bring them to the upriver natural reserve; the man said show them the fish, then we'll bring the ?? and put it on its ?? butt and get all the things there, man.'

Maroon women by contrast, make comparatively little use of external codes because linguistic versatility carries negative connotations for them as it aligns them with the world beyond the community which easily has overtones of _waka_ 'sexual promiscuity.' In order to off-set these associations, women prefer to make use of European languages as they carry associations of learning and proper behavior since they are typically acquired through participation in the school system. My 2013 corpus reveals two uses of code-alternation by women. They use it to mark the performance of non-traditional interactional roles. In Extract (6) a younger woman (30s) in the village of Bethel is engaging an elder of her grandmother's generation to tell her (on behalf of the author) about what life was like in the village when she was young and about her own life. In the interaction Kf is at pains to express herself well and respectfully because she is talking to an elder. However, she nevertheless regularly intersperses her turns with a few elements from other languages, in her case mostly Dutch (and to a lesser extent Sranantongo). These switches mark Kf's speech out as performing a non-traditional speech activity – interviewing – which is not part of the local speech repertoire. Her use of non-Matawai elements highlights that Kf is engaging in a particular non-local speech activity, but also that she is asserting difference to the elder's life world.

Extract (6)

1 Kf: ma di de koti di *konde*, di tyatya an bi dɛ *direkt* ?
   'But when they created the village, the gravel was not there right away?'
2 O: nono, an bi de ne en, de taaki.
   'No, it was not there, they say ...'
3 Kf: fa a ta wasi?
   'how did it come to the surface?'
4 O: fa di tyuba ta kai, di wata ta waasi, bika di mi woyo limbo, nɔɔ hen mi ta si di
5 tyatya, nɔɔ he i si a ta ko, nɔɔ te fa i si i si a sai de.
   'when it was raining, the water uncovered it, because I cannot remember seeing it without the gravel, thus so you see it came and now it is here.'
6 Kf: ma i an sabi *omeni* yai so di *konde* a sa abi fu di a *bestaa*?
   'But you cannot remember how many years the village exists, how long it's existed?'
7 O: mhmm, mi an sabi. 'No, I don't know.'

But code alternation is also used in other interactional functions such as to draw attention to something or to highlight the importance of a wrong doing, for instance. Just before the beginning of extract (7) W had complained to the others present that E did not pay enough respect to the woman basia of the village of Boslanti because he did not bring the author over to talk to her when they had first arrived. E had conceded and thus W, by way of accepting E's apology, also admitted that the basia woman should have been more assertive (line 1). E then repeats his apology (line 2) which is accepted by W (line 3) and emphatically asserted (line 4). E then explains what he should have done. K then uses the opportunity to playfully shame E over yet another issue (line 8). He argues that E had behaved wrongly when he ran off to do his own business upon their arrival in Boslanti. W draws further attention to E's inappropriate behavior by enquiring whether E had even had the courtesy to inform K of his

RESEARCH ON MAROON LANGUAGES

plan (lines 9, 11). To emphasize the seriousness of E's wrong-doing – K is an important kapiten and the kapiten of E's native village apart from being E's younger brother – she employs the Dutch word *melde* 'report, inform' instead of a more habitual local term such as *taagi* 'tell' or *fan* 'say' both of which do not usually have strong hierarchical overtones. By using *melde*, she is clearly establishing a hierarchical relationship between E and K and thus increases the strength of E's disobedience.

Extract (7)

1 W: dam E yaika, den basia muyɛɛ an, den an piki i tuutuu.
   'Elder E listen, the female assistants to the kabiten did not insist on the matter.'
2 E: luku mi fowtu dobu.
   'I made a serious mistake.'
3 W: Okay! 'Ojay!'
   [several voices]
4 W: soo! Om E fowtu.
   'Alright, elder E made a mistake.'
5 E: ná kapten mi bi mu baa en, mi bi mu tya en da di basia muyɛɛ
   'I should not have brought him to the kapiten, I should have brought her to the female village assistant.'
6 K: E, dam E 'E, elder E'
7 E: ya 'Yes'
8 K: mi ku i ko, ma a e dyombo pipa, a sa go a hondi.
   'I came together with you, but he went on his own way to deal with his own business.'
9 W: a melde i no?   <
   'Did he inform you?'
10 K: no, no, i fowtu kaa, ná kuutu moo!
   'No, no, you highlighted the mistake, stop raising the issue.'
   E: [laughter]
11 W: a melde i no? di a go a sembe a melde i?   <
   'Did he inform you? When he went to visit people, did he inform you?'
   [laughter]
12 K: mɛ a an kuutu moo [unclear]
   'Make her stop raising the issue.'

While members of the Eastern Maroon and Matawai community employ code alternation practices selectively to negotiate interactional roles and social identities, it seems that bilingual speech has become the norm among Kwintis

104 MIGGE

in the village of Bitagron on the Coppename River, currently the only Kwinti village that is continuously inhabited. In Bitagron a mixed code involving Sranantongo, a generalized Eastern Maroon code with a few insertions from what are locally identified as Kwinti features (Huttar 1988) appears to have become the unmarked code of interaction (Borges 2013). Extract (8) is a case in point.

Extract (8)

1 A: da fosi, sowtu konde be de ya fosi?
'In the beginning, which village was here originally?'

2 F: a disi *nomo* 'Only this one.'

3 P: a disi 'This one.'

4 A : na a konde 'was the village (that was here).'

5 P : di mi ai e *klin* 'When I grew up.'

6 F : a konde *disi nomo*, da den *suma*, tu man *suma be* de, tu baala be de. –
'Only this village, then the people, there were two men, there were two brothers.'

7 A : ehmm 'Yes.'

8 F : da den be suku **golon plesi** fu tan, we i *no mak* kon <u>*doo*</u>, da i kon taki *direkt* so.–
'they were looking for a place to live; you cannot arrive and speak directly like that.

9 A: ehmm 'Yes.'

10 F: *want* i *no sab* efu te wata bigi efu a e sungu efu a *ne* e sungu, da den

11 luku en *langa* den si en, den luku *dya* anga Kaimansiton. –
'because you don't know if when the water rises it inundates, so they observed it for a long time, they saw it, they looked here and in Kaimansiton.

In Extract (8) the author (A) is visiting with F, an elder from Kaimansiton who is in his 60s and a few other people, among them P. F starts telling A a few things about Bitagron and then launches into a narrative about the founding and development of the village. Throughout the narrative, which was as much aimed at the author as at the other men present, F employs what could be called a generalized Maroon code which is interspersed with items clearly marked as Sranantongo (italics) (e.g. lines 6, 8, 10) and with a few items from what is locally considered to be Kwinti (line 8, bold) although the narrative was comparatively formal – note the intervals (–) left at the end of several of

RESEARCH ON MAROON LANGUAGES

his turns (lines 6, 8, 11). There are also a few items that are more closely associated with Eastern Maroon speech (e.g. line 8, underlined and italics).

The style of speaking exemplified in Extract (8) is widely heard in Bitagron but it is not considered to be 'real' Kwinti by the locals. A bit later during the same interaction, P, a man also in his early 60s, starts telling everyone about his experiences in the Netherlands. One of the issues raised were Maroon – European (Dutch) interactions. P initially starts off in the mixed style but when reminded to speak in proper Kwinti by one of the people – because he had previously bragged that he is well able to speak Kwinti – P and also M, a man in his 30s, launch into a different type of speech pattern exemplified in Extract (9).

Extract (9)

1 P: ... u go a bakaa konde, de o **laafu** yuu, de o **laafu** yuu.
   'We went to Europe, they will ridicule you, they will ridicule you.'

2 M: ya, de o **laafu** yu??? 'Yes, they will laugh about you.'

3 P: eh, da na *grun* fasi de o gwe waka. 'They will travel naively.'

4 M: sa i membe pasa? 'What do you think happened?'

5 P: eh? 'Okay?'

6 M: **yaiki** mi bun ye! 'Listen to me properly!'

7 P: a faya de? 'Is the lighter there?'

8 M: de o **laafu**, san pasa meki de *no* **laafu** a man?
   'They'll laugh, why did they not ridicule the guy?'

9 P: eh? 'Okay?'

10 M: soo! *umdat* a man *no* sabi a *syteem* fu anda.
    'Right! Because the guy does not know how things work over there (Europe).'

11 P: na dati. 'That's it.'

12 M: da den *no* **laafu** a man. a tya, den o wani tya a man pasa anga den.
    'They do not laugh about the guy. They will want to bring the man into their system.'

13 P: *ya tok*, de o tya i pasa anga en.
    'Yes, right, they'll try to bring you into their system.'

14 M: i **saabi** tok. *'You know, right.'*

15 P: Bakaa konde anda.. 'In Europe over there ...'

16 F: bakaa, efu i du wan **saani** *fowt*, a bakaa *nei* lafu yu, a e *verbeter* yu!
    a *sranan*

17 ya, i taki wan **saan** *fowt*, de e lafu i tee i *no* wani *tak* a **saan** *dati*
    moro. ma a

18 bakaa *nei* lafu, a e *verbeter* yu.

106 MIGGE

'Europeans, if you make a mistake, a European doesn't ridicule you, s/he corrects you! Here in Suriname, you say something wrong, they ridicule you to the point that you don't want to say anything anymore. But a European does not laugh, s/he corrects you.'

19 M: a *no* o **laafu** yu. 'S/he won't ridicule you.'

20 F: *tak* wan <u>*neederlands*</u>, i an tak bun, 'Speak Dutch, if you don't speak well,'

21 M: **yaiki** mi! 'Listen to me!'

22 F: da yo yee fa a bakaa o seeka soi i fa i mu taki en.
'You'll hear how the European will show you how you should say it.'

23 M: **yaiki** mi noo! 'Listen to me know.'

24 F: ma a nenge, a lafu a o lafu i 'But the (black) Surinamese, he'll ridicule you.'

25 M: a man ya *nei leisi* mi <u>*yon*</u>! mi taki, a bakaa *no* o laafu yu. soso fu meki muiti fu 26 a poti yu na a **paasi**. efu i *tak* a *san* ya, i an *tak* bun, da a o lei yu fa i mu taki en. 27 i **saabi** *tok*.
'Man, this guy does not understand me! I said a European will not ridicule you. S/he will make an effort to put you on the right path. If you say this thing and
you don't speak well and s/he'll teach you how you should say it, you know, right.'

In Extract (9) all three speakers P, M and F still make use of a mixed type of style involving a generalized Maroon variety (italics)[9] and insertions from Dutch and Sranantongo (italics and underlined) and Kwinti (bold). With respect to the later, it is noteworthy, however, that they only make use of very emblematic or common Kwinti features – lengthening of (initial) vowels and the Kwinti form of the word for 'to hear' yaiki. They also appear to be used in a kind of distinctive way. They are predominantly used to draw attention (lines 6, 21, 23) or to create emphasis (lines 1, 2, 8, 12, 14, 19, 25, 27). In that sense, they are marking the out-of-the-ordinary. A similar pattern of speech was found among younger Kwinti in Paramaribo. They mostly lengthened word initial vowels when 'performing Kwinti' but otherwise spoke in a Sranantongo-type or a generalized Maroon style depending on the context.

---

9 Note that there is obviously some overlap with Sranantongo due to their relatedness. I'm focusing here on how it is perceived locally rather than detailed etymological assessment of each word.

RESEARCH ON MAROON LANGUAGES

The only people that are locally perceived to use a proper Kwinti style throughout are older women – they were also the only ones that the author was sent to to find out about real Kwinti. Extract (10) is a case in point. It comes from an interaction that was taking place while the author was helping O and M, two senior members of the community, peel cassava one afternoon. During that interaction, O is asking M who has always lived in the village, all kinds of questions about the village because he thinks that the author is interested in this. O considers himself less knowledgeable because he lived most of his life in Paramaribo and only returned to live permanently in Bitagron two years ago after he retired from work:

Extract (10)

1 M: ma mi seefi **hain** mi **nan** si en, di de e kai a gaaman Alamu, da u de a???
'But my own eyes, I did not see him, who they call paramount chief Alamu, thus we are???'

2 O: mi *srefi*, a **yei**, mi be si, mi si *wel*, mi *yere* a ?? enseefi osu a ..
'Myself, I heard, I saw, I did see, I heard ?? his own house ...'

3 M: a fowtow 'The picture.'

4 O: a fowtow *dati* be de, a taampu anga wan pikin kamisa f'en, mi taki

5 'san! wan *granman*, en taampu so? Fu wan *konde leider!'*
'There was a picture, he stood there with his little loin cloth, I said "What! A paramount chief, he stand like that? A head of a village!" '

6 M: wan di mi si, **hen** an *trampu* ye. 'The wan that I saw, he did not stand!'

7 O: ohh, en *sdonsdon*. 'Oh he was sitting down.'

8 M: en de sid-, ya, **hen** de da den taa wan, kowonu sama de trampu, ma a gaaman,

9 a de **sidosido**, wan **deikideiki** sama, hen futu opo so, ya.
'He was sitting, yes, and the others, common people stood but the paramount chief sat; a big person, his legs were open like this, yes.'

10 O: a *sdon* so, da den *tra* wan *snap* ne en **bandya**.
'He sat so, the others stood at his side.'

11 M: na ape mi si en, ma mi seefi **nansamben**, hen i si u ko de ya, we dede dede tee

12 we dede teee, we dede enke fa, u kon libi ya, tyokoo, w'an de, w'an sa moo,

13 ma di na *gaado biigi*, da u de, u de ya.

'That's where I see him, but I do not know him ; then you see us come here, we are suffering very much, we are suffering very much when we came to live here, in misery, we did not know anymore, but since god is remarkable, we are still (alive).'

In Extract (10) M uses a style of speaking that is locally identified as 'pure Kwinti'; besides elements that are clearly shared with other Maroon languages, particularly the Eastern Maroon varieties (REGULAR), she regularly uses distinctive lexical forms that are associated with Kwinti (bold) and Srananton-go (italics) only. Note also that apart from initial vowel lengthening (lines 13), she also uses a number of other lexical forms that are locally considered to be characteristic of Kwinti.[10] In contrast to M, O makes comparatively little use of forms clearly associated to Kwinti. Instead he makes use of a fair amount of Sranantongo associated words. There are various reasons that could explain this: his long terms residence in Paramaribo, his desire to present himself as a sophisticated person and possibly also because he did, without being asked, take over a kind of interviewer role during part of the recording (cp. Extract 6) which is traditionally associated with codes other than the local traditional variety because it is a non-local speech activity.

The discussion then suggests that while monolingual codes are still quite present in other Maroon communities, this is no longer the case in the Kwinti community. In fact, they will probably die out once the elders (women) who still use them die. The younger generations appear to have the ability to understand such codes but mostly make use of only a few relatively easily accessible and emblematic features (e.g. initial vowel lengthening). The small size of the rural community which was dramatically reduced during the Surinamese civil war, that had forced many Kwintis to live in Paramaribo, is probably mainly responsible for the demise of the language. Borges (2013), however, also suggests that the absence of a clearly defined leadership system – they do not have a gaanman or viable kapitenships like the other Maroon communities – and thus the absence of a formal domain where distinctive styles of speaking are practiced and preserved are another important reason why Kwinti is on the brink of disappearing; or rather of integrating with a generalized Maroon code. The language is essentially gradually being reduced to a set of lexical forms and distinctive phonological rules that can be selectively employed to either perform Kwintiness, if needed, and/or to create salience.

---

10   Note that some of them, such as the consecutive marker **hen** is also characteristic of Western Maroon varieties such as Matawai and Saamaka, this possibly confirms that influence of Matawai on Kwinti.

Conclusion

This attempt at a brief overview of research on the Maroon languages demonstrates that they have figured prominently in linguistic research. However, most of the research has dealt with only a few of the languages, mostly the Eastern Maroon varieties of Ndyuka and Pamaka and Saamaka; Aluku has received some attention from Kenneth Bilby (2002). Saamaka has also featured but two of the other communities, Kwinti and particularly Matawai, remain largely or completely understudied. In addition to focusing only on some varieties, most of the research efforts have focused on the emergence and development of these languages. However, since this work has mostly proceeded on synchronic comparative data, where synchronic data are investigated to reconstruct historical stages and processes of development, this research has also provided important insights into the grammars of these languages. We could speculate at length why there is so little research on sociolinguistic and pragmatic issues – difficulties accessing these communities, research agendas in linguistics, the lack of participation of members of these communities in research – but instead, I would like to focus on why sociolinguistic and linguistic anthropological work on these communities is important.

Sociolinguistic and linguistic anthropological research aims to analyse patterns of language use and how they link in with socio-cultural issues, such as the role of language in the negotiation of social groupings and identities, social relationships, social interactions, ideologies and processes of change. These issues are, of course, important for applied purpose. For example, from the point of view of language planning knowledge about these things is vital for determining which languages and which varieties of these languages should be instrumentalized for educational purposes and how and for what purposes they can be instrumentalized. These issues also provide insights into language-based discrimination on the basis of which measure can be developed to fight it. This research is equally valuable for determining the social structure and dynamics, including the factors that drive it, of these communities, something that we are still far from clear on. We know about the broad nature of processes of language change, but we still know fairly little about how patterns of linguistic variation mutually interact with particular mixes of social factors to give rise to linguistic change. Most of our knowledge and understanding is still largely based on inferences that we draw on the basis of available historical data and an analysis of structural linguistic data either derived from historical documents or modern conservative data. Both data sources present problems and historical documentation is also hardly sufficiently comprehensive. Thus, observation of the social and linguistic dynamics of a particular contact setting provides unparalleled insights into the development of contact settings both from a social and linguistic perspective. Based on such findings, we can get insights into which aspects of language are most affected by social change, why (e.g. language ideologies) and how these changes emerged and which groups of people in the community are driving these changes. The above discussion for instance suggests that men are the main drivers of contact-induced change while women are the main guardians of more traditional forms of speech.

For instance, if we try to bring our current knowledge about the contemporary development of the Maroon creoles to bear on the question of the differences between Sranantongo and Maroon varieties, it is possible to argue that two processes must have played a role, namely code alternation processes and social differentiation. Essentially, we can assume that the initial linguistic situation was somewhat diffuse, possibly involving variation between more European-based and African-based language strategies. Overtime, these strategies became bundled or focused around different social identities and practices or interactions in the plantation setting. The latter (African) strategies became progressively attached to more conservative or oppositional groupings and with the occurrence of maronage, they (also) became attached to Maroons. By contrast, features that were perceived to be Europeanized became associated with plantation life and more 'progressive' forces. As relations started to change and the oppositional relationship between Maroons and non-Maroon Afro-Surinamese started to ease due to Maroons' greater desire to participate in aspects of coastal society, they started to variably insert more and more lexical forms from coastal languages such as Sranantongo, but also Dutch, into certain discourses, usually those tied to urban contexts. These changes proceeded differently for men and women, being mostly driven by younger men. However, overtime, a kind of metaphorical extension took place whereby non-Maroon forms were used to conjure up a variety of non-traditional local identities, contexts and relationships. Adoption of new, non-local lexical forms clearly played an important role in this process. However, in addition to this, Maroons started to variably omit linguistic features strongly linked to a traditional Maroon life-style from certain of their discourses, leading to the emergence of new, linguistically intermediate varieties.

References

Aboh, Enoch. 2006."Complementation in Saramaccan and Gungbe: the case of C-type modal particles." Natural Language and Linguistic Theory 24, no. 1: 1–55.

Abrahams, Roger D. 1983. The Man-of-Words in the West Indies: Performance and the Emergence of Creole Culture. Baltimore: Johns Hopkins University Press.

Arends, Jacques. 2017. Language and Slavery. Amsterdam: John Benjamins.

Arends, Jacques. 2002a. 'Young languages, old texts: Early documents in the Surinamese creoles.' In Atlas of the Languages of Suriname, 183–205. Edited by Eithne Carlin, and Jacques. Leiden: KITLV Press.

Arends, Jacques. 'The History of the Surinamese Creole Languages I: A Sociohistorical Survey.' In of the Languages of Suriname, 115–130. Edited by Eithne Carlin, and Jacques Arends. Leiden: KITLV Press.

Arends, Jacques. 1995. 'Demographic Factors in the Formation of Sranan.' In The Early Stages of Creolization, edited by Jacques Arends, 233–285. Amsterdam: John Benjamins.

Arends, Jacques. 1989. 'Syntactic developments in Sranan: Creolization as a gradual process' (Unpublished PhD dissertation). University of Nijmegen.

Arends, Jacques, and Perl, Matthias. 1995. Early Creole Texts: A Collection of Eighteenth-Century Sranan and Saramaccan Documents. Frankfurt: Vervuert.

Bickerton, Derek. 1981. Roots of Language. Ann Arbor: Karoma.

Bilby, Kenneth. 2002. "L'aluku: un créole surinamien en territoire français." Amerindia: 26–27, 279–92.

Borges, Robert. 2013. 'Coppename Kwinti: the influence of adstrate languages on a Surinamese creole.' In The life of a language: Dynamics of language contact in Suriname, 181–214. Edited by Robert Borges. Utrecht: Lot.

Bruyn, Adrienne. 1995. Grammaticalization in creoles: The development of determiners and relative clauses in Sranan. Amsterdam: IFOTT.

Bucholtz, Mary and Hall, Kira. 2010. 'Locating identity in language.' In Language and Identities, 18–28. Edited by Carmen Llamas and Dominic Watt. Edinburgh: University Press.

Byrne, Frank. 1987. Grammatical relations in a radical Creole. Amsterdam: John Benjamins.

Charry, Eddy, Geert Koefoed, and Pieter Muysken. 1983. De talen van Suriname: Achtergronden en ontwikkelingen. Muiderberg: Dick Coutinho.

de Beet, Chris and Sterman, Miriam. People in between: The Matawai Maroons of Suriname. Krips Repro Meppel, 1981.

Devonish, Hubert. 2002. 'On the Sierra Leone-Caribbean connection: hot on the trail of the 'toneshifted' items in Anglo-West African varieties.' In Talking rhythm stressing tone, 165–180. Edited by Hubert DevonishKingston, Jamaica: Arawak Publications.

Essegbey, James. 2005. 'The basic locative construction in Gbe languages and Surinamese creoles.' *Journal of Pidgin and Creole Linguistics* 20 (2): 228–267.

Essegbey, James., and Felix Ameka. 2007. ' "Cut" and "break" verbs in Gbe and Suriname Creoles.' Journal of Pidgin and Creole Languages 22, no. 1: 37–55.

Essegbey, James., Migge, Bettina, and Donald Winford. 2013."Cross-linguistic influence in language creation: Assessing the role of the Gbe languages in the formation of the creole of Suriname." Lingua 129(5): 1–8.

Essegbey, James., van den Berg, Margot, and Marlene van de Vate. 2013."Possibility and necessity modals in Gbe and Surinamese creoles." Lingua 129 (5): 67–95.

Gleason Carew, Joy. 1982. 'Language and survival: will Sranantongo, Suriname's lingua franca become the official language?' Caribbean Quarterly 28, (4): 1–16.

Goury, Laurence.2003. Le Ndyuka: une language créole du Surinam et de Guyane française. Paris: L'Harmattan.

Goury, Laurence, and Migge, Bettina. 2003–2017. Grammaire du nengee: introduction aux langues aluku, ndjuka et pamaka. Paris: IRD Éditions,

Haabo, Vinijee. Ms. Saamaka-Holansi en Holansi-Saamaka.

Hancock, Ian F. 1969 'A provisional comparison of the English-based Atlantic creoles.' African Language Review 8: 7–72.

Hoogbergen, Wim. 1990. The Boni Maroon Wars in Suriname, Leiden: E. J. Brill.

Hoogbergen, Wim. 1983. 'Marronage en marrons, 1760–1863: De niet-gepacificeerde marrons van Suriname.' In Suriname, de schele onafhankelijkheid, 75–110. Edited by Glenn Willemsen. Amsterdam: de Arbeiderspers.

Huttar, George L. 1988. 'Notes on Kwinti: A creole of central Suriname.' Society for Caribbean Linguistics Occasional Paper No. 20.

Huttar, George L., Aboh, Enoch, and Felix Ameka.2013. 'Relative clauses in Suriname creoles and Gbe languages.' Lingua 129 (5): 96–123.

Huttar, George L., Essegbey, James, and Ameka, Felix K. 2007. 'Gbe and other West African sources of Suriname creole semantic structures: implications for creole genesis.' Journal of Pidgin and Creoles Languages 22 (1): 57–72.

Huttar, George L., and Huttar, Mary. 1994. Ndyuka. London: Routledge.

Huttar, Mary L. and Huttar, George L. 1997. 'Reduplication in Ndyuka.' In The Structure and Status of Pidgins and Creoles, 395–414. Edited by Arthur Spears and Donald Winford. Amsterdam: John Benjamins.

Kroon, Sjaak and Kutlay Yagmur. 2010. Meertaligheid in het onderwijs in Suriname: Een onderzoek naar praktijken, ervaringen en opvattingen van leerlingen en leerkrachten als basis voor de ontwikkeling van een taalbeleid voor het onderwijs in Suriname. Den Haag: Nederlandse Taalunie.

Léglise, Isabelle. 2007. 'Des langues, des domaines, des régions. Pratiques, variations, attitudes linguistiques en Guyane.' In Pratiques et représentations linguistiques en Guyane: regards croisés, 29–4. Edited by Isabelle Léglise, and Bettina Migge. Paris: IRD Editions.

Léglise, Isabelle, and Migge, Bettina.2015. 'Language Practices and Linguistic Ideologies in Suriname: Results from a School Survey.' In In and out of Suriname: Language, Mobility and Identity, 13–57. Edited by Eithne Carlin, Isabelle Léglise, Bettina Migge, and Paul Tjon Sie Fat. Leiden: Brill.

Léglise, Isabelle and Migge, Bettina. 2006. 'Language naming practices, ideologies and linguistic practices: toward a comprehensive description of language varieties.' Language in Society 35 (3): 313–39.

Lefebvre, Claire. 1998. Creole Genesis and the Acquisition of Grammar: The Case of Haitian Creole. Cambridge: Cambridge University Press.

Lefebvre, Claire, and Loranger, Virgine. 2006. 'On the properties of Saramaccan FU: synchronic and diachronic perspectives.' Journal of Pidgin and Creole Languages 21 (2): 275–336.

McWhorter, John H. 1995. 'Sisters under the skin: A case for genetic relationship between the Atlantic English-based creoles.' Journal of Pidgin and Creole Languages 10(2): 289–333.

McWhorter, John H. 1992. 'Substratal influence on Saramaccan serial verb constructions.' Journal of Pidgin and Creole Languages 7, (1): 1–53.

McWhorter, John H., and Jeff Good. 2012. A grammar of Saramaccan creole. Berlin/Boston: De Gruyter Mouton.

Migge, Bettina. 2017. 'Putting Matawai on the Surinamese linguistic map.' Journal of Pidgin and Creole Languages 32 (2): 233–262.

Migge, Bettina. 2001a 'Negotiating social identities on an Eastern Maroon radio show.' Journal of Pragmatics 43 (6): 1495–1511.

Migge, Bettina. 2011b. 'Assessing the nature and role of substrate influence in the formation and development of the creoles of Suriname.' In Creoles, their substrates, and language typology, 155–179. Edited by Claire Lefebvre. Amsterdam: John Benjamins.

Migge, Bettina. 2007. 'Codeswitching and social identities in the Eastern Maroon community of Suriname and French Guiana.' Journal of Sociolinguistics 11(1): 53–72.

Migge, Bettina. 2006. 'Tracing the origin of modality in the creoles of Suriname.' In Structure and Variation in Contact Languages, 29–59. Edited by Ana Deumert and Stephanie Durrlemann. Amsterdam: John Benjamins.

Migge, Bettina. 2005. 'Greeting and social change.' Politeness and Face in Caribbean Creoles, 121–144. Edited by In Susanne Mühleisen and Bettina Migge. Amsterdam: John Benjamins.

Migge, Bettina. 2004. 'The speech event kuutu in the Eastern Maroon community.' In Creoles, Contact and Language Change: Linguistic and Social Implications, 285–306. Edited by Genèvive Escure and Armin Schwegler. Amsterdam: John Benjamins.

Migge, Bettina. 2003a. Creole Formation as Language Contact: The Case of the Surinamese Creoles. Amsterdam: John Benjamins.

Migge, Bettina. 2003b. 'The origin of predicate reduplication in the Suriname Eastern Maroon Creole.' In Twice as Meaningful: Reduplication in Pidgins, Creoles and Other Contact Languages, 61–71. Edited by Silvia Kouwenberg. London: Battlebridge.

Migge, Bettina. 2002. 'The origin of the copulas (d/n) a and de in the Eastern Maroon Creole.' Diachronica 19(1): 81–133.

Migge, Bettina. 2001. 'Communicating gender in the Eastern Maroon Creole.' In Gender Across Languages, 85–104. Edited by Marlis Hellinger and Hadumod Bussmann. Amsterdam: John Benjamins.

Migge, Bettina. 2000. 'The origin of the syntax and semantics of property items in the Surinamese Plantation Creole.' In Language Change and Language Contact in Pidgins and Creoles, 201–34. Edited by John H. McWhorter Amsterdam: John Benjamins.

Migge, Bettina. 1998. 'Substrate influence in creole formation: the origin of give-type serial verb constructions in the Surinamese Plantation Creole.' Journal of Pidgin and Creole Languages 13(2): 215–65.

Migge, Bettina, and Léglise, Isabelle. 2015. 'Assessing the Sociolinguistic Situation of the Maroon Creoles.' Journal of Pidgin and Creole Languages 30, (2): 63–115.

Migge, Bettina, and Léglise, Isabelle. 2013. Exploring Language in a Multilingual Context: Variation, Interaction and Ideology in language documentation. Cambridge: Cambridge University Press.

Migge, Bettina. and Léglise, Isabelle. 2011. 'On the emergence of new language varieties: The case of the Eastern Maroon Creole in French Guiana.' In Variation in the Caribbean: From Creole Continua to Individual Agency, 207–30edited by Lars Hinrichs, and Joseph Farquharson. Amsterdam: John Benjamins.

Migge, Bettina, and Mühleisen, Susanne. 2010. 'Earlier Caribbean English and Creole in writing.' In Varieties of English in Writing: The Written Word as Linguistic Evidence, 223–244. Edited by Raymond Hickey. Amsterdam: John Benjamins.

Migge, Bettina. and Goury, Laurence. 2008. 'Between contact and internal development: Towards a multi-layered explanation for the development of the TMA system in the creoles of Suriname.' In Roots of Creole Structure, 301–331. Edited by Susanne Michaelis. Amsterdam: John Benjamins.

Migge, Bettina. and van den Berg, Margot. 2009. 'Creole learner varieties in the past and in the present: implications for Creole development.' Aile ... Lia 1, (1)253–81.

Migge, Bettina and Winford, Donald. 2013. 'Fact-type complements in Gbe and the Surinamese Creoles.' Lingua 129(5): 9–31.

Migge, Bettina, and Winford, Donald. 2009. 'The origin and development of possibility in the Creoles of Suriname.' In Gradual Creolisation: In Honor of Jacques Arend, 131–154. Edited by Rachel Selbach, Hugo Cardoso, and Margot Van den Berg. Amsterdam: John Benjamins.

Moomou, Jean. Les Marrons Boni de Guyane. Matouri: Ibis Rouge Editions, 2013.

Moomou, Jean. 2004. Le monde des Marrons du Maroni en guyane (1772–1860). Matouri: Ibis Rouge Editions.

Muysken, Pieter and Smith, Norval. eds. 2014. Surviving the middle passage: The West African-Surinam Sprachbund. Berlin: Mouton de Gruyter.

Parkvall, Mikael. 2000. *Out of Africa: African influences in Atlantic Creoles*. London: Battlebridge Publications.

Postma, Johannes. 1990.The Dutch in the Atlantic slave trade, 1600–1815. Cambridge: Cambridge University Press.

Price, Richard. 1996. Maroon Societies: Rebel Communities in the Americas, 3rd ed. Baltimore and London: Johns Hopkins University Press.

Price, Richard. 1983. First time: The historical visionof an Afro-American people. Baltimore: The Johns Hopkins University Press.

Rountree, Catherine S. 1992. Saramaccan Grammar Sketch. [Languages of the Guianas 8]. SIL: Paramaribo.

Schiffrin, Deborah. 1987. Discourse markers. Cambridge: Cambridge University Press.

Shanks, Louis. 2000. A buku fu Okanisi Anga Ingiisi wowtu: Aukan–English dictionary and English–Aukan index, 2nd ed. (Paramaribo: Instituut voor Taalwetenschap (SIL). [Also online at http://www.sil.org/americas/suriname/Aukan/English/AukanEngDictIndex.html]

Smith, Norval. 2014a. 'Ingredient X: The shared African lexical element in the English-lexifier Atlantic creoles, and its implications.' In Surviving the Middle Passage: The West Africa-Surinam Sprachbund, 67–106. Edited by Pieter Muysken, and Norval Smith. Berlin: Mouton de Gruyter.

Smith, Norval. 2014b. 'A preliminary list of probable Kikongo lexical items in the Surinam Creole languages.' In Surviving the Middle Passage: The West Africa-Surinam Sprachbund, 417–462. Edited by Pieter Muysken, and Norval Smith. Berlin: Mouton de Gruyter.

Smith, Norval. 2014c. 'A preliminary list of probable Gbe lexical items in the Surinam Creole languages.' In Surviving the Middle Passage: The West Africa-Surinam Sprachbund, 63–76. Edited by Pieter Muysken, and Norval Smith. Berlin: Mouton de Gruyter.

Smith, Norval. 2006. 'Very rapid creolization in the framework of the Restricted Motivation Hypothesis.' In L2 acquisition and creole genesis: Dialogues, 49–65. Edited by Claire Lefebvre, Lydia White, and Christine Jourdan. Amsterdam: John Benjamins Publishing Company.

Smith, Norval. 2002. 'The history of the Surinamese creoles II: origin and differentiation.' In Atlas of the Languages of Suriname, 131–152. Edited by Eithne Carlin, and Jacques Arends. Leiden: KITLV Press.

St-Hilaire, Aonghas. 2001. 'Ethnicity, assimilation and nation in plural Suriname.' Ethnic and Racial Studies 24 (6): 998–1019.

St-Hilaire, Aonghas. 1999. 'Language Planning and Development in the Caribbean: Multi-Ethnic Suriname.' Language Problems & Language Planning 23, (3): 211–231.

Thoden van Velzen, H. U. E and Hoogbergen, Wim. 2011. Een zwarte vrijstaat in Suriname: De Okaanse samenleving in de 18eeuw. Leiden: KITLV Uitgeverij.

van den Berg, Margot. 2007. A grammar of Early Sranan. PhD dissertation, University of Amsterdam.

van den Berg, Margot. 2000. ' "Mi no sal tron tongo" Early Sranan in court records, 1667–1767.' (unpublishrd MA Thesis), Radboud University of Nijmegen. (http://home.hum.uva.nl/oz/vandenbergm).

van den Berg, Margot, and Aboh, Enoch. 2013. 'Done Already? A comparison of completive markers in the Gbe languages and Sranan Tongo.' Lingua 129 (5): 150–172.

van Dyk, P. ca. 1765. Nieuwe en nooit bevoorens geziene onderwijzinge in het Bastert Engels, of Neeger Engels, zoo als hetzelve in de Hollandse colonien gebruikt wordt. Amsterdam: De Erven de Weduwe Jacobus van Egmont.

van Stipriaan, Alex. 2015. 'Maroons and the Communications Revolution in Suriname's Interior.' In In and out of Suriname: Language, Mobility and Identity", 139–163. Edited by Eithne Carlin, Isabelle Léglise, Bettina Migge, and Paul Tjon Sie Fat. Leiden: Brill

Veenstra, Tonjes. 1996. 'Serial Verbs in Saramaccan: predication and creole genesis.' Dordrecht: ICG Printing.

Van Wettering, Whilhelmine, and Thoden van Velzen, H. U. E. 2014. Een Zwarte Vrijstaat in Suriname: De Okaanse Samenleving in de 19e eeuw. Leiden: Brill.

Weygandt, G. C. 1798. Gemeenzame leerwijze, om het basterd of Neger-Engelsch op een gemakkelyke wyze te leeren verstaan en spreeken. Paramaribo: W.W. Beeldsnyder.

Winford, Donald. 2006. 'The restructuring of Tense/Aspect Systems in creole formation.' In Structure and variation in language contact, 85–110. Edited by Ana Deumert, and Stephanie Durrleman. Amsterdam: John Benjamins.

Winford, Donald. 2008. 'Processes of Creole formation and contact induced language change.' Journal of Language Contact – Thema 2.

Winford, Donald, and Migge, Bettina. 2007. 'Substrate influence on the emergence of the TMA systems of the Surinamese creoles.' Journal of Pidgin and Creole Languages 22(1): 73–99.

Yakpo, Kofi, and Bryun, Adrienne. 2014. 'Trans-Atlantic patterns: the relexification of locative constructions in Sranan.' In Surviving the Middle Passage: The West Africa-Surinam Sprachbund, 135–174. Edited by Pieter Muysken, and Norval Smith. Berlin: Mouton de Gruyter.

CHAPTER 4

Representations, Sexuality and Male-Female Relations among the Boni of the Maroni Valley, French Guiana, at the Turn of the Twentieth Century

Jean Moomou

Introduction

The gold mining (mawdonenge ten) and logging practiced in French Guiana between 1880 and 1960 also gave rise to the activity of canotage or boating (kulaboto ten) among the Bushinengué (literally 'bush negroes') of the Maroni-Lawa river, specifically the Boni-Aluku, Ndyuka and Pamaka Maroon groups, descendants of Maroon slaves of eighteenth century Suriname. As a consequence, these societies were plunged into a process of material change (through the acquisition of objects from the colonial world of the past or the consumer society of the present), socioeconomic change (with the advent of wage labour), political change (through the emergence of representative power from 1969 onward), and cultural or aesthetic change (including transformations in dietary practices, clothing and hairstyles). This industrial exploration also highlighted the spatial mobility of these riverside populations, an important factor in the recomposition of village space and the altering of traditional perceptions of the territory. The integration of elements of the colonial world led to an upheaval in the ways of living of these sociocultural groups who constructed their history and elaborated their identity and their imaginary around the marronage and through what remains as memory traces of the slavery experience and the forms of knowledge inherited from their African origin.

Among the observed transformations, the present article[1] looks to examine the way in which the *uman nanga man toli* (history of woman and man), the koosi ini toli, kamba toli,[2] the 'use of pleasure' (Foucault 1984), the definition of sexual belonging and the responsibilities assigned to each of the sexes

---

1 My thanks to the ten Boni (4 men and 6 women) who read this article for their remarks and suggestions.
2 Literal translation: a history beneath the clothes, a bedroom history; that is to say, intimate life.

© KONINKLIJKE BRILL NV, LEIDEN, 2019 | DOI:10.1163/9789004388062_006

can provide a reading grid for documenting an evolution of customs in the Boni society of the Maroni-Lawa valley at the turn of the twentieth century. The thematic at the heart of my analysis spans the sociocultural aspects structured not only by education but equally by the history of the Boni (slavery, marronage in the eighteenth century, gold mining at the end of the nineteenth century and the first half of the twentieth) as well as by the socioeconomic and political conditions (like the municipalization of the Maroni-Lawa river system, the acquisition of Dutch and French citizenship over the course of the 1960s) and environmental conditions (rurality and urbanity). It is situated at the intersection of various disciplines: namely, psychology, sociology, anthropology and history. This sensitive topic allows us, on one hand, to inquire into the relationship between 'the female and male sexes' and 'the expression of intimacy' within public space through the observation of ideas and practices. On the other hand, by providing an insight into the intimacy of Boni society itself (rites of passage, betrothals, marriages, polygamy, widowhood, the relation between men and women, the family institution, parenthood, the division of roles within the group or couple ...), the topic is capable of further enriching the study of the dynamics of social change experienced by this sociocultural group of French Guiana.

I immediately emphasize that there is insufficient space in one article to cover such a vast and complex subject. My observations will be limited, therefore, to the preconditions necessary to explore the question of sexual identity; to the factors that have engendered the (dis)continuities in the representations and practices related to sexuality through specific examples; and finally to the tensions that these mutations have generated in the male-female relation and in the family group among this traditional Boni society in transition.

Conceptual and Methodological Considerations

The way in which the relations between men and women are organized in Boni society (which also applies to the other Bushinengué of the Maroni-Lawa) demonstrates that the questions of domination or equality between the two sexes is neither posed nor understood in the same manner as in western societies. The analysis of the testimony of the *sabiuman*[3] and the *sabiman* (the masculine of *sabiuman*) shows us that rather than an asymmetry in the roles

---

3 A central figure of the group, the repository of knowledge, wisdom and knowhow of the Ancients.

REPRESENTATIONS, SEXUALITY AND MALE-FEMALE RELATIONS 119

conferred to each sex (*uman wooko/manenge wooko*),[4] in terms of social and ritual obligations, there existed a complementarity. In the past, this division did not give any power of superiority to one sex over the other. Put otherwise, the social distinction between men and women was not a synonym of inequality in the treatment of one sex to the detriment of the other. Until a recent period, in Boni society or among the Ndyuka and the Pamaka, men were not perceived to be superior to women, nor indeed the inverse. Both enjoyed a complete and jealously defended independence (see Hurault, 1961: 158). Should we see here an attachment to the principles inherited from the history of the marronage, when the ancestors fought to recover their status as free men? Principles that contrast with the behaviour of domination observed on visits to the plantations of Dutch Guiana? Men and women each possessed their own house with kitchen utensils, their own boat, in their respective village. Even so, men or women who failed in their family and conjugal obligations were quickly called to order within public space (during a public meeting) as well as in private space (within the family or conjugal nucleus). The tasks and responsibilities of Boni men and women, very clearly the outcome of a social and historical construction, were not distributed in favour of one sex or the other, but rather to achieve an equilibrium vis-à-vis the living conditions imposed by their new environment. We can note, however, that the question is posed differently today with the introduction of elements foreign to Boni society into their traditional way of life. These mutations have engendered – not unproblematically – a simultaneous reshaping and redefinition of the functions previously assigned to men and women respectively within the couple, the family and the group, but also of the way in which the Boni think about the male-female relation and speak about sexuality. We can highlight the role played by urbanization and the rural exodus; the level of instruction of women and men, and the career paths of each; the social milieu in which he or she develops; the Christianization of morality; and the impact of digital media.

In this Boni society, the individual is determined according to a set of criteria. From among these criteria, here I select just four. The first is the biological sex recognized at the moment of birth. You are female if you possess a vagina, a menstrual cycle spanning from the first periods to the menopause, and able to birth to life. You are a man if you possess a penis. The constitutive incompleteness of the two sexes means that descent is impossible without a meeting of the two. According to the testimony of the *sabiuman* and the *sabiman*, this incompleteness thus places the two sexes in constant dialogue and obliges them to be

---

4 Literal translation: 'women's work, men's work.'

complementary, within a logic of gift and counter-gift, lest they perish. The Boni apply this sex distinction (male and female) to the wildlife and plants of their environment, as well as to the divinities that govern their world. To the biological criterion they add a physiological dimension. To these two criteria, they add the codes of social, sexual and affective behaviour assigned to each sex respectively. Among the social codes, we can cite the use of the traditional clothing until the 1980s, the moment when European dress became democratized. Thus women wore woven palm or banana leaves around their loins from the marronage until the 1880s. They then abandoned this attire in favour of the loincloth (*pangi*) and then, gradually, in favour of European dress. Men, for their part, had used tree bark to conceal their genitals, then a piece of fabric (*kamisa*) which they passed between their legs, before definitively adopting European clothing. An individual can lose the identity of their biological sex of birth if they do not adopt the codes with which it is associated. Hence, a woman who looks male is qualified pejoratively by the expression *manenge uman sondee taka* (a manwoman without testicles: a *hommasse*). For a man who looks female, a number of equally depreciative periphrases are utilized: *gelisi uman, du enke uman* (stop doing things like a woman). Compared to other societies, another distinction operates at the level of a person's biological sex. Among the Boni, the belief system also interferes in the sexual identify of a person: a belief in reincarnation (nenseki), a belief in the presence and the power of the soul (akaa/yeye) and in the 'divinity of the place from which the infant comes' (bun gadu) which are also elements liable[5] to determine, according to the obiaman,[6] a person's sexual orientation (an aspect to which we shall return in due course).

This article is based in part on my own experience as someone of Maroon descent and in part on a long period of ethnographic research conducted by myself for my doctoral thesis (Moomou 2009). This research was continued with the writing of the present article in mind, my investigation focusing on asking women and men about the question of gender. To obtain the information pertaining to this subject, I first adopted the semi-structured interview method, asking my female and male interlocutors open questions and allowing them to answer freely without interruption. As an example: 'Madam, can you tell me what the relations between men and women have been like from your adolescence to the present?' 'Can you tell us about your life?' The men were asked the same questions. A methodology of direct and indirect in situ observation, combined with participant and multiple observation, was also

---

5   Géraldine Renault, conversation, Saint-Laurent-du-Maroni, April 4th 2017.
6   Louis Topo (Boni sabiman-obiaman), Loka, March 12th 2012.

employed. The objective was to gain a better insight into my informants' statements. In total a hundred people were interviewed. I took into account the different age groups, ranging from the age of 18 to the over 60s, so as to obtain a representative idea of their life experiences. Also taken into account were the spaces (villages and towns) where the interviews were conducted, the circumstances in which the observations were made (traditional festivals, patron saint festivals in the communes of the Maroni-Lawa river, washing laundry on the river shore, agricultural activities, the cleaning of places of worship by women, hunting and fishing parties among men, conflict situations in couples and families, etc.) – as many elements as possible that could shed light on informants' replies. Intervening as a researcher (and not as a man with a particular view of women), in this article I have condensed the viewpoint of women and men when considering my analyses. I could have undertaken a study based solely on the male viewpoint of women, or on the female viewpoint of men. I have chosen, instead, to centre my analysis on the two sets of protagonists in order to obtain as complete a reading as possible of the evolution of customs within Boni society. At the same time, I have consulted the ethnographic literature from the second half of the nineteenth century (Crevaux 1877, Brunetti 1886, Coudreau 1893) and the first half of the twentieth (Tripot 1910). This reading informs us about the customs of the Boni and allows us to observe both the ruptures and the continuities. The study is based, then, on the contributions of the work and reflections of earlier authors. Among these, the engineer-geographer Jean Hurault (see 1961: 121–158; 1970), for instance, described relations between men and women in the Boni society of the 1950s and 60s. Anthropologists have also explored the issue, including Diane Vernon (1992) on the division of roles between men and women in Ndyuka society, and Marie-José Jolivet (2010) on the question of gender among the Ndyuka, through a study of polygamy. Richard and Sally Price have addressed the question of gender in numerous works, such as Arts des Marrons (2005: 31–49), among the Saamaka, some examples of Maroon women (Kaala and Panza), as well as among Saamaka men during the marronage (1994: 119–123, 211–218). The same applies to the couple Thoden van Velzen and W. van Wetering (1982, 2004). Diverse aspects have been studied by these researchers: the division of roles between men and women within the group, polygamy, marriage, divorce, the education of girls and boys, kinship and so on. However, the aim of my study is not to produce a critical review of the work of all these researchers, nor to comment on what they have written before proceeding to my own analysis. Drawing from both anthropological and sociological data, the article's objective is instead to explore this material by mobilizing written texts and oral sources simultaneously in order to analyse, *within a more historical perspective*, an aspect that nonetheless has seldom been approached; namely, the construction of sexual identities, the question of intimacy and the changes that have taken place over time.

My interest in the question of the construction of sexual identities among this group stems from having noted, through a comparison between the testimony of the *sabiuman* and *sabiman* and the discourse of the younger generation, a remodelling of male-female relations, as well as a transformation in how 'carnal pleasure' is expressed. This mutation is perceptible from the 1960s and 70s. In effect, from this period on, the transformations of Boni society seemed to be accompanied by a new view of their own sexuality, but also a new understanding of male-female relations both in the marital relationship and in the division and complementarity of the roles that prevailed in the past, for example. A transformation that should be considered in parallel with what happened at the level of women's emancipation, in France and globally. Put otherwise, the destabilization of certainties that occurred over the course of the 1920s and 30s became consolidated during the 1960s. This mutation that began in mainland France spread to French Guiana. This first took place on the Guianese coast and along the Maroni-Lawa valley, through the contact maintained between the inhabitants of the towns on the Guianese and Surinam coasts (Creole) and the Boni of the villages. The relationship to desire, seeking pleasure and sexual practices underwent a significant evolution during the second half of the twentieth century. We can observe a liberation of discussion on the topic of sexuality and the emergence of a degree of self-exhibition, not without consequences for the way of life and thought of this traditional society in transition.

How do we penetrate the mysteries and received ideas surrounding the sexuality of our elders? How do they think about love, sexuality, conjugality and parenthood? How do they conceive the relations linked to sex? How did they make love? Did they hug? Kiss? Raised to be modest, did women show any inhibitions toward men during sexual intercourse? So many questions that the middle generation (between thirty and forty years old) ask themselves concerning the sexual practices of preceding generations, without, though, going to ask them directly. Is there continuity or transformation between the sexuality of the elders, the male-female relations of thirty or forty years-old adults and the younger generations? If there has been a change, when did it start happening? Orally evoking sexuality or male-female relations is easier than putting them into writing, because they concern an extremely sensitive topic that touches on family secrets and the private life of women and men who, on average, are around seventy years old and do not wish to be compelled to disclose their intimate life. Indeed some of them asked me outright: why would we dokoo (rummage/delve) into their private life? What were my motives? Legitimate questions to which I needed an adequate response if I was to establish trust. The questions that

REPRESENTATIONS, SEXUALITY AND MALE-FEMALE RELATIONS

I asked embarrassed them, as well as myself, since the topic provokes shame. My attitude inevitably stems from the respect that I owe them. In this society, one did not discuss sexuality, nor relations between men and women, in front of one's parents or parents-in-law, and it is rare to hear any talk of sex among those Boni born prior to the 1960s/1970s. This behaviour differs markedly from the generations born after the 1970s. For the younger generations, sexuality has become an almost banal subject of conversation. If adults are speaking among themselves, they fall silent when someone arrives of the opposite sex or from outside their family, clan or group. They are also silent in the presence of an adolescent or a child. They judge that children will discover the secrets of sexuality at an adult age when they have their own experiences. I emphasize the fact that the relatives of *sabiuman* and *sabiman* who I interviewed seldom evoked their emotional and sexual life in front of their children, doing so solely to call them to order when they displayed vulgar or deviant behaviour, and then quickly changing the subject. My questions at first met with a certain distrust on the part of the *sabiman* and *sabiuman*. Subsequently, though, it generated a kind of satisfaction since I had shown an interest in them and above all in their knowledge of 'carnal pleasure,' and their view of love, sexuality and male-female relations – all topics on which they had been unaccustomed to expressing themselves. When I asked them such questions, they most often replied with phrases accompanied by laughter, such as: mati/bia, fika mi ye anga u taki![7] This attitude would presage a dialogue potentially rich in anecdotes.

To work around these obstacles, I adopted a variety of approaches during the interviews, so that the *sabiman* and *sabiuman* – without being aware of the fact – were able to provide me with some insight into their intimate lives. My first strategy was to raise the subject of polygamy and its role in Boni society prior to the 1960s. Polygamy was then a matter of pride for Boni men. This involved a man tending to women's material needs to some extent by, for example, working as a boatman, rubber tapper or storekeeper, irrespective of whether he was already involved with another woman. Men thus enjoyed a certain amount of freedom since they were not constantly present at home. By letting them talk freely about their history, therefore, both women and men, contemporaries of the period under examination, provided me with a glimpse into intimate aspects of their lives. Profiting from this opportunity, I gradually steered them toward talking about the relations between men and women, but also the place of each sex in society. Another question were the obligations of the man to his parents-in-law and his wife, and vice-versa, or those relating to the education of boys and girls as the 'closure of personalities' (see Mead 2001),

---

7 'Friend, let me be with your words!'

as well as their place in society. Topics that differ appreciably from what is observable today. I was interested in how couples came together: at what moment of the day (maman ten/mindi dey/baka dina/neti),[8] at what location (in the swiddens, by the shore or on the river), in what context (traditional festivals, mutual aid). One situation in particular permitted young adults to meet: these were the games played on land (kukukuulu: hide-and-seek) and in water (yampa). I emphasize here the latter. In contrast to the present day, aquatic games were highly developed among the Boni until the start of the 1990s. The yampa game was introduced into Boni land in the 1950s by the Dutch school. The story narrated before the game refers to the colours of the Dutch flag, the royal family (Orange-Nassau) and the fish that it consumes, the cod (bakiyawn). The yampa is a very dynamic aquatic game that offers a double chance for boys to approach girls, or vice-versa, and arrange a later rendezvous. Given the lack of opportunities to approach girls in the village owing to the vigilance of their parents, some young adult men profit from this occasion to disappear with the girls behind the boats moored at the jetty, reappearing a few minutes later. An ancestor to this game also exists, the faa. This was most often played with two participants, sometimes more. Less dynamic than the yampa, the person nevertheless had to be a good swimmer to avoid being caught before reaching the resting place. I was equally interested in their games of seduction (*poolo gi uman/poolo gi man*), their way of behaving in society. What kind of seduction strategy did they pursue to approach someone? How did the woman or man react if refused? Finally, I was interested in the arrival of the first child, its place of birth, the choice of name, as well as the rituals that accompanied the birth.

My second strategy was to focus on two cult objects used by Boni men and women respectively. Although I was already aware of their function, I preferred to let the people interviewed explain their use to me since speaking about the two objects would lead to a discussion of sexuality and male-female relations. These items are the bokekete/kelinki (kettle/chamber pot) and the mannengebata (the potion that turns a boy into a man). The young woman receives the first item at the end of puberty (around 17 or 18 years old) during the *gi pangi/dumbi pagi*[9] ceremony (the 'gift of the loincloth'). During this phase of her life, the circle of women teach her about her rights and obligations, along with those of men. She has the right to sexual relations, for example, but pursued

---

8   Respectively : morning/midday/after dinner or evening/night.
9   For boys, the ceremony is called the tey kamisa/gi kamisa ('gift of the kamisa'). In contrast to the women's ceremony, this rite has completely disappeared among the Boni. Nevertheless, even though the rite of passage is no longer practiced, men are still given a kamisa that they can wear at major occasions.

discretely so as not to tarnish her reputation before marriage. From the day of the ceremony until old age, she can use the bokekete. She inserts various kinds of leaves in the pot, leaving them to infuse in hot water. She then tips this liquid into a kelinki/doodo (chamber pot) for her personal hygiene. This preparation, the virtues of which are well-known to women, allows her to avoid infections (vaginal mycosis, stomach aches, discharges, colds). It is used frequently around childbirth. This is an indispensable ritual for Boni women and the Bushinengué in general, whether from the villages or for some in the towns too today. This kettle accompanies the woman wherever she goes. It allows seeka yu seefi fi yu de bun[10] one Boni *sabiuman* remarked. Forgetting to take it during a long or distant journey, you cannot be at ease, it is as though it were your food[11] some of the women declared. This infusion presents another interesting aspect: it has the power to shrink the female genitalia. The second object, the mannenge bata (the bottle that makes you a man/the man's bottle), also called pipi bata (the penis bottle), contains a concoction of leaves and roots mixed with alcohol, which the man, most often in his fifties, prepares himself and drinks before having sex. The potion is said to keep the phallus erect for longer. As sexual impotence is viewed dimly, the Boni man can become a laughing stock of women chatting among themselves as they wash clothes or dishes by the river shore. On account of this problem, a man may remain single all his life.

My third strategy involved asking about the mato (tales recounted in the evening or during funeral rites), such as the tale of baa Anansi anga sa Wenon toli,[12] via the symbolism of art timbe[13] (a geometric image on a wooden base), which often depicts sexuality in an ironic or roundabout fashion. By way of illustration, the painting by Sawani Pinas below depicts a love scene.

I have also used the interpretation of erotic dreams, as well as the odo[14] (adages), nango[15] (parables) and enigmas that emanate from the discursive dynamic

---

10 'Taking care of your body to feel good.'

11 'I no man de bun, na leti enke na yu nian nian.'

12 The story of Anansi and his wife sa Wenon. For more detailed information, see Anelli (1994).

13 For a study of timbe art among the Boni, see Hurault (1970), Abonnenc (1971–1972), R. Price & S. Price (2005), and S.Price (2015).

14 'Kibi du, kumba sa soli' (young woman, you can hide to make love, but your navel will betray you), 'san fu kii rawmma nee gi en bee' (what should have killed the old woman made her pregnant), 'tapu a wali na ini foo-kuukuu ini' (shut an opossum inside a chicken coop).

15 'I be go na waka esi de' (I was walking yesterday evening), 'i be go na wan olo' (I was in a 'hole'), 'i be pasa a pe' (I passed by there), 'a baya de be feni mi/a baya de be go na mi' (that man there had me/that man there entered me).

FIGURE 4.1   Sawanie Pinas, painting 'A pasi fu lobi'
SOURCE: JEAN MOOMOU, 2005

of the Boni. Also included were figures of speech (periphrasis, ellipsis, analogy, metaphor, metonymy, euphemism) and different expressions. To cite some examples: *siibi nanga yu/didon nanga yu* (spend the night/sleep with someone); waka-waka napi to talk about a 'skirt chaser'; *faya ede and pania ede* to designate a frivolous woman; *booko kini* (bend the knees when speaking about a woman to signify her first sexual relation three months after childbirth); *luku bee* (look at the belly, that is to say, make love with one's wife while she is pregnant). According to the account of a Boni *sabiuman*, the practice of *luku bee* was part of the obligations of the Boni man. It was prohibited for him to abandon his wife during pregnancy.

The final method involved inquiring about the repertoire of traditional songs (*awasa singi, songe singi, mato singi, awawa*)[16] of past and present. Among the themes broached in these songs, the following are omnipresent: poverty,

---

16   Parodical songs performed during funeral festivals but also on New Year's Day. For more detailed information, consult Anakesa 2008.

wealth, suffering, the joy of life, social successes and failures, life in society, love, sharing, sexuality and marital relations. As an example, the acoustic recordings[17] made by Jean Hurault between 1957 and 1965, very interesting ethnographic sources, immerse us in the universe of the Boni of this period through the intermediation of Boni singers like papa Eféa, papa Apawlobi, papa Nétoyé and the female singer ma-Tikisi. To this acoustic source we can add the audio cassettes recorded in the 1980s and 90s on which women left messages of love to send to their husbands and vice-versa, or a kapiten[18] from one village to another with the aim of settling conflicts that were weakening a couple. We can note that an insight into the private lives of men and women can also be gained during conflicts between suitors or spouses, or during clashes between rivals while women are washing clothes or dishes at the jetty (lanpeesi). Indeed, the information that transpires through this verbal jousting can tell us something about sexual practices and male-female relations. Other circumstances favour discussion on sexuality and male-female relations. This is the case, for instance, of the moment when women peel and grate manioc to make couac, when rice or peanut harvesting begins, or when they gather in the *munu-osu*. The latter (the 'moon house') is a cabin situated far from the cult spaces in which the woman lives during the menstrual period. Among men, discussion is propitious during a hunting or fishing trip, or during the towing of a boat or the clearing of an agricultural field.

To gain an understanding of all these elements, I asked the interviewees to express themselves freely, taking care not to interrupt them. When necessary, I asked some of my own family to undertake their own inquiries with members of their nuclear family or friends, after indicating the age groups in which I was interested. We then together compared and analysed the results obtained.

What Do These Testimonies and My Observations Show?

Invited to reflect on their 'ego-history' (personal history, marital life, experience of polygamy) or themselves analyse certain tales, myths, timbe symbols, adages and enigmas, the interviewees ended up discussing the theme of interest to us here. An examination of their discursive dynamic reveals the nature of conjugal 'violence' and the way in which conflicts within the couple were resolved. For example, custom permitted a deceived man to use physical

---

17   See Jean Hurault, Chansons boni des années 1950–1960, IRD-CNRS, 1998.
18   The chief of a village.

violence to reclaim his honour when another man wooed his wife. At the time of the loweten (marronage) and until the 1960s-70s, a certain number of Boni men – in part because they lacked the right scissors, but especially for aesthetic reasons – wore different types of plaited hairstyles. Their hair was styled by their sisters, cousins or friends. The problems began when they had their hair styled by another man's wife. Sitting on a bench, his face close to the private parts of the woman doing his hair, the man could take advantage of the situation to seduce her (*begi a uman*). Before the 1960s–70s especially, the women wore loincloths, of course, but usually no underwear.[19] The spouse considered that the man whose hair had been styled had *toobi* ('troubled her life'). The accused could end up receiving a severe beating from his own wife or her brother. He could accept the punishment or choose to flee, but he could also fight back if wrongly accused. We can understand now why mothers advised their adolescent or adult daughters to pay attention to the status of the men whose hair they styled. A woman whose husband was wooed also had the right to inflict physical punishment on the suitor, albeit without shedding her blood or making acerbic comments about her. If the latter was at fault, she would not react. If not, fighting would break out and insults would be thrown.

The different accounts also highlight the *fuusuku uman*[20]/*suwa anga uman* (the fight with the woman, i.e. rape), the du ogi na man osu (adulterers),[21] the *fii a uman* (molestation) and their consequences. Psychological support existed to help a woman who had been subject to severe ill-treatment and severe punishments were pronounced against the offender. The accounts also reveal the strategies adopted by women or men to meet each other, such as the recourse to adages or little songs in which the words distract the attention of those liable to understand them. Some women made use of a set of codes to fix a rendezvous with a man: the form of the knot tied in the cloth covering the meal that she sent to a man, for example. The woman who no longer felt any desire for her spouse, and who had trouble admitting this to him, could use a code of communication: a particular arrangement of the spoon on the table; serving him tepid water rather than cool water to drink, and so on. Having received instruction from his maternal uncles, or sometimes his father, during

---

19 I emphasize that in the absence of underwear, adult women nonetheless could use a small kamisa underneath the loincloth (not to be confused with the kamisa worn by men) which functioned as an undergarment. However this small kamisa was rarely used, save during menstruation or following childbirth.

20 This term probably derives from a corruption of the Dutch expression for violating a woman, wrouw schenden.

21 Adultery is prohibited to women but tolerated among men.

REPRESENTATIONS, SEXUALITY AND MALE-FEMALE RELATIONS 129

adolescence, the man was able to interpret these signs. A man who desired a woman would offer her a craft object (tee, bangi, kankan, mata, tafa, pali, guluma, koja, paytiki ...)[22] on which he had inscribed a message of love. When a relationship became official, there was a marriage contract[23] that involved the exchange of a valuable item between the man and woman. This might be a hammock, an embroidered loincloth or *kamisa*, a jewel, or the like. If a spouse later wished to separate, he or she was obliged to return this item to the other spouse or to a member of the latter's family, who could then accept or refuse it. Separation could not take place if one of the spouses refused to take back the object testifying to the engagement. This symbolic contract engaged the man to take good care of his wife, to protect and feed her, and to take good care of her children (even when not his own), to build a house for his wife in her village, to clear a swidden for her, to provide her with a rowing boat, to respect his parents-in-law and his host family, which he should treat as his own, and to mourn if she died. He should help his parents-in-law with their agricultural activities. This contract also bound him to not beat his wife or make her suffer. If he no longer wanted her, he should take her back to her home village. For her part, the wife had to take care of her husband, prepare his food, behave respectfully towards him and be faithful to him, take care of the children, respect her parents-in-law, and help them with their agricultural work. If her husband died, she should mourn. Despite these strict rules, we can note a degree of 'freedom' in the couple where neither the Boni man nor the woman should feel prisoners to one another (see Hurault: 1961 : 149–150). Either spouse could break off the marriage without authorization. Nonetheless, in reality, both the man and the woman would be called to order by their family were they to fail in their obligations. The couple were considered a stake between two families linked by alliance; the form of 'privatization' observed after the 1990s did not yet exist and the consent of the parents might take precedence over the couple's desires. The 'confiscation' of the couple by the two spouses was not then tolerated. According to the *sabiuman* and the *sabiman* of the 1960s, both joy and woe had to be shared between the three components – the two families and the couple – since both families wished to control the situation and protect those belonging to their lineage.

Their testimony also highlights the importance of the woman's virginity prior to marriage; a primordial condition found among other societies, notably in West Africa or in the societies of the religions of the Book. Until around

---

22   Winnowing dish, bench, comb, mortar, table, paddle, washboard, linen beater, spatula.
23   Bruno Apouyou, interviewed by telephone, Paris, September 8th 2012.

the 1980s, among this matrilineal society with its polygamous patriarchal tendency, the Boni woman had to be a virgin before settling down with a man. Losing her virginity before marriage constituted a dishonour as much for the woman as for her mother or family. It was considered a lack of education and proof that the woman had failed to contain her impulses. This loss of virginity demonstrated the absence of self-esteem, the absence of respect for her body, for her ancestor reincarnated in her, for her soul and for her bun gadu. The man at fault had to pay the price of her lost virginity by offering the young woman an object of value (fabric, a jewel or an everyday object: a gold chain, pot or plate). However, there was no question of her being given money. She should refuse any such gift for fear of being perceived as a *wey uman/lampuweli* (prostitute). It should be emphasized that the young deflowered woman (gaansama en)[24] had to denounce, alongside her aunt or sometimes her mother and maternal uncles, the man responsible for the act who refused to assume its consequences and form a home with her. The men of the family did not hesitate to punish the offender publicly. The aim was to spare the young woman from psychological suffering, shame and to help her escape the logic of *suku mi, begi mi, feni mi, fika mi*.[25] After the gradual emancipation of women and their sexual liberation over the course of the 1970s, which still remained timid at the time, this cult of virginity had completely disappeared, except among Boni, Ndyuka and Pamaka families converted to Christianity, especially among the alternative movements after the 1990s. Moreover, once the girls left to pursue their studies outside the space where their parents live (village/town), the question no longer arises for most of them.

Other behaviours appear in the testimonies. These include the solitary pleasure of the Boni man or woman, and homosexuality. Masturbation exists, even if nobody dares talk about it. The expressions naki gitali (play the guitar) to speak of female masturbation and naki tetey (pull or beat the rope) for men attest to the existence of the practice. As for homosexuality, according to the people interviewed, it seems unthinkable to imagine a Boni man engaging in this practice, which they qualify as molusu sani (something improper), a vice, a practice contrary to the social norms established by the Maroon ancestors who promoted the cult of the strong, skilled, agile man, an excellent warrior who tames his fears and his emotions: manenge nee kee (a man doesn't cry). If a man or a woman engages in this form of sexuality, the elders justify it with an explanation of a religious kind: the practice in this case originates, they say,

---

24 An expression which means give the young girl the status of a woman.
25 He pursued me, he asked for my hand, he had me, he left me, in Méli (a singer of Ndyuka origin), Album CD, 2008, track 4.

REPRESENTATIONS, SEXUALITY AND MALE-FEMALE RELATIONS 131

from the soul, from the bun gadu of the individual in question or their nenseki (Vernon 1992 : 27–31). Given that these different entities are capable of harming or perverting a man or woman's sexuality, preventing them from procreating and keeping them single, it is necessary to pray for them. People may perform the rite of separation (paati nenseki/paati bun gadu) and elevation of the name (opo nen) for the person to recuperate a sexuality that conforms to the social norms established by the group. The objective of these rites is to bridge the gap between the biological sex of birth and the feeling of being a boy or girl. On the other hand, the Boni in the years before 1960, as well as a portion of them today, attribute homosexuality to the customs of urban inhabitants. If some Boni men or women engage in such practices, this is because they have imported them from the town. They justify this origin by turning to the lexicon, for example, in support of their argument. Sodomy is designated bulu by the Boni (from the Dutch boer). The practitioner is called *bulel* (from the Dutch boerer) or *buluman*. The sexual relation between women is called giiti. This term comes from the Dutch glijden and signifies 'slide,' in the sense of female genitalia rubbing together. On the French side, the Boni speak of makumé ('ma commère,' my gossip), according to a lexicon deriving from Creole gold prospectors from the Maroni-Lawa river used at the start of the twentieth century. A certain number of Boni *sabiman-kapiten* and *sabiuman-basia*[26] also cite the existence of two gold prospectors who lived as a couple downriver from Wacapou village during the 1960s and 70s. A Boni suspected of such a relationship may be subjected to humiliating treatment. If a parent catches children of the same sex under the age of 10 in the process of such an act, he or she may think that they are just discovering their bodies and presume that this play will stop when they reach adolescence. A man who is slightly effeminate in his behaviour or performance of a domestic task would be quickly reprimanded by other men. The latter would not hesitate to tell him: *kaba fu du enke uman/kaba fu gelisi uman* (stop doing things like a woman/stop imitating women). Nonetheless, this repressive response does not prove that homosexuality never existed in Boni society. It suffices to pay attention to the lexicon, the expressions to which the *sabiman* and *sabiuman* turn, to talk of this sexual practice. The same is true of the attitude adopted by the Boni to belittle a man with an effeminate appearance or mannerisms. This allows us to ascertain that this practice existed, despite the apparent denial of homosexuality as a reality. Such is corroborated by Malinowski (1989) and Gueboguo (2006), notably in their studies of cultures that similarly condemn these practices. As

---

26   A spokeswoman for the female circle.

in most organized and structured traditional societies, the work of men was differentiated from that of women. Thus the divisions of tasks and activities did not escape the attention of Boni society. This distribution of responsibilities is explained by the history of slavery (the gendered attribution of activities in the eighteenth-century plantations), by marronage (men assigned to combat, women to protecting children during the flight) and by the new experiential spaces formed by the river and forest. A man who did the domestic work of his wife, rather than go about the tasks deemed masculine, was treated as gobisa.[27] This did not mean that a man could not help his wife, or the opposite. But, in the past and still today, Boni society did not look kindly on a man who engaged in embroidery, or a woman who performed timbe, for instance. A man whose attitudes were judged to be feminine had to repress them or else become a figure of gossip. Just as there existed a 'male culture,' there was also a 'female culture.' As I have already mentioned, a woman who displayed a masculine bearing was described as *manenge-uman sandee taka* (a man-woman without testicles) because, in the eyes of both sexes, she appeared to be someone who had rejected their biological sexual identity of birth. The same applied to a man who adopted behaviour deemed to be feminine by both sexes – for example, a man who urinated squatting down (*tsotsootso*) rather than standing up. It is worth stressing, though, that neither sex regarded an androgynous person as a subject of mockery, as we can see from time to time today. This does not mean that there were none in the past. But the androgyne was more often perceived as someone who emanated from God: na gadu meki en so (God made them so) the Elders would remark wisely. Over the course of the 2000s, two new expressions made their appearance among the Boni, likewise among the Ndyuka and the Pamaka. These were *uman toobi manenge* (a woman who grabs a man's wife) and *manenge toobi uman* (a man who grabs a woman's husband). Expressions that illustrate two different actual events that became widely reported: one in the Maroni valley, the other on the coast. We can note, however, that these terms and expressions do not go as far as to exclude the individual or ignore them. It is up to him or her to assume their behaviour, despite the sometimes negative views held of the person concerned. According to the *obiman* and *obiauman*, other practices were also proscribed. These included fellatio and cunnilingus. Their proscription is explained in part by the fact that most men and women, for example, practiced the possession cult (very well described by Jean Hurault in his works) and took the bath of invulnerability (*manenge-obia*). Some communicated by drinking sweli (the

---

27   Such behaviour was common when a woman decided to leave her husband.

REPRESENTATIONS, SEXUALITY AND MALE-FEMALE RELATIONS

drink of the group's guardian divinity). A number of sexual practices were considered antithetical to the principle of the sacred, capable of weakening the spirit (obia) of the woman or man. Moreover, sexual relations were prohibited when taking certain ritual baths or during some ceremonies. Nowadays, this principle is less and less respected and tending to disappear.

From the Unsaid to the Disclosure of Intimacy in Public Space: Multiple Factors

Prior to the 1960s and 70s, sexuality was a sensitive topic, not to say 'taboo.' Everyday discussions centred on agricultural work and crop yields, craft activities, the exploits of hunters and fishermen. Favoured subjects also included sorcery, jealousy, the sharing of inheritances, the devolution of traditional power, knowing how to live and act in society, family conflicts, disputes between clans and the way of settling them to assure harmony. And finally, the obsession with finding a paid job in public administration, due to the end of the gold mining and boating activities and the political concerns, linked to the territory's municipalization (1969). Today's *sabiuman* and *sabiman* recount that the Elders very seldom spoke about sexuality. When they did refer to the subject, they expressed themselves with modesty and sobriety. An attitude that contrasts with that of the young generation. The lexical field of sexuality was expelled from public space. This does not mean that they refrained from speaking of the topic in the public sphere, among men or among women, or sometimes between the two sexes. Indeed, in public space, the Elders talked among themselves using riddles or adages to avoid offending sensibilities or appearing too vulgar; an attitude that I was still able to observe today among certain older people from the villages. As an example, in their discursive dynamic, words deemed vulgar (like soki, teki, nay, bombo, pipi ...)[28] are banished in favour of expressions or terms unlikely to be noticed by children or adolescents. Sensibilities are protected by the use of euphemistic expressions[29] like *siibi anga, go neen, man peesi, uman peesi, takuu peesi, mi sani, mi* ondo. Similarly, a man does not

---

28 Translation: "kiss a woman or man, take a woman or man, sew a woman, vagina, penis ..." I would note that most young people today use these words more readily than adults. There currently exists a degree of 'banalization' of these terms and sexual practices among this age group.

29 Translation: 'sleep with ... I entered here, my male part, my female part, my thing, my bottom ...' These words or expressions are the vocabulary used by adults to avoid appearing disrespectful.

say *mi uman* (my woman) but rather mi *ma-sama* (my spouse), *mi boliman* (the one who cooks for me) to speak of his wife in public. She, in turn, will not say *mi man* (my man), but *mi da-sama* (my spouse). The Elders ensured that the 'good customs' did not become corrupted; they monitored and reprimanded those who flouted the rules. Until the 1970s and 80s, one could speak of a sacralization of the body and the genitalia, taken to be the life-giving organ. From childhood, whenever a boy touch the private parts of a girl, the parents would tell him *yu o dede fi yu oli en moo* (you will die if you dare do that again). Out of fear, children would avoid touching each other until adolescence, the moment when they became aware that their parents had been lying! Such a warning would have little or no impact today.

Sexuality and various practices linked to it were likewise 'taboo' subjects. However, one event[30] would make them public and become recognized as a novelty. This concerns the story of a man from the village of Tabiki (Island of the Lost Child) and a woman from Assissi ede konde which unfolded at the start of the 1960s. One day the woman became seriously ill. Unfortunately, the doctors from Maripasoula were unable to diagnose her malady. During a consultation of the divinities, the inhabitants discovered the cause: the group's guardian divinity announced that, while having sex, the wife and husband had engaged in cunnilingus, a practice disallowed while communicating with sweli (*diingi sweli*). Their experimentation of this kind of practice had thus provoked the woman's illness. In front of the *faakatiki*, the traditional chiefs – including kapiten Kondoku – organized a libation to expiate the couple's mistake by making him publicly acknowledge that they had experimented the practice. Some people directed insults at the offender: *papa x i tingi mofu ye bia! I nian a uman toc!*[31] This was the moment when the practice was first revealed publicly in Boni land.

A number of factors have helped lift the veil on sexuality in the lives of women and men alike. These factors include, on one hand, the exodus to towns on the Guianese and Suriname coasts (1950–1960), plus the urbanization and municipalization that occurred in their living environment from 1969. This evolution was also accelerated by the new relationships made with inhabitants of towns along the Guianese and Suriname coasts, as well as the Creole who lived among them. In effect, the Boni who had visited or conversed with inhabitants from the coastal towns subsequently replicated the amorous rituals of urban life in their own world and practiced them with their partners.

---

30 Bruno Apouyou, interviewed by telephone, Paris, September 8th 2012. I interviewed Bruno again in Saint-Laurent-du-Maroni on 25 July 2015.

31 Papa x, you performed cunnilingus, didn't you! What a dirty mouth!

Among the Boni who lived in towns during the 1960s and especially between 1980 and 1990, black-and-white television with its soap operas and their love scenes,[32] cinema, theatre and access to erotic books all led to new sensibilities and new conceptions of romantic relationships. At the same time, access to education can also be considered a catalytic element. In fact, the arrival of the school in Boni country (its full development on the Dutch side between 1950 and 1970, followed by its introduction on the French side between 1962 and 1970) strongly contributed to a better understanding of the body provided by biology courses[33] (discovery of the functions of the human body, the anatomy ...). The schooled children were able to discuss the topic more easily with their parents, now more trusting, who thus began to express themselves. Nonetheless, communication remained difficult in some families due to the respect shown to parents still, and the adolescents found it easier to talk to their uncles and aunts. Learning to read also allowed the generation of children born at the end of the 1950s to access books discussing the topic of sexuality. Thus some of these young people who continued their studies in Cayenne, Saint-Laurent-du-Maroni, Paramaribo or Albina were able to develop new experiences.

The introduction of a new musical trend, aleke, is the third factor to have favoured the evolution of customs. According to the *sabiuman* and *sabiman* (Boni and Ndyuka), the entry of loonsey music into Boni country at the start of the 1960s (Planchet & Gana 2002: 128) had been initiated by the Kottica-liba sama, that is, the inhabitants of the Cottica river in the Moengo region (the site of bauxite mining) in Suriname. In contact with the Creole population of the Suriname coast, Moengo especially, the Cottica river inhabitants interpreted the Surinamese Creole music in their own way and created a new rhythm in the Bushinengué region. Loonsey or mongo poku (Moengoi music), later called aleke, from the name of the singer who made the style popular, spread along the Maroni-Lawa river and on the Tapanahoni. Over the course of the 1960s, the music and dances of Paramaribo (bigi poku/kaseko) and the Caribbean basin[34] (meringué from the Hispanic islands, the Dominican Republic especially, and the slow of Guyana) also reached the Boni. These musical styles were first introduced by Saïfa Welemu and his father Galimot Saïfa (boatman, storekeeper and rubber tapper). In his father's store located on Lawatabiki

---

32 According to the testimony of the Boni living in Paramaribo, these films were censored. It was rare to see the nude body of a woman or man on television. Scenes of kissing were also censured. The end of censure dates from the 1980s, but erotic films were prohibited to those under the age of 18.

33 Antoine Bayonne, interview, Cayenne, September 18th 2012.

34 Ibid.

island, Welemu organized dance evenings between 1964 and 1968 that attracted not only the Antillean gold prospectors, keen to hear the sounds of their home country (Dominica, Saint Lucia, Guadeloupe, Martinique), but also the Boni who discovered them. The end of the 1970s and the start of the 1980s saw the arrival of melodies (cadence-lypso) sung by the Dominican singer Ophélia Marie, highly popular among the Boni. Papa Basika (an inhabitant of Assissi), for example, husband of ma-Buki (Papaïchton), often played tracks sung by Orphélia on his radio cassette player during the 1980s. Radio[35] performed an important role in the diffusion of music from the town of Paramaribo. By purchasing radio sets, then, the Boni remaining in the village had access to the musical varieties of the town.

These musical styles have the particularity of being danced alone (as in the case of loonsey) or often in couples (a cavalier and a cavalière), thus making physical contact and interaction easier, in contrast to Boni music (awawa) and dances (awasa, songe, susa, tuka) in which men and women dance separately. In 1960, such physical contact was heavily frowned on by elders; according to them, the sensual aspect of this music gave rise to conflicts in couples. The contemporaries of this period recount that men often separated their wife from their dance partner. Some would prohibit their wife from dancing with other men entirely. Among the musical genres that penetrated the Boni villages, only loonsey and aleke were taken seriously by the traditional authorities in view of the enthusiasm that they had aroused among some of the Boni youths of the 1960s. Other musical genres were only heard, never played, because the Boni lacked the financial means needed to buy the right equipment (guitar, piano, drums, flute, cymbals), unlike the instruments used in loonsey, which they themselves could make and which they already used in order to play their traditional music (the drums aside since these had to be longer). Aleke tended to take precedence over traditional music and dance. Called baka sikeyni ('new dance style'), this was forbidden at the start of the 1960s with infractions punished by the gaanman Difou (1937–1965), then reintroduced over the course of the 1970s by the gaanman Tolinga, becoming the most popular music among the Boni. The same enthusiasm spread to the other Bushinengué societies of the Maroni-Lawa and Tapanahoni rivers. Among the themes contained in the songs were social issues, sexuality and above all love. Themes that also exist in the repertoire of traditional Boni music, but which were sung on special occasions (New Year's Day, betrothals, marriages, funerary rites) and which caught the attention of women and men, sometimes causing them to change the

---

35   Ibid.

course of their romantic relationships. In the 1970s and 80s, the most well-known groups along the Suriname coast and on the Maroni-Lawa-Tapanahoni river were Tsotso Pokina, Klemensia, Labi boy (Bley) and Sapatia. Zouk became popular at the end of the 1980s. Melodies from the Guyanese coast were introduced through borrowings from the Creole population of Maripasoula and young Boni who had left to pursue their schooling in Saint-Laurent-du-Maroni and Cayenne. Outside of sensual music, another musical genre was also introduced into Boni country between 1965 and 1966 via Welemu (Wempi). This was Jamaican music,[36] ska (the forerunner to reggae), which the Boni called Jamaika poku (Jamaica music). The reggae of Bob Marley, which appeared at the start of the 1970s, acquired followers along the Maroni-Lawa river and reached its zenith during the 1980s. Thus the first Pamaka-Boni to have adopted the Jamaican Rasta movement in a town (Saint-Laurent-du-Maroni) were two[37] brothers, baa-Manu and baa-Dewini, with a Pamaka mother and Boni father. The Boni from the villages of the Lawa river discovered the Rasta style from the two brothers when the latter stayed among them on two occasions between 1974 and 1975, then again between 1978–1979. The two had adopted the Rasta way of life: the use of herbs, a special diet and style of dress, the use of a cane, reggae music. Later, over the course of the 1980s, the movement grew rapidly.

The acquisition of the bed during the 1970s[38] constitutes the fourth and last factor in the evolution of customs. Its arrival led to changes in intimate relations. Hammocks do indeed make intimate relations uncomfortable and just about anything can lead to a fall: ropes break, knots come undone, hammocks tear. Anecdotes add gloss to the narrative of the sabiuman and sabiman and provoke widespread laughter. Nevertheless, most of the Boni born in the village prior to the 1980s had been conceived in a hammock. We can note that various kinds exist: the ingi amaka (a hammock made by Amerindians), the maypa boto amaka (very small, shaped like a maripas palm coconut shell), the goon tapu amaka (a hammock for everyone/a popular hammock) and the ayundo mi de amaka or boyzili amaka (a hammock produced in Brazil). The evolution of hammock styles had already allowed a change in sexual practices, but mattresses brought comfort and freedom of movement. Acquisition of this item became widespread at the start of the 1990s just when the majority of Boni women began to receive family allowances. The 1960s-80s thus saw a gradual transformation in Boni gender relations and sexuality. This mutation

---

36   Antoine Bayonne, interview, Cayenne, March 9th 2017.

37   Antoine Apouyou (kapiten), interview, Kourou, March 10th 2017.

38   By way of example, Ma-Anini received her first bed in 1978, given by her Ndyuka husband, Baïnon Midaye.

is explained by a certain number of factors cited previously that timidly lifted the veil on a theme difficult to access in the past, one that today has become a subject at the centre of discussions, in the village and in the town, among men as much as women. Dialogue between adolescents and adults has also become freer. Storytellers and singers have played a role in this liberation of speech and in the honouring women and men in public space. Storytellers,[39] especially Ndaati anga ndaagi (debut in 1990), singers of aleke beni (Saafi-Saafi, As System Tranga Noto, Big Control, Wan Tong Melodi, Tsotso pokina, Sapatia, Bigi ten,) and singers of gitali beni today (Djaiut, Kesekoloko, Mely, Norma, Big-Boss ...) have all tackled the themes of love and sexuality without taboo. In 2004, for example, the group Wan Ton Melodi even released a song that spoke about the amorous relations of the Boni gaanman, Paul Doudou. Afterwards they had to apologize to the chief. The singers also speak of the suffering of women and men alike with the aim of changing behaviours. In 2007, for instance, in a hymn to woman (Uman i pina, 'the suffering woman'), the singer Mely denounced the attitude of the frivolous man, someone who is not serious in his relationship with women. The singer places himself in the skin of a woman by imitating her voice: *di mi o dede mi naw u kon uman mo! di mi o dede mi naw u kon uman mo!* ('when I die, when I come back to life, I won't want to be a woman'). Others highlight the mutual deceptions and conflicts within couples.

To their former ways of expressing affection or love – including, among others, the baasa (the hug) and the sign of protection (an obiaman or obiauman who marks with the forehead of his or her patient with their own) – the Boni, like the other Bushinengué populations of the Maroni-Lawa and the Tapanahoni, have imported a new social behaviour from the town: namely, kissing (bosi) with its variations (a kiss on the cheek, a kiss on the lips ...) whose arrival in Boni country dates back to the middle of the 1980s. Kissing on the cheek and especially on the lips were heavily frowned on at the outset, the *sabiuman* and *sabiman* told me. Firstly, it was associated with eroticism and a lack of respect. Secondly, the skin (via transpiration) and the lips (via what the individual consumes) involved questions of hygiene and comprised channels for the transmission of microbes. These reasons why taken to explain the fact that the Boni did not kiss, preferring to hug and exchange affectionate words. The diffusion of the urban way of life via the rural exodus and schooling, as well as the impact of television soap operas, banalized kissing on the cheek and removed its sexual connotation. It became a sign of affection. Thus a mother may barely notice that her children hug her rather than kiss when they pay her a visit in

---

39   Atoman Léo, a Ndyuka singer.

the village. We can note that children still seldom kiss their father on the cheek with hugging preferred. In mixed couples (a Boni woman and a Creole man, or a Boni woman and a white man, and vice-versa), children do tend to kiss their father, though. But it is still rare to see two men kiss each other. By contrast, kissing on the lips retains a sexual acceptation. Among Boni couples today, whatever the age group, kissing indicates a sensual love. In the past, woman's breasts were not coveted as an object of sexual pleasure; they served to 'give life,' the *sabiuman* say.[40] When a Boni woman was surprised naked by a man, she would use her hands to hide her *uman peesi* (private parts), while most Creole or white women would hide their breasts and cross their legs. Curiously, from the moment when Boni women started wearing a bra, an undergarment that first appeared in the 1960s, they adopted the gestures of women from the Guyanese and Suriname coasts. The relationship to the breasts also changed and acquired a second function, the search for sexual pleasure. Among some Boni, Ndyuka, Saamaka and Pamaka women, providing nourishment has been eclipsed as a function by visual appearance. A mother may refuse to breastfeed her child or decide to wean the infant abruptly in order to keep her breasts firm. Men and women's enjoyment during sex also became demystified from the 1960s onward.

Remodelling the Social Bond: Frustrations, Clashes and New Dynamics

In Boni society, the man should bring in money for food, clothing and travel costs for his wife, children, nieces and nephews. He is also responsible for building a house for his wife in her home village; making a rowing boat for her to be able to travel around; and clearing a swidden for her to plant crops. Since the 1990s, most Boni women, married or single, have received social welfare or had a paid job, allowing them to have this work done by artisans who they remunerate. Living in the village, the women buy a motorized boat which they themselves pilot. In town, they invest in a car. In contrast to them, there are some men who do not even own an urban house (Moomou 2013: 27–28), a motorized boat or a car. This leads to frustration among some. The emancipation of women, as well as men, through schooling, paid work, and access (from the end of the 1980s for women) to social rights (family allowances and social security) that provide French citizenship gave rise to a new type of relationship.

---

40   Ma-Toïti, interview, Loka, 15/04/2005.

French family law became mixed with the traditional Boni way of conceiving the family, sometimes leading to clashes with customary law.

New kinds of conflicts made their appearance in conjugal relations and in the way in which family life was managed. Men who should channel their impulsiveness have sometimes become violent. The same has been true of women. Since the 2000s, we can note an increase in the number of suicides with weed killer or attempted suicides of men whose wives decided to leave them. Prior to the 1990s, a woman would often leave her spouse because she considered him lazy or sterile, and vice-versa. But the breakups did not lead to the death of one or the other. We can note, nonetheless, that violence, generally speaking, does not reach the extreme levels observed in the Creole societies of Guyana and the French Antilles, as frequently reported by the local press (France-Guyane and Guyane Première especially) to the surprise of the Boni in the villages. The belief in the spirit of the deceased that returns to torment the family tends to dissuade attempts to kill a spouse. Furthermore, a man who dared to strike his wife ran the risk of receiving a beating from her brothers or uncles. Nonetheless, the ever more frequent 'privatization' of couples has left brothers and uncles more distant from conflicts. This emancipation is interesting but not without its problems given that nothing replaces the traditional relations and values constructed around the loweten which linked men and women to their family and group. Among the Boni, as among other societies, the individual can only live properly through the intermediation of a constructed social relationship.

Another significant transformation has been observed in the domain of polygamy and singlehood. According to the *sabiuman* and *sabiman*, after the flight of the Boni Maroons from the plantations in the eighteenth century, men outnumbered women (see Moomou 2013: 339). From the viewpoint of social equilibrium, women, like men, were unable to stay single due to the necessity to ensure descent: Quand tu mourras qui te mettra en bière, the Boni saying goes: 'When you die who will put you in the coffin?' A l'âge de ta vieillesse qui s'occupera de toi? goes another saying: 'When you're old, who will care for you?' The status of the single man, and woman, prompted derisory remarks.[41] Mothers and fathers can often be found reprimanding their twenty-something sons and daughters who went away to study or work without any official partner, or any children. In Boni society before the 1970s, a man was expected to have a wife and children by the age of twenty. If he

---

41   A view that is changing today.

did not, he was perceived as a bad man (*ogi man*), lazy (*lesiman*), or such like. The same applied to women. In the past and until the 1990s, it was inconceivable for a young woman without any handicap, healthy (*bumbu-uman*), charming (*moy-uman*), hardworking (*wooko-uman*) and having received a proper education (*kya-uman*) to have reached the end of adolescence (*sabi du uman pikin sani*)[42] and still be single without being very ill-regarded or even denigrated. One of the biggest concerns of a Boni, Ndyuka or Pamaka mother – as we can observe in other societies, especially among the Creole populations of Guyana and the Antilles prior to the 1980s – was to see her daughters and sons married. Among the Boni until the 1970s or 80s, the choice of marriage partner fell sometimes to the mother, or an aunt or an uncle from the maternal line, but seldom to the father. Unlike today, the consent of parents usually took precedence over the wishes of the two spouses. Observing a presentable adolescent educated well enough to become a good wife, a mother would not hesitate to approach her parents to ask for their daughter's hand in marriage to her son, arranging that they would live together when they reached adulthood. This practice, almost vanished today, was called *poti mofu na uman* (to put a word on a girl: the fiancée); *poti mofu na man* (to put a word on a boy: the fiancé). It would be wrong to suggest that there was no 'Romeo and Juliet'-type love during the era of the *loweten* or the *mawdonenge ten*. But the practice of *poti mofu*, the reasons for which were multiple, was very widespread. A matrimonial strategy, the *poti mofu* enabled a family that lacked knowledge of a certain practice (especially rites) to gain access this knowhow. It was also a means through which a mother and daughter, often living in poverty, could receive help to clear a swidden, for instance. This was likewise a way of receiving the products of hunting and fishing from a suitor, as well as accessories from the colonial world. Survival conditions were difficult for women: more vulnerable than men during the time of the *loweten*, they were forced to live with a man, even if he was already with another woman. The mawdonenge ten and the *kulabobo ten* offered the Boni, Ndyuka and Saamaka boatmen a real boon by reinforcing the woman's material and particularly financial dependence on her spouse. Each boatman thus had a woman in each village or known *kampu*[43] during the era (1880–1970). This explains why so many of the interviewed men and women have half-brothers and half-sisters dispersed along the Maroni-Lawa and Tapanahoni rivers. Nowadays, polygamy has fallen into decline, due not

---

42   'Know women's know-how.'

43   A temporary habitation. Not to be confused with a village where a faakatiki (Altar of the Ancestors) and a keeosu (House of the Dead) are found.

only to sexually transmitted diseases and the social changes that have taken place within Boni society, but also because of the incapacity of Boni men, in the villages and towns alike, to meet the needs and desires of their suitors given the difficulty of managing their wives equitably as custom also demanded. Finally, the gradual Christianization of morality since the 1990s and 2000s has also had a significant impact. Thus the 'faithfulness' that was once required of women is now also required of men.

By freeing themselves increasingly from the weight of custom, being single is no longer experienced in the same way by individuals due to the new ways of living that they have encountered. Until the 1990s, in fact, a man or woman would see no drawback in having a partner without a paid job. Social status has now become one of the key selection criteria, especially in towns. The dynamics of social change also affect the family. The ever more fractured family group (bee) has given way to the increasingly autonomous family household. The impact is felt in the area of children's education. In the villages, a child would be educated by all members of a family, but so too by members of the clan (lo) as a whole. Now, though, reflecting an issue that is becoming increasingly acute in towns, the mother frequently raises her children alone. During a separation, couples often fight over the custody of the children since the parent responsible for them has the right to receive a family allowance. The application of French family legislation to the Boni family household since the 1990s has not been without consequence. In the past, a father did not have parental authority over his own children, but rather over his nephews and nieces. When he died, the latter would inherit his property, not his children, except in the case of any child that the mother had given him to educate. Nowadays, this rule is often thrown into question. Families are torn apart in both the villages and the towns. Children, through French law, claim their heritage. By introducing the father's authority into the family household, the parental right exercised by the father in relation to his children rendered him less and less responsible for his sisters' children. In the case of separation, if he has a wage and if the children bear his patronym (something that was rare until recently), he must pay alimony. The result is a growing judicialization of relations. And the corollary is frequently a deterioration of the relations between the separated man and woman.

Other elements can be added to this survey of the evolution of customs, such as the use of jeans and shorts by women, over the course of the 1980s, and especially during the 1990s, or the fact that some of these women began to smoke cigarettes.[44] A woman wearing trousers and smoking cigarettes was frowned on by men until recently. Likewise a woman who treated her

---

44   Some nuance is necessary since Boni women did smoke in the past. The oral and written sources dating from the twenty-first century confirm this fact. Nevertheless, men from the

REPRESENTATIONS, SEXUALITY AND MALE-FEMALE RELATIONS 143

hair with straighteners (1960–1970) or later with the use of softeners (1990–2000) or who wore a wig (balata uwii)[45] would be reproached for rejecting the body given to her by nature. The 'liberalization' of relations and the management of the female body met with harsh criticism from men. It was a new behaviour. In sum, women's appropriation and interiorization of customs linked to urban practices were deeply unpopular among the men contemporary to these changes. Nonetheless, this female revolution has now been accepted and integrated into the social body of Boni society. Such emancipation has allowed some women to become actresses of their lives and escape certain constraints imposed by custom. The same goes for men. A shift has occurred, in effect, from a traditional society where the individual and the group were as one to another where, as observed elsewhere in the world, the individual is emancipated and where the bonds of solidarity and mutual support are becoming more and more institutionalized. It is important to stress, though, that despite the changes in customs, traditional festivals and cultural activities still reintroduce men and women into their respective customary functions.

By Way of Conclusion

The article has enabled an apprehension of the representations linked to sexuality and male-female relations in Boni society at the turn of the twentieth century. A study that allows us to gain access to the psychology of their behaviour and show that it can be a source of analysis and understanding of the evolution of customs. The approach also reveals that the utilization of data relating to sexuality and male-female relations by the historian can prove a fertile source of information when writing about the social and cultural history of the Boni of the Maroni-Lawa valley.

Thus we can ask, when it comes to Boni experiences, where each sex has bitterly defended its space of intervention, is gender – such as formulated in the debate in Europe and in North America, a word with no real equivalent in the Boni language – sufficient to encapsulate the full complexity of being? The apparent difficulty is explained in part by the multiplicity of approaches to gender resulting from the encounter between the epistemological approaches of North

---

1970s and 1980s believed women should not smoke cigarettes because it made them seem frivolous.

45   'Plastic hair.'

America (Scott 1988 in particular) and Europe (among others Bourdieu 1998, Bereni et al. 2008, Berger 2013), discordant sometimes due to the conflicting or opposite ideologies involved, as well as the resulting semantic shifts. The feminist current, for example, uses gender as a tool to deconstruct male domination. Among the Boni, the question of domination is not yet posed in these terms, at least for the moment. This does not rule out the future, though, where it is already possible to glimpse the social and cultural changes under way.

References

Anakesa, Apollinaire, Musiques et chants traditionnels busikondé sama de la Guyane, CADEG RADDO AVPL 61, 2008, notice 28 p. Notice double CD audio.

Anelli, Serge, ed. 1994. Mato: contes des Aloukous de Guyane. Paris: Conseil international de la langue française.

Cottias, Miriam, Burguière, A., Downs, L. L., Klapisch-Zuber, C., Jorland, G., and Le Goff, J. 2010. Le corps, la famille et l'état: hommage à André Burguière. Rennes: Presses Universitaires de Rennes.

Berger, Anne Emmanuelle. 2013. Le Grand théâtre du genre. Identités, sexualités et féminisme en Amérique. Paris: Belin.

Bereni Laure, Chauvin Sébastien, Jaunait Alexandre, Revillard Anne. 2008. Introduction aux études sur le genre. Bruxelles : Editions De Boeck.

Bourdieu, Pierre. 1998. La domination masculine. Paris: Editions Seuil.

Brunetti, Jules. 1886. La Guyane française souvenirs et impression de voyage. Tours : Alfred Mame et Fils.

Coudreau, Henri Anatole. 1893. Chez nos Indiens: quatre années dans la Guyane française (1887–1891). Paris: Hachette.

Crevaux, Jules. 1877. Le mendiant de l'Eldorado: de Cayenne aux Andes. Paris: Phébus.

Foucault, Michel. 1984. Histoire de la sexualité, Tome 2, L'usage des plaisirs. Paris: Gallimard.

Gueboguo, Charles. 2006. « L'homosexualité en Afrique: sens et variations d'hirer à nos jours. Socio-logos. » Revue de l'association française de sociologie, n. 1 (Online: https://journals.openedition.org/socio-logos/37).

Héritier, Françoise.1996. Masculin/féminin. La pensée de la différence. Paris: Odile Jacob.

Hurault, Jean. 1998. Chansons boni des années 1950–1960. Paris : IRD-CNRS.

Hurault, Jean. 1970. La vie matérielle des Noirs réfugiés Boni et des Indiens Wayana du Haut-Maroni (Guyane française). Agriculture, économie et habitat. Paris: La Haye, Mouton.

Hurault, Jean. 1970a. Les Africains de Guyane. Paris: The Hague.

REPRESENTATIONS, SEXUALITY AND MALE-FEMALE RELATIONS 145

Hurault, Jean. 1961. La vie des Noirs réfugiés boni de la Guyane français., Dakar: IFAN.

Jolivet, Marie-José and Vernon Diane. 2007 « Droits, polygamie et rapports de genre en Guyane », Cahiers d'études africaines [online], 187–188.

Malinowski, Bronislaw. 1989. La sexualité et sa répression dans les sociétés primitives. Paris: Payot.

Mead, Margaret. 2001. Mœurs et sexualité en Océanie. Paris : Editions Pocket.

Moomou, Jean. 2013. Les Marrons boni de Guyane: luttes et survie en logique coloniale (1712–1880). Paris: Ibis Rouge.

Moomou, Jean.2011. « Habiter et construire en pays bushinengue : l'architecture, l'une des clés de lecture des mutations de la vie matérielle (xviiie-annees-1990). » In L'esclavage de l'Africain en Amérique du 16 au 19 siècles-les Héritage, 191–194. Edited by Eadie Emile. Perpignan: Presse Universitaire de Perpignan et Association Dodine.

Moomou, Jean. 2009. Les Boni à l'âge de l'or et du grand takari (1860–1969). Ph.D. Dissertation, Paris, EHESS.

Norman, Sante. 2009. « Poötie uma », U de nen kaba. CD, Diesel Production.

Oakley, Ann. 1972. Sex, gender and Society. London: Temple Smith.

Planchet, Gael, and Emile Gana. 2002. 'Les Noirs Marrons de Guyane.' Hommes et Migrations, 1237(1): 125–130.

Perrot, Michelle. 2009. Histoire de chambres. Paris: Editions Seuil, Paris.

Renault, Géraldine, F comme Femme. Broadcasting in 2005, Télé Guyane.

Price, Richard. 1975. Saramaka social structure: analysis of a maroon society in Surinam. Puerto Rico: Institute of Caribbean Studies.

Price, Richard and Sally Price. 2005. Arts des Marrons. Paris: Editions Vents d'Ailleurs.

Price, Richard and Sally Price. 1994. Equatoria. London: Routledge.

Price, Sally. 2015. « Tembe: un art qui s'adapte. », In Sociétés marronnes des Amériques, Actes du colloque, Saint-Laurent-du-Maroni, 368–376. Edited by Jean Moomou. Matoury: Ibis Rouge.

Stoller Robert, J. 1968. Sex and Gender: On the Development of Masculinity and Femininity. New York: Science House.

Thompson, Victoria E. 2008. «L'histoire du genre: trente ans de recherches des historiennes américaines de la France.» Cahiers d'histoire. Revue d'histoire critique, 96–97 (Online: http://chrhc.revues.org).

Thoden van Velzen H.U.E and Willelmina van Wetering. 1982. 'Female religious responses to male prosperity in turn-of-the-century Bush Negro societies.' New West Indian Guide 56 (1–2): 43–68.

Thoden van Velzen H.U.E and Wetering, Willelmina van. 2004. In the Shadow of the Oracle Religion as Politics in a Suriname Maroon Society. Long Grove: Waveland Press.

Tripot, Jean. 1910. La Guyane: au pays de l'or, des forçats et des peaux-rouges. Plon-Nourrit.

Vernon, Diane. 1989. « Femme qui cuisine; Homme à fusil: perspectives du marriage Marron. » In Familles en Guyane, 31–38. Edited by Observatoire Régional de la Santé en Guyane et l'Association des psychologues de Guyane. Paris: Editions Caribéennes.

Vernon, Diane. 1992. Les Représentations du corps chez les Noirs Marrons Ndjuka du Surinam et de la Guyane française. Paris: Éditions ORSTOM.

Wallach, Scott Joan. 1988. Gender and the Politics of History. New York: Columbia University Press.

CHAPTER 5

New Lives for Ndyuka Women: "Everything's Changed but the Men"

Diane Vernon

Since the 1980's sweeping changes have occurred in the lives of Ndyuka women from the villages of the Tapanahony river in Suriname. The days of seeing women as "hearthstones" as the Saramaka Maroons sometimes put it (Price 1984:33) or, "sitting on your own door sill," as the Ndyuka say of respectable feminine conduct,[1] is all but forgotten in the new female immigration to coastal Suriname and French Guiana. Recently still defined by the late paramount chief, Gaanman Gazon, as "where men go (temporarily) to make money" Paramaribo and particularly Saint Laurent have become the permanent destination of mothers without husbands, houses, and cash, while the men, finding few jobs on the coast, return to the forest to mine gold. From the single-model career of child rearing and subsistence farming in the forest villages, Ndyuka women immigrants to coastal Suriname or French Guiana now branch out in diverse ways with great individual mobility, increasing their independence from lineage authorities, and taking on a wide variety of economic and productive activities. For all those who, on the French side, are illegal clandestine immigrants and handicapped in this new environment by lack of literacy and local language, the variety of activities is dictated less by opportunities than by the necessity of fending for themselves and their children, with or without husbands. Most of them still practice subsistence horticulture. At the other extreme, young women who are second or third generation of immigrants, who have enjoyed the backing of their families to pursue their education, have entered professions such as nursing, teaching, psychology, accounting, administration, social work and even politics[2] They complain that despite their professional status, their husbands still boss them around, still play around, and still take second wives. Occupying the middle ground are women married to men

---

1   These are to be understood as norms and only usually announced by elderly women. In fact, within the river territory, women were very mobile, moving from village to kampu and often had houses in both.

2   In the last municipal election in Saint Laurent du Maroni, one of the candidates was a thirty-year old woman of mixed Saamaka and Ndyuka origin. The present mayor, re-elected, has in his team a Ndyuka nurse who works in the hospital.

© KONINKLIJKE BRILL NV, LEIDEN, 2019 | DOI:10.1163/9789004388062_007

148   VERNON

with secure salaried jobs, and/or women entitled to French family allowances who enjoy a relatively comfortable life.

The former divide between married women (enjoying a husband's contribution of new fields, riches and coastal products) versus single women (usually older, without husband, scraping a living out of old gardens) is now situated in the French administrative realm: between those with residence cards who enjoy the generous French child allowances, and their sisters who hang on desperately in hopes of the magic papers that will bring them a basic living. It is situated in the cultural divide: between women who are literate and speak French, who drive cars and get jobs, and those who cannot read or write or speak French, and who not only are not independent, but are ever searching for intermediaries to depend on.[3] This chapter tries to scan some aspects of the sea-change in Ndyuka women's lives as they invent new ones in the foreign urban setting of Saint Laurent du Maroni.

$$\cdot\ \cdot$$
$$\cdot$$

Women were, in the early years of this society, few,[4] precious, and in great demand and men's concern was to settle them – sisters or wives – in safe hiding, a practice which continued into the 20th century of never allowing them to move out of the territory unless accompanied by men. Until the end of the 70's, this restriction of women's mobility to the confines of village, grounds and kampu was still defined as protection from the dangerous Bakaa world, though it had become reinforced by male jealousy and codes of behavior that ordained that women not wander in places where they had no business.[5] Until the early 1980's mothers still concealed most of their children by not declaring their births: even the list at the health center at Stoelmanseiland[6]where

---

3 This is a constant complaint of their choice "intermediaries" – the health and social workers in St. Laurent

4 Tales recounted of marooning women stress the difficulties of escaping, babe in arms, or in the last months of pregnancy. Even thirty years after the signing of the peace treaties (1760), the first villages all the Ndyuka clans founded together was named « Kiyoo kondee » « Guys' village » because the majority of its population was male.

5 Women living in the river villages in the twentieth century could do business by proxy: sending down ground produce with brothers going to the coast to sell for them and make purchases to send back.

6 In 1950, acting on the advice of the missionaries Mr. and Mrs. Axwijk who had been visiting the Lawa river, the Moravian Mission sent a young doctor, Dr. Doornbos to found a health clinic on the edge of Ndyuka territory at the island of Stoelmans. Success was slow in coming and it was only after two years of medical presence and a cultural adaptation on the part of the doctor, that the first, desperate maternity case was presented. The successful delivery

NEW LIVES FOR NDYUKA WOMEN

names of mothers and their children were noted showed only one or two of their many offspring.

While the core value for Maroons is ancestry, the back-up of legal authority, constantly renewed in funeral rites, ever appealed to for life, health and blessing, the single most sacred task of men and women is to perpetuate society (grounded in the extended kin group) by giving life. The importance of people is reiterated in every kind of situation: nothing, not land nor river nor gold is important without people. The dominant value accorded to human life is followed through by pro-life laws, even in the case of rape, bringing immigrant families into conflict with French law in Guyane, but potentially in line with fundamentalist Christian pro-life movements.[7]

The supreme social work of making people falls to women: the matrilineage derives from them and thrives, with husbands being thanked for their help. Each woman makes her paansu, a "sprout" of lineage: grandmother, her children and the children of her daughters, which quickly becomes an osu unit, then a mama pikin (four generations). As this is essential family on whom each member depends to settle his problems and come to his defense, the segment of the lineage where interactions are the densest, I see the mama pikin unit as the most probable family to survive eventual lineage disintegration. Factors Ndyuka themselves have cited as weakening the matrilineage are demographic and migratory. Villagers in Bilo Ndyuka in 1977 could not remember all their grandchildren born and raised in Paramaribo and pointed out the houses of families who had not return in years. The importance of the avenging spirit kunu which Richard Price called the "lineage charter" (Price 1973), obliging all lineage members to gather and propitiate, was also true for Ndyuka, but has lessened over the years, going from a week's celebration to three days. Now it is put off year after year. Unlike the Saamaka, where lineage fission is realized thanks to the production of new kunus, Ndyuka lineages do not seem to split along new kunu lines, redrawing new social frontiers. Other factors weakening matrilineages are their non-recognition in French law. Customary law, working on social relations within these parental groups can be contradicted by French law, freeing members to ignore lineage injunctions. And conversion to

---

opened the door to a Ndyuka clientele at first mostly maternity cases and dental problems, necessitating the construction of a hospital.

7 Excepting cases of incest, if a rape results in a pregnancy, Ndyuka law dismisses the crime to favor the new life expected. The rapist must attend to the pregnancy as any lover or husband would and as he will now be the father of the child, there can be no pursuit against him, for it would create a situation of fio-fio (spiritual conflict) that could bring illness or death to mother or child.

Christianity protects wayward members from lineage kunu retaliation and ancestor sanctions.

The emphasis, with children, is on quantity, as a quality – for the inherent talents or vices of any particular person are attributed to a combination of many spiritual sources that affect his nature, such as incarnated ancestors or an earth spirit responsible for his conception. Mothers are aware of the importance, for their own reputation, and for their children's future, of a large fraternal group. Neither immigration from the forest villages to urban dwellings nor the impact of biomedicine on the number of babies lives[8] saved has discouraged their multiple maternities except in the yet rare cases of girls highly motivated and encouraged toward professional careers. As one woman divorcing her husband afflicted with AIDS said, "I have only four children so far, and I must supply them with siblings so they will have people to fall back on." In this matri-group as adults, brothers are expected to help sisters without husbands, and come to their defense in problems with men. Moving, with age, up the scale in life, men and women become aunts and uncles to advise and manage the young and from there, rise to the superior authority of great aunts and uncles, who by then are all the more important and precious since age is reducing their numbers as lineage heads.

"Having one's people" abi sama, is to have support, backing and insurance against need and attack; not to have people leaves one in a weak and vulnerable position. Recently, a candidate for kabiten-ship in the village of Malobi was advised by his family on the coast to refuse the honor: none of his close family still lived in the village to support him against possible conflicts. Men, though more often assuming a limited role as fathers in this matrilineal society, are also committed to reproduction through any number of marriages and a wide dispersal of their seed, as they move about in the world, gathering riches to bring to the wives and mistresses (riches referring both to material goods and the lineage's riches: progeny conceived during a man's visit which adds to the population of the woman's lineage he visited). Polygyny is arguably instrumental in this pro-birth project.

Uman na a basi: ne en meke wi (man speaking: "Woman is the boss: she makes us"). The women make people, the men manage them. Male management (kabits, basias, elders holding kuutus, counsels) however, tends to take center stage, women giving voice back-stage or bed-side, as advisors; or

---

8   During my meeting with him in 1977, Dr. Doornbos estimated that within the ten years of his practice in the health clinic at Stoelmanseiland, 50% of lives had been saved. This has ushered in a demographic explosion, at least in Saint Laurent du Maroni, where births have finally stabilized at 2500 per year for a population of roughly 40 000.

NEW LIVES FOR NDYUKA WOMEN

front-stage as spirit mediums. Subordination to lineage decisions is more a respect of relative age and of status, and it affects young men as well as women. Male macho attitudes are deployed by older brothers toward younger sisters[9] and in conjugal unions, which husbands by marital right dominate.

Traditional Marriage

If you asked a man why he married, his first reply would be to have the right to beat up any man who paid court to his wife.[10] It is less often remarked that wives, too, have the right to attack a rival who shows her face, so a second wife keeps out of sight until the first has accepted officially to greet her (gi odi). Both cases of permitted attacks are hemmed in with rules: the beating must be public, administered only once unless the guilty party fights back, with fists only, and during daytime, and (in the case of a betrayed husband) only so long as the case has not been tried in council. In the long run the first wife is expected to relent and accept the co-wife, but not all do so, and men's only power of negotiation is the threat to leave – which, if he cares for his children, is a loss for him. As one kabiten remarked during a council meeting dealing with such a problem, "If the (first) wife refuses the second, he is faced with a choice: either to stay with the first and give up the second or to leave the first and go with the second." Otherwise, if a wife-fight ensues and someone is injured or killed, it will be his fault." Opposition from the first wife may be stronger than death: if the second potential spouse dies before the first has accepted her in the ritual ceremony of "gi odi," she will now be obliged to concede (under threat of death by the ghost of the dead) and recognize the co-wife in an enactment of the above ceremony with the matrilineal family of the deceased standing in for its deceased relative.

There is, however, one advantage to be gained by the first wife if she recognizes the second: this new one, usually younger and firing the man's passion, will be blamed if the husband begins to ignore his first spouse. The family of the first, defending her right to equal time and goods, will then descend on the young rival and beat her up for having kept the husband to herself. Such a husband who dotes on his second wife but wishes to avoid trouble with the first wife's family will often encourage the first to leave him by staying with her but making her life miserable.

---

9   Within a sib-ship, age difference allows for hierarchical relations: respect and responsibility, subordination and domination. Often an older sister raises a child.

10   For more details on traditional mariage, see Vernon (1989).

No woman in the village in the 1970's ever expressed the wish to be financially independent of her husband, but complaints against polygamy and obligatory monthly menstrual retreats were a constant thorn in their sides. For both men and women marriage is a badge of respectability and seriousness. For a man, it attests to his sense of responsibility. A woman, also, validates her reputation by marriage. Unmarried women are said to be na gaanda – there for the taking. As one Ndyuka woman said, "It's when you're not married that you can have man" (sex). A first marriage for girls was once more or less guaranteed through arranged unions. One form, still practiced in the early twentieth century, but now long gone, naku bee ("tap the belly") consisted of asking for the child before its birth. If it were a girl she would be his wife (or one of them); if a boy, then a mati (close friend). Poti mofu – asking for a prepubescent girl – was still practiced in the 80's and has not even now completely disappeared on the river. To a certain extent this was a security for both partners, since the seriousness of the boy and girl could be weighed. The girl's physical maturity was estimated by her breasts falling to her chest, (probably a better rule of evaluation than going by years) and the potential husband's on his resources to maintain a household. An older man could often make a better offer both as husband and as son-in-law than a young one starting out. Both this age difference and arranged marriages would later become red flags in the French context of Saint Laurent de Maroni teenage pregnancies. The age of sexual consent in French law is fifteen and a half years. The law labels anything under that, committed with a partner who is over eighteen, a rape of the younger by the elder. Nor does French law recognize customary marriage, even when the affinal lineages have gone through all the stages of initiating and concluding an official customary union. Most cases both of love affairs and adolescent marriages escape scrutiny by French legal authorities until teen pregnancy brings them to the attention of the maternity unit and social services, which issue a signalement to the juge des enfants. There will be no follow-up, however, unless a complaint is brought.

Arranged marriages were reassuring for families also because they were not based on that dangerous emotion, passion. The lad for whom his family chose a young bride would necessarily be pleased with the best his family found, certain that love would grow slowly out of mutual respect while other attractions would not be forbidden him. The girl would perforce be faithful – it was for her a marital duty. She could theoretically refuse the union if she disliked the man, but more frequently, young and under pressure, she would give it a try and would divorce him early on if she were unhappy, and try her luck with someone later. But by then she had received her skirts of womanhood, was obliged to be responsible for her own grounds, and life was hard till she found

NEW LIVES FOR NDYUKA WOMEN

a new husband. If she had already had a child with him, she should know that a new husband is often not good to another man's progeny.[11]

As Sally Price has described for Saamaka Maroons, Ndyuka women have traditionally been dependent on husbands to prepare new grounds to plant, to provide canoe and paddles to reach them, and to supply almost all consumer articles from on the coast, including the cloth with which they make their skirts, the utensils with which they cook and hoe, and the bedding for themselves and the children. The wife's lineage also transfers to the husband her medical expenses which up-river would mean taking her to the clinic and/ or traditional healer, but in an immigrant situation would mean, in Paramaribo paying hospital bills, and in Saint Laurent, arranging Aide Médical d'Etat papers which allows her to be treated free, and could be a symbolic first step toward legal residence. Residence papers would be added to the provisions a husband owed his wife as immigration toward the French side quickened in the 1990s after the outbreak in 1986 of the Surinamese civil war.

All marriages were contracted between the two lineages, in protracted palavers, in the woman or girl's village. The agreement was concluded with rum and libations to the ancestors and the couple was informed as to their respective marital obligations. Taking the wife away required a much longer waiting period and any number of palavers.[12] Her first house she would make for herself and her children in her family kampu (a hamlet next to the grounds).

Her husband would eventually build her one in her own village, if the marriage lasted, but that would be many years later.

Each contracting lineage took on responsibility for its member's behavior up to the termination of the marriage by divorce or its prolongation until the end of mourning in the case of demise of a spouse. No valuables were held in common, nor children nor houses nor money (and land, of course, was clan property). Separation was limited to the dyadic relation, ended by a symbolic return of an article of clothing. Affines remained affines, with marital taboos intact. Divorce was easier for women who could justify their complaints of irresponsibility or cruelty on the part of a husband. A man had somewhat more difficulty: he could return the bride on grounds of misbehavior, but even in the case of adultery, a council (lanti) might insist he take her back, though he was only really obliged to do so symbolically out of deference to a higher judgment. Obviously, this close surveillance of marriages by lineages depended on the

---

11 See below "Men are tired of raising women's children."
12 In 1980, in the village of Tabiki, a kabiten from the Cottica region seeking a wife to take with him was obliged to wait there three months, bored, teased , and heckled by village children before his wish was granted.

FIGURE 5.1　House in an agricultural hamlet, Gaakaba
SOURCE: DIANE VERNON, 1979

strength of lineage power over their members, which would begin to wane in the new millennium.

As for children, they belonged solely to their mothers to keep and to raise or to distribute as foster children. The first one or even two she traditionally gave to the mother who raised her, but a mother might also offer a child to any relative who loved the child or that the child fancied, or who was without progeny, or who could procure him or her certain advantages. And husbands would try to coax a wife into giving them dada pikin ("father's child"). The father would then transfer the child to the care of his own matrilineal family – his mother, his sister ... to ensure against losing the child in case of divorce. Fostering of children is still common in the immigrant situation. It is a necessary social insurance for children who will always be taken in by a relative when tragedy strikes; but it runs up against French laws on recognition of autorité parentale, (official guardianship) and the rights to social benefits that go with it. The French administrative transfer of official guardianship to distant relatives (cousins, aunts, uncles, etc.) cannot be made without the mother's permission so that in cases where the mother is unreliable, drug-dependent, mentally deranged, living elsewhere or even dead, fostering sisters or cousins have been

FIGURE 5.2　House in the village of Malobi, constructed 1950s
SOURCE: DIANE VERNON, N/D

unable to obtain legal guardianship. Hence fostering relatives in the coastal situation take on a heavy financial burden raising a child in school.

Pregnancy Outside of Marriage

In Ndyuka, children used to be raised in kampu, (horticultural hamlets) and young girls were kept close to mothers who tried to guard them from too early sexual experiences by sleeping hammock to hammock. Women now fifty tell me they believed their mother's warning that early sex could kill them; and, of course death in childbirth still occurred to substantiate this claim. But young gallants took up the challenge and sometimes managed to thwart the best mother's intentions with the result that a young girl might at any time find herself on the way to motherhood. After a scolding, the mishap would be quickly resolved by calling in the genitor's mother, delivering the message to his family, and allowing the genitor's recognition of paternity and his tending of the pregnancy, luku bee. From then on till the birth, he would live with the girl, equipping her with hammock, mosquito net, cloths for skirts and cooking utensils and supplying her with meat and firewood. (For a mature woman only meat and firewood are necessary.) Whatever her age, he would have to stick around until three months after the birth to be assured that the mother survived and that he would not have to go into mourning to protect himself from her ghost. Once her health was assured, he was free – to request marriage or to leave. If he did not take her to wife, he must desist and not bother her again. It was only in 1984 that I witnessed the first case of a genitor's flight from responsibility. But the girl was a single Ndyuka woman in Grand Santi and the man, an Aluku French politician, was only passing through.

Starting in the second half of the twentieth century, three important developments would slowly transform the traditional world. The first was migration of men toward new jobs opening up on the coast; the second was the introduction of Western medicine in the interior. The Medische Zending (medical mission) of the missionary Hernhutters founded, on the edge of Ndyuka territory first a clinic, then, in 1956, the Johannes King Hospital. Regular mosquito control teams sprayed consenting houses to keep malaria down. By 1970, according to Dr. Doornbos, there was a 50% increase of lives saved.[13] Thus began what would become a demographic explosion, one to which the possibility of migration would speak. The third would be the outbreak in 1986 of the Surinamese civil war and its multiple consequences, notably on female mobility and immigration.

Migration of Ndyuka men to the coast, taking wives with them and raising children in schools in Paramaribo, had been developing since the sixties and had extracted large numbers from the river villages by the late seventies. As one kabiten of the single-clan bilose village of Tabiki (where some 500 persons were absent) put it, "It's fortunate they're not here: where would they live? There's no more room on the island." But as one elder warned, "People move to the coast and settle right there where their ancestors had been slaves. Bakaa (the Whites) can just throw a net over them and re-enslave them. Those times will come again." The women who remained – either in the village or more frequently in the kampu or going and coming between the two, farmed their grounds, sending any surplus via brothers to be sold in coastal markets. Wives in waiting for their husband's return twice yearly, had by then found a use for contraceptive pills: to delay their period if it fell during the short reunion with their husband or a festive ceremony. The delight of husbands' returning with love and presents waned, however, if they outstayed this joyous period and hung around bossing wives already taxed with grounds and children. As one

---

13   Doornbos, personal communication 1977.

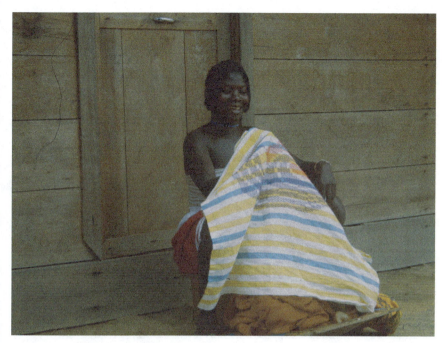

FIGURE 5.3 Young woman embroidering a pangi, Tabiki 1977
SOURCE: DIANE VERNON, 1977

wife said, "No, thank god he's not here all the time." Only she didn't want that absence to be a presence by another wife's side.

Other cultural opportunities open to women in the villages – decorative sewing, calabash carving, mid-wivery, healing and spirit mediumship were still frequent and important practices (see figures 5.3 and 5.4). Mediumship not only carried weight in the social and political realm; it was an advantage for women in the domestic scene: husbands had to tread more softly with a wife protected by a spirit. But with the increasing influences from the city in their lives, angry, railing spirits of victimisation, the bakuu, a sorcery linked to commerce and money, were becoming more numerous in the pantheon of women's mediumship (Vernon 1980:1–50).

Money had entered exchanges in village life, and women could pick up a few coins by selling eggs or fruit; some qualified for potiman moni: a Surinamese poverty allocation. A few women had found jobs cleaning and cooking at the hospital at Stoelmanseiland – an extension of domestic labor. But two women from Grand Santi, a commune on the Lawa river in French Guiana had trained for professions and crossed the gender-defined vocational border. At the first signs of illness they decided to back off, convinced their audacity had

FIGURE 5.4 Lavishly decorated pangis
SOURCE: DIANE VERNON, 2012

provoked sorcery retaliation. This anxiety of entering professional life would continue in the later urban context, with psychosomatic complaints and trance possession frequent now among high school girls.[14] Men occasionally arrived now with loud speakers and canned coastal music to hold a dance in the village, and celibate women were afterwards railed against by elders for their too blatant acceptance of passing men's favors. A few single women had run loose in unacceptable fashion in St Laurent, and an important busi sikootu ("forest policeman")[15] tried writing a letter to the French gendarmes to pick up these stray creatures and bring them back home.

By the 80's schools had opened on both rivers, the Tapanahony on the Surinamese side, and the Lawa on the French Guianese side. Now in addition

---

14   Crises of possession by bakuu spirits have been reported in lycées and colleges in SLM, Mana and Grand Santi.
15   A traditional function, the busi sikootu was a man appointed by Gaanman to apprehend an accused. The position disappeared with the death of this last representative, Da Balansi from Tjontjon, having become superfluous since state troops were now stationed at Stoelmanseiland.

to the boarding school at Stoelmanseiland, some children on the Tapanahony were getting a little Dutch up-front in village primary schools that the civil war (1986 to 1992) would soon close. More Ndyuka children on the Lawa river were being schooled in French in a Grand Santi primary school. As the first graduates of these classes were ready for collège, not yet available in Grand Santi, parents began to worry about their futures, now definitely considered dependent on schooling. Mostly boys were being sent down from Grand Santi to stay with relatives in Saint Laurent and go to school on the coast. Several children lacking relatives there were found together in a house in SLM looking after themselves. Meanwhile the situation of growing tension in Paramaribo subsequent to the coup d'état of 1980 culminated in the 1982 December murders in Paramaribo of fifteen leading citizens by the dictator Desi Bouterse (see below). In response, the Dutch government cut off the funding it sent to its ex-colony and the Surinamese economy plunged. The French side of the Maroni, and notably the little town of Saint Laurent du Maroni seemed more and more a promising land. A mother would move all her children to SLM and settle with a relative as soon as her first child finished the basic courses in Grand Santi. This safer future has been the major reason given by women for immigration.

A second reason Ndyuka women gave for immigrating was celibacy. Some women, with up to five co-wives, had not seen nor heard from their husbands in so long they were not certain they still had one. Single women, especially after a first marriage had failed, were no longer finding husbands in the villages, so defied the authority of uncles and moved to where the men were. The third reason women gave for migrating to Saint Laurent was medical. In a study made in 2014 on the traditional mobility that allows a flow back and forth ("migrations pendulaires") between French medical aid at Grand Santi-St. Laurent, and Suriname, Dr. Jolivet attempts to ascertain to what extent the motivation behind giving birth in the St. Laurent maternity unit by women living on the Surinamese side was the quest for papers and/or family allowance. Women interviewed recognized that they hoped for social advantages, and agreed that giving birth in French Guiana might make such acquisitions easier, but as they never gave this as a motivation she concludes from her interviews that the search for health or proper maternity care is initially the sole factor responsible for a decision to resettle permanently in more than 1.3 % of the cases. The occasions were several and variable: pregnancies followed at the clinic in Grand Santi in anticipation of complications, began to be relayed by that local clinic to SLM, safely conveyed by the medical boat, eliminating the need for male chaperoning. The expansion and modernization of the Saint Laurent hospital's maternity drew pregnancies from up-river and across, with women staying on after birth for ablutions in some of their own or a husband's family. Births were registered on the French side and were a first step toward obtaining papers. Post-natal complications, child illnesses, including kwashiorkor, malformations,[16] or later, in the 90's, discovery of chronic complaints such as diabetes or AIDS[17] made moving closer to medical facilities sensible. Husbands responsible to the affinal lineage for their wives' health could be pressured into settling them near the hospital in Saint Laurent. Lineage authorities could not object to a doctor's advice that a woman's pregnancy be closely monitored, especially for cases of diabetes, anemia, high blood pressure, HIV. During the 80's and 90' s residence cards for health-related problems supposedly not cared for by one's native land (Suriname) were still easily come by, and child allowances for mothers soon convinced women that the French appreciated the importance of their task: they were no longer making children just for their lineage, they were also making them for the French.[18]

A final reason given by women since 2000 for their move was their increasing isolation due to family mobility, immigration or death. Grandmothers in the villages used to raising a grandchild for help and company lost them to the new era of schooling. The last daughter to have cared for a father or mother closed the house on the parent's death and moved down-stream. Migration was becoming a vicious circle, which made living in the village or kampu untenable. All the cases I know of since 1996 of women moving back up-river to farm kampu are those from Paramaribo who had to abandon studies due to lack of funds after a divorce or a father's death. Once settled on the coast, women found another reason for staying on, even under the most difficult conditions: the food – so basic, so scarce and expensive in Ndyuka. No one ever

---

16   In cases where the mother's choice is to continue the pregnancy and give birth to a handicapped child, specialized care and allocation of funds will persuade her to settle on the French side.

17   To date HIV infections still open rights to carte de séjour pour soins, hence, residence in French Guiana, as do many other illnesses such as diabetes, cancer, hepatitis B, HTLV 1, even though Suriname now has programs for supervision and medication.

18   Maroon men boast, with some justification, that they (Maroons) have made the sleepy town of St. Laurent into a city of 40 000 that will, with its rate of growth, easily outweigh Cayenne in the future. "La croissance démographique est estimée à plus de 8,4 % par an et les projections mentionnées dans le Projet d'Aménagement et de Développement Durable (PADD) annoncent plus de 70 000 habitants en 2015 et plus de 100 000 habitants à l'horizon 2020 ce qui en ferait la ville la plus peuplée de Guyane. Plus de 50 % de la population a moins de 20 ans. » Rapport I – analyse de contexte et état des lieux de l'habitat spontané sur le ZAC St. Maurice et alentours, p. 27.

NEW LIVES FOR NDYUKA WOMEN

expressed nostalgia for village life, though most were happy to return for short periods – ritual treatment, ceremonies or vacations.[19]

Bad Weather, Mobility and Commerce

The shock of the December murders had convinced villagers that they should be a separate nation; that what happened in Paramaribo had nothing to do with them[20] and that they should ask the kind Dutch queen to take them back. Some men felt that Gaanman should be able to coin their own money. And when in 1986 the first Ndyuka child was killed in the Cottica, there was talk of marooning as their ancestors had done – but to go where? The world turned when a fourth attempt to oust the dictator Bouterse was led by a Ndyuka from the Cottica, Ronnie Brunswijk. There followed the massacre of civilians by the Surinamese army that triggered the flight of 10 000 Ndyuka refugees from the Cottica region to French Guiana: Apatou, St. Laurent du Maroni and Mana. As the guerilla war raged on, Ronnie's band, the Jungles, moved up the Tapanahony river in a predatory occupation of Ndyuka territory. In retaliation for the Maroon support of the guerillas, Bouterse abolished the national currency, which effectively led to the destruction of local savings (women's in particular) up-river where inhabitants were unable to reach the capital within the three-day limit to change their money into the new currency the dictatorship issued.

The six years of refugee camps were for SLM and the rest of French West Guiana a time of suffering, fear, anxiety, excitement and anger. Independent female mobility increased when the war made a new commerce available to women, replacing men in retailing goods between Paramaribo and SLM, while men did less visible dealing in drugs. After the war men then took over from women on a larger scale and women's resale activity was reduced to wheel-barrowing articles around town, or for a few who could afford it, holding a legal stand in the bi-weekly market. But the possibility of independent female mobility had been established. While women continued to

---

19   There are, nevertheless, men and women who left the village fleeing sorcery, and others, often in churches, who have little or no village experience but imagine the interior villages as the heartland of witchcraft and have no desire to visit them. Third generation Ndyuka raised in Paramaribo who still cherish an identity with the mother village complain now (2012) of being treated as "city folk" by villagers when they return on holidays.

20   Between December 7 and 9, 1982, the Surinamese dictator Desi Bouterse, who had seized power in a coup on February 25, 1980, had fifteen of the most prominent male citizens arrested, tortured and shot at Fort Zeelandia, Paramaribo, in response to their criticism.

FIGURE 5.5 Maroon woman in market, SLM
SOURCE: DIANE VERNON, 2012

farm plots whenever and wherever possible, their inclusion in the formerly male preserve of jobs and commerce was now tolerated by uncles and even by husbands as a financial necessity, and their mobility to this end was understood.

Sex

A second aspect of the end-of an-era atmosphere of the war was the sexual license of refugee youth yanked out of schools or work in Suriname and facing an unclear future. Occasional prostitution helped adapt to uncertainty, and in the Bakaloto in the Charbonnière an Aluku boy ran a clandestine brothel. My interviews with men and women in the SLM and Mana districts at this time in conjunction with an AIDS research program[21] noted an evolution of men's

---

21 The research preparatory to constructing an adapted prevention message was conducted by myself in the summer of 1991, financed jointly by Aides-Guyane of Cayenne and ORSTOM. The following year a prevention program was carried out on the French side, reaching from Saint Laurent du Maroni to Maripasoula. It was then evaluated in 1993, and a second program followed in 1994. All reports on the research and programs are filed with Aides-Guyane, Cayenne. For the most recent report on new sexual practices along

NEW LIVES FOR NDYUKA WOMEN

gifts traditionally offered in Maroon amorous encounters, diverging into gifts explicitly in exchange for sex. This troubled period would seem to have left its mark locally as a high tolerance for casual and remunerated sex among the young that they do not recognize as prostitution. In 2012, Stephane Barbosa, an éducateur specialisé doing research for AIDES-GUYANE, came out with a paper entitled "Un regard sur la jeunesse" which exposed considerable sexual experimentation and trade (several boys hiring a girl, couples filming themselves on the cellphone and "sharing" with friends). This report has been taken very seriously by all the institutions in SLM and has been followed up by a questionnaire in lycées that appears to confirm the practice of prostitution among boys as well as girls, in exchange for valuables such as phones or financial support; but also for no more than a sandwich and soft drink.

Since the 90's, the maternity unit of the St. Laurent hospital has been sending out alerts on the increasing number of teenage pregnancies among 12–14 year olds. This is seen as a recent development called on the French side "grossesses précoces" but is it anything more than a multiplication of earlier incidents when youngsters initiated secret young love at a tender age, in the same way as gifts to a mistress slide into payment for sex?[22] On the male Maroon side, modern sexual license and the advent of AIDS is attributed to a change in women's ways. "Men," the argument goes, "are just doing what they've always done; it's since women run about that we have AIDS." In 2002 a kabiten from the Charbonnière in St. Laurent pointed out a handful of girls setting out together for town at 11 o'clock at night, "You see what I'm talking about: den mocho!" ("They're whoring") Had they been boys, I don't think he'd have noticed. It is disquieting for men to see girls now doing what the boys do. Ndyuka parents trying to nurture and rear in the immigrant situation complain their children are "fire," "we make them to kill us," that beatings no longer help. A couple came to consult the hospital psychiatrist after the wife's new husband was called before the judge for having beaten her older boy unconscious. Mother and stepfather were desperate: the eldest, 17 and his younger brother, 16, were out of control, and now the thirteen-year old had also begun to sleep in derelict houses. Unfortunately, psychiatry had no solution for them.

---

the river see the report by Thomas Polime, "Anthropological expertise mission for Hepatitis B-C-D project on the Maroni River," september 2016.

22   "Nous signalons toutes les grossesses de moins de 15 ans au Procureur de la République, certaines avec abus sexuels manifestes, mais malgré nos courriers, c'est le laxisme le plus total": citation d'une gynécologue exerçant à l'hôpital dans "Un regard sur la jeunesse," enquête de Stéphane Barbosa, Aides Guyane, 2009.

Mothers having difficulty coping threaten to give the children to the French lanti (DDASS). Of course, Ndyuka mothers were used to holding forth in a rhetoric of affectionate criticism of their children from the days of their birth: baby was "lazy," little tots had "hard ears," all of them poli," spoiled rotten!" That said, and even accounting for the intergenerational rhapsodizing of the "good old times" or the disparaging of the rebellious young, there is a real concern by mothers trying to raise ten children in crowded urban conditions. Next-door neighbors are not family, but kids to fight with, resulting in adult conflicts; or they are mati (pals) who can teach one's kids bad ways. Mothers especially, finding it difficult to raise boys by themselves, buy TV sets to keep the children inside. Parents now trusting the school with their child, feel they have no control over what the child does or whom he sees. "We send our girls to school to get pregnant and our boys to sell drugs," remarked one parent. "They find mati there to teach them new ways." "Girls are no longer afraid of getting pregnant," offered one father. "They know women don't die in childbirth anymore." Several Saamaka women in Saint Laurent maternity maintained that the skirts of womanhood are now given to Saamaka girls systematically at twelve years to guarantee against pollution from menstrual blood that is sullied by unrecognized sexual relations –a recognition of the weakened family control over their young.[23] The three factors – new female mobility, massive female migration to the coast and easy access to young girls away from their mothers most of the time – create the impression among Maroon men and women of a surplus of women now easily come by, which weakens the bargaining power of lineages for respectable treatment of their girls as potential wives. And women must lower their expectations with regard to husbands and lovers, making themselves ever easier to come by and to leave.

Churches

A possible counter to the increasingly free sex may eventually come from the burgeoning new churches, whose dogma and social pressure together with the individualistic values taught in schools, is having a detrimental impact on lineage coherence. The third contribution of the war era has been the penetration of new evangelical movements, prominent among them, the Jehovah's

---

23 The ritual giving of what the Ndyuka call gi pangi recognizes a sexual coming of age that entails ablutions morning and evening for which a night pot is also provided. Cottica Ndyuka, long touched by urban Dutch-Creole culture, maintain the pangi was always given at 18 years.

NEW LIVES FOR NDYUKA WOMEN

Witnesses. Brought over from coastal Surinam, the Witnesses and the "God's Trumpet," another evangelical cult, infiltrated the refugee camps on the pretext of visiting family, giving hope of a better tomorrow through material gifts and promises of papers, and above all, protection from sorcery which appears to be the handmaiden of conversion. Jehovah's Witnesses was formerly confined to Cayenne. During the war it established church in SLM, then moved up the Maroni River and into Gaa Kaba, where it had never been tolerated before. There it developed into a powerful institution, drawing in the surrounding population, afraid to counter it.[24]

Women's sufferings and disappointment with obia have usually been the reason for their family's being drawn into the congregation. Other improvised evangelical churches are springing up everywhere founded by ambitious young Maroon men who feel themselves called upon to do the work of obiaman looking into the spiritual dimensions of suffering. With their clairvoyance they detect the spiritual knots, call down blessings and offer up prayers and syncretic therapeutic rites. Churches have answered the need for community by filling up more and more time and demanding more and more contributions from more and more faithful and enthusiastic congregations, the bulk of whom are women. Intra-family disputes, which can bring upon the most vulnerable member of the family unit (often a pregnant woman) ancestral punishment, necessitate a cleansing ritual called "puu mofu" – "remove the words spoken" and which consists of each member present spewing water from a calabash (where articles such as coal have soaked) onto the presumed victim while delivering a command to erase the bad talk. New church therapists replace this rite by eliciting confessions from the guilty, followed by prayers. Women derive intense enjoyment from the high sociability: outings nicely costumed, frequent and lengthy services offering singing, dancing, trance-possession by the holy spirit, spontaneous confession, witnessing, praying, healing and bible study.

The role of Maroon women as important spiritual healers appears not to have been pursued as a lucrative vocation in the immigrant situation. This may be because male obiaman have, for the last fifty years, invested in this opportunity to reach an international clientele, coming down-river where they receive patients in their kampu outside the city. Women have not come with

---

24   The New Year festivities traditionally drew back to the major villages its migrant workers bearing the fruits of their labor and becoming immersed for a time in intense cultural and socio-judicial activities. The years 2012 and 2013 have seen empty villages in the bilosé as the Jehovah's Witnesses gathered the population into its fold.

FIGURE 5.6 In a Catholic church in La Charbonière
SOURCE: DIANE VERNON, 2013

such intent and they encroach very little on this territory. Apart from two professional healers – Ma Atema of Charvein and Ma Rita outside Albina – a few minor mediums practice in the homes of their husbands but most are mediums representing victimization to malevolent bakuu spirits rather than spirits of nature, medicine, war, or divinity. And in those roles it is not the power to cure that these mediums enjoy, but rather to harm through bakuu accusations. H.U.E. Thoden van Velzen has given us a chilling description of their reign of terror in the Mi Gaanda cult.[25] In SLM in 2004, such an accusation unleashed an attack on an over-ambitious kabiten who was successfully chased from the city, and two other industrious Ndyuka citizens were also accused. Women in SLM have discovered an equivalent source of power in the severity of French laws on rape. The kabiten chased away by bakuu accusations was later pursued from the same source by threats of a rape accusation to make sure he didn't try to return. These cases are now so familiar that the mere threat is enough to cow a man or his family.

---

25   See Thoden van Velzen and Wim Hoogbergen (2011: 33, 305–7, 309, 311–3, 315), and also : DVD's of prosecutions « Tuu tuu doo, lei lowe » shot by the team of the antisorcery cult, Mi Ganda.

Husbands and Papers

In addition to their various financial activities, a source of income for women with French identity or carte de séjour are the family allowances, which swell with the number of children. No one ever gave this as a reason for immigrating, but it might be subsumed under the major motive: school the children. For women with children born on the Guyanese side, French nationality or carte de séjour are a ticket to comfort and an insurance in divorce, as they give women rights to child allowance for any babes born on the French side and, for three children or more, rights to lodgings.[26] These all-important papers, nevertheless, depend traditionally on husbands; first of all, because by custom, a married woman couldn't seek papers without her husband's consent. Secondly, while husbands know their way around this Bakaa world, in-coming women, married or not, speak neither French nor Creole on arriving, inter-lineage jealousy is rife and the only family willing to help them are mothers and fathers or later their grown children when these are legal residents. Husbands, however, are supposed to set up wives in proper housekeeping, and papers are seen as an element of this domestic scene. But a husband's goodwill in obtaining for her what amounts to a semi-independence that would allow her to move about freely, or to move away, with both family allowance and the children, requires a lot of coaxing. Husbands often string along their wives for years, supposing that they would be less obedient if the state allowance for children gave them independent means. On their side, women often stick with husbands when the coming of a new co-wife has made their relation unbearable. "I'm only going to stay until he gets me papers," announced one wife, "Then I can leave." "Oh you mustn't take that risk," replied another, "Remember Keleda!"

The drama of Keleda took place in 2003. A salaried Ndyuka worker in St. Laurent had gone to the Opu on the Tapanahony river to take as wife a village woman who already had six children by former men. He brought her back to SLM, had 4 children with her and obtained a 10-year residence card for her. With his salary and aid from the CAF they were able to acquire a house in a new housing development. Unfortunately, they were obliged (against traditional practice) to sign joint ownership of the property. According to the president of the association for victims, Savip, such duel ownership of houses very often leads to domestic quarrels, each side wanting the house for himself. I suspect this may occur after some time has passed and the man becomes interested in another partner. In this case, Ali took a second wife,

---

26   Unfortunately these rights are often not respected. See Léobal (2017).

and Keleda, in revenge, took a lover in their common domicile and became pregnant by him. In a traditional move, Ali embarked Keleda and the 10 children in a canoe and returned all to her lineage in the river village. But Keleda, with French papers, was a free woman, and she returned with the children and re-established them and her lover in the joint domicile. Ali moved into a shack with his second wife and left Keleda the house, which after all, the importance of the progeny had helped them acquire. Keleda was then receiving allocations (child allowance) for her four children with Ali, plus the latest with her lover. But her oldest daughter also shared the house with her own four children and no allocations. So to improve their lot, Keleda applied for a special allowance (probably advised by the CAF) as a single mother. She received this until the CAF informed her she must pursue the children's father for child support. This she did, won her case, and money was retained from Ali's monthly wages. It seems this was not enough yet for all ten children, one of whom, a daughter, living there, had by then four children of her own, also dependent on Keleda. And, of course, there was the lover. So she again was helped to file a court order. This time Ali was away in Saül, and had to leave his work to come to the court in Cayenne. Keleda didn't bother coming, but once again she won her case. This was too much for Ali. He stormed up to her house with a rifle and demanded she evacuate. She refused, fleeing with the lover to the bedroom, the daughter begging Ali not to shoot. (Such a plea usually has the power to stop an aggressor in his tracks, as it is said such a plea goes directly to God.) But he came in firing, killing Keleda and wounding the lover. He then jumped into his car, drove to the gendarmerie and gave himself up. Meanwhile the news reached Ali's mother, nearby, and she fell wailing to the floor, knowing that the whole clan, and she, above all, would have to pay for this murder in service and in kind. The house, jointly owned, given to Keleda orally by Ali, was, for her family, a moral claim: Ali could never have had the house without her. A reflection of Ali's kabiten was that it should by right be Ali's, since he had gotten her the papers and the children to buy it.

Houses are another right that comes with French papers and progeny. A study of spontaneous habitats made recently by the NGO, GRET, for the SLM mairie's rehabilitation project revealed that 2/3 of the structures belonged to women raising their children (see figures 5.1 and 5.7). In 2009 I drew up a list of 48 Maroon potential house-owners who had paid huge sums over the years to a building company that absconded with their money. My list revealed the same percentage of women owners. This cannot be taken as an indication that there are more women than men. Men always travelled light, between sisters and wives, and their houses in urban areas were simple structures. Women, on the other hand, must have houses to raise children. Just as boats and outboard

FIGURE 5.7   Cluster of spontaneous Maroon dwellings in SLM
SOURCE: DIANE VERNON, 2011

motors are a part of male identity, so women's are houses. One young woman in her early thirties with only one child complained bitterly that the government didn't give her a house so she still had to live with her mother. If in the future, father-headed households come to dominate, this might be reflected in more cases of joint or male-owned houses.

Paternal Recognition

Ndyuka children are as yet rarely born to couples married by French law. Of course French paternal recognition flies in the face of Ndyuka matriliny by according rights and duties that forever link father and child. And although for the time being this public is unaware of all the duties and privileges entailed in a legal paternal recognition, it happens that the baby's mother, traditionally married or not, allows the father to recognize the child at the mairie. But interestingly, Maroon fathers do not take these legal steps without the mother's permission, even if he is a French citizen and she is an illegal resident. The Sous-Préfet, on a tour of Papaïchton, was surprised to find an Aluku father had not recognized his children who could have French citizenship through him. He explained that his (Ndyuka) wife had not consented. She may have refused, as do many, interpreting it as a gift of the child to the father on the order of dada pikin (in which case he could remove the child from her influence and have it raised by his sister.) Paternal recognition is ever an honor a woman is free to bestow or withhold. One woman had six children by the same father, but only five carried his name. A boy in the middle of the sib-ship carried the mother's last name. Asked why, she explained he'd been away during her pregnancy (not luku bee) nor had he come for the birth, so she didn't let him recognize the child. One young woman discovering the marvels of cultural difference said she let her husband recognize the child because "it looked chic."

Through paternal recognition a man legally resident (supposedly the genitor) may obtain child allowance for the family instead of getting papers for the mother. Some Maroon men ally themselves with women illegally in French Guiana who have children born on the French side. These men recognize the children, and collect the allocations, some of which they share with the many mothers. One man was being investigated for receiving money for 48 children! In another case, a polygynous husband had established his two wives and their grounds in two adjacent houses on the road to Mana. After a CAF's inspection he was ordered to decide which was his concubine and children and send the other party packing. Even concubines must be monogamous. A mother of a French-born child does not necessarily depend on her child's father to obtain an allowance if she has no papers: she can ask her brother to recognize the child. This is of course illegal, but there is a matrilineal logic at work here whereby the authority of the uncle is over his sister's children, and a brother is close family, not someone who will divorce or abscond with the funds. In the cases I've seen, the husband doesn't mind – it's his brother-in-law, who, in any case, should help him out with his sister, usually in cutting a field, and is here helping recuperate money to raise the children the clandestine parents could not otherwise have. The fact that this is not only a lie, but is administrative incest doesn't bother its practitioners: after all, it's only paper.

Single mothers are beginning to discover that they can obtain papers and child allowance without a husband's assistance. This may be revealed through a serious health problem necessitating a prolonged legal stay, and requires the intervention of a social worker. But it is also enough to have a child born, raised and schooled on the French side till the age of 13. The mother can then request an early recognition of the child's French nationality, giving her the right to legal residence. Her educated adult children can accompany her in filling out the forms and feeling her way through the formalities.

So women can do without husbands. But who wants to? Many women with papers, finding themselves single at some moment, will take in a man who hasn't. Women without papers now accept even an impecunious man or " 'wan bookofutu man' ("a no-good man"). Nor are money and valuables still a one-way street; women, who formerly tapped their crotches saying "That's my bank account," who would have felt humiliated if the lover did not give a gift, now bestow gifts on male partners. A mother coming down to SLM from Grand Santi where her daughter was going to school, was shocked to find her postal account emptied of 4000 euros: the daughter had bought a second-hand car for her love.

It is a common assumption among the non-Maroons of SLM that Maroon women have large families for the allocations familiales, and this further infuses the negative ethnic stereotype Maroons suffer. Even Maroon boys in school lambaste their female counterparts for what they suppose is an easy way to find a living without succeeding in school or going to work. Men are facing more difficult times than ever before, and a certain envy emerges with regard to fertile women's easy access to money. When they are not thanking them for contributing their allocations to funerals, Maroon men accuse them of using the money for their own pleasure.

Libi Foto Fasi

In this new coastal environment, many young women no longer wait for the man to apply to their families for marriage, but move in with him and raise children, always hoping he will validate the marriage by taking her up-river to officialize the union. (One young woman was warned by her mother she should not stay with the man who had just fathered her child, but return home and wait for him to call on her. She did not heed the advice and within months he threw her out.) Worse yet, mothers complain that the genitor continues after the first pregnancy to frequent their daughters and produce offspring in the mothers' house.

In 2003, a case drew all the Maroni river kabitens of SLM and 20 people in a series of kuutu over inter-clan threats of death from the family of a woman with four children by a lover who beat her and threw her out, then took her back. The families were unable to separate the couple, the gendarmes refused to interfere in domestic quarrels, six kuutu (council meetings) had already declared them separated, though they had never been officially joined. Nor could the girl's family send her up-river to resettle there and scrape out a living for the children because all their members had emigrated, leaving village and kampu empty.

In another case, an unofficial couple who had already parented two children were riding the man's scooter when they collided with a car and the girl was thrown over the top, her head smashed on the street. The girl's family took the children and accused the man of having stolen their daughter and killed her. They refused him mourning, thereby leaving him to the vengeance of her ghost. In a show of sincerity he attempted suicide, leaving the local kabiten, as lanti, (authority) to plead his case, marrying them after the fact. Such shacking up leaves families at a loss as to how to deal with affinal relations that do not formally exist. Their default solution, in the absence of serious conflict, is to treat the irregular living together as an official marital state.

The Flight of the Genitor

In the context of weakening lineage control, it is not surprising that lovers may suddenly disappear at the announcement of pregnancy, since some fathers of large families also do so. In the study of teenage pregnancy I conducted from 1996 to 1998 in the hospital of SLM where they were presented, in 19 cases the girl's lover assumed responsibility for the pregnancy, but in 16 cases he did not. The difference appeared to be partly a question of resources – older married men with money accompanied the girl; boys disappeared, with no contribution from their families, leaving the pregnant teenager and her mother waiting to see if the man's family would come for the birth with a few baby clothes. But it was also more frequent with girls under the age of fifteen, who, not yet in the marriageable category, appear as children to whom the pregnancy comes as a mistake, rather than as young women about to become mothers.

We seem to have a problem of male responsibility as fathers or genitors. With the weakening of the framework that underpins inter-lineage relations, and therefore marriages or genitor recognition, what sort of family system can we expect to see emerge from the disempowerment of lineages and the new, casual live-ins? From the determinedly polygynous males and the long-suffering women – as Christian converts or independent professionals? From a generation growing up between the family Maroon model, two Créole models – Surinamese and French – and the latest metropolitan French multiple choices: monogamy, with divorce and recomposed families, with PAC's or long live-in's and even unisex marriage? Though polygamy has traditionally been a status symbol among Maroons, monogamy is a status symbol in a wider world. Men reaching for a more international recognition may choose to present to the outside world an image of classic monogamy. Then, as with French Creoles, legal church marriage might be sought as a stamp of success – not for moral or religious reasons, but seized upon most often at a socially ascendant point in life. Legal French matrimony, renouncing polygamy (though not necessarily

NEW LIVES FOR NDYUKA WOMEN

marginal amorous relations) could eventually tempt ambitious Maroon men as an asset to their outside professional image.

At present, polygamy evolves in a fair field, with an apparent over-abundance of potential wives and a readiness of women to accept living-in arrangements as a surrogate marriage. The same easy-come, easy-go couplings now mar the stability of polygamous unions. In the case of a man attracted to a new wife, the announcement of yet another pregnancy by the usual one now often ushers in a liminal period of maltreatment to encourage the now undesired wife to leave, or of outright abandonment of her (at the very moment when customary law requires his attendance). "Men are tired of raising women's children," one elder said. Serial polygamy resulting in reconstituted families means many men are raising another man's children. Husbands would like to have dominion over their own children; charismatic men have managed it in the past, some even settling two young wives together early on, and keeping them and the children around them till death. But a long-ingrained structural principle pulls in the opposite direction: for men, the children belong to the women unless given them as dada pikin, and when the marriage has gone sour (often due to the arrival of a new wife), or a greater love beckons, they pull out altogether. In 2014, a Ndyuka father who had recognized his new-born son by a French woman abandoned both, saying, "Let her raise him, and when the boy becomes a man, he will seek out his father, and I'll explain to him ..." According to the Ndjuka anthropologist Thomas Polime, this is indeed what happens: men are not afraid to leave their children behind, because they have no problem drawing them to their bosoms later on regardless of the fact that they have neglected their formative years. These sons and daughters, ever forgiving of the absent father, rally around in his declining years and supply him with income and attention. Boys and men all the way to Holland know this and boast happily about leaving all the work to the mothers and reaping the advantages later.

In the study I made between 1996 and 1998, out of 21 teenage pregnancies, between the ages of 12 and 14, an unexpected detail emerged: all but two came from matrifocal homes, and in one of the two non-matrifocal ones was a stepfather. Where did the fathers go? In the study earlier referred to by the GRET, based on the interviews of 355 inhabitants of these spontaneous dwellings, 31% were a couple with children, but 49% were women alone with children. Again, where are the men? The stability of marriage (traditional or legal) may have a direct influence on the futures of the children. Seeing young adults through studies towards diplomas depends much on a father's contribution, as demonstrated by the several cases I know of students in Paramaribo having to leave school and return to the forest or the grounds when a father dies. Most of the cases known to me of successful professional careers by Ndyuka women of SLM have been the product of stable unions, often families established there before the war, and integrated in the traditional economic niches. If Ndyuka women are to climb the social ladder of the new territory they have chosen, to enjoy real independence through economic autonomy, like boys, they will need the backing of families where fathers stick around to finance their grown children's studies. There is no longer a model of family or adulthood but an open market of increasingly numerous experiments with conflicting ideologies and contextual individual interests, and it seems likely that this situation will continue in the future with a variety of individual choices. It is still the women who make the children but whether they make them for the lineage, for their paansu, or for future patriarchal fathers remains a moot question.

Conclusion

We have tried briefly to scan the transformations in the lives of Ndyuka women from the 1970's until today (2013).[27] Men's lives in essence have remained the same: moving in all directions to find work, but finding work more difficult today to come by. Dependent on other lineages to grant them wives, now often taking a woman they want without asking her family.

As for the women, in the 70's and 80's, women's travel outside the traditional territory depended on male accompaniment and their access to coastal riches, largely on husbands. Young, they were under the gaze of their extended families or, if a husband so placed them, in the care of his family. Older, they were part and parcel to the protective matri-structure. Financial autonomy had never been a woman's dream. Now, for many, it was thrust on them. Freedom from male dominance had never been a worry: husbands came for holidays bearing gifts and returned to what work they could find until the next visit. Now it was becoming difficult to find a responsible husband. Girls and women in the villages used to love to be taken on trips – by fathers or uncles, or taken to live on the coast by husbands. Now it was they, with their small children who sought out sisters and cousins in and around urban areas to move in with and

---

27   This corresponds to the period during which I have worked with and among the Ndyuka, first doing research in the Bilo rivers villages of the Tapanahony (traditional medicine, spirit possession) 1976–1986 in a series of research programs, then research in preparation for health programs (1990–1994), and finally in a position of applied anthropology as cultural mediator in the hospital (CHOG) in Saint Laurent (1996–2013), by which time, the majority of Ndyuka women were living in or around an urban setting.

school their children. Three complaints only had been voiced by village women: the lack of food, the obligation to scurry into the tiny "moon house" at the first sight of a menstrual period, and polygamy. Living in the coastal area, food is more plentiful, there are no "moon houses" in the city, and it has become acceptable practice for a woman to sleep in another room and decease from cooking for others. Polygamy, ever more shunned by women, nevertheless has a tough hide. Worse, even getting a real marriage, recognized by both lineages and surveyed by them is becoming difficult. Women must now imagine making it on their own. Here the mama pikin remains crucial to insure its women alone or in between husbands in their struggle to feed, lodge and raise children in this challenging new world.

References

de Groot, Sylvia. 2009. Agents of their own Emancipation, Amsterdam: de Groot.

GRET (Association des Professionnels du développement solidaire), Renaud Colombier, Bérangère Deluc, Virginie Rachmuhl, 5 mars 2012. Rapport I analyse de contexte et état des lieux de l'habitat spontané sur la ZAC Saint-Maurice et alentours, DEAL Unpublished.

Jolivet, Anne. 2014. Migrations, santé et soins en Guyane] Thèse de doctorat d'épidemologie et sciences de l'information biomédicale. Paris: Université Pierre et Marie Curie.

Jolivet, Marie-José and Diane Vernon. 2007. "Droits, polygamie et rapports de genre en Guyane." Cahiers d'études africaines XVII, 3–4:733–752.

Léobal, Clémence. 2017. "Osu," "baraques" et "batiman": redessiner les frontiers de l'urbain à Soolan (Saint Laurent du Maroni). These de doctorat de Sociologie, Université Paris Decartes.

Price, Sally. 1984. Co-wives and Calabashes. Ann Arbor: University of Michigan.

Price, Richard. 1973. "Avenging Spirits and the structure of Saramaka Lineages." Bijdragen tot de Taal-, Land- en Volkenkunde, 129(1), 86–107.

Price, R. 2008. Travels with Tooy: History, memory, and the African American imagination. Chicago: Chicago University Press.

Vernon, Diane. 1980. Money magic in a modernizing Maroon society. ILCAA, Tokyo, pp. 1–50.

Vernon, Diane. 1980a. "Bakuu: possessing spirits of witchcraft on the Tapanahony." Nieuwe West-Indische Gids, 1 :1–38

Vernon, Diane. 1989. "Femme qui cuisine; Homme à fusil: perspectives du marriage Marron," dans Familles en Guyane, Observatoire Régional de la Santé en Guyane et l'Association des psychologues de Guyane, Editions Caribéennes, Paris, pp. 31–38.

Vernon, Diane. 1993. "Accès à quel droit pour les peuples du fleuve?" In L'accès au Droit en Guyane. Actes du colloque organisé par le Conseil Départemental d'Aide Juridique de la Guyane, 109–116. Edited by Didier Peyrat et Marie-Alice Gougis-Chow Chine, Cayenne, Editions Ibis Rouge.

Vernon, Diane. 2015. « La coutume immigrée » In Sociétés marronnes des Amériques, mémoire, patrimoines, identités et histoire au XVII au XX siècles [Actes du colloque Saint-Laurent-du-Maroni, Guyane française], 451–461. Edited by Jean Moomou and AFPOM. Cayenne : Ibis Rouge.

Thoden van Velzen, B., & Van Wetering, Willelmina. 1988. The Great Father and the Danger: religious cults, material forces, and collective fantasies in the world of the Surinamese Maroons. Dordrecht & Providence: Foris Publications.

Thoden van Velzen, H.U.E and W. van Wetering, 2007, "Violent Witch Finders and the Suspension of Social Order in a Suriname Maroon Society." in: "Wildness and Sensation: Anthropology of Sinister and Sensuous Realms, pp. 157-176. Ed. Rob van Ginkel and Alex Strating. Apeldoorn/Amsterdam: Het Spinhuis

CHAPTER 6

Performing Ethnicity as a Way of Contesting Removals: Bureaucratic Strategies and Affirmation of Busikonde Ways of Dwelling in Soolan (French Guiana)

Clémence Léobal

I once walked past a wooden house like many of those that can be seen from the roads of Western French Guiana, enclosed in vegetation. The Ndyuka friend I was with asserted: "This is a Ndyuka house." It made me wonder: how could a Maroon newcomer identify these houses as being inhabited by Maroons at first sight, without any doubt? The production of urban forms conveys much information on the social identifications of a city's inhabitants. Houses are statements addressed to the observer of the house, like my Ndyuka friend who assumed that the dwelling we were looking at was occupied by Ndyukas. This information can be interpreted in different ways, depending on who is observing it: a Maroon could recognize a Maroon house, and also see in it the marks of social class; state agents could see an "insanitary" dwelling, occupied by generic poor Maroons, supposedly illegal, to be eradicated.

French Guiana is in a postcolonial situation where French law applies, since it is a département (administrative region) of France. This includes legislation relating to urban planning and development: wooden houses are categorized as failing to conform to French urban norms, and are defined as "insanitary", "unhygienic", "illegal", or more recently "spontaneous" dwellings. This categorization has been used many times as a justification for demolition by the authorities. By targeting houses, they also implicitly target their inhabitants (Poupeau and Tissot, 2006), unwanted in the city center. In Saint-Laurent-du-Maroni (Soolan in Ndyuka), a city which lies on the Maroni river that forms the border with Suriname, the presence of Maroons dates back many decades. Their language, businenge tongo,[1] has become a lingua franca in these

---

1 Maroon languages are often designated by the name of the group that speaks them: Aluku tongo, Ndyuka tongo and Paamaka tongo. These three languages are mutually intelligible, and are frequently termed Businenge tongo in French, in opposition to Saamaka tongo. Linguists also identify it as Nenge(e) tongo (Léglise and Migge). Nevertheless, my Ndyuka

---

© KONINKLIJKE BRILL NV, LEIDEN, 2019 | DOI:10.1163/9789004388062_008

neighborhoods. However, they remain a minority – in the political sense of the word – marginalized along class, race and national lines. Maroon houses are threatened by the urban authorities whenever they become too central, in the context of new construction projects. Maroon inhabitants face a racialized spatial domination materialized through removals.

Anthropologists have mostly taken contemporary Maroon ethnicity for granted, analyzing given Maroon communities in rural areas rather than in urban contexts (Thoden van Velzen and Wetering, 1988; R. Price 1983; S. Price 1987; Hurault, 1965; Vernon, 1992; Hoogbergen, 1990; Moomou, 2009). Literature on Maroon migration to towns initially tended to focus on negative aspects of their acculturation in cities (Hurault, 1985; Delpech, 1993). However, some authors analyzed how ethnicity is shaped in interaction with other communities (Jolivet and Collomb, 2008): Jean Moomou examined the process of "intégration" of Bonis in French Guiana (2007), and in one chapter of his dissertation, Kenneth Bilby (1990) studied the Maroon riverside pile dwellings in Saint-Laurent-du-Maroni, showing how a pan-Maroon sense of belonging emerged in these neighborhoods. More recently Olivia Gomes da Cunha (2018) has analyzed the changing relationship to space and time among Ndyuka inhabitants of the town of Moengo. Linguists Isabelle Léglise and Bettina Migge have studied the issues at stake in the evolution of the vehicular language in coastal Western French Guiana, and how language denominations emerge from the contact situation with other languages (2013).

Drawing on these works, I seek to analyze the making of Maroon ethnicity in the urban context of Saint-Laurent-du-Maroni. I will closely look at Maroon practices and ways of living, and at the practices of the State regarding demolitions. I will analyze Maroon discourses about themselves as well as the discourses of state agents. If house and body are the most intimate elements of our everyday life, urban forms can be considered as an expression of social identification. In the case of removals, houses that would not be described ethnically in other contexts come to be categorized in terms of Maroon ethnicity, both by public agents and by inhabitants.

I argue that ethnicity is contextual: it depends on power relations involved in a given situation. In his study of Copperbelt, Clyde Mitchell already outlined the urban reshaping of ethnicity called "tribalism", as it emerged out of the

---

interlocutors also use the term of nenge tongo to describe the language of young urban Maroons, which is closer to sranan tongo, the Creole language of Paramaribo, in contrast to pure Ndyuka tongo or Aluku tongo. However this may be, the three languages constitute a common spoken by all Maroon inhabitants of Saint-Laurent: people frequently elude these problems of denomination by simply saying "a tal" (the language).

context of social and political conflicts (1956). Frederik Barth showed that the boundaries of ethnic groups are "in flux", produced by actors who use selected "cultural stuff" to legitimate the existence of those groups (1968). Considering the house as an extension of the body (Carsten and Hugh-Jones, 1995), I build on the hypothesis that these houses are in themselves performances of ethnicity: in the ways in which they are constructed and used, they constitute an affirmation of belonging to a group, even if this process is not necessarily a conscious act of presentation of the self. I am using the concept of performance as developed by Judith Butler, among others, in gender studies, as a "practice of improvisation within a scene of constraint", that exists "beyond oneself in a sociality that has no single author" (Butler, 2004: 1). Maroon ways of life and their everyday practices constitute an affirmation of an alternative life in the city, different from Bakaa (Western or White) norms of urbanity.

To begin with, I describe the context of the arrival of Maroon migrants as a minority in the French Guianese town of Saint-Laurent. I then present ethnographic data on these residents' ways of dwelling, where matrilineal kinship is materialized in urban forms. I describe how they have been subjected to several evictions within the town, as a consequence of French shantytown elimination policies and racialized spatial domination. In this conflictual situation, where residents are threatened by bulldozers, the affirmation of an urban Bushikonde way of life, contrasting with the French system, is a resource for resisting the injunction to leave.

From Saint-Laurent to Soolan: The Emergence of a Maroon City

Saint-Laurent-du-Maroni was founded in 1857 by the French state, as a base for a colonial prison. Prior to this, the Maroni basin was remote from European centres of colonization, which were concentrated around Cayenne (for French Guiana) and Paramaribo (for Suriname). For this reason, it was an area occupied by Amerindians and by Maroons who had escaped the Surinamese plantations. Following the closure of the prison in the 1940s, the population of the town grew as Creole, Amerindian and Maroon people migrated from upriver. From 1986 on, the Surinamese civil war amplified this growth, with the arrival of many Maroon and Amerindian refugees from Suriname.[2] Maroons now make up a large proportion of the 50,000 inhabitants of Saint-Laurent-du-Maroni.

---

2   An anthropological survey based on life histories of refugees provides information on refugee camps during this period (Polime and Thoden Van Velzen, 1988).

Political life remains dominated by Creoles – descendants of slaves who were freed during abolition – and the metropolitan French employed in local state agencies. Like the colonial situation defined by Georges Balandier, this is a situation where the numerical majority is a political minority in terms of class and race power relations (Balandier, 1951).

Many new neighborhoods have been created, following a recurring pattern of development. People settle in unoccupied areas on the margins of the city, clearing the forest, and building wooden houses. Presented with this process of urban development that does not fit in with French standards, the Creole and French authorities have started to act against these dwellings, at least when they are located in central parts of the city.

Initially, Maroon migrants settled on the river bank near the city centre: they built stilt houses with one door opening toward the city, and another door to the river and Suriname. These dwellings formed a "Maroon city in the city" (Bilby, 1990: 304). From the 1980s on, various removal policies displaced Maroon residents to more remote areas. The stilt dwellings were finally demolished in the 1990s. Residents who were entitled to social housing have been relocated to peripheral districts previously devoted principally to agriculture, including the "Vampires Road", on which I now focus.

This paper is based on ethnographic fieldwork I conducted in 2013 and 2014, in a neighborhood on the Vampires Road that I call Lebi Doti. A newcomer taking the Vampires Road coming from the Cayenne Road would start out on a wide, recently asphalted road. She would pass state-built social housing estates, small individual houses built along side roads, and vast schools. From time to time she would see, in the middle of these estates, small groups of wooden houses that remain from the earliest occupation of the area, prior to government construction. All around the public housing, she would see large numbers of dwellings built from wooden shingles: people have built these there to take advantage of neighborhood facilities – electricity, water supply and roads.

She would then reach a bend where the asphalt is replaced by a broad laterite track. The landscape no longer appears urban: the path winds up and down, through dense vegetation. At the bottom of a downward slope, she will cross a little wooden bridge over a small river, the Vampires creek: there is a good chance she will see children bathing there, women washing their dishes or men their cars. At times, she will be able to see small houses, made out of wooden shingles and concrete, with corrugated iron roofs, standing in the middle of clearings, where the smallest blade of grass is plucked out daily. Fruit trees and decorative plants frequently add to the bucolic picture. Some hints might suggest that more than a few people actually live here. An opening in the trees reveals the valley of Chekepatty, where there are 300 to 400 houses. At some

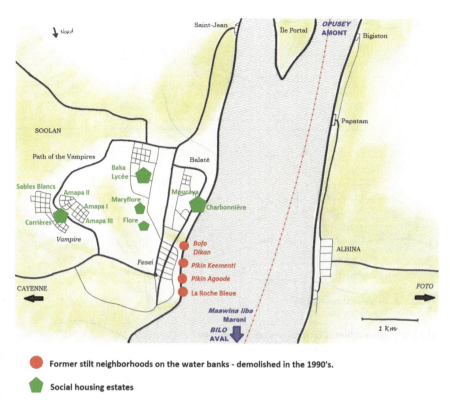

MAP 6.1 Old and new neighborhoods after removals
SOURCE: CLÉMENCE LÉOBAL, 2018

of the places where paths branch off the main track, the numerous letterboxes indicate the presence of many inhabitants, invisible from the Vampires Road.

At some point, a great gap opens before our visitor, and large leveled surfaces appear in front of her, where boys come to play football in the afternoon. Three-story buildings are under construction, soon to become the "Pôle Médico-Social" [health and social care center], a billboard announces. Large blocks of social housing apartments are also being built. On the flanks, and sometimes in the middle of these wide spaces, stand a few small hills with wooden houses on them. Taking a muddy road along the building site, you arrive at a flat area, a location called "Allée Bois-Canon" on the French maps, and "Lebi Doti" by the inhabitants. When I started my fieldwork in January 2013, I was struck by the violence of this spectacle: in the middle of the machine-leveled grounds these houses, which could have been lovely in a green environment, seemed suddenly fragile, ready to fall. The construction of the biggest housing project yet implemented, which will involve their demolition, is beginning there.

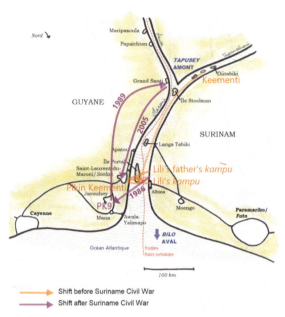

MAP 6.2 Lili's residential trajectory: a transborder life
SOURCE: CLÉMENCE LÉOBAL, 2017

Since the 2000s, the municipal authorities have sought to link together all the pre-existing peripheral districts through an overarching urban plan, with the creation of a central zone known as the Saint-Maurice Zone d'Aménagement Concertée (special planning district, ZAC) that would connect all of them. The plan includes building 4,000 homes, 60% earmarked for social housing, but also facilities, schools, etc. For a long time the planners drawing up this project failed to take into account the presence of many existing residents in this area. It was only two years ago that a study of "spontaneous dwellings" in the zone was commissioned from an NGO: with the help of aerial images, the authors estimated that in 2011 more that 6,000 people were living in the zone and the surrounding areas.[3] The implementation of the ZAC project thus implies their removal. Demolitions have already taken place at the site where the first building is being constructed: during the initial earthworks, the company in charge of the project[4] had the bulldozers dig very close to the dwellings present there,

---

3 DEAL Guyane, L'urbanisation spontanée en Guyane: appui à la mise en œuvre de modes d'aménagement alternatifs, Groupe de Recherches et d'Echanges Technologiques, Renaud Colombier, Bérangère Deluc, Virginie Rachmuhl, 3 reports, March 2012.
4 The Senog, Société d'Economie Mixte de l'Ouest Guyane, which is 80% owned by the municipal authorities.

PERFORMING ETHNICITY AS A WAY OF CONTESTING REMOVALS 183

with the aim of intimidating the inhabitants into leaving. Those who were French citizens or had French residence documents were sometimes offered social housing if they had not already left. The others, being "illegal" migrants, had no right to social housing. This intimidation strategy actually worked for most of them: only one house still stands there, in the middle of a space of flattened ground.

As I noted above, these demolitions belong to a three-decade long history of removal policies and demolition of "insanitary" neighborhoods (insalubres). The French administration uses ethnic categories to categorize the residents of the Vampires Road. The 2011 survey estimated that 90–95% of the inhabitants were Ndyuka and Aluku Maroons.[5] This estimate is not based on an exhaustive census and I doubt it is accurate. During my fieldwork, most of the inhabitants of the Vampires I met were Ndyuka Maroons, although their neighbors included Haitians, Brazilians, Creoles, Surinamese Creoles, and Saamaka and Pamaka Maroons. Ethnic categories are used by the government to make its population "legible" (Scott, 1998) and do not reflect the various auto-identifications of the resident. They also mask class and race domination: when the State agents are using the word "Businenge", all working class Black people are denoted, possibly including Haitians or Guyanese residents under this generic category. The French-speaking authorities racialize the inhabitants of these dwellings: they are categorized as Maroons, now under the generic appellation of "Businenge", which replaced the previously used term "Bosh".

Multiple ethnic denominations among Maroons in Saint-Laurent

Ethnicity involves multiple and changing categories. In current French Guianese political discourse, Maroons are referred to as "Bushinengué" ("men of the forest" in bushinenge tongo). This new term succeeds many others, such as "Bosh" or "Boni", formerly used by non-Maroons to refer to Maroons in Saint-Laurent-du-Maroni. Internally, they define themselves in terms of six group identifications (nasi), the Saamaka, Matawai and Kwinti (whose traditional villages are on the Suriname, Saramacca and Coppename Rivers respectively) and the Aluku, Ndyuka, and Paamaka, whose traditional villages are upstream along the Maroni River, the Lawa River (Aluku) and Tapanahoni River (Ndyuka). This geographical partition parallels a language difference between Nenge-tongo-speakers from the Maroni region and Saamaka-Matawai speakers from inland Suriname.[6] In addition, since the late nineteenth

---

5   DEAL Guyane, L'urbanisation spontanée en Guyane: appui à la mise en œuvre de modes d'aménagement alternatifs, GRET, Renaud Colombier, Bérangère Deluc, Virginie Rachmuhl, 3 rapports, mars 2012, p.39.

6   Kwinti language is close to Aluku, Ndyuka and Pamaka. For details on their history, see Hoogbergen (1992).

century numbers of Ndyuka have emigrated to the Surinamese coastal region of Cottica and are known as "Cottica Ndyuka". Another historical division separates the Aluku from the Ndyuka and Pamaka on the basis of nationality. Whereas the former have been recognized as allied to France since 1892, the latter were initially considered Dutch, and then Surinamese – even though many of them have more recently become French citizens.

Beyond race and class, the ethnic categorization also interferes with national lines. As the relocation was implemented, the state had to redefine this population, less in ethnic terms than in terms of national adherence. What now matters is to know who has French citizenship or residence rights, and who has not. Only the former are entitled to social housing. But in the current discourse of the state and municipal agents, Maroons are frequently referred to as undocumented foreigners and illegitimate occupants of the territory. Deportation of undocumented migrants has been analyzed as a sociopolitical regime whereby the state reaffirms its sovereignty, by "illegalizing" migrants (De Genova and Peutz, 2010). Here it is not only the presence of the migrants that is deemed illegal, but also their homes.

I shall now describe some of the urban Maroon ways of life created by the residents I came to know in Lebi Doti, improvising in a context of exclusion. I shall then go on to show in more detail how the authorities stigmatize these ways of life, and how the residents develop strategies and discourses that allow them to stay on site in spite of the development project.

Space and Kinship: The Creation of Urban Maroon Ways of Life

In 2013, the anthropologist Diane Vernon introduced me to Lena, the mother of a disabled child being treated at the hospital where she was working, who was living on Vampires Road near the building site. I did not find it easy to establish a relationship with her, mainly because I was shocked by her precarious situation and did not know how to handle it. Her situation was extremely difficult: neither she nor her husband had French residence rights (titre de séjour), meaning that they had no income to support Lena's three children. She would have liked to get social housing but could not even apply for it, as an undocumented foreigner. Neither did she have a field (goon). She was dependent on her family, on the jobs that her husband Bobby was doing, and on food issued by a municipal agency, the Centre Communal d'Action Sociale (Community Social Action Centre) each week. Aligning me with the other white women she knows, social workers from the hospital or other statutory bodies, she would always ask me for help in buying food for her and her children – which I did,

PERFORMING ETHNICITY AS A WAY OF CONTESTING REMOVALS 185

but felt very bad that I could not help her further. After six months, her child died following an operation, increasing my compassion for her and deepening my feelings of guilt. For months I visited her regularly during the day, and I gradually met other residents of this neighborhood. As we wandered through the district together with her daughter, I met various shopkeepers and neighbors, including Gisela Asaiti, the owner of the only house still standing within the building site, who agreed to tell me why she refused to leave. Through other acquaintances in Saint-Laurent, I also came to know other inhabitants of this neighborhood. Here I build on these encounters to reflect on the diverse ways of urban living that these people are reinventing, thus proposing an alternative to French norms.

The stories of how people came to settle here exemplify the common process of urbanization in Saint-Laurent, in which deforestation and agricultural practices drive urban development, where residents progressively transform cleared spaces in urban neighborhoods, in a combination of illegal settlements but also of a redistribution of land by the local authorities. One local authority worker recalls that after the civil war, he proposed to the "refugees" – which in this case meant Maroons from the Cottica region of Suriname – that they should develop agriculture along the Vampires Road. In the 1990s, although the war was over, many former refugees actually stayed or came back to French Guiana. "In those times, it was far away from the city," this official explained,[7] "so we put them there." In Lebi Doti a farmer from Charvein, Stephan, told me that he settled there in 1995 with verbal authorization from the municipal authorities, cleared an area of forest and built a big farm. Many relatives came to live on "his" land. Other people settled without permission from the authorities: Franz Clark, the cousin of Lena's husband, who was then living in neighboring Djakata, looked for land along the Vampires Road in 2003, and found his site, which was unoccupied. He first cleared the land, and planted cucumbers to sell, before starting to build houses for himself and his relatives. In like manner, Gisela came to live with her brother, who already had social housing in Baka Lycée, but had decided to clear a field and later built houses for himself and his relatives. The urban settlements of Lebi Doti thus derive from agricultural practices: they approach the Maroon upriver model of the kanpu, where someone decides to clear a site in the forest for cultivation and eventually settles with their relatives.

The houses are not isolated but built in small groups. For example, to get to Lena's place, I had to go uphill to a small group of houses above the big leveled area where trucks were driving toward the building works. The first

---

7 Yves-Charles Castagne, July 30th 2014.

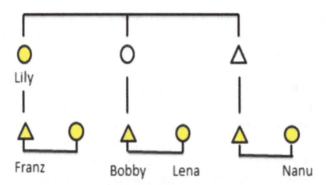

FIGURE 6.1 Lili's genealogical tree
SOURCE: CLÉMENCE LÉOBAL, 2017

things I would pass were remains of old cars, completely dismantled, and the traces of an attempt to build a house in concrete, invaded by vegetation and apparently abandoned several years earlier. Finally I would arrive at two wooden houses (paanga osu), where many people lived, surrounded by many other smaller wooden constructions.

In those settlements, matrilineal kinship ties end up being concretized in the urban forms. Lena told me that their two houses were shared by four households, all members of which were related to one elderly women, Lili. Lili's son Franz lived in one of the houses with his wife and their ten children. The second house, a little bigger, was shared between three households: that of Lili, Franz's mother; that of Lena's husband, Lili's sister's son, and Lena's three children; and that of Lili's brother's son and his wife and children. The settlement grew as after clearing the site, Franz first had a house built for his mother, where she lived with her nephew Bobby, Lena's future husband. Later, he built another bigger house, with money from his cousin Kiki, for his mother and for Kiki: it was built on a slab, partly in concrete and partly in wood. Finally, after he separated from his first wife, he decided to build a house for himself and his new wife Julia. He first built a paanga osu (wooden house) on a concrete slab base and started to make a siton osu (in concrete), but construction of the latter came to a halt when he saw the municipal bulldozers arrive in 2011.

This inscription of kinship in space through the layout of houses is common to many Maroon homes that I have visited, in this neighborhood and elsewhere. Gisela had her concrete house (siton osu) built near her brother's, which has now been demolished: her son built his own wooden house (paanga

PERFORMING ETHNICITY AS A WAY OF CONTESTING REMOVALS   187

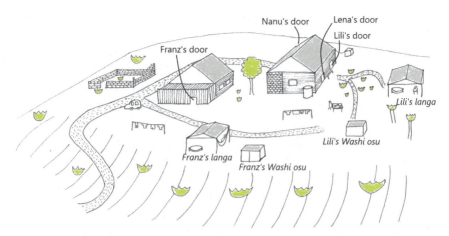

FIGURE 6.2   The houses of Lili's family
SOURCE: CLÉMENCE LÉOBAL, 2017

osu) in front of her house. Similarly, Stephan Pinas came to settle on the land cleared by his brother and built a hangar where he lives with his chicken. Many of his relatives came to settle near him, and his nephew recently built a villa a little further away. Joyce Apagi settled on Stephan's land because she was a relative of his wife: her husband built her a sodoo paanga osu (stilt wooden house). Later, her daughter had her own paanga osu built nearby. The material differences between concrete and wooden houses reflect class differentiation between these inhabitants: as a long-time French citizen, Gisela could afford the concrete house that Franz did not complete, and Lili never started. Notwithstanding these varying levels of income, all these settlements are organized according to the matrilineal kinship ties of their inhabitants.

Another characteristic of these settlements is the importance of life outside the house, in domesticated private outdoor spaces. Each house has separate constructions outside: one langa (open annex) for cooking, and one washi osu (toilets and washroom), as well as a place to wash the dishes, and a place for doing laundry. At Lena's place, one washes dishes on a simple table, but Joyce has put together a kitchen sink outside her house. Rainwater is collected in water tanks, which are sometimes old fridges. All these constructions delimit a yard where people like to sit, to spend time together, to receive friends, to play with the children. These yards were carefully cleared, and planted with fruit trees, decorative and medicinal plants. At Lena's place, it was only after many visits, and after seeing photos of the place before the works had begun, that I noticed this esthetic, because my overwhelming first impression was of a great precarious mess and of deprivation. Likewise, the bigger siton osu of Gisela is oriented toward the garden outside: whenever I come, she sits on a pretty, decoratively tiled terrace, looking at her garden, which is still beautiful with its many fruit trees. Sometimes, she rests in her hammock under one of the trees. One completely forgets, being there, that one is in the middle of a building site. These outdoor ways of living are not here connected to agriculture: Franz used to have a field here, as did Gisela's brother, but it was destroyed by the authorities in 2011. But Franz has a field on the Apatou road, far from here. Neither Joyce nor Lena have ever had a field. In an urban context, these ways of living outside the house are not necessarily connected to agriculture.

Life inside the house is limited to particular activities during the day: taking care of the children, talking in private, cooking. Gisela even put her stove and kitchen outside the house, on the terrace, so that she cooks outdoors. At Lena's place, there are two rooms: the first is the bedroom, with just one bed for the couple and all three children. The second is the living room, with car seats by way of a couch, a hammock, and a TV that is never on during the day, since Lena only switches on the generator in the evening. Behind this is the kitchen, the pans hanging on the wall reminding me of the traditional interiors of up-river Maroons photographed by the Prices (2009). Behind the kitchen there is a terrace, which is shared with the other occupants of the house, Lili and the family of her baala pikin (nephew). There is a bed and seats, and large cooking utensils such as a pestle and mortar. Lili also uses this terrace in the back for her work as healer. She is a fervent Catholic but she "works with stones", and with the Bible, to heal people. In the other houses I visited in Lebi Doti, I was only invited in the living room. Joyce's and her daughter's first room is the living room, with a sofa, TV, and walls decorated with many knick-knacks, toys and photos. But most of the time, they received me outside to talk.

Lebi Doti residents live in close connection with other homes in the area, in Soolan or on the other bank of the Maroni: they could be said to belong to a "configuration of houses" (Marcelin, 1996). Lena regularly returns to her family in Baka Lycée, where she used to live. She goes there frequently, for example to charge her phone. It was here that everyone gathered when her child died. She is also close to her adoptive mother, who used to live with Lili in the Chinatown area in the city center, but now has been allocated social housing. They are also closely connected with Lili's sister, Lena's mother-in-law, who lives just the other side of Vampires Road. She owns land on the road to Cayenne, but prefers to stay here, not too far from the center, for the sake of her grandchildren who go to school. They also frequently visit Bobby's family in Midina Kanpu, a village on the other side of the border 30 minutes upriver from Soolan. Lena and Lili evoke this kanpu with delight: they call it "tapsey", which means upriver; they say it is a peaceful place, with a beautiful creek. They still have relatives there, who regularly come to see them – it is only half an hour by boat. They go there sometimes: this is where Lena stayed when her child died. Lena could imagine going back and living there, especially now that Surinamese president Bouterse has introduced an allowance for mothers.

There is some turnover and exchange of homes in line with life events. In 2013 Lena and her husband had been living here only two years: they took the house of another niece (baala pikin) of Lili, Kiki, who had actually paid to build the extension of the house with a concrete floor. Prior to this, Lena used to live at her cousin's place in social housing in the Baka Lycée neighborhood. When he was a young boy, her husband Bobby also used to live there with his aunt Lili. In 2014, Lena and Bobby had moved to Midina Kanpu, to the home of Lena's foster mother. Their lives are thus closely connected with those of others homes nearby, and there is a great deal of circulation within the configuration of houses.

A striking feature of these ways of life is the strong connection the residents have with other places outside Soolan, on both banks of the river. Life histories are often characterized by multiple residence. Maroon inhabitants frequently travel to places where they used to live. They often say they love to be in Soolan because from there they can easily go to Foto (Paramaribo), upriver, or to Cayenne. For example, Lena was raised by a cousin of her mother in Paramaribo. She came here ten years ago to seek healthcare for her eldest daughter. Lili, was born and raised in Keementi, on the Tapanahoni. At the age of 14 she went to her father's kanpu near Papatam, a few kilometers upriver from Soolan, on the opposite side of the river. Lili had to leave the kanpu because of the civil war: she went to a refugee camp for a few weeks, before going to Grand Santi to stay with her second son. She came back to Saint-Laurent eight years ago, when this son died, asking Franz for shelter. It was at this time that Franz started clearing the site and building a house here in Lebi Doti.

Likewise, Joyce came from Papaichton ten years ago after getting her French National Identity Card (known as a pièce). She came so that her children could go to high school (lycée), since there is none upriver. Her husband is a boat driver (botoman): he regularly travels upriver, and she often goes herself, when there is a funeral or a feast. Gisela was born in Aluku, on the Lawa: she has been coming and going all her life, between her place upriver near Papaichton, Boniville, Saint-Laurent on the river banks, and Cayenne. But unlike the Ndyuka people I have met, she is not familiar with Paramaribo. She came in Soolan so that her grandchildren could go to school, and because of her health problems which require her to regularly see a doctor. Stephan came to French Guiana from Albina just before the war, as the problems in Suriname had already begun. To begin with he had no French papers or status. He worked one year for the space center in Kourou, and then got a 10-year residence card. He used to live between the Mana road, where he farmed, and Kourou where he would sell his produce. He came here to Lebi Doti in 1995 after he and his wife, who was from Mana, separated. These people's life histories are characterized by frequent physical journeys to these different places of belonging.

These residential patterns are occasionally said to be specifically busikonde, as one inhabitant put it: "That's how Busikonde sama are, they have many places to live".[8] However, this reference to ethnicity only comes out in comparison with the Bakaa system. In this urban situation, where the inhabitants face a racialized spatial domination materialized through removals, houses and ways of life become defined in ethnic terms.

Trajectories of Migration and Exclusion

In Soolan, these people had experienced various trajectories of progressive exclusion from the center of the city. Franz for example was born on the island of Portal, near Saint-Laurent, where his father, a Ndyuka from Albina, was working. His birth was never registered by authorities, and until recently he did not have any documentation of nationality. He was living with his mother, Lili, coming and going between their kanpu near Bigiston and their rented house in Sineisi, on the Maroon fringes of the city at that time. Later, his father bought a wooden house in another riverside neighborhood, Awaa Ondo, which lies south of the center, near La Charbonnière. After many years, when his father had died and his mother had gone upriver, Frank heard that this neighborhood was to be demolished by the government. He knew he could not be allocated social housing, since he had no documents. He sold his house to someone who wanted to reuse the timber and searched for another place to live. He gained permission from Saamaka people living in a neighborhood known as Vietnam, near the Baka Lycée housing estate, to build there. After a few years, he and all his neighbors were expelled by the municipal authorities, who wanted to build a school there. They were all resettled in a place called Djakata, at the entry to Vampires Road. In the meantime, Frank had obtained a French national identity card, so he decided to look for a place to build the house in Lebi Doti. His residential trajectory in Soolan is thus one of progressive displacement from the center and from the river, paralleling the history of the city's development, with the demolition of shantytowns and the creation of peripheral sites.

---

8 Julia Abakamofou, 25th July 2014: "Na so den Busikonde sama e tan: den abi fulu tan peeshi."

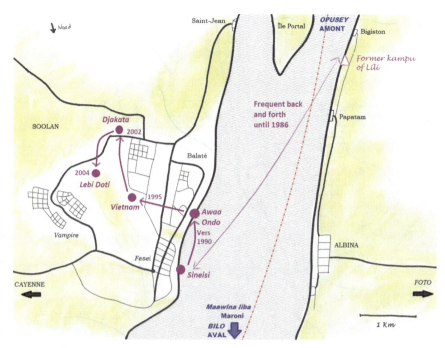

MAP 6.3 The residential trajectory of Franz in Soolan
SOURCE: CLÉMENCE LÉOBAL, 2018

Gisela also has a long history in Saint-Laurent, coming and going from her Aluku village on the Lawa. She used to live in the Pikin Agoode neighborhood of stilt houses with her first husband, who was also Aluku. Later she lived in another of these riverside areas, in Baka lopital, before the houses were demolished. After this she moved to Charbonnière, sharing a house with one of her nieces. Finally, she came here in 2001. She sums up: "The Frenchmen are like this: they always pull the Busikonde sama and put them somewhere else".[9] Here she uses the term "French" (Faansiman) to qualify the authorities, in opposition to the Maroons (Busikonde sama): even though she has French citizenship, she feels like a foreigner.

Also originating from the Aluku upriver region, Joyce did not come to Saint-Laurent during the time of riverside dwelling. When she arrived in Saint-Laurent after she obtained her national identity card, she first rented a wooden house (paanga osu) from a Haitian in the neighborhood of Paul Isnard. But

---

9 "Den Faansiman de so kaba: den puu den Busikondesama puti go de." Gisela Asaiti, July 12th 2013.

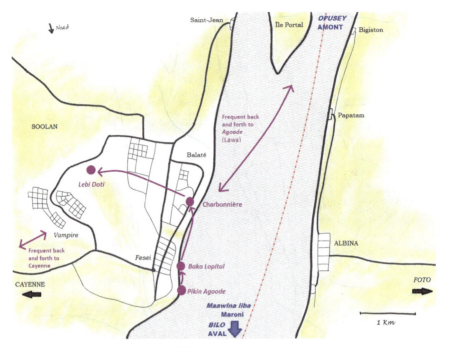

MAP 6.4 The residential trajectory of Gisela in Soolan
SOURCE: CLÉMENCE LÉOBAL, 2018

when she went upriver for three weeks, on her return her landlord had thrown all her stuff out, even though she had paid the rent before leaving. "Haitians have bad manners," she comments. So she stayed for a while with someone in Charbonnière, before finding a house to rent here in Lebi Doti by asking Stephan's wife, a cousin of hers. She had to pay 120 euros in rent, but the landlord said she should not declare this to the government when she was filling out the forms for welfare allowances (CAF). Her husband finally built her this wooden stilt house, so she no longer has to pay rent. She also came here after finding it impossible to find anywhere to live in more central areas of the city.

Life in Lebi Doti is characterized by isolation. Residents are remote from the rest of the city and far from any public transportation. Men have scooters and cars but in their absence, women have to find taxis (2-euro wagi) to go to the center. Children have to walk for nearly an hour to reach their school in the housing estate. For shopping, people frequently ask me to take them to the center in my car. Otherwise they buy everyday food from various houses in the neighborhood that sell products at very high prices. I went to some of these places with Lena's five-year-old daughter: small shops are constructed in front of some houses, or she had to ask people sitting in front of the house directly if they had this or that. She had to pay cash, but apparently her mother is in debt to some of these vendors, since they asked for their money. Itinerant sellers – mostly young Maroon men – are also constantly passing by with barrows selling vegetables, clothes, soap, etc. at a high price.

Their life histories of exclusion lead these people toward a collective identification. Sometimes, this identification takes the form of class consciousness. Lili calls herself "potiman" (poor), as does Stephan. Joyce describes her house of "pina osu" as a miserable one and complains: "We suffer only in this country."[10] But more frequently, this experience of exclusion is expressed in ethnic terms opposing "Busikonde sama" to "Bakaa". The inhabitants I met in Lebi Doti thus shared this common reference to Busikonde sama ethnicity, both positively in their everyday way of life, and also negatively in their experience of being excluded in Saint-Laurent by non-Maroon people. They indeed face the process of domination stemming from race, class and nation-state categories materialised through urban development policies.

Unviable Dwellings, Unviable Lives: Development as Justification for Removals

The presence of these houses is seen as unacceptable by the authorities, since they stand in the way of the state's building project, which requires that they be demolished. Legally, the inhabitants are accused of being in breach of regulations on many levels: first, they do not own the land; second, they have no construction permit; and third, they are often themselves undocumented foreigners, so are not allowed to be in France. However, the normal procedure for confiscation of property is very long in France, unless the state makes a public health order (arrêté d'insalubrité) that speeds up the procedure – but no such order has yet been issued. This is why the company in charge of the project decided to intimidate the inhabitants by excavating around their homes.

To justify this procedure, the houses themselves are stigmatized and refused the classification of house: agents of the municipality call them "shacks" ("baraques") or "huts" ("cabanes"). In practice, the "insanitary" dwellings are not the only ones to be demolished, since the authorities are obliging all residents to leave. In a 2008 census, Gisela's house was actually identified as "in good state",[11] but it was also included in the eviction order. Thus, one of the

---

10   "Wi pina namo na a konde disey!" Joyce Apagi, April 13th 2013.
11   SENOG. ZAC Saint-Maurice Secteur 1. Enquête socio-économique et bâti. August 2008, C2R.

local authority agents in charge of development stigmatizes both the strategies of the "poor" who she suggests build their houses here precisely in the hope of being entitled to rehousing, and the houses themselves which are seen as unworthy of the term "house":

> Because it was announced in 2007 that there would be a ZAC, people came there to be relocated! We had 50 people, by now they are 5,000. We talk about "participatory projects", but the reality is that we have a population which is so deprived that when we have a plan, the less we talk, the better it is. We arrive in the morning with a bulldozer, and that's it. Because their things are not viable, these are poky little places ...[12]

This discourse conceals the diversity of the constructions: many of them are built on a concrete base, and some of them are partly or totally in concrete. Moreover, this official minimizes the trauma of demolition, since the inhabitants just have to "take their boards and their sheets" and go away. This official also stigmatizes these families' way of life, suggesting that they have many children to benefit from family welfare allowances:

> Here, there is some kind of polygamy, yes ... there are people who have several wives and who calculate so they have an even number of children with each one: half for her, half for him. I had a man like that who came here and showed me his income declaration: he had 20 declared children and received 50,000 Euros, non-taxable! I thought that I should do the same ... But we don't have the same criteria: to raise a kid without any clothes, just one outfit for the school, we can't, so we would ruin ourselves.[13]

---

12 Jacqueline Duvert, May 31st 2013: « Le fait d'avoir annoncé en 2007 qu'il y aurait une ZAC: les gens sont venus pour se faire reloger! On est passés de 50 à 5000 personnes! On parle de projets participatifs, mais la réalité c'est qu'on a une population tellement démunie, que lorsqu'on a un projet, moins on en dit, mieux on se porte! On arrive le matin avec le bull, et voilà. Parce leurs trucs, c'est pas viable, c'est des cages à lapin... »

13 Jacqueline Duvert, May 31st 2013: « Ici, on peut assimiler ça à de la polygamie oui... il y a des gens qui ont plusieurs femmes et calculent pour faire un nombre pair d'enfants à chacune, la moitié pour Monsieur, l'autre pour Madame. J'ai un Monsieur comme ça qui m'a montré sa déclaration d'impôt, il avait 20 enfants déclarés et touchait 50 000 euros non imposables... Je me suis dit, je devrais faire pareil! Sauf que nous, on n'a pas les mêmes critères : élever des enfants sans aucun vêtement, avec juste une tenue pour l'école, on sait pas faire, donc on se ruinerait. »

FIGURE 6.3 "Awassa dead-end" in the final housing project
SOURCE: CLÉMENCE LÉOBAL, 2017

Not only the houses but also the inhabitants' way of life is declared unviable. The legal argumentation of the urban planning authorities masks a racialization of Maroons, implicitly described as unwanted foreigners. They are accused of trying to profit from the French social system. The French dominant norm in terms of housing and lifestyle thus expresses itself in words and in acts of demolition. In a way, some humans are recognized as less than human, and "that form of qualified recognition does not lead to a viable life" (Butler 2004: 2). Ethnic categorization is a way of euphemizing the race and class domination processes at work in the development project. Maroon ethnicity is referred to in the street names of the standardized housing project, all in concrete, that was finally built after the demolitions of the Maroon houses: the streets are called after elements from Maroon culture, like "Aleke" or "Awassa".

Refusing to Quit: Alternative Norms as Resources

Judith Butler asserts that it is only at the end of a process of recognition in terms of norms that an individual is constituted a viable being. The terms and the norms according to which the human is recognized as human are socially articulated "depending on its race, the legibility of that race, its morphology, the legibility of that morphology, its sex, the perceptual verifiability of that sex, its ethnicity, the categorical understanding of that ethnicity." Maroons thus have to escape the norms by which recognition is awarded, and "articulate an alternative, minority version of sustaining norms or ideals" (2004: 3). In Lebi Doti, not everyone accepted the idea of moving into social housing (batiman). Even after the arrival of the bulldozers, some of the residents who had the necessary resources stayed there, refusing to protest, like Gisela. State agents ridiculed these people, calling them "the last irreducibles",[14] in reference to cartoon hero Astérix, the "last rebels",[15] or "Grandma plays Resistance"[16] – in reference to Gisela's age and to a French comedy film of the 1980s.[17] In their view these people who "resist" are French citizens who are aware of their rights, and thus do not want to go, but they are very few. Still they hinder the building project.

One day as I walked past these houses perched on earth mounds that some state agents call "mushrooms", a boy called me over and introduced me to his grandmother Gisela. This family was seeking to gain support for her struggle against eviction. Gisela explained that she did not want to leave because she had no other place to go, and because she had paid a lot of money to build this siton osu. Her brother had told her that the land belonged to him before she had her house built, but he actually did not have legal title. His own house was demolished, along with his fruit trees, and he asked the government (lanti) to indemnify him for the fruit trees but they refused. Gisela now stays there alone with her son and her grandchildren. She has consulted a lawyer for help. She would like to keep the house by paying for the land, adapting herself to the customs of the white people:

> They could have let me have my house and I would pay for the land. But anyway, it is how it is in the land of the Bakaa (Bakaakonde), it is like that. Anyway when you are here in that land, you keep paying for all! I want my own house and I would pay for it, I pay, I stay. Because I put all my money already in it, I spend it all.[18]

---

14   Hubert Fijol, May 21st 2013.

15   Jacqueline Duvert, May 2nd 2013.

16   Françoise Ambert, June 3th 2013.

17   Papy fait de la résistance, 1983.

18   "Den be sa fika en gi da mi e pay a peeshi. Na so! Ala fasi na so a Baakakonde gi en, na so a de. (...) Ala fasi a Bakaakonde te I de na en kaba na so so pay! (...) Mi wani mi eigi osu da mi e pay, mi e pay, mi e tan. Bika mi lasi kaba ala mi moni, mi lasi ala." Gisela Asaiti, June 4th 2013.

But she categorically refuses the idea of living in a social housing apartment, even if she was offered one:

> I don't want a batiman (apartment block), I don't like that. I don't like to stay indoors. I like to walk. I have a walk, I clear the garden. I don't like to stay in the house, I feel warm. I am not used to that, Busikonde sama are not used to that. Some people like it! But all of us do not like that. (...) Yes, [in your own house] you have fruit trees, the wind blows ... you can't buy that![19]

In the threat, the question of ethnic identity is activated: Gisela describes her way of life as being "Busikonde sama". She does not want to live in social housing because she likes living outside. Lili also valorizes her way of life: she says that their place used to be the "best place in all Saint-Laurent" before the bulldozer destroyed their surrounding plantations. They had many fruit trees, growing avocado, lemons, custard apples and pineapples. Even now, she likes sitting on the yard "teke winta", enjoying the breeze. Gisela also compares this unfair treatment to the situation upriver: "Upriver, the Whites (Bakaa) cannot come and remove you, they cannot be that annoying."[20] She is conscious of her rights being violated in comparison to the upriver regions, where this does not happen. She defines the authorities here by the term "Bakaa" Whites.[21] For her, Saint-Laurent is a Bakaakonde, land of the Whites, which is why it is so different.

Performing ethnicity through dwelling practices offers resources in this conflict. Multiple residences give some of them the possibility of ignoring orders to leave: Gisela says that if the government were to demolish her house, she would go back to "her land" (mi liba), where she has social housing (Bakaa osu) in Papaichton, upriver. She also has the possibility of going to another house in her residential grouping in Charbonnière. She develops an alternative discourse to the French injunction to leave, and refuses to reproduce French

---

19   Mi na wani batiment mi an lobi en. Mi na lobi tan a ini wan osu ini. Mi lobi waka. Mi e kiin peeshi, mi waka mi e kiin peeshi. Mi na lobi tan a ini wan osu, mi e waam. Mi an gwenti, Busikondesama an gwenti den sani de. Soms lobi en! Ma a na wi ala lobi en. (...) Weeno. I abi sii. A winta booko. I na bay dati Gisela Asaiti, June 4th 2013.

20   "Tapu a liba, den Bakaa no man kon puu yu, den no man konkuu so." Gisela Asaiti, June 4th 2013.

21   This specific category of Whiteness is shared across the Caribbean regions, for example with the békés in Martinique, or the bakra in Suriname. All the variations of this term refer to the colonizers. In Ndyuka, bakaa sometimes includes the Creoles, but many of my interlocutors were using it as a synonym of White (weti sama).

norms in terms of housing, using ethnicity as a resource to affirm alternative collective norms in terms of "good living".

∴

By the time this chapter will be published, most of the residents I met in 2013 and 2014 will certainly have been evicted and sometimes relocated in social housing. The first parts of the housing project have been built on the former site of Lebi Doti. However, other parts of the Vampires Road are still occupied by wooden houses: some inhabitants of the Vampires Road have succeeded in obtaining title to the land and are thus entitled to stay there.

Maroon inhabitants are thus facing urban policies that lead to their marginalization along class, race and nation lines. The struggle of the people I have met is based on the register of ethnicity, categories on which they both act and in which they are acted upon (Butler 2004: 2). Maroon ways of living result partly from the political and social exclusion they face, but also from specific ways of dwelling: as such they convey a message in terms of ethnicity. They express, by their very ways of living and occupying this space, their claim for a different kind of urban life than the one planned by the authorities, which they define as Busikonde. The physical characteristics of dwellings, as well as the ways they are used in everyday life, constitute an affirmation of alternative Busikonde urban ways of living vis-a-vis the dominant political order.

References

Bilby, Kenneth. 1990. The Remaking of the Aluku: Culture, Politics and maroon Ethnicity in French South America. Baltimore, Maryland: John Hopkins University, 1990.

Balandier, Georges. 1951. "La situation coloniale, approche théorique." Cahiers internationaux de sociologie, 11 (1951): 44–79.

Barth, Frederik. 1968. Ethnic Groups and Boundaries. The Social Organization of Culture Difference. Boston: Little Brown.

Butler, Judith. 2004. Undoing gender. London: Routledge.

Carsten, Janet, and Hugh-Jones, Stephen, eds. 1995. About the house: Levi-Strauss and beyond. Cambridge: Cambridge University Press.

Casimir, Valérie and Moomou, Jean. 2010."La guerre civile du Suriname 1986–1990: Les nouvelles donnes de l'axe fluvial Maroni." Revue Guaïana: 16–20.

Collomb, Gérard, and Jolivet, Marie-José, eds. 2008. Histoires, identités et logiques ethniques: Amérindiens, Créoles et Noirs marrons en Guyane. Paris: Édition du Comité des travaux historiques et scientifiques.

Cunha, Olívia Maria Gomes da. 2018. "In Their Places: The Cottica Ndyuka in Moengo." In Ethnographies of U.S. Empire, 247–279. Edited by John Collins and Carole Mc-Granahan. Durham: Duke University Press.

De Genova, Nicholas, and Peutz, Nathalie, eds. 2010. The Deportation Regime: Sovereignty, Space, and the Freedom of Movement. Durham, NC: Duke University Press.

Delpech, Bernard. 1993."Les Aluku de Guyane à un tournant: de l'économie de subsistance à une société de consommation." Revue Cahiers d'Outre-Mer, 46 (182): 175–192.

Hoogbergen, Wim. 1990. The Boni maroon wars in Suriname. Leiden, Brill.

Hoogbergen, Wim. 1992. « Origins of the Suriname Kwinti Maroons ». NWIG: New West Indian Guide / Nieuwe West-Indische Gids 66, no 1/2: 27–59.

Hoogbergen, Wim. 1993. The Boni Maroon Wars in Suriname. Leiden: Brill.

Hurault, Jean. 1965. Africains de Guyane. La vie matérielle et l'art des Noirs Réfugiés de Guyane. Paris: Editions Mouton.

Hurault Jean. 1985. "Pour un statut des populations tribales de Guyane Française (1968–1984)." Ethnies, 1, (1–2): 42–49.

Marcelin, Louis Herns. 1996. "L'invention de la famille afro-américaine: famille, parenté et domesticité parmi les Noirs du Recôncavo da Bahia, Brésil." PhD diss., Rio de Janeiro, Universidade Federal do Rio de Janeiro.

Migge, Bettina and Léglise, Isabelle. 2013. Exploring Language in a Multilingual Context: Variation, Interaction and Ideology in Language Documentation. Cambridge: Cambridge University Press.

Mitchell, J. Clyde. 1956. The Kalela dance: Aspects of social relationships among urban Africans in Northern Rhodesia. Manchester: Manchester University Press.

Moomou, Jean. 2007. « Les Bushinengue en Guyane : entre rejet et intégration de la fin du XVIIIe siècle aux dernières années du XXe siècle ». In Comprendre la Guyane d'aujourd'hui Un département français dans la région des Guyanes, par Serge Mam Lam Fouck, p. 51–82. Matoury (Guyane), France, Guyane française: Ibis Rouge.

Moomou, Jean. 2009. "Les Bonis à l'âge de l'or et du grand « takari » (1860–1969): temps de crises, temps d'espoir." PhD Dissertation. Paris: EHESS.

Parris, Jean-Yves. 2013. Interroger les morts. Essai sur la dynamique politique des Noirs marrons du Surinam et de la Guyane. Matoury, French Guiana: Ibis Rouge.

Poupeau, Franck, and Tissot, Sylvie, 2006. "La spatialisation des problèmes sociaux." Actes de la recherche en sciences sociales, 159: 4–9.

Price, Richard. 1983. First-Time: The Historical vision of an Afro-American people. Baltimore: John Hopkins University Press.

Price, Sally. 1987. Co-wives and Calabashes. Ann Arbor: The University of Michigan Press, 1987.

Price, Richard. 2007. Travels with Tooy: History, Memory, and the African American Imagination. Chicago: University of Chicago Press.

Price, Richard and Price, Sally. 2011. Les marrons. La Roque d'Anthéron: Vents d'Ailleurs.

Price, Richard. 2011. Rainforest warriors. Human Rights on Trial. Philadelphia: University of Pennsylvania Press.

Polimé, Thomas and Thoden van Velzen, H.U.E. 1998. Vluchtelingen, opstandelingen en andere bosnegers van Oost-Suriname, 1986–1988. Utrecht: Instituut voor Culturele Antropologie.

Scott James. 1998. Seeing like a state. London, New Haven: Yale University Press.

Thoden van Velzen, H.U.E. and Van Wetering, Wilhelmina. 1988. The Great Father and the Danger: religious cults, material forces, and collective fantasies in the world of the Surinamese Maroons. Dordrecht & Providence: Foris Publications.

Vernon, Diane. 1992. Les representations du corps chez les noirs marrons Ndjuka du Surinam et de la Guyane française. Paris, Editions de I'ORSTOM.

PART 3

Incorporations

∴

CHAPTER 7

Spirits and Pain in the Making of Ndyuka Politics

Stuart Strange

What does Ndyuka metalanguage of pain tells us about Ndyuka understandings of the political? For the Ndyuka people I worked with, pain appears to be conceived primarily as a social relationship. Not merely a representation, pain compels people to recognize themselves as made from relations with others. Because of this elementary identification, I contend that pain acts in important ways to constitute Ndyuka politics. Protracted, persistent pain invites political descriptions of how people live with each other, indexing the categories of relatedness available to people to talk about both the ontological grounds for, and the pragmatic experience of, sociality. This invites the re-conceptualization of Ndyuka political life through their assumptions about what a person is in relation to others, showing how the paradigmatic categories of Ndyuka discourse like the matriline and the clan, are created in tandem with Ndyuka descriptions of persons and the phenomenology of subjectivity. For Ndyuka, pain is socially powerful because it compels descriptions of how people suffer as explanations of why they suffer together.

In this way, Ndyuka focus on what might be called the poetics of pain. As Roman Jakobsen notably stated, "The poetic function projects the principle of equivalence from the axis of selection to the axis of combination" (1960:358). This moves our awareness to "the constitutive device of the sequence" (ibid), in "the foregrounding of message form" (Fleming and Lempert 2014: 471). Poetics is a "dimension of persuasion" (ibid), part of the larger rhetorical work of creating social relations. Poetics emphasizes the combined characteristics of things like words, sensations and gestures as a patterned aggregate. While pain is often thought of in anthropology as resisting language (Daniel 1996; Das 2007), Ndyuka often emphasize that unintelligibility as a semiotic quality of pain to create equivalence between its sensation and the social existence of the person experiencing it. Still, pain is not language and, while construed as needing to become a socially legible communication, it still must be described. Such descriptions—the metalanguage of pain—provide the rhetorical force that allows pain to combine with the wider contexts of the sufferer's social relations, imbuing these with explanatory force. Pain is poetic because it calls attention to the formal properties of Ndyuka persons that render them legible as combinations of relations, whether through descent or residential proximity. Pain

© KONINKLIJKE BRILL NV, LEIDEN, 2019 | DOI:10.1163/9789004388062_009

assumes "iconic-indexical" (Silverstein 2003) features. In suffusing a person, pain points to the relationship that causes the pain by resembling it; by taking on that relation's salient properties the pain indicates that these relations are physically real. Pain is maybe the most active sign of Ndyuka dialogical models of subjectivity that conceive of the thoughts and feelings as signs of the shared presence of spirits and ancestors in personal consciousness. Pain speaks. In evincing a sufferer's specific relationship to another person or spirit, pain also speaks beyond that relation, convoking an imbricated family network in which the afflicted is subjectively and substantially situated. When winnowed by the specifics of Ndyuka epistemology—the interpretation of who has the capacity to know and about what—these issues become particularly consequent for the management of explanations that ascribe responsibility for suffering to others, the central concern of Ndyuka political life.

It should be noted that the formal category of politics (*politiki*) has almost exclusively negative associations of trickery. Instead of doing politics, Ndyuka strive to rhetorically embody their political aims through speaking as the ancestors. This politics is concerned with fixing the often-uncertain conditions of such dialogical personhood. As personhood extends to many other than human beings like spirits and animals, Ndyuka politics is about managing the relations that compose persons to decide which relations matter for attributing personal responsibility as collective culpability. These evaluations depend on divinatory logics that allow the truth about these relations to be made clear. This process is not simply about invoking prior "systems" like kinship. These divinatory forms play an active role in establishing and redefining these relations, grounding a given controversy in an account of the specific social dependencies from which it emerges. Through divination, moral adjudication based on objective knowledge about the world is made possible, fixing who and what acts within and between persons to cause suffering and death. Pain is the evidence of these relations and of the need for intervention. It plays a signal role in communicating the *a priori* reality of these relations, their moral foundations, and the collectivities so assembled. This chapter will explore this process, detailing how the divinatory metalanguage of pain poetically interweaves personhood and collective responsibility. In doing so, I will demonstrate how pain constructs the explicitly dialogical subjectivity of sufferers and thus the ontological grounds of Ndyuka political practice. While the examples that follow are not ones addressing wider political concerns, I hope to show how personal crises participate in the same forms of communication addressing the Ndyuka people as a whole.

Once, when I was with Da Mangwa, an obiyaman (oracular medium) friend, he decided to divine the causes of a sore throat from which I was suffering. His

SPIRITS AND PAIN IN THE MAKING OF NDYUKA POLITICS

diagnostic means was a *luku*, a divination device composed of a bell (*gengen*) suspended from a cloth cord. This was one way that his tutelary spirit, Da Lanti Winti ([respect marker for elder]), communicated. Da Mangwa informed me that if Da Lanti Winti was to "possess" him (*bali ne'en tapu*), I would be unable to understand him. So he spoke through the bell, which he could directly translate for me.

Placing the bell on a stone wrapped in a white cloth, he sprinkled it with clear rum and prayed to his ancestors (*gaanma, gaanda*). Picking up the bell, he suspended it from his left hand, and with very little visible effort, allowed it to swing. He proceeded to pose a number of questions. He asked the luku if I had had the sickness before. It rang wildly. He then asked if I was suffering from a *kowownu siki*, a meaningless illness. It remained silent, a negative response. He then inquired if "*sama be du en wan sani*" (someone had done something to me), meaning that I was a victim of witchcraft. The luku responded negatively. Finally, after inquiring with increasingly specific yes/no questions, Da Mangwa arrived at a diagnosis. He said that it was not me who had the sickness, but rather one "Da" (*a á yu di abi a siki disi, a be de wan Da di be abi en*). A senior man in my family—he was not sure if it was my grandfather or one of my uncles—had been afflicted with the illness and had come back (*nasi*) as my *nenseki*—one of the constituent souls that reside in the deceased's descendants and grants elements of their personality and appearance.

My suffering was the result of my being and not being my nenseki. My unknown ancestor resided in me, and in an important respect was I, determining important contours of the particular make-up of my character. And yet, it is equally true that as a nenseki, he is distinct from me. Since he is I, I was implicated in the same suffering which had killed him. My suffering was not the result of some property of my own unique body or my actions. My body, an iteration of the substance of the matriline—the *bee*—conveyed my *nenseki*, inviting him to live as me. And, as this pain had killed him, he resided in me as this final pain. He had become defined by this suffering and, in determining me, imbued me with the same suffering. In being diagnosed as suffering from my nenseki's sickness, continuity and rupture were equally emphasized. The pain was thus external to me, an element of my existential dependence on the past. This past remained, my own embodied subjectivity predicated by the intergenerational social relations from which I, as an individuated but not individual person, materialized.

As this example shows, for many Ndyuka, as a quality, pain is causally predicated by a number of different sets of relations and relational aggregates. The discrete character of the pain combines with my body as a bundle of relations to indicate the transitivity between the pain, my aggregate self, and the lineage.

When so combined with these categories as invoked in divination, pain becomes the clearest proof that these categories are relations embedded in the body. The relationship affords pain, which acts as evidence that the category is objectively present. In this case, the category is the lineage and its comprising kin terms/roles. The quality of pain comes to existentialize the lineage (*bee*) as a discrete, bounded fact, collapsing feeling and definition. This transforms pain from merely a contingent property of an embodied self, into a sign of the priority of the lineage as a containing ontological category. Such a move "ontologizes" convention, uniting material properties and habits of description. This "obviation" (Wagner 1978) of the pain extends the predicating power of the lineage. This serves to unify analysis and feeling, allowing pain to naturally index the lineage as the ontological grounds for thinking about the character and consequence of relatedness. Even where relations with other causal agencies like spirits and witches are postulated, these afflicting beings can only be motivated by the sufferers' membership in a category that could justify suffering.

Pain demarcates rupture in the fluid maintenance of these practices, pointing to the body as a "chronotope" (Bhaktin 1981), a summary of the chronological succession of relations seen to have produced the body and its abilities. Pain indicates all of this, while enforcing rupture from the basic abilities seen as innate to bodies and selves. This alienation from habit elicits definition, broadening the implication of pain to include immediate intersubjective relations with neighbors, kin, and the conceptual categories they token. This extension of pain is not perceived as limited to bodily sensation, but includes the full variety of incapacities, from underemployment to conjugal discord. As Giofani, a young Ndyuka gold miner said to me: "I have to bathe (seek healing), as I have problems with money" (*Mi musu wasi omdat mi abi toobi anga moni sani*). Suffering moves beyond pain to become an ambient quality of intersubjective experience, discord leading to illness and death. As this process of diagnosis unfolds, suffering is subjected to multiple interpretations. The extent to which these descriptions are held to fix the cause is the degree that a given therapeutic strategy is held to be effective.

Da Sabun's Calling

One of the works of pain is to demonstrate that relations with spirits and gods are rarely voluntary. Spirits impose upon humans, imprinting their hosts with their presence. Their invisibility presses in. Present or absent, it is all the same: spirits colonize every corner of their hosts' lives. Spirits predicate what it means to be related, adding an additional, hidden motive force; moving a

SPIRITS AND PAIN IN THE MAKING OF NDYUKA POLITICS

person's actions into new realms of narrative qualification. No longer do simple stories about desire or enmity suffice. Spirits call their human hosts, inflicting suffering to enforce compliance. These stories are never simple. They unfold, building towards sure resolution, but tentativeness and uncertainty remain basic to these narratives. According to mediums, pain and spirits share a phenomenology. Pain is clear; it registers on faces, in voices, and yet, defiantly, remains just beyond the comprehension of others. Pain, and its generalization in suffering, lingers indiscernibly, a floating reminder of the limits of bodies and the entanglement of destinies. This affinity between the evasiveness of spirits and pain brings them together. Spirits, in their imminent invisibility, like pain, are present, but somehow defy surety. Spirits create through this intangible proximity, weaving their agency into accident, transforming happenstance into necessity.

Da Sabun is a popular medium (*obiyaman*) in his late middle age. He has been a medium for the past twenty years. His story is typical, moving inexorably from initial accumulating crises to a resolution in full mediumship and symbiosis with his occupying spirit. The first signs of Da *Sabun's* relations with the spirit world were in the form of sickness. While working for the government in the forest, a tree fell on him, injuring his head. This left a still visible scar. Three years later his problems resumed. His house in the Paramaribo suburbs burnt down. Then, while working again in the interior, he broke his leg. This is when he began to understand that he had a lingering problem, but was still unsure as to its nature. Lastly, while on a gold dredging pontoon, he pulled a nerve while changing a battery. He was unable to work for thirty days. He returned to one of his three wives' villages, Moi Taki, sharing an island with his own native settlement. There they treated (*deesi*) him, washing him with herbal formulas, keeping him locked in his wife's home. He stayed like that for thirty days, but nothing happened.[1] Another man from his ancestral village was then seized by an idea. He went out to the forest and gathered some leaves that he knew. He washed himself with the leaves while sitting on a stool and had Da Sako do the same. It was then that the spirit came. It was an Ampuku (forest) spirit, and he came with full force, stamping (*bate*) the ground and crying (*bali*) his name. The spirit took responsibility for everything that had previously befallen Da Sabun. He had been searching for a mouth through which to speak. Da Sabun's own ancestors had predicted this, and so, after lying dormant, the spirit

---

1   Three and its multiple are an important ritual number signifying ritual work and its fulfillment.

tried to claim his proper place, his power taking shape through misfortune.[2] Da Asaigoontapu (Father he is enough for the world) had announced himself. Other obiyaman prepared the stool (*bangi*) where he would sit, and made him a shrine table (*obiya tafaa*) to keep his offerings and medicines. This formalized their relationship, allowing Da Asaigoontapu to consult with clients through Da Sabun, though he did not start doing so regularly until about five or six years after Da Asaigoontapu presence was confirmed by the village authorities (*lanti*).

As we can see from this narrative, Da Sabun's mediumship was informed by a slowly accumulating attentiveness to his interdependency with Da Asaigoontapu. Wrapped up in his own being was another, who expressed his claims obliquely, sowing signs of his presence through chronic ill luck and affliction. Pain, whether of a direct physical nature or through financial strain and loss, divulged the spirit's presence. Once it became manifest that Da Sabun was not in control, that his body, his life were not his own, resolution became possible. This dawning awareness of limits allowed Da Sabun to remake himself as a hybrid of human and extra-human. He was simultaneously his own person and the aims and desires of this other being, whose control and authority redefined him. Da Sabun's "intersubjective spacetime" (Munn 1992) became explicitly constrained. No longer was he the support for his large family of three wives and children. This restriction on his own capability served to infuse his body with the mediating capacity that paradoxically expanded his field of influence through the spirit's penetrating, encompassing power. While his body was present, the expansive consciousness of the spirit enabled the corporeal Da Sabun to transmit reality as it really is. Da Asaigoontapu's intervention reinvented Da Sabun's dispositions, his intentions, and his life. Once Da Asaigoontapu was seated and settled he promised to support Da Sabun, attending to his financial needs through his healing powers. Da Sabun became solely a conduit for Da Asaigoontapu's superior capacities to know and to act. From that moment on, Da Sabun began to ply his trade as a consulting healer, the "horse" (*asi*) of his tutelary spirit. Now Da Sabun consults from his shrine in a neighborhood immediately outside of Paramaribo. He does a thriving business. His clientele, while predominately Ndyuka, is diverse, consisting of Creoles, Guyanese, Chinese, and others. On a regular consulting day he will see

---

2 *"Da a man go da a broko uwiri san a sabi, da a masi poti ini wan krabasi. Te u go meke a man sidon tapu wan bangi, da wi wasi a man, da den man pot mi tapu wan bangi da den was mi. Baka den be wasi, da a winti kon bari. Da a man bari, da a bate* (stamp his feet), *da a man teri eng nen, taki mi na so wan sma. Na wan Ampuku. Ala den san be psa na mi be du den sani. Dati bigi wan be go suku eng mofu, den bigi sma fu mi be suku eng mofu a fesi. Taki di a tan te a doo na antal yari, di a fii, da a kon bar' now."*

SPIRITS AND PAIN IN THE MAKING OF NDYUKA POLITICS 209

upwards of twenty people, spending between thirty minutes and an hour with each person or group. This popularity provides him relative affluence, sustaining his three wives, many children and grandchildren.

Da Sabun's story is routine and illustrates how suffering changes persons into hosts and the consequences of this transformation. Pain results from an inability to recognize the grounding relation with the spirit. The spirit is integral to its host's personhood and destiny. Despite this, such relations are difficult to discern. The necessity of this co-definition can only be made explicit through the undeniable authority of pain. This pain does not call attention to the discrete, irreducible humanity of the sufferer. Rather, the pain registers the enfolding intimacy of the relation with the spirit. The person is reframed, from an agent with relative volitional autonomy, to a dependency of an incorporeal actor possessed of contextually transcendent knowledge and ability. The role of medium reduces a person to a conduit of this greater capacity, into the material means allowing humans in their finitude to communicate with the invisible potency of the spirit world.

The ethical implications of this are important. A medium cannot be measured as a fallible human in a precise sense. Spirits, while transcendent in comparison to humans, are by no means unbounded in their powers. Spirits are imagined as another, but very human, order of being. They live in houses in their own native countries, speak their own languages, and have husbands, wives and children (Thoden Van Velzen 2004; Price 2008). The major difference is their immortality, invisibility and resulting superior facility to act. Da Asaigoontapu is an Ampuku, a forest spirit. Ampuku are the original inhabitants of Suriname's immense interior. They live in the wilds in particular species[3] of trees, in termite mounds or stones, where people frequently stumble across them. When someone burns an Ampuku's home while planting a garden, the Ampuku will take revenge by becoming a *kunu*—dedicating themselves to the destruction of the matrilineage. It can also happen that while a human is wandering in the bush that an Ampuku will chance to see them and become attracted and want to be part of their lives. Both of these are means to mediumship, each situation needing resolution through a clear spirit voice speaking through a human host.

As Martin Holbraad (2013) has observed for Cuban Ifa divination, Afro-Atlantic ritual systems pose a problem for how Anthropologists think about the philosophical and theological mainstays of transcendence and immanence. For my Ndyuka informants, this is not a problem of an abstract nature.

---

3   Most notably Kankantii and Nkatu.

Spirit imminence or transcendence is intrinsic to how spirits are able to act in the many efficacious ways that define them. Spirits are at once invisible and superhuman and intimate and knowable. This does not present a contradiction. Instead, this exemplifies Ndyuka sociality as implicit in all elements of the world. Spirits, rather than embodying the complex mysteries of incarnation and absence, actualize the extent of morally legible sociality across domains of village and bush, "nature" and "culture." As in the case of spirits and hosts, spirits are complex hybrids whose hybridity qualifies social relations in the creative ways necessary to produce the salient collectivities of Ndyuka society.

Pain, as I mentioned earlier, presents a similar paradox of transcendence and imminence in descriptions of how spirits are known to act. Pain, as that which is at once most personal and general, focuses the problem of interpretation, intentions and shared being. Da Asaigoontapu was the pain he caused in the same way he is a voice in Da Sabun's body. Speaking with pain makes the feeling of pain but another texture of the intentional totality of the spirit, the host, and the host's lineage. Each relation indexes the whole of which it is part. Pain, as that aspect of individual experience most revealing of humanity *qua* humanity, has a peculiar sort of scalar transcendence, allowing narratives to focus on different levels of causation and intersubjective participation. Pain is both limited and generic, individualizing experience while indexing different, nested collectivities'—the immediate family, the matrilineal sub-segment or the clan—moral and genetic accounts of obligation and con-substantiality. As Da Sabun's narrative demonstrates, this qualified transcendence accords with that of spirits. Pain as an individualized warning of failing to observe inherited prohibitions (*kina*) is different in how it enforces collective participation from pain as a sign of failure to appease a matrilineal avenging spirit (*kunu*). Spirits provoke pain as a sign of their intentional agency, relieving it when their presence is recognized. Spirits are not reducible to pain, but pain is the condition of presence most insistently indexing spirit existence and offering it as a cause.

Pain occupies an intermediate position. Pain, as a state, is necessary as what is most in need of interpretation. Pain insists on description, beseeching intervention. To effectively intervene requires that the pain be a decipherable sign. For my Ndyuka collaborators, intentional agency is the grounds for this legibility. That pain is rooted in relationships with other beings is a basic claim. Pain thus represents both an epistemological and moral problem. To recognize pain as being of a particular kind is to say that you can know how symptoms entail causes. To do so is to make claims about what enables such connections. The authority to assert continuity between a pain and its cause, while seemingly practical, is bound to the moral authority to know accurately. An obiyaman

SPIRITS AND PAIN IN THE MAKING OF NDYUKA POLITICS

is accurate to the degree that their moral authority ultimately rests in the re-velatory power of their spirit. This braiding of knowledge, cause and effect, enables the exterior perspectives a given kin group requires to substantiate its authoritative existence.

Da Sabun's story removes his motives from consideration. The productive value of his entire life was called into question by his inability to recognize the spirit's presence in defining his existence. Pain, occurring at the inter-section of his body and his productive endeavors, undercut his sense of self-directedness. The more he strove to accomplish what was obligatory for his own and his family's flourishing, the more he suffered from physical and fi-nancial catastrophe. It was only when, retreating to his wife's native village,[4] someone from the neighboring *bee*, empowered by their own spirit, was able to address his problems for what they were. Da *Sabun's* narrative frames the many ways he was defined by and yet unaware of the spirit's hold on him. It was only by ending up in a site where unambiguously authoritative knowledge could be said to reside that the conditions were established for this relationship to be explained. The man whose spirit revealed this to him was ideally situated to disclose this knowledge, being a member of the same matrilineage, but not matrilineal sub-segment. This position placed him in human terms in a similar place to his own spirit—linked to his matrilineage through inherited ritual expertise. Da Sabun is, at least in his telling, relieved from signaling the motives of anyone other than his *bee* and his spirit. He is truly a medium, a node in a much larger, intergenerational coordination of the lineage with the spirits' power. Da Sabun, as a fully moral person, is distinct in demonstrating this fact, passively enacting the ancestral interests predicating the present and conditioning the future. He becomes the means of expressing the lineage by simultaneously standing within and outside it. His body and his words become distinct, the voice of the spirit protecting the body, and by extension the entire lineage, from the corrosive vengeance transfused by the blood/substance of the matriline. Pain enables all of this, facilitating the positive form of both the spirit and the lineage. More im-portantly, the pain provides a means of reflection for framing the spirit as a prerequisite. The pain is evidence which accounts for the spirit, revealing the hidden influences disturbing the smooth flow of the everyday. This dis-closure, however, is also a reflection upon that flow. In accounting for the snags, the counterintuitive currents, Da Sabun produces spirit presence as

---

4 Mooitaki, an up-river (*opo se*) Misidyan village is just above Futupasi, the location of the major cataract on the Tapanahony.

a meditation upon the trials of subsistence, the pain of the quotidian. The spirit emerges from this as both a discernable entity and a reason. The pain is justified and the moral coherence of Da Sabun's life restored by active relinquishment of the proposition of his independence from these inherited constraints. In recognizing that, rather than being constraints, these are in fact the means of his personal consequence, Da Sabun transforms and is transformed by these limits.

Da Sabun's story expresses the integrality of pain, lineage and spirits. The struggles of life are experienced as inevitable interruptions of a self that assumes its sufficiency. Da Sabun is called back to the grounds of his existence. This process takes place when pain begins to inhabit the voices of those around the sufferer. This intersection of sensation and language is critical, the feeling rhetorically translated into an imperative. Pain, as an imperative, compels multiple acknowledgments, commanding assent from the sufferer and their kin. This is not seen as unjustified, not a cruel demand upon another's volition. Instead, compelling pain is a sign of election, the transformative fact that allows a new synthesis of human and spirit. Since it is precisely this melding of worlds that allows humans the knowledge that makes the world comprehensible, that provide certainty and healing, such a relinquishing is seen as a necessary good. Spirits then are not merely pain. They are also knowledge and its potential.

Invoking the Invisible Dead

Spirits are a particular kind of constituting and ratifying otherness. Spirit otherness to the human world acts to frame the appeal of the unknown. One description of forest spirits is that they are almost identical to humans but with their noses twisted to the side. This kind of dissonant similarity acts to open and remodel the strangeness of more human others—even one's closest kin—reshaping them as simultaneously comprehensible and bizarre. Spirits define humanity in ways questioning and testing the boundaries of humanness. Voice plays a key role in demarcating this difference, making it register in the commonplaces of daily life. Death is the major event that transforms a person from a bounded material body to a circumference of evidential signs without a visible center. Death is the most socially impactful pain, reverberating to signal the integrality of the categories of relation binding people together in mutual grief. Despite the spectral insecurity this creates, this uncertainty is not confined to the dead or other spirits. In their dissembling faces the living equally radiate an aura of inscrutability. Pain, for all its adamancy,

SPIRITS AND PAIN IN THE MAKING OF NDYUKA POLITICS

participates in this complex of certainty and doubt as both the feeling of loss and the experience of death. Making these feelings make sense is the prime goal of the preponderance of Ndyuka political-ritual activity, seeking to clarify pain, its cause and its consequences through fluid, embracing rhetoric and collective labor.

Johana, a woman in her mid-thirties resides in one of the many predominantly Maroon neighborhoods ringing Paramaribo. She is a medium for Da Tyoka, her classificatory brother. Thieves shot and killed him during the course of a burglary at his house in an adjacent settlement while stealing his sizable savings. Ba Tyoka had been a successful gold miner and entrepreneur acquiring a considerable reputation as a wealthy man (*guduman*). As the result of his tragic death, he came back as a *koosama*, a ghostly victim of untimely death. The circumstances of his "ugly death" (*takuu dede*) made this inevitable. Unable to achieve the solace of old age and extensive progeny, he had returned to receive emotional acknowledgment and help defend the *bee* against additional misfortune, transformed into a spirit of the family (*A be toon winti kaba ini a famii*). Unfortunately, when Ba Tyoka was initially recognized and given a shrine (*poti a bangi*), it had been performed incorrectly.[5] This had angered the spirit and he had seeded misfortune until his displeasure was recognized and a new shrine installed in Johana's home.

The installation ritual shows how ritual practices use talk about pain to reveal spirit presence, employing rhetoric and the material of the shrine to make Da Tyoka and his kinship incontestably real. Through the synchronous invisibility of speech and the spirit, the spirit becomes present through the medium's discourse. After carefully disassembling the previous shrine and building a wholly new one in the same location in Johana's son's room, the time came to summon the spirit. At that point the preparations had been in process for at least two hours; Da Sabun, the obiyaman discussed above, had methodically pried apart and reconstructed the shrine's paraphernalia of flags and bound bottles while giving a running commentary to my field assistant John and I about the purpose of each step. Moving from the basic materials of the shrine, the time came to test these preparations and make the spirit manifest. This would insure that the work had been done correctly so that the new shrine would properly assuage Da Tyoka's anger.

---

5   This was for two reasons: 1) the man who prepared the shrine was a member of the same matrilineage and you cannot "prepare your own things" (*seeka yu eigi sani*) 2) the shrine had been prepared with the paraphernalia of another class of spirits.

214   STRANGE

In what follows, I will carefully examine the order of this dialogic invocation. While the material preparations are integral to the Da Tyoka's final animation, in what follows I will focus on how rhetoric in interaction coordinates ontological facts about spirits to generate and project their presence and power. This will demonstrate how language weaves talk into a fertile context for spirit appearance, while using their lingering invisibility to guarantee the knowledge produced.

Da Sabun summoned Johana and her aunt into the shrine room and invited them to take their places. Da Sabun addressed John formally, initiating the backchannel affirmations that distinguish Ndyuka formal oratory from everyday speech. First, John was accorded respect as a mature man (*mannengee*) and then Da Sabun acknowledged the older woman, stating that this was Johana's aunt who, while not her mother, "brought her into the world" (*ne'eng tyai a uman ye ya kon a goontapu*), had cared for her (*ma a tia ne'eng e solugu*). Then Da Sabun continued:

1. Da Sako:	Da na leti enke fa a de a wi libi sama a ini busi kondee.	This is right, like how it is there for us (i.e. how it is done), the living, in the forest (i.e. in the Ndyuka homeland).
2. John:	A so a de baa da.	That is how it is, Brother Father.
3. DS:	Ma yu a si tide a winti fu a famii.	But you will see the spirit of the family today.
4. J:	Na so Baa Papa.	That's so, Brother Father.
5. DS:	Ma yu á si da wi kon poti eng a bangi. A be wasi kaba, a be toon winti kaba a ini a famii.	But you have seen how we have given him a stool. It has been washed; he has already become a spirit.
6. J:	Na so tuu ye	It's true, listen.
7. DS:	Ma di á be toon winti kaba wan pikin buya, wan pikin fanya kon ne'eng.	But when he had already become a spirit, there was a little trouble; he encountered a slight difficulty.
8. J:	Na leti so baa.	That's exactly right, Brother.

SPIRITS AND PAIN IN THE MAKING OF NDYUKA POLITICS   215

9. DS:	En sani á be waka moi.	His affairs (literally "thing") did not go well.
10. J:	Na so baa.	That's how it is.
11. DS:	Da tide na a dei.	Then today is the day.
12. J:	Ya.	Yes.
13. DS:	Ne'en si u kon ne'eng baka fu kon poti wan ana gi eng baka. Ná anga nen fu mi, ma anga nen fu den winti.	It is him who sees us come after him to extend a helping hand. Not in my name, but in the name of the spirits.
14. J:	Na so tuu baa.	That is true, Brother.
15. DS	Bika da Asaimundu be e yeepi a mundu kaba.	Because Da Asaigoontapu (Da Sabun's tutelary spirit) has already been helping the world.
16. J:	Na so tuu ye.	That is true, do you hear?
17. DS:	We da ne'en a taa winti seefi abi wan fanowdu.	Then it is the other spirit who needs his (Da Asaigoontapu's) help.
18. J:	Na so baa da.	That is so, Brother Father.
19. DS:	A e yeepi goontapu di a kon bali.	He assists the world by coming to speak (literally yell).
20. J:	Na leti so.	That is right.
21: DS:	Da ne'eng i si wi kon poti eng a bangi ye. Bika da efu yu mu seeka baka gi eng, da yu á poi teke eng taki anga a gaandi wan di a be go a bangi. Yu o go kai eng.	Then it is him you see us coming to place on the stool, understand. Because, if you must prepare the stool again for him, then you cannot receive his words and those of the elders who have [already] been seated. You will call him (when you want to speak with the dead).
22: J:	Kwetikweti papa.	Certainty, Father.

(*cont.*)

23. DS:	(referring to the women)	Da yu a fu poti eng a bangi tu enke fa a twalufu anga a tin na dii be e wooko.	Then it is you who has to seat him as the Twelve (meaning the twelve Ndyuka clans) and the Thirteen (the total number of Ndyuka clans when the paramount chief's clan is included) do it.
24. J:		Na so a de Baa Da	That is how it is, Brother.
25. DS:		Da u begi eng anga ala lesipeki di wi o wooko anga eng, meke a kon a wi moi moi, da wi taki moi moi.	Then we pray to him with all due respect that we will work with him, make him come to us beautifully, that we shall speak with him pleasantly.
26. J:		Na so a de baa.	That's how it is, Brother Father.
27. DS:		Te a kai na a yuu da a kibii fu eng baka.	Until the hour arrives for him to again conceal himself.
28. J:		Na leti so baa	That's how it is, Brother.
29. DS:		Taki tide u kon poti eng a bangi.	That's how we speak with him.
30. J:		Ma yu a ye, baala yu a ye?	That's right, Brother. Do you here? Do you hear, Brother?
31. Johana and her Aunt:		Ai, u yee, yu seefi yu a ye?	Yes, we hear! And you, do you hear yourself?
32. DS:		Soo, Pa Tyoka luku ya wi kon poti yu a bangi ye, tide na a dei... u poti yu a bangi oo. A lanti, a twalufu, a tin na dii, poti yu a bangi. A lanti fu Saamaka, Matawai, Kupanamu, fu a hii Ndyuka liba te doo a den lebi	Today we have come to seat you on the stool. So, Father Tyoka look here we come to seat you on the stool, understand. Today is the day... We will seat you on the stooooool. The people (meaning the present assembly),

lebi ingii anga den weti weti bakaa. U Poti yu a bangi yeeeeeeee. Soo. Iya, papa Tyoka yu a si oo...da u kon poti yu a bangi. Fu di yu be kon a dei, u be kai yu, a tan langa wi anga yu be taki mofu mofu. Da di wi anga yu be taki, u be taki te a kai na a dei da wi o kon da wi meke wooko, da i si tide u kon meke wooko. Da di a wooko meke kaba enke fa u be taki. U tyai yu a baka kon poti a osu. Da wi kon begi yu gaantangi fu yu kon a wi so tyuwa, da u taki wan mofu makandii anga a famii da yu kibii fu yu baka ye. U begi so gaantangi anga lesipeki, ee meke u taki so kolo da i kibii fu yu baka ye. (They clap their hands, praying for him to come) Efu sani bun da wi taki makandii, efu sani á bun tu, da soi wi da wi wooko makandii ye. U begi so gaantangi. Iya!

the Twelve, the Thirteen, will seat you. The governments of the Saramaka, of the Matawai, of the Kwinti, of the entire Ndyuka territory as far as its borders with Amerindians' and White peoples' lands, we seat you on the stool, listeeeeeeeen. So. Yes, Father Tyoka you seeeeee, that we have come to seat you. It is for you the day has arrived, we have called you, stay with us for a while so we can talk, face to face. Then, when we have talked with you, until the day comes when we shall work. Then you see that today we have come to work. Then, when the work will finish as we have discussed. We bring you again to install you in the house. Then we come to say thanks that you have come to us, that we can speak together with the family that you protect. We thank you with all due respect, please talk with us clearly that you protect yourself, understand. If it is good, then we will speak together, if it isn't good, then reveal to us how we will work together. This is what we ask. Yes!

33. Tyoka:	(Crying)	Heeei... hnhn... ai yoo sweli gadu... hnhnhn.... ai oo da Anado, ai oo da Asamaya hnhnhnhnhnhnhn. ... Mi yonkuu yonkuu Tyoka oo Gadu! hnhnhnhnhnhn. ... wani mi á wani mi go hnhnhnhnhnh hn hn hn hn ooho ooho nnhmm nnhmm hnmm hmmmm. ... Den gaansama di sidon ya mi e gi wi odi!	Heeei... hnhn... yes, yoo (ideophone of response) God of oaths... hnhnhn... Father Anado, yeeees, Father Asamaya hnhnhnhnhnhnh... I'm young, young Tyokaaaaa, God! Hnhnhnhnhnhnhnh... wants, I don't want to go hnhnhnhnhnhnh hn hn hn hn ooho ooho nnhmmm nhmmm hmmm hmmmm... The elders who sit before me, I greet you!
34. Everyone:		Odi oooo	Greetings!
35. T:		Mi e bali odi mi bali odi, mi e bali odi baa.	I cry greetings! I yell greetings! I give greetings!
36. Everyone:		U dee oo, wi de.	We're here, yes, we are here.

The above interaction clearly demonstrates how metalanguage precipitates spirit and lineal presence to overcome the haunting pain of sudden death and its ramifications. This is done through the language used to sow indexical signs of the spirit's attentive proximity. The final success of this largely depends on the spirit's invisibility, his ability to stay in soft focus until born forth in voice. Initially (until line 30) Da Tyoka is not spoken of as present. The conversation is conducted as a dialog between Da Sabun and John for the benefit of Johana and her aunt. However, already from the commencement of the backchannel call and response of authoritative speech, Da Sabun begins playing with the pronominal indexes of identity, creating the denotative framework for the spirit's sudden, spectacular emergence. To initiate backchannel affirmations, John uses two respect markers, Ba, a generic for men of the same generation, and Da, reserved for older men—particularly one's father's age or older. Combining these honorifics increases respect, endowing the speaker's statements with greater authority. This attribution of respect is intensified by the formulaic affirmations of factuality that the responses represent. Within the basic structure of the dialogical form of ritual speech, we find implicit claims of epistemic authority.

This virtue is not confined to the conventions of honor surrounding age. Such discursive conventions exhibit how voices can iconize the correct transmission of knowledge. This plays on a fundamental ambivalence in Ndyuka ideas about age and representation. While this is tied to significant understandings about the origins of gerontocratic authority, this heightening of respect with increasing (and in some sense contradictory) honorifics implies spirit presence while not declaring it. This underdetermination supports the premise that all reliable knowledge is actually transmitted from the spirit world, either through ancestors or non-human spirits. Such standard affirmatives fix the speaker as a particular kind of knower, someone whose age and experience qualifies them to speak. This authoritative speech is not an expression of self-mastery. In keeping with Ndyuka notions of influence, it displaces agency, positioning the speaker as a mediator, a membrane through which the invisible sources of true knowledge pass themselves. That this is so is declared in Da Sabun's statement that "you will see the spirit of the family today" in line 3. This implies that Da Sabun has the knowledge to make Da Tyoka appear, while foreshadowing that appearance and implying that the spirit is already near. Before the spirit can appear, however, Da Sabun must establish that the conditions are appropriate for his apparition. To constitute the rectitude of the context, Da Sabun must explain who the women are, specifying the relation of nurture between Johana and her aunt. These identities are from the perspective of the deceased, emphasizing his presence while making no positive claims about it. Further, in making these statements before John, Da Sabun affirms him as an audience who can himself witness the spirit's witnessing as a member of another matriclan, and as an adult male with political rights.

As the dialog progresses, Da Sabun includes more and more information, shifting perspectives, invoking not only the deceased but Da Asaigoontapu, his own possessing spirit. In doing so, he harnesses an essential ambiguity about his role as a speaker. Invoking Da Asaigoontapu raises questions about his co-presence, signaling the uncertain boundary separating Da Sabun's statements from those of his spirit. This is necessary, as is Da Asaigoontapu's awareness that the shrine has been constructed and the séance convened. Tacking between first person and third person statements accentuates and elides an ontological gap, implying both Da Asaigoontapu's power and proximity. Power, in that he can be said to be listening without revealing himself, and proximity, by showing that this awareness transcends basic restrictions of the apparent physical world. Power is this ability to be felt, to rise up from nowhere and fundamentally alter the material conditions of life. This marks the spirit's qualified omniscience and omnipotence, revealed not by absolute control but through relatively greater degrees of efficacious intervention compared to human beings. This Da Sabun's confirms when he says: "It is him who sees us come after him to extend a helping hand. Not in my name, but in the name of the spirits"(line 13). This line collapses Da Sabun's authority into that of Da Asaigoontapu, while confirming that Da Tyoka is waiting and will accept the intervention because it is Da Asaigoontapu who is guaranteeing the work. Such a play underscores the "indeterminacy of participant roles" (Irvine 1996), heightening the stakes while obscuring responsibility for who speaks and with what consequences.

An important part of what is established over the course of the dialog, first between John and Da Sabun, and then Da Sabun and Da Tyoka, is that those present are capable of recognizing the ritual protocol followed as correct. Human relations must also be politically specified, making sure that the connections between people substantiate claims to spirit knowledge. Da Sabun, Da Tyoka's patrilineal classificatory brother, shares familial substance and is known to the deceased as one who can be addressed by a designation of affiliation. Later, after Da Tyoka manifests in Johana's body, Da Sabun further specified the degree of relation between each person present and the ghost to underline the legitimacy of the rite.

This is demonstrated when Da Sabun redirects talk from particular spirits (Da Tyoka, Da Asaigoontapu) to the most generic categories of political identity undergirding ritual discourse. Equivalence between the bedroom shrine and the village where such rites are supposed to be performed is asserted in line 1 by Da Sabun saying that what is to be done will be done right, the same as it is done in "the forest" (*busikondee*), the Ndyuka homeland. As he develops this parallel further, Da Sabun amplifies this association, shifting from a general statement of equivalence to, in line 23, directly addressing the women present as the authors of the correct installation. Da Sabun here invokes the twelve clans comprising the Ndyuka "nation," and its completion by including the Paramount chief's (*gaanman*) clan (*Otoo*), which is held to ratify Ndyuka as a political unit. This is yet another equivalence between the proper authority allowing reference to the Ndyuka as a homogenous ethnic-political unit (*nasi, sama*), and to those present as legitimate tokens of that whole. This is important in that it imbues the women with the qualities of discerning knowledge and mediating familial substance to effectively fulfill their responsibility as though a village assembly (*kuutu*) of senior persons had been held. Such an assembly would be the most accurate evaluator of truth and propriety. By addressing them as such an assembly, Da Sabun presents those present as a quorum who can serve as trustworthy evaluating witnesses (*lanti*) to the dead.

When the spirit does arrive, Da Sabun immediately provides kin labels for those present (with the careful omission of myself) from the mutual perspectives of the dead and the living. Da Sabun is described as a patrilateral brother (*tu baala pikin*), Johana as a classificatory matrilineal sister. John, a member of another matriclan, is described as a "child of Ndyuka" (*Ndyuka pikin*). A basic concern of Ndyuka kinship is isolating the correct, reciprocal kinship terminology between people. The deixis of kinship terminology produces an initial warp that calls crucial issues of seniority and authority into question. When people meet, or in discussions about others, these issues must be settled as soon as possible. After Da Tyoka "possesses" Johana, one of the first things Da Sabun explains to him is the kind of relatedness connecting them, saying "the father sitting here, when he was alive he was my little brother because we are the children of two brothers" (*A papa di dede ya... A ini a ten fu libi ten fu en a be de mi pikin baala... da na tu baala meke wi*). This contextualizing mirrors the initial explanation of the relationship of care and generation between Johana and her aunt. In making such connections, it becomes possible to define what relations are supposed to obtain between relatives. This need to affix designations, however, indexes a certain conceptual indeterminacy, a suggestion that, just as in the case of the spirit, positive discursive work must be done to maintain these descriptions as accurate. The ambiguity of relations is paralleled by the indistinctness of the spirit's other than linguistic proximity. In the same ways that the appropriate terms of classification are made clear, a moral ontology is established for the terms of kinship. It is because of how they are related that these specific persons must be in attendance; it is right for Da Tyoka to speak through Johana to her aunt, John and Da Sabun. Such ascriptions underline the quality of their commensality, representing the women's ministrations as ethically proper care. Such talk emplaces the spirit as a particular person emerging from a network of relations, each with its situated obligations. The consequence of these relations turns on the way kinship categories intersect with the interpretation of appropriate ethical actions. Stipulations governing expectations about moral practice inflect what knowledge can be effectively produced through spirit speech.

As Bowker and Star (1999) remind us, much of what makes for classificatory order is invisible to us. The invisible matrix of our categorical scaffolding is one of the most interesting and persistent problems in the anthropological literature (Durkheim and Mauss 1963, Lévi-Strauss 1966). I want to suggest that, as with pain, spirits are ontologically implicated in certain schemas of classification. In epistemic regimes like that of Ndyuka mediums, there is an intimate connection between the self-evident existence of the dominant categorical abstractions of kinship and spirit presence. Dissolving any predisposed distinction between formal structure and pragmatic relations, we have instead an account of the co-determination of positions of moral value. A sister (*sisa*) is so by the coordination of multiple forms of affect and action in relation to the meaning of kinship. To speak coherently about the meaning of the label brother is more than just to occupy a place within a structure of related terms. It is an expression of certain definitional moral expectations that may or may not be fulfilled. As the Ndyuka saying goes, "Life makes family" (*Na libi meke famii*). This value, however, is not *a priori* fixed. These values emerge from the complex interplay of interaction and its political evaluation. These evaluations are not separate from the content of another's intentions. These are not transparent, and can only be produced definitely by modes of epistemic authority emphasizing the existential priority to a system of relations.

The ethical entailments of this ambiguity animate a variety of adjacent ontological principles. Most importantly, they establish spirits as beings who can make claims about the content of relations, adjusting expectation to the hidden reality of others' motives. Conversely, these ambiguities help guarantee spirit presence, excavating a foundation of uncertainty that is embedded in the forms of talk used to enact spirits and kinship. In lines 1 through 30 of the above dialog, the spirit is implied to be present as a listener while importantly accentuating the identities of the living as a justification for Da Tyoka's continued presence on earth. This presence is produced at two levels: first in the scope of address which moves steadily to coax the figure of the spirit from the ground of the audience seated in front of the shrine; secondly, in the shift from third to first person at the moment of possession itself. This rhetorical foregrounding of Da Tyoka's imminent appearance becomes axiomatic only when he begins to speak through Johana's mouth. The dialog between John and Da Sabun is for an audience, one of whom will make Da Tyoka co-present, the other who will act as a witness to affirm his testimony. Each piece of the dialog assembles some pragmatic element necessary for Da Tyoka's manifestation, starting with the implication that he has been co-present all along because these are his kin.

The continual inter-indexing of substantial relatedness and adequate ritual performance accentuates the social conditions for producing truth in collectively agreed upon statements. This, in turn, foregrounds the spirits as necessarily present. In an important respect, Ndyuka ritual practice as I observed it emphasizes truth as co-presence. Truth here, as is apparent in the technique of backchannel responses, entails acknowledgement. This affirmation signals a generative logic of similarity and difference, proximity and distance, representing truth as consensus between times and places. This consensus is more than accord between the living—though such accord is treated as significant

SPIRITS AND PAIN IN THE MAKING OF NDYUKA POLITICS   223

evidence for the presence of the ancestors and other spirits. For speech to be
authoritative it must channel the ancestors, implicating the speaker and their
message as continuous with ancestral authority. This is not conceived of in
terms of the logic of representation. A speaker is held to speak as their lineage, making the cumulative authority of the dead substantially apparent in
their body, through the accuracy of the claims made. This isomorphism is not
automatic. It must be achieved through the sufficient arrangement of indexes
into the cumulating iconicity of the speaker. This spatio-temporal-substantial
co-presence is the ideal of rhetorical performance, the *sine qua non* of truth.
The more that oratory can be invested with signs of mediation, the more likely
the orator is speaking accurately (cf. Keane 1997 on Anakalanganese oratory).
Presence is the effect of this ontological logic making speech and identity continuous with the lineage.

It is this kind of presence that Da Sabun's authoritative speech tries to make
clear. In weaving together the semiotic infrastructure affording the rectitude
of speech, each statement is compelled to be a claim and its confirmation.
Within the pragmatics of call and response, a mirroring is achieved between
assertion and reality. From this internal fulfillment, the spirit's voice is culti-
vated, Da Sabun playing off of ambiguities of reference until the figure of the
spirit emerges from its dilogical ground. This process is best displayed in lines
25–31. Here we see Da Sabun employ the third person (*a* or *en*) in illocutionary speech, in an act that is simultaneously invocation and instruction. While
Da Tyoka has been the subject of the whole conversation, at this moment Da
Sabun moves from describing of who Da Tyoka is and what he wants, to actively addressing him. This transition has the force of direct address. While the
previous statements have all construed Da Tyoka as nearby, insinuating that he
can overhear to freely affirm or deny, at this moment Da Sabun launches into
a formal address insisting on a response. No longer does Da Tyoka flit referen-
tially in and out of John and Da Sabun's formal dialog, but jumps, with the full
emotion of his un-assuaged pain, to life.

The moment when Da Tyoka verbally appears demarcates a "transduction"
(Keane 2013) between degrees of presence. Moving from implication to instantiation, Da Tyoka emerges as a voice clothed in the emotions of his death.
As discussed earlier, death is held to modify the deceased—particularly in
cases of tragic or unjust death. Their manner of death becomes paradigmatic
to the character of their voice, a resonating event validating the continued
strength with which the dead speak. But as Da Sabun's statement in line 5
that Da Tyoka has become a spirit indicates, he has already undergone an
essential transformation. This metamorphosis is at two levels, that of physical death and burial which decomposes the body into its related, animating

parts, and the ritual recognition of the spirit as a valid and authoritative voice through ritual installation. Ritual installation recomposes the spirit as an aggregate of objects and actions, a punctuated event appearance and the ritual objects that point to it. While this reduces Da Tyoka to the conditions of his death, it also newly animates him, making his voice rather than his body the primary sign of his presence. This reconfigures the evidence as it affords interpretation about the nature of his co-presence. Da Tyoka's presence is now primarily induced from verbal iconization, his mastery of the metalanguage of pain and its resolution, not deduced from the body that animates his appearance.

Rather than the ideal relation that is supposed to pertain between a living speaker and their lineage for which they speak, possession reverses the connection between voice and body. In councils, as in most formal rhetorical performances, the lineage, in the form of the corporate ancestors who are notionally the source of correct speech, has to be read from the body of the speaker. Positioning the speaker within the categorical logic of kin relations accomplishes this identification. That this has been achieved is registered by the responses of the other council members. For the dead to speak, however, their identity has to be inferred from the correct presentation of iconic properties in speech, particularly the pain of death that separates them from the living and justifies their return. This is shown in Da Tyoka's wailing appearance, where the wail iconizes the pain of dying: "I'm young, young Tyokaaaaa, God! Hnhnhnhnhnhnhnh... want, I don't want to go hnhnhnhnhnhnh (line 33)." Instead of a speaker ventriloquizing the lineage by virtue of the physical matrix composed by its members, the lineage allows the spirit to emerge as a vocal projection of its collective being. That spirits are who they say they are is dependent upon who is present to witness and confirm the spirit's performance of the defining icons of their identity—as a particular spirit and a member of a class of spirits. If the dead person speaks through the wrong mouth, or uses the wrong cues to signal their presence as a particular person, the ghost is liable to be dismissed through exorcism.

This, when taken with how the structure of dialog and the play of reference involves and then invokes the spirit, amply demonstrates the force of pain in grounding and actualizing spirit and lineal presence. The metalanguage of ritual enables this tightening spiral of implication to become positively embodied in voice to resolve pain. Beyond this, it is the spirit's death that permits the authoritativeness of any of these forms of speech. The accumulating discursive implication produced by statements about the spirit and those present ignites in the moment of possession. The realization of the spirit suddenly accomplishes the political power of language to make reality appear.

Ndyuka language ideologies stressing the essential continuity of reference, denotation and objectification support this ontologization of spirit presence. This causal identification of words and things is also a description of the process of generation and event. From within the context of designation, the ontological coherency of the world as an assemblage of categories emerges. As authoritative speech is crafted from the consensus of councils of witnesses, so words are imbued with their authority by the mutual recognition of a name by a speaker and the object spoken about. When Da Sabun invokes Da Tyoka he is representing both Da Tyoka as an actor and the possibility of his action. While Ndyuka do not attribute agency to everything, invoking something compels it through the direct relation of nouns as names to the actions denoted as the essence of things; Da Tyoka is not only a ghost: he is the specific death that results from others' destructive greed. His death is a moral state, a message interpellating his kin as a collectivity and a field of action where he can express the pain of his death and justify the horrible consequences he will reap on the guilty.

In this ideological framing, language, or, more accurately, talk, has many of the same qualities as spirits. It is invisible but efficacious. In Ndyuka, this efficacy is called *kakiti* or *makiti* (from the Dutch *kracht* and *macht*, meaning force and power). It is common to hear people say to spirits that they will accomplish something "with your power" (*anga i kakiti*).[6] *Kakiti*, as with the English word power, invokes a sense of efficacious influence and personal capability. Language is held to have the same sort of influence—the power bound up into both the illocutionary and perlocutionary potential of locutionary speech acts. Language, like spirits and the influence they are said to embody, is generative, creating the conditions of relations between otherwise disconnected things. One Ndyuka obiyaman explained to me that, in reality, it is only the force of words that cause events to happen. He said this was equally true of everyday Ndyuka and the various spirit languages, both of which he related to the power of Sanskrit mantras used in Hindu ritual. While his position—that all power is actually verbal and not in the materials used to make things like *obiya*— is controversial, it provides insight into the power of naming in speech as a "grounding conceptualization for knowledge" (Strathern 1992: 194). Language, in its transitivity between subjects and objects, relates and renders, imbricating practices and categories, differentially planting agency "effects" through the ontological descriptions it provides.

---

6 Among younger people this can also be used as an affirmative means of saying goodbye, a little like saying "good luck."

Another way to think about this relation is to consider the limited forms of Ndyuka perpetual kinship. A child and all their siblings can be referred to by the name of the father. This situated corporate group is shallow, only existing in relation to the inseminating father and not transmissible to the children's children. Such a group and the onomastics associated with it demonstrate the strong linkages that pertain between practices of naming and generation. The children are metonymically part of the father. This however, is generally only true in relation to an elicitation by a senior person. By responding to the name of the father, each person performs an identity continuous with the initial act of conception. This seems to indicate, that, while different, in moments of formal address, shared paternity makes all siblings equivalent to each other and the father. The father is present in his name and in the effects of his actions (his children). Similarly, it is the name of the dead as a index of kinship that enables ghosts to return, linking each instance of pain and its voicing to the deceased personage to mark the echoing misfortune of living as death that is the fate of *koosama*,[7] Ghost possession is a complex performance of the metalanguage of pain as a relationship, of the extent to which healing is a political exercise of bearing that pain so as to recognize it as a shared property of all those who are summoned by the tragedy of untimely death.

Pain and the Diagnosis of the Political

Pain comes in genres. Rather than being a simple, forthright experience, how pain produces tentative, doubting awareness has important consequences. A good friend of mine, Da Sudati, an Ndyuka man in his seventies, lost his voice. He was consternated about this, as was his family. There was an open question as to the cause. While I took him and his wife to the hospital and he was diagnosed hesitantly with cancer, he and his family began to settle on a verdict of witchcraft. He was a *basiya* (a traditional title/political role combining oratory, surveillance and enforcement) in his native village, and it was suspected that others who were jealous of his position where bewitching him, depriving him of the powers of speech necessary for the work. A *basiya* is defined by his voice. The Basiya calls people to major ritual/political occasions like funerals and councils (*kuutu*). They provide the ritual backchannel affirmations that allow the framing of speech as formal and consequential. *Basiya*

---

7 The noises that accompany the spirits appearance represent basic problems with mediating appearance.

SPIRITS AND PAIN IN THE MAKING OF NDYUKA POLITICS

act as mediators for the living while embodying the binding authority of the dead for which the strength and clarity of their voices plays a defining role. The lingering loss of this most characteristic element of his capacity to fill this role was crushing to him. The specificity of the condition, its compromising of rudimentary ability, suggested such a reading. To return to the question Evans-Pritchard (1938) made classic: why him? And why like this? The combinatorial properties of the absence, the clarity of the connection between authority, its iconization in the voice, and the concurrent loss of both, seemed to compel this reading as jealous witchcraft (*wisi*) by unknown assailants from his matrilineage (*bee*).

Despite the clarity of this reading, one supported by the majority of his children and grandchildren, there were other opinions. By the time I became involved, Da Sudati had been sick for many months and had undertaken some costly healing sessions. That these had not produced unambiguous improvements did not faze him. Obiya, as a means of healing, is semiotically dense to the degree that its benefits can be multiple and underdetermined. He continued to hunt for the cause. In accordance with this, we went to visit his younger sisters' son at his obiya kampu (shrine) south of the city. His nephew, Ba Frans, was insistent that he was not a victim of witchcraft. At the time, Da Sudati's daughters by his third wife were both living more or less permanently at Ba Frans' healing center. One of them had become pregnant by her classificatory brother. This is considered incestuous and *kina* (interdicted). After an arduous labor, she gave birth to a child who soon died. This loss hung over the family, but was seen as unmistakable evidence of a clear disregard for incest prohibitions. This, however, was not Da Sudati's problem. He was rather inflicted by *fiofio*.

Fiofio names a complex agent emergent from Ndyuka linguistic ideology. Most Ndyuka I worked with hold speech to clearly entrain its referents. For my Ndyuka collaborators, language obviates theorization. Description maintains a translucent relation to reference/denotation. Language exists to describe things. Despite this, language is problematic in two senses. First, this direct relation with the world enchains its objects. Once when I mispronounced the name of the village of Saneki as Sneki (snake), my friend Aki whisperingly chastised me, warning me that I would call snakes. Language, of course, does more than frame truth statements, as ordinary language philosophy and linguistic anthropology have well demonstrated (Austin 1962, Bloch 1975, Tambiah 1981). Of particular consequence is the ambiguity of language in expressing sentiment. According to many Ndyuka, language both instantiates emotional states and conceals true motives. Words may directly denote the reality of things, but do not necessarily encode the reality of thoughts. This contradiction is productive and goes a long way to explain why pain must index relatedness. When words are seen as unambiguously expressing emotion, particularly anger, the coalescence of words and emotion are objectified as a *fiofio* spirit. The anger of the words hypostatizes the sentiment. Importantly, this is not in every instance, but only where a conflict remains unresolved. Unless the consequences of such conflicts are assuaged, the anger itself, as expressed in words, runs the risk of metamorphosing, becoming an agent of vengeance defined by the conceiving emotion. As a number of my Ndyuka friends have said, "talk brings danger" (*a mofu taki tyai ogii*). It is the facticity of the denotative quality of words that impedes their ability to adequately represent thoughts, held to be unknowable by other humans. When the expression of emotion becomes incontestable, it is reified into a being that condenses the tone of the relationship from which the words and feelings emerge. Emotions coalesce from interaction, providing, along with the categories of relation, the means of defining the essential moral qualities of the people related.

This principle of emergence was what Ba Frans was referring to when he, while possessed by his spirit, Da Kotombli, asserted that Da Sudati was afflicted by *fiofio*. His daughter's incestuous relations with her classificatory brother, and her subsequent possession by a demon (*bakuu*), where clear signs of a storm of ruptured interdictions, strained interactions and antisocial sentiments. These had become charged to the point where they had transformed into a living fury, wreaking havoc on the collective health of the family, particularly Da Sudati, the senior progenitor of a large group of children and grandchildren.

Da Sudati on the other hand, was not willing to accept this diagnosis. He scoffed at the séance at which this was revealed. The consultation ended with Da Kotombli challenging him with rapid-fire Kumanti. Kumanti, an emblematically masculine esoteric spirit language, is used to provoke, bringing people into agonistic performances of volatile knowledge. Da Sudati refused to take up this challenge. He walked away laughing nervously, waiving his hand dismissively at Da Kotombli's incitements. In a choked whisper, Da Sudati told me, despite having a reputation for being a master storyteller and expert singer, that since he had lost his voice he could no longer engage in such activities. Da Sudati rejected Ba Frans' explanation, holding to the origins of his sickness in the malevolent envy of those in his natal village.

This example demonstrates important facets of pain as relatedness. Pain is accounted for in terms of final causes, in the intentions of others, but these final causes must be seen as according with the symptoms of the affliction. These textures—the quality and location of the pain—must further accord with the dominant disputes and anxieties within a person's social field in a "poetic" combination. While Da Sudati was amply willing to recognize *fiofio* and the lineage *kunu* as being responsible for the sudden death of his grandchild, as far as his own suffering was concerned, he failed to see why it would take the form of losing his voice. He was free by virtue of being a medium for his own spirit (that of an escaped slave) and his position as Ba Frans' *gaan tiyu* (eldest maternal uncle), to make up his own mind and go elsewhere for the appropriate diagnosis. Further, Da Sudati resented Ba Frans' attempts to enroll him as an exclusive devotee of his shrine. His vulnerable status as a title-holder, however, exposed him to a wider range of animosity. Losing his voice deprived him of the most basic quality of a successful *basiya*. This was too clear a proof to be ignored, and, in his other dealings with obiyaman, it was this facet of the illness that Da Sudati, his wife, their children and grandchildren were most intent on emphasizing. His ability to be an effective political figure had been compromised in the most galling of ways. Such cruel provocation could not be epiphenomenal of a less personal, more general problem within his extended family; it must have been a targeted act of usurpation.

That the character of the pain should so easily invoke the rough realities of interpersonal politics is illustrative of how pain, in its sheer ubiquity, conditions the political. Presenting a limit, pain creates a speculative impulse, motivating reflection upon what relations should be like. Da Sudati's suffering forced him to consider what kind of sign feeling is. In doing so, the indeterminacies of relation were opened up. This hedging recognition accumulated momentum until settling on a script. The narrative, to the degree it could be circulated, created the moral conditions for establishing identification with Da Sudati and his suffering. The pain indexed a whole potential set of relations, the collectivity of his progeny and their partners who could be presumed to identify with his suffering, to use it to motivate their own descriptions of ethical necessity. It also included a host of kinsman who, jealous of his prominence and oratorical skill, wished to pry his title from him. This interface between highly subjective experiences of suffering and the cultivation of collective destiny is basic to Ndyuka conceptions of the political. This, mirroring the logic of segmentary opposition made famous by Evans-Pritchards (1940) or the fractal person invoked by Roy Wagner (2008), requires conceiving of pain as a quality of a whole system of relations. Pain, to the extent to which it is intra- or inter-generationally transitive, is one of the most pervasive basis Ndyuka assume to substantiate the ontological grounds of their collective existence.

In this fractal logic, as outlined by the above description of *nenseki*, a single person contains the relations that they instantiate, and potentially, the power to extend or contract relevance to different quantities and distributions of these relations, from a village house cluster (*pisi*) to the Ndyuka nation as whole. The con-substantiality that relation implies enables an escalating logic of ethical involvement. As Bernard Williams has addressed the problem, to talk about ethics is to address questions of importance (1985: 182). Da Sudati's case forcefully presents how pain and its diagnosis rhetorically create this kind of collective ethical concern. Objectified notions of substantial descent and discourses of moral obligation are mutually constitutive. The discourses that suture pain, to substance, to collective action, produce descriptions in which personal pain is always a shared element of a collectivity and its ethical regulation. As Da Sudati's story demonstrates, these discourses are bound up into the networks martialed by the sense of substantial participation in the segmentary parts of the Ndyuka lineage. Lineages, as composed of simultaneously nested and branching elements, imply concentrations of concern in tandem with proximity of descent. The three major scalar divisions, *lo* (matrilineal Clan), *bee* (matrilineage), *wan mama pikin/paansu* (matrilineal segment), are political units and measures of consubstantial co-participation. In practice, the *bee* and the *wan mama pikin* represent the distinction between factional and aggregate interests, the *bee* being invested with political titles and comprising the aboriginal ground upon which consanguinity is reckoned. What is of consequence here is how each one of these designations depends on producing a description of consubstantiality as a positive value as a function of talking about pain in terms of kinship.

Da Sudati's account of the origins of his sickness could be accepted solely due to his genealogical priority, and, even more notably, the substantial flow this implied. Interestingly enough, none of the children who most closely identified with Da Sudati's initial account of the origins of his sickness in witchcraft are technically members of his lineage or clan. They are Misidyan, members of the largest Ndyuka lineage from which Da Sudati's wife, Ma Koni, comes. Despite the matrilineage being the formal holder of land, personal property, and political representation, the father's lineage (*dda bee*), plays a defining role in the guarentee of matrilineal reproduction. The father's lineage provides support through access to the world, to the forest and the coast, outside the village and its politics. The father has rights to the degree that he and his lineage can intervene on the behalf of their progeny who are always by definition members of other clans. They do this by supplying heavy labor, meat, commodities, and maybe most importantly *obiya*. It is the father who provides the nourishment and wealth that insure that the matriline will continue. This, combined with changing residency patterns emphasizing ambilineal descent, have produced a preference for patrilineal identification, if not a change in the conduct of Ndyuka lineage politics. In these terms it is the father's *bee* that will intervene to protect its children from collective substantial guilt, or predatory witchcraft transmitted through the blood of the matrilineage. This is precisely what Da

Sudati did for his children, who now prefer to label themselves members of his Dyu clan.

Pain produces descriptions of importance, but only to the extent that such descriptions coordinate with other evaluations of essential concern. Da Sudati's pain does not but passingly produce reflection on the general human condition, but rather underscores the metalanguage of substantiality as relatedness. This enrolls pain as its primary evidence, making it identical the moral issues seen to be at stake. Descriptions of motive emerge from within varying accounts of these interests. Such interests, however, need to be positioned in terms of the constitutive relations that allow for their social recognition and elaboration. Pain, as a compelling starting point, metastasizes to the web of relations encircling any person. Through narratives of targeted malfeasance against Da Sudati, pain becomes the medium demonstrating the unshakable primacy of descent, enforcing participation in the lineage. Da Sudati's pain becomes a metonym for his progeny and affines as a whole, is seen as these relations, and an instantiation of clan politics. His pain is also the spirits produced by tensions within his fracturing descent group. All of these are open to diagnosis to the degree that the true dispositions of those within these groups can be recognized by spirits, both Da Sudati's own and those of the obiyaman he consults.

Kinship then both conceals and reveals descriptions of the content of clan relations. Segmentary logics produce persons by designating them extensions of lineages, accentuating common concern through shared substance and the ethical practices it underwrites. In doing so, however, such assumptions place greater emphasis on what is shared. Psychological accounts seeking to objectify others' subjective goals tend to focus on traits that are divergent from the notional goals of a putatively unified collective. This divergence produces ambivalent accounts of moral dispositions, concealing intentions that are perceived as threatening to a given corporate group. This contradiction simultaneously impels Ndyuka to make strong epistemological claims not to know about others and develop techniques for circumventing them. Spirits provide a solution to the impasse that results from the moral insistence on the ontological primacy of the collective and a psychology convinced of other persons' jealous self-interest and intentional inscrutability.

Spirits act to open up and label these relations. It is from the position of exteriority to the present, to the lineage, to the press of ordinary resentments that roil the everyday that spirits speak. Visiting from outside of these categories of relation, spirits define who and what belongs to them, creating sets of relations and descriptions of those relations. People whose goals and desires remain unobservable to other humans are rendered transparent by a spirit's gaze. Even when their advice is resisted, spirits produce the facts that enable people to assert the existence of political categories of relations like the *bee* or the matrisegment (Price 1973). Pain serves to signal the "holographic" (Wagner 2008) character of personhood, a rhetorical projection from the grounds of consubstantial transitivity of kinship, enabling spirits to erupt from and into this corporate continuity. As should already be clear, spirits are pain in intricate ways. It is this play of competing meta-claims about what is essential in a given situation that allows particular assertions to be authoritative, to be important to a community. The rhetorical entanglement of spirits and pain produces descriptions enabling categorical abstractions like the lineage. Pain is always united with language in ways that make political categories felt, not only by sufferers, but by all those who can be rhetorically motivated to share in it. It is that power that underwrites the authority of the politics regulating the complex contradictions of a kin-based polity.

References

Austin, J.L. 1962. How to do Things with Words. Oxford: Clarendon Press.

Bakhtin, M. M. 1981. The Dialogic Imagination: Four Essays. Austin: University of Texas Press.

Bloch, Mark. 1975. Political Language, Oratory and Traditional Society. London: Academic Press.

Bowker, Geoffrey and Susan Star. 1999. Sorting Things Out: Classification and Its Consequences. Cambridge: MIT Press.

Daniel, E. Valentine. 1996. Charred Lullabies: Chapters in an Anthropology of Violence. Princeton: Princeton University Press.

Das, Veena. 1997. "Language and Body: Transactions in the Construction of Pain." In *Social Suffering*, Edited by Arthur Kleinman, Veena Das, Margaret M. Lock, 67–92. Berkeley: University of California Press.

Durkheim, Emile and Marcel Mauss. 1963. Primitive Classification. Chicago: University of Chicago Press.

Evans-Pritchard, Edward. 1938. Witchcraft, Oracles and Magic Among the Azande. Oxford: Clarendon Press.

Evans-Pritchard, Edward. 1940. The Nuer: A Description of the Modes of Livelihood and Political Institutions of a Nilotic People. Oxford: Clarendon Press.

Fleming, Luke and Michael Lempert. 2014. "Poetics and Performativity" in The Cambridge Handbook of Linguistic Anthropology, Edited by N. J. Enfield, Paul Kockelman, and Jack Sidnell, 485-515. Cambridge: Cambridge University Press.

Holbraad, Martin. 2013. Truth in Motion: The Recursive Anthropology of Cuban Divination. Chicago: University of Chicago Press.

SPIRITS AND PAIN IN THE MAKING OF NDYUKA POLITICS

Irvine, Judy. 1982. "The Creation of Identity in Spirit Mediumship and Possession." Semantic Anthropology, 241–60. Edited by D. Parkin. London: Academic Press.

———. 1996. "Shadow Conversations: The Indeterminacy of Participant Roles" in Natural Histories of Discourse, Edited by Michael Silverstein and Greg Urban, 131–59 Chicago: University of Chicago Press.

Jakobson, Roman. 1960."Closing Statements: Linguistics and Poetics." Style in language edited by T.A. Sebeok, 350–377. Cambridge: MIT Press.

Keane, Webb. 1997. Signs of Recognition: Powers and Hazards of Recognition in an Indonesian Society. Berkeley: University of California Press.

———. 2007. The Christian Moderns: Freedom and Fetish in the Mission Encounter. Berkeley: University of California Press.

Lévi-Strauss. Claude. 1966. The Savage Mind. Chicago: University of Chicago Press.

Munn, Nancy. 1992. The Fame of Gawa: A Symbolic Study of Value Transformation in a Massim Society. Durham: Duke University Press.

Price, Richard. 1973. "Avenging Spirits and the Structure of Saramaka Lineages." Bijdragen tot de Taal-, Land-, en Volkekunde 129: 86–107.

Price, Richard. 2008. Travels with Tooy: History, Memory and the African American Imagination. Chicago: University of Chicago Press.

Silverstein, Michael. 2003. "Indexical order and the dialectics of sociolinguistic life." Language and Communication 23: 193–229.

Strathern, Marilyn, 1992. After Nature: English Kinship in the Late Twentieth Century. Cambridge: Cambridge University Press.

Tambiah, Stanley. 1981. A Performative Approach to Ritual. London: British Academy.

Thoden van Velzen, H.U.E. and Willelmina van Wetering. 2004. In the Shadow of the Oracle: Religion as Politics in Suriname Maroon Society. Long Grove: Waveland.

Wagner, Roy. 1978. Lethal Speech: Daribi Myth as Symbolic Obviation. Symbol, Myth and Ritual Series. Ithaca: Cornell University Press.

Wagner, Roy. 1981. The Invention of Culture. Chicago: University of Chicago Press.

Wagner, Roy. 2008. "The Fractal Person." Big Men and Great Men: The Personification of Power in Melanesia, edited by Maurice Godelier and Marilyn Strathern, 2008. Cambridge: Cambridge University Press.

Williams, Bernard.1985. Ethics and the Limits of Philosophy. Cambridge: Cambridge University Press.

CHAPTER 8

Funerals, Rhetorics, Rules and Rulers in Upper Suriname

Rogério Brittes W. Pires

As a neophyte ethnographer in Botopasi – an Upper Suriname village associated with the Moravian church – the aspect that most bewildered me about Christian Saamaka mortuary rituals wasn't how strange the actual rites were, even though they were completely different from anything I had ever seen. After all, the anthropological canon on funerary rites – from van Gennep (1960[1909]) and Hertz (2003[1907]), to Metcalf & Huntington (1991[1979]), and Bloch & Parry (1982) – provided me with reasonable explanations for most rituals. What seemed truly eccentric to me was the way everyone restlessly gave orders to each other. I would soon learn that, even though there are many differences between Christian and non-Christian Saamaka rites, this aspects remains constant. Furthermore, in seemingly every sphere of Saamaka life, this attitude of constantly telling each other what to do was present.[1]

There is something doubtlessly peculiar, even if perhaps not totally unique, about the way the Saamaka place great importance in rules (weti) and simultaneously debate them ceaselessly, almost as though they were not meant to be followed. Starting with this problem, in the following pages I will present some ethnographic episodes involving funerary rules in Upper Suriname, and then gradually climb to higher levels of abstraction, in order to reach a rough outline of an ethnographic theory about how collective actions and decisions are undertaken in Saamaka. By discussing the ways life is regulated in Saamaka, I hope to better understand some principles of a Saamaka political philosophy, and thus engage in debates with works written about the Guiana Maroons.

In particular, I will tackle a widespread – but under-debated – trope in this literature: the idea that Businenge communities are "states within a state". More specifically, I will argue against the unreflective use of the concept of "state" in several works about the Businenge, while suggesting alternative approaches

---

1 Previous versions of this chapter were read at the NAnSi Seminars (Museu Nacional) and at the International Colloquium "Maroons and Businenges in the Guianas" (Casa da Ciência). I thank everyone who commented and contributed to earlier versions, particularly Olívia Gomes da Cunha, Marcio Goldman, Richard Price, Sally Price, and Genia Corinde.

© KONINKLIJKE BRILL NV, LEIDEN, 2019 | DOI:10.1163/9789004388062_010

FUNERALS, RHETORICS, RULES AND RULERS IN UPPER SURINAME

to talk about Maroon polities. The main argument will turn on Saamaka ideas about weti (rules), which point to specific forms of plasticity given by debates, deliberations and reinventions that balance different forms of authority, hanging between tradition and creativity, control and flight. My argument rests on the idea that politics and life are ultimately indiscernible: the nomos elicited by a style of life should not be detached from the authorized power structures that sustains it. And, in Saamaka, I argue, this structure is not state-like.

Washing a Corpse, Digging a Grave

I remember when Baaa Bino[2] died, in mid-2011. I was starting to understand Saamakatongo, and for the first time it became apparent to me that the tasks related to his exequies – from building a tent in front of his house and notifying relatives to washing the corpse and digging the grave – were discussed and conducted as duties, obligations. Everything *had* to be done the proper way, following customary village prescriptions. At each of the many council meetings (kuutu) held during the funerary cycle, all the tasks that had already been done and everything else that was yet to be accomplished were recapitulated, often highlighting that the rites should be executed, as they say, "the way we're used to" ("kuma fa u guwenti"). But who exactly was deciding how things would be done, I could not tell. The village leaders were present, the family seemed to be on top of things, and there were special ritual positions assigned for "those who wash the dead" (wasidedema), "gravediggers" (baakuma), and "funeral overseers" (dede basia). Still, people with no special task or position were also laying out rules.

The washing and shrouding of the corpse was particularly striking. It was done by a group of four wasidedema assigned at the council meeting. With Bino's house already emptied of furniture and personal belongings, they placed a white bedsheet on the floor, lowered the body from the hammock where it layed and proceeded to systematically clean its skin with a white piece of cloth, soaked in one of the three calabashes placed in the corner of the room. Two contained plain water at different temperatures; the other, a lukewarm solution of camphor, white rum, lemon juice and black tobacco in water. The corpse was later dried with a towel and put in a provisional coffin, where a complex shroud was prepared using koosu[3] and bedsheets of various colors

---

2 All names are pseudonyms.

3 Koosu are pieces of cloth, usually bought in Paramaribo, used for clothing, decoration, and as "ritual currency". See Pires, 2017, S. Price, 1993[1984].

and patterns. Some textiles were arranged vertically, other horizontally, some were folded, other open, and the resulting ensemble wrapped the body like a cocoon. The wasidedema manifested great concern in counting and recounting the amount of koosu being used, repeatedly asking each other how many more were necessary, which led to contained but firm arguments. It then seemed to me they were deciding the exact number as they worked, in some sort of game of rhetoric, improvisation and obsessive attention to detail. Later, they would explain to me that there is no improvisation at all: there is a rule that says that the right amount of koosu should be around 30. If they are excessive, the deceased might think there is enough for more than one person and, therefore, try to take someone with him to the land of the dead. Inversely, if they are too scarce, the deceased might take it as a sign of avarice, and, enraged, bring misfortune to the living.

A similar rule applies to the work of the baakuma. Grave-digging is a task mainly executed by young men, and I was able to help with it many times. After cleaning the leaves and roots at the place chosen for the new grave, the dimension of the hole is accurately demarcated. The rigor with which the size of the grave is determined lasts from the beginning of the work until the final moments at the cemetery, when the gravediggers zealously measure it, retouch it, flatten its base and sides. Those details entail arguments and discussions – in a tone less sober than in those that happen during the shrouding of the corpse, but still serious. Once more, when one is unacquainted to Saamaka funeral practices, it may seem like there is improvisation, but there is not. Precisely because the exact size of the grave is one of the most fundamental rules in a burial, it leads to controversy. The grave has to be only slightly bigger than the coffin – around half a thumb larger – in order to fit it precisely. If the hole is too tight, the deceased might feel mistreated and seek revenge; if it is too wide, they might want to take someone else with him to his grave.

In both cases, the ritual procedures follow a somewhat accurate calculation – around 30 koosu, about half a thumb of room – still, they were subjects of lively arguments. It took some time for me to understand that the debates themselves were, on a different level of abstraction, a crucial part of the rituals. A funerary ritual is not just about burying the dead the right way, or about properly honoring the deceased and his family; discussions regarding the best means to carry out such tasks are also vital. During their fieldwork in Dangogo in the 1960s, Richard and Sally Price (1991:194) also noticed lively discussions in funerary rituals. They would concern, for instance, exactly how many libations to the ancestors were necessary. According to them, "[W]ashing the dead, like other parts of funeral rites, remains a privileged occasion for heated – and much appreciated – disputation about ritual details; 'There are no burials without argument', approvingly runs the proverb " (p. 44).

The danger posed by an activity is not what makes it more or less regulated or discussible. The tone of the argument among the men building a tent is not that different from the tone they use when digging a grave. In Botopasi, a game of rhetorics called politiki humorously expresses the multiplication of rules that takes place during the funeral cycle. In that context, playing politiki means trying to find out rules someone might have broken; such rules are often obscure, marginal, or almost irrelevant. The underlying reason to finding broken rules is to charge fines (butu) in beer, liquor or soda, which will be consumed by everyone present. Accusations like "you did not come to the tent yesterday" or "red should not be worn in front of a dead person's house" often come up. The accused has to be witty and explain why he did not break any rules or to point his accuser of having committed other faults, making him also pay a butu. Since the goal is to have fun and drink together, one should not always be too eager to "win" the argument – buying rounds for everyone is also a part of the game and a way not to come across as a stingy.

Defining Rules

"There are no burials without argument", but there are arguments outside burials. Building a house, planting a garden, washing clothes by the creek, behaving in front of one's in-laws. In any situation, it is likely that an argument concerning the right style of doing things might commence. There are rules for seemingly every activity.

The concept of weti[4] or "rules" often comes marked with a qualifier: there are "church rules" (keiki weti),[5] "obia rules" (obia weti),[6] rules for cutting a garden (koti goon weti), rules for a matrilineage (bee weti) and so forth. This is because rules are always localized: they are relevant to a specific village, to a lineage, to mediums of a certain kind of spirit (gadu), to followers of a specific

---

4　See discussions about "rule" and "law" among the Ndyuka and the Matawai, respectively in Köbben (1969b) and Green (1977).

5　"Church rules" are hardly ever taken dogmatically, even in a Christian village where the "church rules" and "village rules" somewhat overlap. How to follow the Moravian rule that people should not work on Sundays, for instance, was object of much debate in Botopasi.

6　Obia weti are the prescriptions each magical formula demands from an obiama or his patient so that it can achieve its desired effect – avoiding sex or certain kinds of food during treatment for instance. Because healing is one of the primary functions of obia, these rules are often similar to "doctor's orders", although some obia weti might be equated with taboos (tjina).

religious denomination, etc. They can be even more narrowly defined: specific areas in the forest often have their own weti, associated with spiritual beings that dwell therein, or with important events that took place there. Perhaps catching a certain species of fish is forbidden, or members of some clans are unwelcome.

As previously mentioned, funerary cycles are particularly rife with weti. When a corpse is lying on its hammock, no one should pass underneath it. While washing or shrouding the body, the living's clothes, sweat or tears should not come in contact with the corpse. When a coffin is crafted at the village, scraps of wood and sawdust should be disposed at a specific spot at the grave-yard. The gravediggers have many rules to be wary of: not only the size of the grave must be perfect, they also have to make sure that the deceased's head points West when the coffin is lowered, since the souls of the dead inhabit where the sun sets. If the deceased is a woman, men should only enter the grave to dig it through the side the head will rest; otherwise, it may resemble a sexual gesture. Also, for a whole week after the burial, the gravediggers must sleep at the deceased's house, where a constant source of light must be kept lit, and they should only eat food especially prepared for them.

There are rules even for apparently trivial actions, such as harvesting and processing kumu. While gathering such berries at the bush with a friend, he taught me that once the palm tree has been cut down, one should not go over its trunk before gathering the fruit. Also, the berries should be plucked one by one, and never yanked out of a branch at once. Finally, when extracting the juice, the pestle should gently crush the berries, and never be dropped heavily on the mortar. When such rules are not followed, the kumu will taste unpleas-ant, like unripe bananas. Surely, these "rules" may seem like little more than attention to detail while preparing such a cherished delicacy. The problem is that not all recommendations are considered weti: checking the tree for spi-ders and scorpions before picking berries is very much recommended, but it is not a weti. One of the village captains taught me a similar lesson on handling shotguns: "we, the dominenge [people of the Dombi clan], have a lot of tjina [taboos, here as a synonym for weti] about guns. I know you white people do not have so many ". One should not walk over a gun when it is on the ground; one should not put it on a dugout canoe if there are other people in it; a gun should not be left at one's door-post. Other recommendations that may sound essential – and perhaps even more commonly observed –, such as not cleaning a shotgun while loaded, do not fit the category of weti.

My exposition on the pervasiveness of rules in Saamaka life may have given the false impression that a heavy burden of regulation weights on people's ev-ery demeanor. That is not the case. The constant attention to detail stands out,

FUNERALS, RHETORICS, RULES AND RULERS IN UPPER SURINAME   239

but the people I have met in Saamaka are not anxious about doing everything right all the time and I do not think most of them feel "oppressed by tradition". It would be a mistake to create a picture of a "cultural personality" in the Upper Suriname that would in any way resemble what psychiatrists call "obsessive-compulsive disorder". Actually, the rules we are talking about are rather loose guidelines of conduct. Whether to follow them or not is a choice that can be understood as risk evaluation; if something goes badly, the violation might explain what went wrong. People often find out about a weti (or tjina) by investigating the reasons behind a misfortune.

Many more examples could be added, but the ones so far are enough to untangle the meanings of weti. Depending on context, "rule", "law", "prescription", "principle", "norm", "taboo", and "doctrine" could all be suitable translations for weti, as the word covers much of the semantic field relating to the dos and don'ts of a particular situation. However, some guides for conduct are not weti. To start with, some imperatives do not fit the category of weti because they are mere common sense. Cleaning a shotgun while it is loaded or carelessly putting your hand where a scorpion might be are simply imprudent acts, foolishness. There is nothing to argue about here – hence, they are not weti.

As hinted above, the concepts of weti and tjina intertwine. The core meaning of tjina refers to food taboos inherited from a "supernatural genitor" (neseki); in this sense, tjina are not considered weti. In other contexts, however, the meanings overlap: saying a widower has "tjina of sex" is the same as saying that not having sex is a weti they must adhere to. The difference between "rule" and "taboo" seems to lie in the fact that a taboo, when broken, brings forth consequences that are almost mechanical, without any need for reprehension or punishment by humans. An essential element to the core meaning of weti is the possibility of it being discussed, since there might be doubt about its relevance or the way it should be handled. There are arguments about "the proper way of doing" almost everything, for there are many rules; in each and every aspect of life, plenty of details must be taken into account.

In some cases, weti can simply mean "law", as in "mamaweti" (literally "mother law", the Constitution of a country) and "sikoutu weti" ("police laws", enforced by the police). But the extent to which the idea of weti is used greatly exceeds its legal meanings. Moreover, the idea of law – at least according to the universalist principles of the Surinamese state – presupposes that its prescriptions are indiscriminately and equally valid to every Surinamese citizen or person living in the territory defined by its authority. Weti, on the other hand, are unwritten and rely on casuistry; disobeying them rarely results in "lawful" sanctions. The dependence on casuistry also makes "norm" a bad translation for weti: if the rules are always localized, they are not about normal or normalized standards of behavior.

In order to define what Saamaka call weti, we must then focus on what really stands out: the fact that everyone seems to lay out rules (buta weti) for almost everyone else. We can thus claim that weti are "rules" in the sense of principles, precepts, recommendations coming from all sides. Even though rules are plenty, they are not followed by everyone all the time. Weti are localized, specific for a place, time and group of people, they do not stem from transcendental, universal or indisputable morals; therefore, they are always questionable. A statement such as "this is how to do it" can always be followed by an adversative conjunction: "but it is not always so ..."; "Although there might be an exception ...; "Yet, in a similar situation, we had to do it otherwise ..."

Perhaps the preceding is enough to define, at least provisionally, what weti in general are, but it is still necessary to understand how each particular weti is pragmatically defined. Arguments are an essential element of the Saamaka concept of rule, but not everything is always open to discussion; furthermore, there are also rules about how discussions take place. Freedom to define one's conduct is restricted by shared morals, by an episteme, and by specific forms of construction and distribution of authority.

There are certain kinds of arguments considered valid to define or to modify a rule. Some of the most common might be: how many times someone has already done the task at hand; how they do it in another village; how our ancestors used to do it; what happened when someone violated this rule. Secrets, esotericism, knowledge, experience are part of the discussion, and so are the evaluation of precedents and risks. Generally speaking, such arguments seek to delineate why and how to regulate an activity for a specific group of people at a specific time and place. There are rules not everybody is aware of and rules with obscure purposes. Some of them are simply followed because "this is the way we are used to doing things"; they are legitimate because "this is how the ancestors did it", often pointed out by name: "this is what I have learned from basia Bakaa" (or some other authoritative figure from the past). Considering that weti are often specific for a clan, a village or a matrilineage, we can understand that, even though they point to general Saamaka ideas (about death, food, kinship, etc) each rule ultimately emerges from a specific history of localized customary practice.

When rules have to be discussed or reshaped, the main aspect to be considered is custom. During a funeral council meeting I heard an iconic phrase: "here, we walk behind the old folks" ("a gaan sembe baka u ta waka aki"), in other words they do things the way their elders and ancestors used to. That does not mean Saamaka society is resistant to changes – the way they tell

FUNERALS, RHETORICS, RULES AND RULERS IN UPPER SURINAME

their history makes it clear that transformations and innovations are and have always been incessant. However, the most common way of publicly announcing a decision – say, the choice of date for a ritual – is to say they will do it "the way we're used to" ("kuma fa u guwenti"). When choosing among possible routes, the path of custom is the surest.

The fondness for rhetorics and esoteric knowledge only partly explain Saamaka debates. In order to win an argument about weti, people can use examples from another village, but the stronger arguments are: how it is done here; how it used to be done here; how it was eventually done here – in that order.[7] People ask each other questions such as: "how did we handle the situation the last time something similar happened?"; "What was the outcome?"; "How did we handle it in other occasions?"; "Are there first time (fesiten) stories that tell how a certain course of actions has been taken?", "If so, who knows the most complete version of the story and who did they hear it from?" Investigating the past is preparing for the future. The idea is to follow the footsteps of the ancestors – "those who walked in front of us" (de sembe di waka a fesi) – but only to the extent that it still makes sense in the present. When a custom changes, the new way of doing things becomes more relevant than the old folks' ways. However, the past might still be recovered when new customs prove to be problematic. An ethnographic episode should help to make this clearer.

A Death in the City

In an afternoon of April, 2013, a council meeting was called to notify the village that Soola had died. She passed away at a hospital in Paramaribo, where she had been admitted a few months before. Since Soola died in the city, the village leaders were still unaware of further details about how and when her body would be brought to Upper Suriname. By the end of the meeting, most of the attendees gathered at Soola's front porch and talked about the deceased. Soola had been ill for quite a while, everyone knew, but her younger brother, who had recently been in the village, should have warned her friends that her death was imminent. Someone attributed his attitude to his "city manners" (foto fasi): after living in Paramaribo for years, he was no longer accustomed to the right way of dealing with death in Botopasi. During the next couple of days, death was the main topic of conversation in the village: people chatted

---

7   Herskovits & Herskovits (1971[1934]:191) report the same kind of statements during their fieldwork in the 1920s.

about problems in recent burials and about how hard it was to know about the health of those living in the city. Some of Soola's relatives spent part of their days sitting in front of her house receiving visitors. When I went by to visit, they told me that the part of the family that lived in the city held a meeting there to decide about the burial.

The following morning, the decision was formally announced to the villagers at a council meeting attended by most of the village elders and leaders, including basia Hesi, the oldest man in the village and a member of Soola's matrilineage – an authority figure for the occasion, if there was one. The meeting started, as usual, with regular formalities, after which the death announcement was repeated and the most important events that ensued were summarized. Only after that, a kabiteni declared that Soola's relatives in the city called him the night before to say they had decided to bury her in Paramaribo. Actually, most people – if not everyone – already knew, but the captain's speech made it official. After long uncomfortable silences, old basia Hesi took the floor and energetically demanded Soola's body to be brought to Saamaka – she was beloved enough to receive the proper honors. She did not go away to live in the city, like so many do, she was a Botopasi person that just happened to die away from home. Hesi said he did not like the way people bury the dead in the city, tossing dirt directly on top of the coffin, and that he was sure that both her matrilineage (mama bee) and her father's matrilineage (tata bee), much like the people of Botopasi (lanti), were against burying in the city and should clearly express their dissatisfaction. Everyone at the meeting seemed to agree with Hesi, and Soola's brother even mentioned that only last year, one of their relatives was also to be buried in the city, but the family in Paramaribo ended up giving in to the pressure of the villagers who wanted the exequies in Botopasi. "The pressure might work again", he claimed, and it was collectively decided that a phone call should be immediately made to Soola's brothers in the city – and that the authorities attending (elders and captain) should talk to them. Basia Hesi and two kabiteni made the call and, with the village attentively listening, the leaders reminded the city men that, during the last funeral rites held in Botopasi, a few months before, it was agreed in a kuutu that every denizen of Botopasi who happened to die in Paramaribo would be buried at the village's graveyard, preferably on weekends, so that the people who lived in the city could come. The two men on the other end of the line said they would meet to discuss the subject and would have a proper response by evening. A couple of days later, I went to sit by Soola's house, where the family, still receiving visitors, told me her brothers had not given in. Soola's burial was scheduled to take place in Paramaribo.

Those discussions turned on an unstable rule. Today, it is common for a person from Botopasi to pass away in Paramaribo, considering half of its population live in the city and the gravely ill often seek medical assistance there. According to R. Price, until the 1960s, if a Saamaka died away from Upper Suriname, their remains would not be buried in their village's graveyard, only a proxy coffin with hair and nails would go upriver to be used for divination. It was said "dead people cannot be brought over Mamadan Falls" (1990:311n11). However, these rapids, that used to mark the boundaries of Saamaka territory, are now under the Brokopondo reservoir (Price, 2011, pp. 32–4), which means the rule changed for most – if not for all – Upper Suriname villages. It still seems to be a topic open to discussion in which cases a body should be buried in traditional Saamaka territory and in which ones the funeral might take place in the city. One of Soola's nephews told me in an unofficial conversation that their matrilineage had the custom of always burying their dead in Upper Suriname, even if other lineages in Botopasi did otherwise. In the event of an "ugly death" (a violent accident or killing), they would rather have the funeral in the city to avoid contact with the dangerous corpse. It would also not be a problem to bury in Paramaribo a member of the lineage that had not lived for long in Botopasi – and thus had few relations in the village. But Soola's burial in the city – her being a regular Botopasi villager who died a normal death – would open a precedent anyone not willing to bring a deceased upriver could follow from then on. The elderly seemed particularly adamant to this kind of change: during the discussions triggered by the affair, I heard one of them angrily saying that "old people are the bosses" and that "the people in the city" should have followed their decisions. Others acted resignedly, saying they disagreed, but that once the family in Paramaribo reached a decision, there was nothing else to be done.

Burying in the city is not unusual, but it is not desired. The problem it brings is more "social" than "metaphysical": I was told it was unlikely that Soola's spirit could get angry due to the burial being held outside Upper Suriname, as long as it was properly taken care of in the city; but allowing it to happen could make such a decision even more common, further emptying Botopasi. Nowadays, the village is rarely lively outside funerary cycles, and the people still residing there do not like it that way – they want visitors, parties, they want their friends and family around. Besides that, the village leaders had taken a clear stance about the issue – even if it was not always the rule, they had made it the rule by officially pronouncing it at a village kuutu.

However, the problem evinced by Soola's death is one about the changes in funerary rites brought forth by new socioeconomic conditions presented for the Saamaka – the problem of development (ontwikkeling). And for decisions regarding development, the words of elders and village leaders may not carry as much weight as in other matters, seeing as they are, quite literally, bearers of traditional authority.

Political Structure

The Saamaka structure of official political offices - much like that of other Businenge groups – is headed by the gaama, the paramount leader, below whom there are offices he authorizes and ceremonially legitimizes, acting at regional or village level. In the villages, there are kabiteni (captains) and their helpers, the basia (usually four under each captain). Populous villages can have many captains and dozens of basia. The gaama also appoints some hedi kabiteni ("head captains") and fisikai ("fiscals"), the former acting as the leaders of captains for a particular area (a pisi wata or "stretch of the river"), the latter responsible for even larger areas. Aside from having basia working directly under him, in his village, the gaama additionally keeps contact with other basia scattered throughout the river, called hedi basia ("head basia"). Appointment for these lifelong positions is based on matrilineal principles, but that does not mean the incumbent's sisters' sons are their rightful successors; because an office is said to belong either to a village, a clan, a matrilineage or a matrisegment, it is often expected that the position should rotate among lineages of a clan or segments of a lineage.[8] This means the structure of official offices is parallel and is mutually interfering with the segmentary lineage system.[9]

The positions of gaama, basia and kabiteni were originally legitimized by the Dutch colonial government, in the peace treaty of 1762 and, even though their legal status is today dubious, the Surinamese government still validates them by paying a "compensation".[10] Intermediary offices of hedi kabiteni, hedi basia and fisikai were later institutionalized, but are also paid for by the government.[11] The incumbents wear military-style attire in official occasions and

---

8 See the distinction between "family captains" and "lanti captains" (Pires, 2015:85).

9 Using a somewhat old-fashioned anthropological jargon, we may translate the levels in Saamaka segmentary system as: tribe (nasi); clan (lo); matrilineage (bee); matrisegment (wosu dendu) and minimal segment (bobi). Except for the bobi, all levels could be classified as corporate groups, whose divisions are defined by shared vulnerability to the same avenging spirits (kunu) and by their collective relation to matrilaterally transmitted land and political offices.

10 In practical terms, this is almost the same as a civil servant salary. However, the fact that it is not called a salary, but a "compensation", "subsidy" or "fee" (vergoeding or tegemoetkoming in Dutch) is relevant, as Genia Corinde suggested (personal communication, 2016).

11 According to R. Price (personal communication, 2015), until the mid-20th Century there were only two hedi kabiteni – one downriver, one upriver –, while fisikai and hedi basia are offices created in the last few decades inspired by similar positions existing in Aluku and Ndyuka.

also carry scepters (pau), where the souls (akaa) of former holders of the same office dwell, which explains why older scepters and positions are said to be "heavier". Therefore, in a very literal sense, the leaders are bearers of ancestrality and political power in Saamaka. They embody the traditional authority of a village, clan, or lineage.

Such description may suggest a pyramidal power structure, a strongly territorialized chain of command through which the gaama's authority would branch through the river and its villages. One could think this is a system of political representation in which those assigned with offices act as representatives of increasingly larger collectivities. However, this is not what usually happens; the "chain of command" hardly, if ever, becomes actualized. Sometimes the words of a prestigious basia can bear more weight than those of a kabiteni; a "regular" captain is more relevant to the everyday affairs of a village than a head captain living in the same village; and, in places far from the gaama's village, the paramount leader's authority tends to be somewhat vague, for most issues. The gaama will influence affairs such as the choice of a new incumbent for an office, or inter-clan conflicts relating to boundaries and usage of natural resources, but for most issues – intralineage conflicts, infrastructural problems in the village, etc. – kabiteni and basia will be more relevant. Because rules are localized, variable from a village to another, the gaama's suggestions will not be effective if they are not accepted (and often adapted) in local spheres. And even the authority of the most powerful gaama or kabiteni is never despotic. For one, because they should not interfere with problems that can be solved internally by the families or persons involved. Furthermore, because there is no "monopoly of legitimate violence". Finally, because a leader should never act or decide alone – they always work in cooperation with the village council (lanti), composed of all the kabiteni and basia, plus an elder from each of the core matrilineages of a village.

One of the most important concepts of Saamaka political philosophy is lanti. In one sense, it is the opposite of family (famii); talking about a thing (or person) as pertaining to lanti means talking about its public character, about concerns, qualities, substances or goods that do not belong to a lineage, a segment, or any kin-related groupings. However, a simple split between public and private does not stand in Saamaka, considering the transmission of lanti offices works matrilaterally. Also, no competent kabiteni would take an important decision without previously consulting with the elders of their lineage. Furthermore, it will be shown that the split between a domestic and a political sphere does not hold up either. To put it briefly, when a kabiteni speaks for lanti, he speaks for a village as a whole, not as a part of his family.

But the meaning of lanti is double. In one hand, it refers to the kabiteni, basia and elders, the council that governs a village, usually translated as bestuur in Dutch (management, board, committee). A country's government can be called lanti. On the other hand, lanti refers to those who are not a part of the government or the council: it means the population in general, every adult that is not an elder nor holds a political office – divided between "young men" (kijoo) and "women" (mujee). Therefore, lanti means a political summit and the people it is responsible for. This duplicity sounds paradoxical under a representational view of the sphere of politics as external and opposed to the society it governs. Far from the idea of a transcendent Leviathan, the concept of lanti points to the fact that the "government" should be a synecdoche of the "people", not its representation. A village's "committee" (its lanti) should ideally be an extension of its people (its lanti), they should be a part of the population foregrounded as responsible for deliberative functions, due to their wisdom and experience (in the case of elders) or to the fact that they embody ancestrality through the office they hold (in the case of kabiteni and basia). A village's council is encompassed by the population, it is a part of it at the same time it is opposed to it. Therefore, their "decisions" should encompass the will of the entire village, they should be as consensual as possible.

The Saamaka usually compare the attributions of the kabiteni and the gaama to that of a boatman, who must steer a vessel without deciding where the passengers (a group, the people) goes. What they do is to conduct, to lead (tii), they are "guides" (tiima), cardinal, but not autocratic. A leader should be mindful of the problems or quarrels affecting the village and help settling them, besides serving as the voice of the people when meeting a foreigner. For this reason, a captain should be respectable, and avoid improper conduct such as getting drunk in public or being involved in gossip. A kabiteni with a bad reputation will not lose their position, but might lose their prestige, which means a village with a disreputable captain might also be ill reputed. To a lesser extent, the same is true for a basia.

The authority of a kabiteni resides in their reputation. The main characteristic of a good leader is being a good speaker, specially (but not only) in public situations, such as the kuutu. They should be a role model, so that what they say is heard by the entire village, so that they can convincingly defend the rights of those who they speak for. Ideally, they would not wield decision-making power; rather, they should make the village sound as one by regulating dissent. Together with the elders and the council, they are the spokesmen for a final word that should be as close as possible to a consensus. One last ethnographic episode should show how deadlocks are overcome and consensus is achieved.

A Death on New Year's Eve

When the bells rang around 6pm on December 31st, 2011, most people thought they were calling the villagers for the Old Year's ceremony, to be held that night at church. Few knew that, actually, Wenu had passed away. Altough his death came as no surprise, it happening in the last day of the year was something very serious: New Year's (jai) is an important celebration, that should set off a party lasting a fortnight, with lots of music, food, fireworks and fun. But how could they celebrate? When there is a body left unburied in the village, the weti say there should be no dancing. Not to mention it was getting dark and they would not have time to get everything ready for the wake, that usually starts at 10pm. Ignoring some complaints, a group of men led by a member of the deceased's matrilineage started raising a tent in front of Wenu's house. When it was set, a quick council meeting decided the wake would not be held that night, for the corpse had not been washed yet. However, the deceased should not be left alone, there had to be at least one person by his side at all times. In the morning, they would determine if the wake would take place the following night or if the burial would happen without a wake – which is something completely unusual, but plausible due to the unprecedented situation. In the meeting, lanti decided that one of the first of two Christian cults scheduled for the night would not be held, but at 11:30pm everyone should go to church. The words of Jozef, one of the village elders, were clear enough: "the people in Botopasi should celebrate the New Year's Eve, but not thinking about death".

After finishing all that could have been done for Wenu that day, everyone went to their homes and got ready for church. Arguments could still be heard: someone said the wake could be done without washing the body, something they had seen in Klaaskreek; others argued about how the problem would be dealt with in Futunaakaba or the in city. The church was crowded for the last cult of the year, and while the priest was mentioning Wenu in his sermon, firecrackers could be heard outside. After midnight, people warmly saluted each other, left church and started going around the village, paying visits to friends. Soon, a great number of mainly young people gathered and started a celebration that lasted until dawn, walking and singing around the village, knocking on people's doors to ask for beverages to be drank during the next two weeks of parties. Not that different from how New Year's Eve is celebrated every year, but this time, with Wenu lying dead on his hammock, there was no dancing, most of the music was "gospel" and some crying could be heard amidst the singing. The night was not as cheerful as usual, but it was loud enough for some people to complain that, with all the noise, it did not seem as if someone had just died in the village.

On the morning of January 1st, a kuutu was set up to decide the tasks necessary for Wenu's funeral, and even those who spent all night celebrating attended. During the day, the corpse was washed, the grave was dug, and, at night, the wake was held, and Wenu was buried the following morning, according to custom. After the burial, the usual baakuma kuutu – a meeting to assure that everything had taken place properly – was held, in which the elders gave their verdict about the New Year's celebrations. Their words made official what most people already presumed: New Year's parties would happen – or yet they had to happen, as Jozef once again asserted –, but they would have to balance mourning and festivities. He was resolute in saying that "New Year's should be celebrated" ("jai musu njan"), for it is an important custom in Botopasi, and that "nobody should complain" ("sembe an musu ta hon"); but at the same time, everyone should remember to spend time under the tent by Wenu's house. His declaration, an order-word, was not at all the village council's one-sided decision, for it took into account a relative consensus reached in the last 24 hours, weighing the importance of customs and the dangers of ignoring either the proper way to conduct a funerary cycle or of ignoring New Year's.

Surprisingly, what seemed like a difficult dilemma was solved without much distress. Botopasi figured the way out of a deadlock, celebrated New Year's and honored the dead with a proper funeral. The village chose for a middle ground. There were some protests, but it was clear that a mournful silence could not be kept in the village during the first week of the year, because that is not just a time for fun – it is a moment of excess and renewal, customarily celebrated in the village.

Kuutu Rhetorics

The Kuutu is the most important Saamaka political institution, and the privileged site where the voice of authority takes shape. It is a formal meeting, in which the rhythm and mode of speech follow a highly stylized etiquette. Even the way seats are placed in a kuutu reveals relevant differences in age, gender and political status: there are areas set apart for the elders, kabiteni, basia, facing the rest of the participants; women and men tend to seat separately, and children usually do not attend. In the past, only members of the village council were allowed to speak; although today there is more flexibility, women rarely speak, even those who are basia. Elders, kabiteni and basia are the ones who speak more often, conducting the meeting.

To take the floor, one must wait for a moment of silence and call someone to be an "answerer" (pikima), usually a basia. The speaker will address the pikima,

FUNERALS, RHETORICS, RULES AND RULERS IN UPPER SURINAME 249

no matter if the speech is actually directed to another person or to the whole of the assembly. One must speak haltingly, so that after each sentence the pikima can answer with a standardized back-channel response – "yes", "so it is", "is that so?" – allowing the speaker to proceed. At the end of a speech or at an important point in it, the answerer will ask if everyone heard the message, to which the crowd answers in unison: "we heard it". Before someone else can take the floor, the pikima asks if the speaker is finished. Every time any speaker thanks someone for something, the crowd follows the expression of praise with rhythmic clapping, and the words "gaan tangi, tangi, tangi!" The crowd should otherwise be quiet, but brief expressions of support or disapproval often take place. If a discussion reaches a point where a particular group – a family, the gravediggers, all the young men, etc – has to make a decision, this group can "go aside" (go a se), leaving the space where the kuutu is being held to deliberate without having to follow the formal mode of speech. But very often a group already comes to meeting with a position previously decided.

Redundancy, interruptions and roundabouts are commonplace in kuutu. The most important topics are often left to the end of a meeting and discussed less vehemently than apparently trivial subjects. If someone takes the floor and interrupts a topic being discussed, they will not be reproached. It often happens that a meeting arranged to discuss a certain issue barely debates it, or that someone declares a decision without presenting the conflicting points of view that justified the very kuutu. Meetings often end without any kind of resolution for a problem.

Saamaka rhetorics have their noblest materialization at kuutu. Knowing how to speak in "kuutu mode" is a praised virtue. When opening one's speech in a formal setting, the most fitting is not going straight to the point: for instance, when a kabiteni announces someone's death, he will start from where he was and what he was doing when he heard the news. Indirect information must be acknowledged as such – if the speaker has not seen something, they must say they heard it somewhere else. When accusing others, their names are usually not mentioned, even if everyone knows who the target is. An experienced public speaker makes abundant use of allusions and metaphors.[12]

A kuutu can take place at different levels – from big "river kuutu" that should be attended by representatives of every village, to private family, lineage or segment meetings. Some kuutu are arranged only to report a decision that was reached beforehand; others will announce a proposal to be debated

---

12   Marrenga & Paulus (2011) wrote a didactic introduction to Saamaka rhetorics, with useful examples concerning village decision-making. See also Köbben's (1969a:238) description of the Cottica Ndyuka kuutu and Migge's (2004) linguistic analysis.

afterwards. Sometimes a kuutu is called simply to give someone thanks officially; sometimes one is called to admonish someone to change the way they are acting towards something important. Many kuutu settle a dispute between two parties (persons, lineages, clans, villages, etc) with the aid of neutral mediators – preferably a kabiteni. Ultimately, any dialogue can turn into a kuutu if the topic and the situation fits, for the kuutu is, above all, a mode of speech. I have watched, quite a number of times, a casual public conversation reaching a serious subject and suddenly becoming much like a council meeting – the cluster of chatter fades and people start taking turns to speak and calling on a pikima to punctuate their sentences. This change immediately grants the speeches with a solemn tone.

The kuutu is somewhere between a conclave, a meeting, and a conversation. They are not exactly an arena for "democratic" decision-making or deliberation, but rather a space where controversies are officially made public – arguments perhaps exposed and evaluated, but not necessarily adjudicated. When a decision is presented after one or several kuutu, the judgment is not reached then and there as a product of official speeches – it emerges from a partial consensus attained through less formal channels, not always made explicit at the meetings. After a problem is introduced at a previous kuutu, or if it arises without being formally declared, ideas quickly disseminate throughout the village: women talk by the riverside, men over a bottle of beer, private family meetings are held – in those contexts, opinions unfitting for a formal setting can be more freely expressed. After some time, the collective decision should be clear enough to be made official in a kuutu, even without a vote or an explicit debate. A village council meeting (lanti kuutu) is in fact a synecdoche of the discussions pervading a village for a stretch of time. Marrenga & Paulus (2011:50) call this process "village democracy".

Looking at Wenu's death we can see how it works: an unprecedented problem came up; for two days, people took stands through words or acts (suggesting, working, partying or complaining); and when the time came for the official meeting after the burial, the villagers already knew a decision had been reached. In the actual kuutu, pros and cons were not raised, there were no arguments, for that had already been done; an elder made the resolution public and official and that was all.

A recurrent aphorism maintained by the men in Botopasi is that "the women's meeting house (kuutu wosu) is the riverside". Women do not usually speak at lanti kuutu, but they do share their views while washing clothes and dishes by the river, and during family meetings. They do voice their positions on important issues and have considerable political agency. That is not to say there is no gender inequality, but it must be made clear that women's voices are not

FUNERALS, RHETORICS, RULES AND RULERS IN UPPER SURINAME 251

at all muted in Saamaka – some can have prestige and authority enough to
rival with the power of an elder sitting at the village council. Politics must not
be approached by detaching public displays of authority from everything else,
for domesticity also has its political dimension (cf. Strathern, 1988, pp. 74ff).
In Saamaka, women's political influence is surely less visible than men's, in-
asmuch as it departs from the most obvious institutions where politics are
performed. But the fact is, politics are also performed – issues are actually discussed and decided – by a neighbor's front porch, or during a work break at the
garden. Visible, formally performed authority is not always what counts, and
while hierarchies are made obvious in kuutu, the authority of captains and
elders in those meetings should be more about communicating a decision –
not always followed, as Soola's burial attested – than properly about deciding.

Rhetoric and power are related. When someone holds considerable influence in a particular place, it is said they "have a voice there" or "may speak
there" ("a sa taki de"). A kabiteni is considered competent when he is able to
present solutions by firmly and elegantly expressing them, bringing order and
doing away with conflict, but he does not command – his moral and legal authority do not make his words definitive orders. The role of an incumbent of a
political office in Saamaka is that of a mediator or arbitrator, his importance
lies in the connections he is able to establish, by the fact that he will be consulted and informed of most of the relevant issues going on in the area he is responsible for. Furthermore, political office holders share authority with elders,
who are the "heads" of their kin-groups, which means authority is fragmented
throughout a village and throughout the river, even though it concentrates in
certain places, objects and persons.

"Village democracy" works by combining respect for the authority of leaders
and elders with freedom as a cardinal value. Herskovits & Herskovits offer an
interesting insight on how the principles that guide Saamaka politics associate
authoritative values inherited from Africa with an ideal of liberty derived from
their ancestors' struggles against slavery:

> At the core of this word [kuutu] we found two ideas. One was the necessi-
> ty of direction. "When the boat lacks a steersman, it sleeps quietly ", these
> people say of a village whose chief is dead. Direction, authority, was their
> legacy from Africa. Their ancestors had known the rule of dynasties, and
> the power of men who reigned.
>
> But there was also the idea of the importance of free discussion, the
> need to weld authority and the will of those over whom it was exercised.
> [...] the experience of the white man's slavery was a crucible in which the
> ownership of man by man, and the unquestioning obedience which men

owed to those of higher rank, were destroyed, leavening only the idea of free men. [...] A "man nengere", an adult Negro, was above all, a free man, and it was as a freeman that he was governed, for though ordinate to chiefs, and though above the village chiefs were clan chiefs, and over them all the Granman, yet the final word rested with the members of each subsidiary body, and not with its leader (1971[1934], pp. 189–90).[13]

Ignoring the North-American liberal hue in the Herskovitses' description of what a "free man" should be, the idea that Saamaka ideals of leadership combine respect for authority with the refusal of subjection is powerful. Elders and leaders are the ones who should have "the last word", but gerontocracy and hierarchy are never absolute. Rhetorics is the main tool for concentrating and performing political power; violence is only used as punishment on rare and specific occasions – and never under the political leaders' order. No one has definitive command authority.

The Ethics and Aesthetics of Flight

The ethnographic problem with which we began this chapter was the fact that details about "how things must be done" are avidly discussed in Saamaka, particularly during funerals. This seemingly anecdotal trait led me to examine the idea of "rules" (weti) and how they are constantly debated through localized interpretations of custom – which demanded expositions of the local political hierarchies, and of the rhetoric in "council meetings" (kuutu). I hope to have shown that kuutu rhetorics are able to undo, to a certain degree, the seeming rigidity of the political hierarchies. In an ideal scenario, the directive capacity to define weti should be an extension of the single-voiced (i.e., produced as a synecdoche of many debates) opinion on these rules – not an expression of family, corporate or individual desires. The following pages will take a different tone, departing from concrete instances towards a delineation of Saamaka political philosophy.

Life in Saamaka seems profoundly imbued of morals – with "musts", "ought tos" or "shoulds". Human agency is seen as one of the main sources of misfortune in the world, and actions have effects lasting for an extraordinarily long time, making rules inevitable for a good life. According to Foucault (1990 [1984]:28), "for an action to be 'moral,' it must not be reducible to an act or a

---

13   Granman is the Sranan version of gaama and man nengre the Sranan version of womi nenge, meaning a "real man", or literally "black man". The Herskovitses relied on interpreters during their fieldwork in Upper Suriname.

series of acts conforming to a rule, a law, or a value. Of course all moral action involves a relationship with the reality in which it is carried out, and a relationship with the self ". In order to grasp a style of life – or an aesthetics of being – as important as the explicit content of rules or actions are the ways people relate to them. I maintain that, if the very idea of weti turns on the importance of arguments, debates and reformulations, the continual (re)construction of legitimate ways of acting is at least as relevant to understand Saamaka institutions – such as funeral rites or the lineage system – as are their contents – such as ritual gestures or the transmission of land, substances and offices. Particular ways of arguing seem to be at the core of both Saamaka politics and funeral rites: they are part of what remains constant throughout the frequent changes in their norms and institutions. I contend that forms of debating are among the most basic elements of Saamaka sociality and historicity, at the core of an ethics and aesthetics guiding relations to people, lineages, authority, friends and spirits. Through arguments, Saamaka constitute their world.

Perhaps that is not particular to Saamaka: to some extent, rules are anywhere flexible and open to interpretation. What is indeed particular in the concept of weti is the way these abundant rules are constantly recreated through arguments – in kuutu and elsewhere – and the specific ways people make use of the past and of authority to produce their customs. As mentioned, everyone seems to be "laying out rules" for almost everyone else, all the time, and the almost paradoxical result is that, ultimately, no one really rules over anyone else. There is authority, but there is no commandment or sovereignty. The many rules are flexible, undogmatic and breaking them does not lead to punishment, which is a result of each person sustaining their own definition of the situation, based on precedents and experience.

A Saamaka understanding of rules breaks away from a legal interpretation of norms or laws existing as given, self-sustaining tenets of social existence – such as in Napoleonic and Germanic legal systems, as well as in contractualist and structural-functionalist theories. According to Wagner (1972), norms and rules derive their moral and social effect from their relationship to other meanings in culture – social actions create or modify, follow or eschew more or less standard behaviors that can, through repetition, elicit rules. Rules emerge from the ways people relate to each other, to the world, and to rules themselves. Life, politics and philosophy are entangled. Weti regulates life according to the way it is lived, and to the way one wishes to live – i.e., according to a political philosophy, a complex of ideas about what a good life ought to be, ideals that are also regulated. Only when there is a state there can be an impression – a false impression – of the autonomy and uniformity of laws. The Saamaka hierarchy of political offices – even though it is not acephalous, even though it is legitimated by the Surinamese state – does not follow a state-like model of politics. For even if weti help organizing sociality by defining actions a "moral person" should or should not take, each person's definition of a "moral person" is also flexible, which means individuality acts as the control of tradition and shared ideals (Wagner 1972:608).

Deleuze (1995[1986]:98) opposes "constraining rules" (contraignants) and "optional rules" (facultatives): rules that appeal to transcendental moral values in order to judge actions as right or wrong; and rules that evaluate actions depending on the ways of existing they elicit. This idea of "ways of existing" or "styles of life" connects ethics and aesthetics:

> Yes, establishing ways of existing or styles of life isn't just an aesthetic matter, it's what Foucault called ethics, as opposed to morality. The difference is that morality presents us with a set of constraining rules of a special sort, ones that judge actions and intentions by considering them in relation to transcendent values [...]; ethics is a set of optional rules that assess what we do, what we say, in relation to the ways of existing involved. We say this, do that: what way of existing does it involve? (Deleuze 1995[1986]: 100)

Thus, the statement that Saamaka life seems profoundly imbued of morals needs rephrasing. It would be better to say that Saamaka sociality has its ethics anchored on the balance between freedom and (optional) rules that work as guides for the production of styles of life that allow coexistence—with the living, the dead, other Maroons, foreigners, states, religions, etc.

Among Maroons, the past is activated in a way very different from Common Law legal systems. Office holders bear scepters where the souls of ancestors reside, meaning leaders "represent" the living and "embody" the dead at the same time, in a bi-directional relationship, simultaneously metonymical and metaphorical. This why they tend to defend customary practices when a dilemma opposes them to "development": their decisions must please not only the living, but also the dead. The usage of "precedents" or "jurisprudence" does not amount to the mobilization of past instances (or higher courts), but to people (alive or dead) and events (from the past) that still have a direct effect on the present situation. A past that is both constituted of fesiten ("first times", ie., when ancestors ran from plantations, fought the Dutch, established the first villages) and recent memories (decisions took in the last years, or even in the last kuutu). Authority, in Saamaka, is transmitted through lineages and authorized by memory – it is a materialization of the past. However, it is an ever-charging materialization, for tradition – when taken seriously, as it is in

FUNERALS, RHETORICS, RULES AND RULERS IN UPPER SURINAME   255

Saamaka – is unable to (and refractory of) covering all virtualities of action. Tradition, custom – or, as the Saamaka candidly put it, "the way we're used to doing things" – is composed by comparisons, additions, reevaluations, because there is a continual necessity to accommodate actions.

Saamaka references to the past connect the present to multiple temporalities, but their ultimate reference is to fesiten: their ethnogenesis during their struggles against slavery. Authors such as Graeber (2004: 55) claim that an ethnogenesis can always be understood as a political project: a group is formed by shared ideals and desires – of resisting a certain kind of oppression, for instance. For Maroons, this is little more than a truism. It is obvious that the Saamaka style of life is founded as a response to the domination exercised by the colonial state. However, it is still necessary to investigate how (and if) this resistance is expressed in the way they exist today.

In an article about tembe (Maroon visual arts), Bona (2009) speaks of an "aesthetics of flight", interpreting the curls and curves of Maroon woodcarving as reminiscent of the rhythm of a flight through the jungle. Even if we ignore his debatable interpretation of the formal aspects of Maroon arts, it is still useful to retain Bona's parallel between the dynamic Businenge arts and their history of struggle for autonomy against the background of a foreign/white world. Once more, ethics and aesthetics go hand in hand: Saamaka performances – rituals, artistic creations, formal and informal arguments, displays of authority – express or elicit their particular style of life through the revealing and concealment of continuities and discontinuities with the foreign world. Their art is profoundly affected by foreign forms and techniques, and at the same time distinguished by their unique creativity and logic of transformation.[14] The same is true for the way Saamaka people deal with politics. Flight, the founding event of Maroon communities, is an ethical and aesthetic leitmotif, a foundation of their political philosophy.[15]

Of course, flight should not be the only relevant theme when approaching Maroon communities. By now, the largest share of their history was peaceful, and everyone knows there are ways of dealing with foreigners other than flight and war. Nonetheless, when their land is under threat, they are not hesitant in saying they will start a war again, if necessary – and indeed they waged a civil

---

14   See also Price & Price 2005[1999] and their interesting use of the idea of a "changing same" to speak of a stability, not of forms, but of logics and aesthetics guiding the transformation of Maroon arts.

15   There are many variations on this theme. Most relevant here is that clans are based on bands of fugitives from a plantation area and the current division of land among them is a result of displacements compelled by the flight from the colonial army.

war during the 1980s. One of the main teachings of first time history, according to R. Price 2002[1983], is that "those times shall come again". Freedom, the Saamaka know, is always provisional, and it demands constant alertness and resistance.

A State within a State?

The Maroons of the Guianas are insistently described as "states within a state".[16] There are two sides to this expression: it is a statement on the position Maroons occupy in relation to the nation-states that surround them; but it also suggests a reproduction of the state-form within Maroon societies. However, when anthropologists and historians talk about Businenge populations as "states within a state", I believe they are mainly concerned with the first statement – they linger on "within", but not on "state". I was never able to find in the available literature any explicit elaboration on why exactly Businenge political and social structures could be described as "states". Tellingly, Edward Green, characterizes the Matawai as a "state within a state" on the very same page he described them as a "simple, stateless society" (1977:107). Like him, authors using the expression did not bother to qualify what they understand as "states". From those unreflective usages of such a complex concept, we can infer an implicit comparison with one or more of the following forms of polity: the African kingdoms some Saamaka ancestors were a part of; the colonial state against which they fought; or the postcolonial states they today are subjects of. There is no reason to discard any of them as sources of inspiration for Saamaka political philosophy, but it would be necessary to look closer at each in order to take a stance on whether and why the Guiana Maroons could be aptly described as states. What follows is but a rough sketch of such inquiry.

African "States"

Two decades-long historical-anthropological debates make it troublesome to approach the sort of African data I am about to discuss from an Americanist

---

16   The expression appears in: Junker, 1932; Köbben, 1968:57, 1969b:127; Green, 1977:107; de Groot, 2009[1985]:182; Bilby, 1989; de Beet, 1992; Scholtens, 1994; Parris, 2004; Thoden van Velzen & Hoogbergen, 2011; Thoden van Velzen & van Wetering, 2013. It has been used to describe the Businenge at least since 1918 (cf. Kambel & McKay, 1999:68) and was also applied to Amerindian groups in Suriname such as the Trio (Carlin, 1998:6).

standpoint. The first debate is about the measure of continuities and ruptures between African and Afro-American sociocultural domains. The second is about the possibility of describing certain African pre-colonial political structures as states, which calls for a definition of what a state is. I will mostly avoid the first debate, which, as Scott (1991) noticed, is particularly sensitive in studies about Saamaka. On the second debate, what follows does not come near to exhausting the vast bibliography nor capturing all its nuances. My objective is merely to highlight the difficulties in defining "states" based on African data.

Guiana Maroon societies easily fit the category of "segmentary societies". Going back to the origin of the concept, Fortes & Evans-Pritchard (1940) created it as a sort of midpoint between "simple societies", and "primitive states" –, i.e., between societies where recognized kinship structures and the politico-jural community are conterminous; and societies where these spheres are clearly distinct, there being a specialized bureaucracy and/or political body. The structural complexity of "stateless segmentary societies" could distinguish them from "simple stateless societies", while the absence of a central political authority would distinguish them from "primitive states". According to Goldman, "the central idea is that, in the absence of a state, some other institution would perform the functions attached to it" (2001:67, my translation.) In the classic image of segmentary societies, the unilineal descent systems is the institution substituting the state.

However, that does not mean segmentarity is fully incompatible with state-like polities. After African Political Systems, complex typologies for segmentary societies were developed. The idea was to accommodate societies in which there was some form of segmentarity – understood as a nesting pattern on segmentary levels of complimentary opposition – but not in its simplest, pyramidal form (Middleton & Tait, 1970[1958]). Out of the many categories in these typologies, Southall's "segmentary states" come close to what I am looking for:

> [...] one in which there is a central kingship and many peripheral rulers. Political sovereignty is only exercised by the king within the central domain (which is indeed defined by this fact) and is also exercised autonomously by each peripheral ruler in his own domain. The sometimes minuscule kingships of the peripheral domains are replicas of the central kingship writ small. (1988:65)

Arguably, Guianese Maroon political systems could fit Southall's definition of segmentary states. However, his definition is merely morphological: much like most of the typological fine-tuning that followed Fortes and Evans-Pritchard, it says nothing on issues about political sovereignty – which is only passingly defined as the monopoly over the means of force.[17] One crucial element of political, state and segmentary structures is often left aside in this debate: the ideas people have and the way they act towards politics, a native theory of power relations. Perhaps – as MacGaffey (2005:197) insinuates – this element was left out because certain African political philosophies were a little too suggestive of anarchy.

Furthermore, those typologies still retain an evolutionist feel – the idea of a transition from kin-based to land-based structures, or from mechanical to organic solidarity. "Segmentary states" would be morphologically transitional, something between "pure segmentarity" and "pure state" (while "pure segmentarity" was already a transition between "state-like" and "stateless"). In that perspective, the ideal type of state is the European state, against which pre-colonial Sub-Saharan examples could structurally be measured. Thus, the state was defined by different authors through a checklist of characteristics found in Europe: territorial sovereignty; a centralized government; specialized administrative machinery; the monopoly of the legitimate use of force; etc.

The most controversial issue was the relationship between kinship and political organization. Vansina's definition, for instance, claims "a state would then be a political organization where kinship ties are not used as a basic principle of organization in the pattern of delegation of authority" (1962:324n4). Miller (1976), focusing on Mbuntu history, follows a less rigid definition of political structures as "stateless", "state" or "state-like": both "state" and "state-like" structures are characterized by "cross-cutting" institutions, wide-spreading and long-lasting enough to establish relationships among people unrelated by kinship; while only "state" structures are further characterized by centralization, territorial sovereignty and monopoly over the legitimate use of force.

Looking at the Saamaka and other Maroon communities in the Guianas, it is clear that kinship and politics cannot be divorced. The segmentary lineage model and the hierarchical structure of political offices are parallel and mutually interfering and, much like what happens in Kongo, as described by MacGaffey, segmentary oppositions work as an "agreed formula for making

---

17   Southall (1988:52) works with Nadel's (1942:69) threefold definition of state, into which the Saamaka most surely do not fit: their political unit is not "inter-tribal or inter-racial"; there is no "centralized maintenance of law and order"; nor the privileged ruling group is "separated in training, status and organization from the main body of the population". See next footnote.

FUNERALS, RHETORICS, RULES AND RULERS IN UPPER SURINAME 259

political claims" (2005: 198) – although not only political claims, I would add. Most of the other characteristics that were used to define the state – monopoly of violence, a system of taxation, territorial sovereignty, specialized administrative machinery – are absent in Saamaka.[18] In the end, attempts to define African "states" still leave us aimless on the question about whether it is useful to apply the concept of state to Businenge kin- and land-based socio-political configuration. The eurocentrism, typologism, morphologism and functionalism of those debates leave aside the most crucial elements for this inquiry: the substantive relationship between people occupying segments and centers. Following Goldman (2001) and MacGaffey (2005), I understand segmentary opposition – the nesting of subdivisions in virtually coexistent levels that are activated only in specific situations – not as a type, but as a characteristic or perspective. In other words, any political system can make use of various forms of segmentary oppositions. What defines the system as state-like is the rigidity of the segmentation – and the ethical, aesthetic and philosophical principles that allow for certain modes of rigidification.

The Colonial State and the Nation-State

Moving on to the relationship between the Businenge and the colonial and postcolonial state, other problems arise. To start with, it may seem paradoxical that, in those Maroon communities, political office holders wear uniforms in the very style of the colonial military their ancestors fought against, and that the scepters they carry are adorned with the Dutch or Surinamese coat of arms. Also, their titles are derivative of colonial roles such as captains (kabiteni) and overseers (basia).[19] But that is only paradoxical if we start from impoverishing dichotomies such as resistance versus submission.

R. Price oscillates in his opinions about the influence colonial models have on Businenge political forms. In an earlier work, he makes a generalizing claim for all Maroon communities of the Americas:

---

18 Legitimate physical punishments are not applied under the decision of the gaama or of a kabiteni, but by the family of a victim of rape or adultery. The gaama's, kabiteni's and basia's "fees" (see note 10) are not paid for by the Saamaka people, but by the Surinamese state. Clans have more sovereignty over their territory than the gaama. Given their attributions, I do not think that holders of political offices in Saamaka can be described as "administrative machinery", although that point is debatable.

19 On the etymology and history of the title basia, see Price, 1990, pp. 285-6n3 and Davis, 2011, pp. 947ff. Davis describes the black as a mediator between slaves and masters.

In contrast [with communities formed in the 16th and 17th centuries, mainly by African-born ex-slaves whose leadership models were based on African monarchies], after the beginning of the eighteenth century, maroon leaders only very rarely claimed princely descent from Africa, tending instead to style themselves captains, governors, or colonels rather than kings. (R. Price 1996[1973]: 20)

Years later, he asserted that:

[...] it would certainly be an error to assume that these offices were largely imposed from the outside [...] Rather, I would argue that in Saamaka, formalized political offices [...] existed from early runaway times, based firmly on African models of leadership, and that the treaty simply added to them an extra measure of authority. Before the treaty, Saamaka political office was already deeply bound up with notions of sacred authority, what Africanists call "mystical values". (1990: 314–5)

This oscillation is coherent with the theory of creolization (Mintz & Price, 1992), and with Price & Price's (2005/[1999]) take on Maroon arts: contemporary forms are the result of a New World history, but the underlying logic for transformation is guided by an African grammar. Ndyuka anthropologist Pakosie (1996) takes a similar position, claiming that their paramount leader's power ultimately stems from divine origins, and that their authority was only further validated by the colonial state through the peace treaties. I would add that, contemporaneously, nation-states have become parameters against which Businenge ideas of power are measured – as demonstrated by recent innovations such as adding secretaries and treasurers to village councils. Eventually, when upset with the attitudes of certain kabiteni or the gaama, my Saamaka interlocutors would entertain the idea of adopting a voting system for captains. Furthermore, in official events in Botopasi and other villages, Surinamese flag is raised and the national anthem is sung. Most certainly, "state-effects" (Trouillot, 2001) are visible in Saamaka displays of authority.

I understand that African "states", old colonial states and contemporary postcolonial states are all models used as background by the Saamaka to think about themselves, rather than direct inspirations or external impositions to their polity. Whether or not African pre-colonial kingdoms fit to it, the definition of a state I would go for is the one brought forward by Deleuze & Guattari (1987[1980]), who speak of a state as an abstract form of organizing power, which is never completely identified with its particular, concrete actualizations. Instead of a checklist of institutions, it makes more sense to think about the state as a mode of organizing authority, a machine that creates resonance among centers of power, codifying, through multiple institutions, territorialized forms of domination, making them referent to the same focal point. The state turns "optional rules" into "constraining rules" and "supple segmentarities" into "rigid segmentarities" – it is an apparatus of capture. In this sense, the structure of authority in Saamaka is anything but a "state within a state". On the contrary, it is a way to suppress state formation, even when eventually flirting with it. After all, nothing could be more opposed to an apparatus of capture than a congregation of runaway slaves.

Another way of defining the state is to approach its philosophical conditions of possibility, as does Agamben (1998[1995]). He claims that, ultimately, the political philosophy that originates the state is founded on the paradox of sovereignty, that is, on "the fact the sovereign is, at the same time, outside and inside the juridical order" (p. 17), being able to install a state of exception that denies the very rule of law that grants their authority. The sovereign state is able to break the rule of law by committing acts of violence which should be their very duty to suppress – it is, therefore, founded on violence. Maroon ethnogenesis shows that their political foundation is a rebellion against this very paradox, against the supposed inherent killability of the slave, against a form of state of exception we may call "social death" (Patterson, 1982) imposed on the black population. Never did the gaama have the capacity of installing anything like a state of exception – and their marginal roles in the recent civil war are a proof of that. Maroon politics is not founded on an imagined act such as the social contract, but on an act remembered and recurrently revisited through oral history: the act of flight. The model for belonging to Maroon polities is not citizenship, but membership to a lo, a clan put together by quasi-kin bonds among runaway slaves.

Certainly, time has brought changes. After the peace treaty, Maroon existence changed from what could be described as a semi-nomadic guerrilla style of life to a much more sedentary and territorialized one. Those changes had direct effects on the expected role of a leader: if during runaway times, there was need for a warrior, after the treaty, Maroons needed a negotiator (R. Price, 1990). Furthermore, a comparison of the authority held by gaama Agbagó Aboikoni – as described by R. and S. Price, who did the fieldwork while he was in charge (during the 1960s-70s) – to the way I experienced his grandson (ZDDS) Belfon Aboikoni's authority in the 2010s, it is quite evident that there have been a decrease in the gaama's concentration of decision-making power. Most of the Saamaka I spoke with about the issue agreed, and explained it by the simple reason that Agbagó was a better, fairer and wiser gaama.

That means we are back to the key issue on what qualities are expected from a leader in Saamaka, what makes people respect and listen to a gaama or a kabiteni – which shows a proximity to what Clastres calls "the philosophy of chieftainship" in "primitive societies". For Clastres, the essential quality of a chief – in what he calls societies against the state – is not the capacity to exercise power or violence over the community.

> What does a chief without power do? He is responsible. essentially, for assuming society's will to appear as a single totality, that is, for the community's concerned, deliberate effort to affirm its specificity, its autonomy, its independence in relation to other communities. In other words, the primitive leader is primarily the man who speaks in the name of society when circumstances and events put it in contact with others. [...] the primitive leader never makes a decision on his own authority (if we can call it that) and imposes it on his community [...]. He has only one right, or rather, one duty as spokesperson [...] (1994[1980]: 89)

In Saamaka, that is accomplished by segmentarity: the kabiteni is responsible for affirming the specificity of his village in relation to others; the hedi kabiteni, for affirming the specificity of a clan (or stretch of the river) in relation to others; the gaama, for affirming the independence of the totality of the Saamaka in relation to other populations and in relation to the state. But the levels are not concentric or rigid, they do not centralize the powers of decision and overcoding on higher levels of hierarchy. Rules are optional, and never become decrees or laws, which does not mean that there is no power.

> The central state is constituted not by the abolition of circular segmentarity but by a concentricity of distinct circles, or the organization of a resonance among centers. There are already just as many power centers in primitive societies; or, if one prefers, there are still just as many in state societies. The latter, however, behave as apparatuses of resonance; they organize resonance, whereas the former inhibit it. (Deleuze & Guattari 1987[1980]: 211, emphasis removed)

It is apparent, from the way the Saamaka face the authority of their gaama and captains, that a state apparatus of resonance or capture is absent. Power centers are scattered, the capacity to define rules, morals and situations is diffused over the social fabric, even if they tend to concentrate in certain poles – more on those who hold political offices than on those who do not; more on elders than on young people; more on men than on women. Like the above

FUNERALS, RHETORICS, RULES AND RULERS IN UPPER SURINAME 263

ethnographic episodes show, such tendencies, however, are often inverted in concrete situations.

On internal affairs, Saamaka leaders, like the chiefs described by Clastres, are heard because they have prestige. Attention paid to their words "never goes so far as allowing it to be transformed into a word of command, into a discourse of power". They do not rule, but regulate internal conflicts "by appealing to reason, to the opposing parties' good intentions, by referring constantly to the tradition of good relations [...] bequeathed by the ancestors ". They do not appeal to a transcendental law of which they would be the organ, they do not sanction relationships of command-obedience, they only reinforce "the discourse of society itself about itself, a discourse through which it proclaims itself an indivisible community and proclaims its will to persevere in this undivided being ". (1994[1980]:90). The power of speech is also the duty of speech – the art of rhetorics should be mastered not to pronounce orders, but to counsel, communicate, unite (Clastres, 1987[1974]). A prestigious kabiteni knows how to speak in a kuutu, his political skill is measured by the capacity of his voice to take effect. That is why an authority figure can also be called a takima ("the one who speaks"). Prestige, unlike power, is revocable. Even if a kabiteni holds his office for life, he might lose his prestige, which means his words will be effectively ignored by the community. Businenge groups are not states within states, because their leaders do not act by violence and overcoding, but by rhetorics and respect, which allows for a greater extent of resistance (or flight) by the least powerful.

That is what one should have in mind when regarding the problem established at the beginning of this chapter, the fact that "there are no burials without argument", or rather, that almost no relevant collective activity is performed without discussions on the proper way to do things. If almost everyone "lays out rules" for almost everybody else, there is no such thing as "obedience" in the sense of submissiveness, or subjection. More than specific forms or ritual gestures, the arguments are what set the tone of Saamaka funerals – whether in the ceremonial aesthetics of kuutu or in the joking games of politiki. Those arguments point to the fact that rules are optional, and thus, not conveyors of a morals of right and wrong, but rather, an assessment of the possible effects and risks that a decision on whether or not to follow a custom might have over people's lives. Tradition is taken seriously, because it represents a safe path taken by previous generations, but people can go where they please, and define the situation from their perspective.

If the ancestors of the Saamaka had followed the rules that were imposed to them, they would not have run away, and the community we know today would not exist. Their elders inaugurated a style of life, a path through space and time that opened the way for their descendants to move freely. The political hierarchy founded by those ancestors is based on optional rules, which means it is unlike political hierarchies of the state-form. Without a real center of power, without monopoly of violence, police or written laws, Saamaka polity is closer to what Clastres defined as a "society against the state". However, it would be more accurate to say Maroon societies are "societies against a state", because their reference is to specific materializations of the state-form. Clastres' "primitive societies" intuitively reject inequalities, they fight against a virtual centralization of power, whereas Maroon societies have lived in the past through those inequalities, and rebelled against them. Their political institutions were built as counterpoints to the colonial state, and they still act today as lines of flight to their successor, the postcolonial nation-state. Maroons are clearly able to learn from the various materializations of the state-form, to negotiate with them, and even be influenced by them, but they still strive against incorporation by them.

References

Agamben, Giorgio. 1998[1995]. Homo Sacer: Sovereign Power and Bare Life. Redwood City: Stanford University Press.

de Beet, Chris. 1992. "Een Staat in een Staat: Een Vergelijking tussen de Surinaamse en Jamaicaanse Marrons ". OSO, 11(2), 186–193.

Bilby, Kenneth. 1989. "Divided Loyalties: Local Politics and the Play of States among the Aluku". New West Indian Guide, 63(3/4), 143–173.

Bloch, Maurice, and Parry, Jonathan, eds. 1982. Death and the Regeneration of Life. Cambridge: Cambridge University Press.

Bona, Dénètem Touam. 2009. "La Naissance d'un Art Marron. Le 'Tembé'". Africultures, acessed September 18th, 2018, http://africultures.com/la-naissance-dun-art -marron-8499

Carlin, Eithne B. 1998. "Speech Community Formation: A Sociolinguistic Profile of the Trio of Suriname ". New West Indian Guide, 72(1/2), 4–42.

Clastres, Pierre. 1987[1974]. Society Against the State. New York: Zone Books.

Clastres, Pierre. 1994[1980]. The Archeology of Violence. New York: Semiotext(e).

Davis, Natalie Zemon. 2011. "Judges, Masters, Diviners: Slaves' Experience of Criminal Justice in Colonial Suriname". Law and History Review, 29(4), 925–984.

Deleuze, Gilles. 1995[1986]. "Life as a Work of Art (Conversation with D. Eribon)". In Negotiations (1972–1990), 94–101. New York: Columbia University Press.

Deleuze, Gilles, and Guattari, Félix. 1987[1980]. A Thousand Plateaus: Capitalism and Schizophrenia. Minneapolis: University of Minnesota Press.

FUNERALS, RHETORICS, RULES AND RULERS IN UPPER SURINAME 265

Fortes, Meyer, and Evans-Pritchard, E. E. 1940. African Political Systems. London: Oxford University Press.

Foucault, Michel. 1990[1984]. The Use of Pleasure: Vol. 2 of the History of Sexuality. New York: Vintage Books.

van Gennep, Arnold. 1960 [1909]. The Rites of Passage. London: Routledge.

Goldman, Marcio. 2001. "Segmentaridades e Movimentos Negros nas Eleições de Ilhéus". Mana, 7(2), 57–93.

Graeber, David. 2004. Fragments of an Anarchist Anthropology. Chicago: Prickly Paradigm.

Green, Edward C. 1977. "Social Control in Tribal Afro-America ". Anthropological Quarterly, 50(3), 107–116.

de Groot, Sylvia W. 2009[1985]. "A Comparison Between the History of Maroon Communities in Surinam and Jamaica ". In Agents of their own Emancipation: Topics in the History of Surinam Maroons, 175–184. Edited by Sylvia de Groot. Amsterdam: Eigen Beheer.

Herskovits, Melville, and Herskovits, Frances. 1971[1934]. Rebel Destiny: Among the Bush Negroes of Dutch Guiana. New York & London: Books For Libraries Press.

Hertz, Robert. 2003[1907]. "Contribution à une Étude sur la Représentation Collective de la Mort". In Sociologie Religieuse et Folklore, 19–64. Chicoutimi: Université du Québec.

Hoogbergen, Wim & Thoden van Velzen, H. U. E. 2011. Een Zwarte Vrijstaat in Suriname: De Okaanse Samenleving in de 18e Eeuw. Leiden: KITLV.

Metcalf, Peter, and Huntington, Richard. 1991[1979]. Celebrations of Death: The Anthropology of Mortuary Ritual. Cambridge: Cambridge University Press.

Junker, L. 1932–3. "Een Staat in den Staat". De West-Indische Gids, 14, 267–280.

Kambel, Ellen-Rose, and Fergus MacKay. 1999. The Rights of Indigenous Peoples and Maroons in Suriname. Copenhagen: IWGIA.

Köbben, Andre J. F. 1968. "Continuity in Change: Cottica Djuka Society as a Changing System". Bijdragen tot de Taal-, Land- en Volkenkunde, 124(1), 56–90.

Köbben, Andre J. F. 1969a. "Classificatory Kinship and Classificatory Status: The Cottica Djuka of Surinam ". Man, 4(2), 236–249.

Köbben, Andre J. F. 1969b. "Law at Village Level: The Cottica Djuka of Surinam ". In Law in Culture and Society, 117–140. Edited by Laura Nader. Chicago: Aldine.

MacGaffey, Wyatt. 2005. "Changing Representations in Central African History ". Journal of African History, 46, 189–207.

Marrenga, Menno & Paulus, Etto. 2011. Talking with Saramaka People. Paramaribo: Ralicon.

Middleton, John, and Tait, David. 1970[1958]. 1970 [1958]. Tribes Without Rulers – Studies in African Segmentary Systems. New York: Humanities Press.

Migge, Bettina 2004. "The Speech Event Kuutu in the Eastern Maroon Community". In Creoles, Contact and Language Change: Linguistic and Social Implications, 285–306. Edited by Geneviève Escure & Armin Schwegler. Amsterdam: John Benjamins.

Miller, Joseph C. 1976. Kings and Kinsmen: Early Mbundu States in Angola. London: Oxford University Press.

Mintz, Sidney W. & Price, Richard 1992. The Birth of African-American Culture: An Anthropological Perspective. Boston: Beacon Press.

Nadel, Siegfried F. 1942. A Black Byzantium: The Kingdom of Nupe in Nigeria. London: Oxford University Press.

Pakosie, Andre R. 1996. "Maroon Leadership and the Surinamese State (1760–1990)". Journal of Legal Pluralism and Unofficial Law, 37/38, 263–277.

Parris, Jean-Yves. 2004. "Entre Forêt et Côte: l'Inclusion Négociée des Marrons Ndjuka du Surinam." Autrepart, 31(3), 21–34.

Patterson, Orlando. 1982. Slavery and Social Death: A Comparative Study. Cambridge: Harvard University Press.

Pires, Rogério B. W. 2015. A Mása Gádu Könde: Morte, Espíritos e Rituais Funerários em uma Aldeia Saamaka Cristã. PhD diss., PPGAS/Museu Nacional, Universidade Federal do Rio de Janeiro.

Pires, Rogério B. W. 2017. "Dinheiro, Tecidos, Rum e a Estética do Eclipsamento em Saamaka". Mana, 23(3), 545–577.

Price, Richard, 1996[1973]. Maroon Societies: Rebel Slave Communities in the Americas (3rd ed.). Baltimore: Johns Hopkins University Press.

Price, Richard. 1990. Alabi's World. Baltimore: Johns Hopkins University Press.

Price, Richard. 2002[1983]. First-Time: The Historical Vision of an African American People. Chicago: The University of Chicago Press.

Price, Richard. 2011. Rainforest Warriors: Human Rights on Trial. Philadelphia: University of Pennsylvania Press.

Price, Richard. & Price, Sally. 1991. Two Evenings in Saramaka. Chicago: The University of Chicago Press.

Price, Richard. & Price, Sally. 2005[1999]. Les Arts des Marrons. La Roque-d'Anthéron: Vents d'Ailleurs.

Price, Sally. 1993. Co-Wives and Calabashes. Ann Arbor: University of Michigan Press.

Scholtens, Ben. 1994. Bosnegers en Overheid in Suriname: De Ontwikkeling van de Politieke Verhouding 1651–1992. Paramaribo: Afdeling Cultuurstudies/Minov.

Scott, David. 1991. "That Event, This Memory: Notes on the Anthropology of African Diasporas in the New World ". Diaspora, 1(3), 261–284.

Southall, Aidan. 1988. "The Segmentary State in Africa and Asia ". Comparative Studies in Society and History, 30(1), 52–82.

Strathern, Marilyn. 1988. The Gender of the Gift: Problems with Women and Problems with Society in Melanesia. Berkeley: University of California Press.

Thoden van Velzen, H. U. E. & van Wetering, Willelmina. 2013. Een Zwarte Vrijstaat in Suriname. De Okaanse Samenleving in de 19e and 20e Eeuw. Leiden: E.J. Brill.

Trouillot, Michel-Rolph. 2001. "The Anthropology of the State in the Age of Globalization: Close Encounters of the Deceptive Kind". Current Anthropology, 42(1), 125–138.

Vansina, Jan. 1962. "A Comparison of African Kingdoms ". Africa, 32(4), 324–35.

Wagner, Roy. 1972. "Incest and Identity: A Critique and Theory on the Subject of Exogamy and Incest Prohibition ". Man, 7(4), 601–613.

CHAPTER 9

Self-Fashioning and Visualization among the Cottica Ndyuka

Olívia Maria Gomes da Cunha

I had recognized Bina's father and mother from Manjabon village in a video bought from a Ndyuka salesman in Saramakastraat in Paramaribo.[1] When I showed Bina the film, she made an observation that, for the first time, caused me to think that contact with death among my Maroon interlocutors was not only feared but also something carefully avoided. Though not appearing in the video, Bina told me that she too had attended the ceremony. On the day in question, she had left her younger children with her oldest son and taken a boat to Manjabon. 'I don't like taking the children to these places,' she remarked. 'Today children go to the cemeteries and have contact with ceremonies held for the dead. That wasn't permitted in the past. Only the family was allowed to visit the place of the burial. The funeral ceremonies were completely barred to children and strangers. After the [civil] war everything changed. Maroon people see their neighbours worshipping their dead and doing these things in the open and want to do the same. ...' These neighbours were Maroon groups with whom some of the Ndyuka lived and married, but also non-Maroon people – *bakaa* (outsiders) of a different kind.[2]

Bina's comments do not contradict the fact that funerary ceremonies like *puu baaka* shown in the video combine sombre family obligations and the more festive enjoyment of Maroon and non-Maroon guests. The transformations in funerary rituals among Maroon peoples, whether held in the villages or in urban contexts in which non-Maroon are also present, have been noted by other anthropologists (Polimé 1998; van de Pijl 2007, 2016; Pires 2015). As

---

[1] Printed on the DVD cover is the title Poeroe-Blaka. Kapitin Djante Ronan. Manja Bong [funerary ceremony in honour of the captain of Manjabon village, Djante Ronan], reel 1 (15/09/2006).

[2] The fieldwork on which the material presented here is based was conducted over various periods between October 2013 and October 2016, supported by funding from CNPq (the National Council for Scientific and Technological Development). A first and substantially different version of this article was presented at the conference 'Anthropology and Photography 2014,' organized by the Royal Anthropological Institute at the British Museum, Clore Centre, London, May 29th 2014.

SELF-FASHIONING AND VISUALIZATION AMONG THE COTTICA NDYUKA

Kenneth Bilby (1990) pointed out in his work on the Aluku in the late 1980s, these meetings mobilize money, work, resources, food, ceremonial exchanges and obligations, as well as the need for kin who are living on the coast and inland to travel to the forest and the villages. Such changes can be associated with migration from the interior to the Guianese coast, a process that increased in the late 1960s and intensified after the Interior War (1986–1992). These transformations also included new relationships between migrant families and the non-Maroon population, along with the first wave of conversions to Christian and Pentecostal churches. Funerary rituals became not just a family obligation but also a spacetime for multiple encounters: places and moments in which people could reconnect with parents, gods, spirits, ancestors and other Maroon, as well as *bakaa* interlocutors. These encounters simultaneously permit the 'reaffirmation of the bonds and ritual obligations of the deceased's family members with their matrilineal villages and the tenacity of the Maroons vis-à-vis their Others and vice-versa' (Bilby 1990:360).

Bina's remark that Maroon people 'want to do the same' as other people, along with her immediate interest in watching the video, as she announced on this and various other occasions when we watched such films together, can be seen to illustrate a double movement. Her acknowledgment of the dangers associated with funerary rituals, combined with her interest in participating in their visualization, reveal an interesting mixture of meanings and perspectives concerning the process of incorporating alterities. The recognition of the possibilities opened up by new interactions with the *bakaa* world signals an ambivalence: on one hand, the fear of losing the authenticity and control of Ndyuka traditional knowledge after contact with different spiritual universes – such as, for example, Christianity and the winti practices of the Creoles; on the other, the Maroon capacity to establish dialogues, incorporate new ideas, and absorb ritual, aesthetic and semantic innovations into their everyday lives. The transformations that Bina saw happening in funerary rituals were noted and, above all, experienced in different manners. Movements could be perceived that incorporated practices, aesthetics and forms of knowledge attributed to the relations with non-Maroons and, at the same time, generated unexpected effects. These effects are the object of traditional knowledge, such as the myths, narratives and therapeutic procedures associated with the proliferation of strange creatures brought by bakaa or attracted by their presence in Maroon territories, and also the object of rituals that aim to purge bodies of the contact with money and other objects from the white world, purchased and brought by prosperous migrants returning to the villages (Vernon 1980, 1985; Thoden van Velzen & van Wetering 1982; van Wetering 1992). The Cottica villages were historically more deeply affected by the constant presence of *bakaa*, whether the latter were missionaries belonging to different Christian denominations, officers from the colonial government, workers hired from India, Indonesia and China, and, after 1975, cooperative members, or workers from the mining and logging industries. In the Maroon apperception, this problematic proximity has not just been responsible for innumerable forms of environmental and spiritual damage. The slow depopulation of the villages through migratory processes that bring people closer to the world and things of the *bakaa* – objects, wealth, money, habits and relations with unknown non-human agencies – also affects the universe of interactions that make the Maroon person a 'composite' (Price 2008:288) of relations involving spirits, gods and ancestors.

The terms in which Magnus Course examines the relations between the Mapuche and the whites, in which potencies, materiality and knowledge all participate, provide us with some insights into processes already documented by the literature on Maroon peoples of the Guianas since the colonial period. Their complex relations with non-Maroons cannot be limited to an endless clash between predefined alterities. On the contrary, they comprise movements and shifts that are conflictual but also creative, involving modes of incorporation and 'continuous transformation.' Describing the Koyong, clowns that embody the presence of white people in Mapuche sociality, Course observes that they are 'not so much about the positive incorporation of the Other into the Self, but rather as the instantiation of the moment when it ceases to make sense to speak of the relationship between Mapuche and winka in terms of Self and Other, which instead become visible as converging points on a continuum of transformation, a transformation also visible in the shifts in identity wrought by the forced urban migration' (2013: 773).

For Bina, seeing a funerary ritual recorded on an electronic device was not the same as experiencing it. There was no continuity between visualization and participation. As an observer, she took part in a practice of instantiation and could see *kulturu*[3] being what it always had been, something continually transformed by all kinds of human and non-human agencies. Visualization, in turn, allowed her to see *kulturu* as the *bakaa* see it. The transformative capacity of ancestral knowledge and practices in the composition of the Ndyuka person enabled her to envisage the Self from the Other's perspective. But as a lived experience, the shift between cosmological universes caused her some

---

3   A Sranantongo word used to describe materiality, knowledge and practices owned and/or inherited by a people, but also religious practices, glossing over any references to healing and witchcraft (Pijl 2007; van Wetering 1996).

SELF-FASHIONING AND VISUALIZATION AMONG THE COTTICA NDYUKA   271

concern: it had the potential to produce effects in the bodies of her family members. Bina's fears are no mere idiosyncrasy.

Marilyn Strathern observes that very often an element adopted from a neighbouring group does not signify a large-scale 'cultural transformation' (1981) but a kind of obviation – a particular usage, a metaphor of something. An object or name imported from the non-Maroon world, for instance, may capture a sense of innovation, and perform a dynamic role as a powerful element. A unique person immersed in a diverse set of social relations can thus be created. Although not without tension and conflict, the introduction of a person, an item of knowledge, or an unexpected artefact is always a surprise. Ever since their earliest times in the Guianese forests, Maroon people have learned how to face the unknown and prepare themselves, both spiritually and materially, to negotiate with all its potential consequences, forms or powers. The ability to creatively face and transform the unknown is the aspect that, in my view, most typifies what many of us recognize as Maroon 'traditional knowledge.'[4]

In order for us to comprehend the effects of these creative processes, it should be noted from the outset that the producers of photographic or cinematographic images did not wish to document a specific ritual dynamic in a realistic fashion. Instead, recording the event allowed relations between kin and ancestors to become singularized, separated both temporally and ontologically. At least in the view of those individuals responsible for organizing the event, all of them converts to Christianity, utilization of this recording technology allowed the interruption of certain direct connections to the villages, spirits and animals of the past, and also made possible new engagements with social practices and relations with non-Maroon people in the present. The making of images of an artificially created public event seemed to inaugurate new 'ways of seeing' and looking at the self. More than a mirror, less than a document, the images spun their optical effects, revealing different perspectives and intensities in the relations making up the Maroon person.

This chapter sets out to describe the creation of visual artefacts to cope with the ontological transformations experienced by the Cottica Ndyuka Maroon population living in the small bauxite town of Moengo, as well as the villages situated along the Cottica river and its affluents, in the Marowijne district of Suriname's eastern coast. It describes some of the effects arising from the creation of a 'public event' called the Poolo Boto Show, a parade of boats in which groups of men and women performing traditional dances and music, dressed

---

4   A movement of producing 'continuity-in-change' (Price and Price 1999:308), incorporating the Other as part of the Self, as ethnologists have formulated in relation to other traditional peoples (Viveiros de Castro 1998; Santos-Granero 2009; Course 2013).

in specially produced clothes, took part in a contest that attracted widespread interest and participation. Electronic devices were employed to capture performances inspired by ceremonies from the Ndyuka funerary calendar, recording them as 'traditional knowledge' (*koni*) – related to life in the villages and how the ancestors lived in the past – to be viewed by kin and new generations of Maroon born or now living in the cities. Digital images were also taken during the preparations for the festival and have played an important role as artefacts used for discovering 'how things were in the past.' First I describe some of the controversies that surrounded the preparations for the first boat parade. Next I consider contemporary processes of learning about the 'past' and 'traditional life,' showing how these are related to an older and still on-going process of differentiation between the Cottica Ndyuka and other Maroon peoples. In the conclusion, I return to the theme of incorporation, a dimension central to my argument, so as to discuss how the creation and learning of things done 'in the past' can erupt into accusations, criticisms and ontological apperceptions concerning Maroon persons in the present.

This Is Not a Ritual

Recent ethnographies have called attention to the dangers of the weak differentiation made – in general by outside observers – between 'traditional' and 'non-traditional' knowledge. While the former is seen to be marked by signs of authenticity and withdrawal from any attempts to make them 'representatives' or 'artefacts of culture,' the latter are taken, by contrast, to be distorted versions of the former, contaminated by a market logic and the consumption of cultural products. Yet not only does this opposition continue to reinforce stereotyped views of practices and artefacts designated 'traditional' and 'non-traditional,' held by those who produce them and those who study them alike, it also precludes us from learning more about the meanings attributed to these designations as they continually shift and change relational form (Battaglia 1995b; Sahlins 1999; Clifford 2004). Moreover, it obscures the constant fabrication of contents and how these are linked to creations and meanings attributed to both terms by preceding generations.

The creation of a public event inspired by traditional knowledge implied a rearrangement of the relations between the Cottica Ndyuka and diverse practices and subjects. It encompassed the former's connections with their others, local or foreign, their neighbours and kin who had converted to different forms of Christianity, and a new generation of children and young people born and raised outside the villages. Simultaneously, it weakened the meanings attributed to a number of everyday practices, such as the execution of funerary ceremonies, backed by the involvement of traditional authorities and cosmic forces that have traditionally participated in a set of rites designed to carefully separate the dead from the living within the space of the villages. Among those converted to Pentecostal denominations of Christianity, the interruption of this practice, which they take to be firmly set 'in the past,' has not only generated conflicts within the matrilineages, but also caused disturbances, suffering and other dilemmas experienced at a personal level. For many people, though, knowing or revealing the 'past' in order to experience it aesthetically as a cultural artefact – one transformed into a public event, held outside the villages and not limited to the participation of kin, thus making it devoid of the ontological implications that mark ritual actions and the potential presence of spirits – involved some considerable risks. As I shall show later, there was a unanimous denial that the public event was intended to reproduce or represent a ritual practice linked to the calendar of funerary ceremonies. Even so, the realization of practical actions, the formation of political assemblages and the efforts to convince neighbours, members of Christian communities and village authorities were all preceded by considerable conceptual investment in its design. The proposed event was not a reproduction or representation of a ritual performed in the villages and part of the funerary calendar, but a creation, a public event.

On this point, a curious convergence can be noted between the debate that took place among the Cottica Ndyuka who participated in the conception, organization and realization of the event over precisely what it was that they were creating, and the efforts employed for years by anthropologists to specify the exact boundaries of actions performed as part of rituals and public events. This merits a brief detour. A wide range of conceptual approaches have been employed to accompany analyses of rituals and their links to social structures and practices (see De Coppet 1992). Procedures designed to describe and classify actions taken to be part of a specific set of practices that encompass rituals have diverged not simply in terms of the elements selected for inclusion, but also, and above all, in their problematization of the epistemological implications informing the conceptual approach. Frequently separated and contrasted through the relevance attributed to aspects denominated either secular or religious, and distinguished thanks to the emphasis on their orders of immanence and transcendence, the relations created, reaffirmed and transformed in ritual practices were, to a certain extent, limited by this polarization. Ethnographies based on exercises of separation and classification are more inclined to conceal than reveal the forms, contents and relations that define a set of practices as ritual (Asad 1993). Both anthropologists and historians have called attention to the dangers of weak differentiation, in general made by external observers, and the need to examine the multiplicity of engagements and 'truth regimes' in which the making of these events are immersed.

At the same time, other authors have problematized reinterpretations of so-called 'secular rituals' (Moore & Myerhoff 1977) and 'public events' (Connerton 1989; Handelman 1990), sometimes characterized as engagements that enable the 'recreation' or realization of practices to 'protect' the knowledge or 'traditional culture' of specific groups, turning them into public spectacles in urban, national or migratory contexts. Ethnographic accounts based on comparative approaches have expressed concerns about the ways in which the people involved in these activities describe them and, at same time, are self-fashioned through them. The aims of these ethnographies have been to highlight local conflicts over the 'meanings' attributed to public events and performances considered part of 'traditional' and 'non-traditional' culture, which cannot always be characterized by the elements typically attributed to rituals. Unlike diverse forms of 'celebration' involving ritualized performances, practices, and rites, sometimes grounded in myth and traditional knowledge, public events cannot be defined exclusively by their capacity to promote actions based on 'formality,' 'replicability,' 'intentionality' and a coherent 'symbolic formation.' As Don Handelman aptly observed, because of their capacity to mobilize ideas, actors, users, social relationships and places of reference, as well as performances that evade the definition of ritual due to their explicit inventiveness and creativity, so-called public events are epistemologically and ontologically marked by a 'state of confusion' (1990:14). Handelman, however, emphasized dimensions related to form, design, structure, enactments and 'intentionality' that frequently comprise and differentiate public events from rituals. For this author, these can be seen as 'abstractions' but 'profoundly existential, since no event qua event can exist substantively as a phenomenon apart from its practice' (1990:17).[5]

Examples from other ethnographic contexts also offer interesting analytic treatments and can be productively compared to the ethnographic material discussed in the following sections. Sometimes allusions are made to practices conceived as traditional through the use of metaphors and the linguistic and symbolic manipulation of elements that elicit a memory, or an element identifying the actions of the present with those of the past. Pnina Werbner, for

---

5 The analysis of Sally and Richard Price (1994) of the dilemmas and limits of their participation in the Festival of American Folklore, promoted by the Smithsonian Institution in Washington D.C. in 1992, offers us a privileged insight into the ambiguation arising from the participation of the Maroon in the creation of a 'public event.'

example, explores the ethnic and political assemblages surrounding the re-reading of the *mothei* puberty rituals among girls in tribal areas of Botswana, transformed into *bojale*, a public celebration organized amid competitive activities and promoted by urban-dwelling Tswana. In the native experience in the villages, Werbner argues, initiation rituals involved a series of markedly private corporal interventions that signalled an ontological transformation: girls began their adult life through ritual activities associated with commensality, the exchange of presents, solidarity between women, and local recognition. By functioning as 'indexical dimensions of the ritual' (Werbner 2014:378), corporal inscriptions, aesthetic productions, and the occupation of the space of the village and houses by movements and dances all comprise important symbolic elements that confer dignity and recognition to the girls who became adults thanks to the participation of the community, especially women and elders. By acquiring a re-reading and a public dimension in an urban context, the *bojale* version of initiation rites – conducted, as the author observes, with inventive-ness, improvisation and the intense participation of family and ancestors – is subject to rules, competitive norms and criteria for participation tuned to a political reading in which Tswapong women are 'liberated' from the physical violence that 'subjugated' them traditionally. By becoming public, puberty rit-uals are transformed into celebrations in which not only the bodies of women as indices of gender differentiation, but also those of Tswapong migrants, are reterritorialized within a multiethnic context. Werbner's example also reveals an important dimension of the material discussed below. The puberty rituals held in the villages consist above all of practices of self-knowledge, enabling the girls to learn about their bodies, the universe that they inhabit and their re-lations to kin and ancestors. Ritually transformed, their bodies became socially recognized to the extent that they both perform – through movement, music, dance and other ritual dynamics – and materialize their relations with Others.

The material analysed by Debora Battaglia is also concerned with prob-lematizing the translation of practices and cultural creations. She concen-trates on the production of knowledge surrounding the 'traditional' planting and harvesting of yams associated with the First Annual Trobriand Yam Fes-tival. Organized by, among others, a Trobriand islander and a government of-ficer, the festival had, among other objectives, the aim of revealing the traces of a 'tradition' in a setting marked by migration and the constant movement of people between village and city. The festival was conceived as almost a reproduction of traditional Trobriand competitions, the *kayasa*. In Port Mo-resby, the competition would involve the population that grew yams in yards. Battaglia observes, though, that, 'the kayasa armature was kin-based relations of alliance; the yam festival invited participations of other ethnic groups'

(1995a:79). Battaglia describes the way in which urban Trobrianders living in Port Moresby comprehend and transform the meanings of the practices associated with land and yam growing. Rather than emphasize the similarities between the forms of planting and using yams in the native plantations, the 'House' gardens (1995a:77) of the Trobriand Islands, elegantly described by B. Malinowski, or even explore the growing relevance that both the planted species and the relations to land seem to have acquired in the present, Battaglia observes the forces that activate these processes as 'vehicles' for producing knowledge. The accent on the active and performative aspects of these practices allows the author to question the scope and effects of these modes of creating connections with the 'past.' With its evocation of the affective and aesthetic values attributed to land cultivation – but also to what she calls a 'sense of future' (Battaglia 1995a: 78), an idea that reflects how the control of the time of planting and the transformation of crops into recourses for other forms of consumption reinforce new and potential relations of Trobrianders living intermittently in urban contexts – the Trobriand Yam Festival reveals the new relations maintained by islanders living today in Port Moresby.

The material described by Battaglia allows us to formulate various comparisons with the Cottica Ndyuka, both in terms of the tense interactions and dialogues that preceded and enabled the first three editions of the Poolo Boto festival to be held, and in terms of the local political effects of the two examples. In Port Moresby and Moengo alike, 'local,' 'regional,' 'national' and 'ethnic' were politically powerful inscriptions in circulation, enabling diverse convergences to be identified between the Trobrianders and the Cottica Ndyuka in a 'symbolic economy of alterity' (Viveiros de Castro 1998). What seems to me more relevant in Battaglia's analysis, however, is the fact that she offers a specific viewpoint, a particular mode of understanding an element present in the material analysed below: namely, the way in which the use of technological artefacts functions as an instrument for acquiring knowledge and for elaborating and constructing the self (see also Battaglia 1995b).

The analysis of the movements that enabled the creation of the event as culture and, simultaneously, of the effects and new relations that became established as a result, eschews any attempt to comprehend such events as a representation, mimesis, invention or even metaphor of lost cultural practices. An event can only be understood as an invention insofar as its meaning is exclusively associated with the unexpected, the creation of something new that reinscribes and transforms relations that render other practices comprehensible (Wagner 1981). In the case of the boat parade, this invention happened when its proponents argued for the close proximity – contested by many – between the parade and various practices associated with funerary ceremonies. Neither was the boat parade conceived as an allegorical version of practices understood as cultural, though: it was an expression aesthetically and historically linked to Cottica Ndyuka modes of existence in the present. This enables the continuity of creative expressions in which their relations with their non-Maroon others become aesthetically and politically visible. It was unnecessary, therefore, to add new meanings to the evocation of the time when certain things and practices existed. The references to the past – the spacetime of the villages, the ancestors, the gods and the spirits that inhabited the forests and protected the matrilineages – are simply part of the everyday life of the Maroon person and his or her multiple belongings, selves and connections (Vernon 1988; Strange 2016). In sum, the festival was not created as a fabrication involving a return to supposedly lost traditions, nor as the nostalgic expression of a universe of relations between kin, living or dead, who no longer exist. On the contrary, as we shall see, those who invented the festival as a way for the Cottica Ndyuka to celebrate cultures in the plural, imagined the event as an aesthetic apperception of ontological transformations that form part of the everyday experiences of Maroon persons living in Moengo.

Making Difference Differently

In August 2013, the extensive and complex network of Ndyuka families living in Moengo – connected to relatives, friends, government representatives, companies and non-governmental organizations, but above all directly associated with the villages of their matriclans on the Cottica river – could be seen in full motion. Marowijne became one of the Surinamese districts to host Carifesta, the famous Caribbean Festival of Arts, held annually in different Caribbean countries. A local Commission was set up and representatives of the Maroon, Amerindian, Creole, Hindustani and Chinese groups were invited to program a day of festivities involving theatrical, musical and choreographic groups from the district and abroad: music bands from Jamaica, Cuba and French Guiana were invited to perform on the stage assembled and decorated in the centre of the small town.

Significantly, the edition of the festival was named after an Okanisi expression that emphasizes the importance of self-knowledge: 'Carifesta XI Marowijne: Sabi yu Seefi' ('Know yourself').[6] A small group of Cottica

---

6   Terms in Okanisi (also Ndyuka or Aucaner) will appear in italics, followed by their translation. In relation to orthographic convention, I use the grammars produced by Huttar & Huttar (1994) and Goury & Migge (2003).

Ndyuka women and men worked actively on the Commission to organize the events. The idea was to combine presentations by foreign groups with shows by local artists. However, 'local' participation had to involve a composition of Marowijne cultures and not just a manifestation of the Cottica Ndyuka, despite their substantial presence in the villages of the Cottica area and in the bauxite town of Moengo. So as to maintain good relations with non-Maroon groups in the region and with the descendants of Javanese, Chinese and Creole populations, such facts were never openly stated. Nonetheless, this did not prevent constant disagreements within the Commission. I witnessed various divergences of opinion during the preparatory meetings held in Moengo in July and August 2012, often expressed in different languages and fairly private situations.[7] Although everyone knew that each representative was there to act on behalf of their respective communities, their cautious interventions seemed to partake of the same rhetoric: any complaint based on particular motives was deemed politically inappropriate. Instead a 'poetics' was employed in which distinct forms of self-presentation performed imaginary roles and ambiguities, but also generated 'coalitions,' as Stuart Strange (2016b) defines them, a dimension not always recognized in public. Marowijne's participation in the festival had to expose this ambivalent and shared discourse metonymically.

The main difficulties faced by the Commission's small group of Maroon participants when it came to organizing the activities were not the disagreements between Ndyuka and non-Ndyuka members. The problems, in fact, appeared in more intense and durable form among the Maroon themselves, over the course of the different attempts to imbue life into an idea that grew out of the following questions: how should Cottica Ndyuka people living in the region be represented? How should the Maroon fashion themselves and cope with the festival format, including its projection of 'culture' as an artefact or an expression of one specific group or people? The festival did not erase old disputes and conflicts, yet it did allow new relationships to form between Cottica Ndyuka and non-Maroon. We could speculate that openly neglecting their own interests was a strategy, since the Cottica Ndyuka who participated on the Commission made their presence effective. By foregrounding a discourse that emphasized a pluriethnic view of the nation, Maroon people made themselves visible, though not in the same way that state and private institutions tried to frame their presence during the festival. Perhaps this is because, to quote

---

7 For the use the language as an aesthetic and political marker of difference in Suriname, see R. Price & S. Price (2015:254), and Migge & Léglise (2015). On the use of Sranantongo and Okanisi in Moengo, see Migge & Léglise (2015).

SELF-FASHIONING AND VISUALIZATION AMONG THE COTTICA NDYUKA   279

Battaglia on the problem of 'ambiguation' among urban Trobrianders performing in the 'national festival,' their 'form of agency embodied other doublings,
other bifocalities, including those of organizers enacting figure-ground rever-
sals of "modern" and "local" identities' (1997:508).

The debate in the Commission led to a tacit agreement: the hosting of the
Carifesta festival in Moengo would maintain its multicultural character with
each 'people' and 'country' duly represented. As well as the Creole kaseko
groups from Paramaribo and French Guiana, plus the foreign music bands,
Marowijne made its presence felt through the presentation of its own 'traditional population': one group formed by the Kali'na de Galibi and Albina, the
other gamelan formed by descendants of Javanese residents from the Won-
oredjo district. The Cottica Ndyuka were represented by an awasa group and
an aleke band coming from the village of Ricanaumofo.[8]

There are various ways, though, for us to perceive the ambiguities, nuances,
disagreements and tense relations that permeated not only the composition
of the Commission, but the way in which the Cottica Ndyuka were represented on it, validating other affinities, their different ties to diverse matriclans,
villages, political and personal interests, and, in some cases, experiences of
conversion to Christianity. Among these we can pick out one element that, in
principle, can be identified as generational and would seem to encompass all
the other dissimilarities. It allows us to connect the plurality of positions to the
event that all of them were working to create.

The life histories of the families of the commission's members – Bina,
Yvonne, Bas and Marcel[9] – are directly connected to the outbreak, experiences and impacts of the civil war. As Bina observed at the start of this
chapter, many things changed afterwards. The stories told about these experiences are very similar, differing only in intensity, in the topography of
exile, and in the way in which they individually affected the members of
the same household (*osu*). When conflict erupted, their family members fled
from Moengo and the nearby villages, taking shelter in refugee camps in the
interior or in the homes of kin in French Guiana and Paramaribo. From 1992
a large number of families that had been living in refugee camps established

---

8   Kaseko is a Creole musical style and Aleke a Maroon style. Awasa is a dance traditionally per-
    formed by Ndyuka and Aluku in funerary ceremonies; over recent decades it has also been
    performed by cultural and musical groups in cities (Bilby 2010:8; Campbell 2012).
9   To protect the anonymity of my interlocutors, I have used pseudonyms and changed factual
    references, conflating situations that involved different people, as well as employing other
    narrative devices that help prevent identification of their actual names. The only exception
    is where the authorship of an idea, an event or an artefact needs to be registered.

by the French state, assisted by humanitarian aid agencies, finally returned, not to the villages though, but to semi-destroyed and abandoned houses and other buildings in Moengo, which were promptly invaded. In the following years, according to agreements established by the Kouru Treaty, some new residences were built to house the returnees, though insufficient to absorb the large influx of families that began to concentrate in one of Moengo's districts.

The families of Bina and other Cottica Ndyuka differed in terms of their relationships to Moengo prior to the war. What they did share, though, were intense experiences marked by dispersion and distancing from the traditional territories where their predecessors and ancestors had once lived. Bina, Yvonne, Bas, Marcel and Pili are all around the age of 40 and were still children during the time of exile. About 20 years after their families returned to Moengo, and thanks to some degree of schooling, they were working, directly or indirectly, for government bodies as teachers and public workers in the districts of Marowijne and Paramaribo. Their families are scattered in villages like Peetondo, Manja Bon, Adjuma and Damtapu, but also in Paramaribo and Charvein (French Guiana). Today they live with their children and, in some cases, grandchildren in neighbourhoods of Moengo. Their houses and adjacent terrains form territories of affinity and intense cooperation, which extend to the villages to and from which family members leave and arrive daily. In some cases, the dwelling is home to authorities from the villages, who visit kin, make purchases in the local markets, use medical and bank services, and sometimes go to religious services in the numerous Catholic and Pentecostal churches scattered throughout Moengo. The local houses are points of intercession, places for exchanges, meetings and family work that extend to the universe of the villages.

One of the Cottica Ndyuka on the Commission was Marcel Pinas, an internationally recognized visual artist who headed various local cultural projects, like the Tembe Art Studio (TAS) and the Kiibi Foundation, supported by agencies and foundations based in Paramaribo and internationally. Also on the Commission were Bas, who had converted to a Pentecostal church some years previously and had participated actively in the logistical tasks; Bina, who works in the local public school; and Yvonne, a public worker. Since one of the Commission's objectives was to turn the event into a source of income, linked to the state's policy of attracting development projects to the region, Yvonne was responsible for establishing contacts with the traditional authorities. This contact between the Commission's members and the Maroon villages – which, for their part, also made use of different networks associated with the importance of the lineages within and between the villages, as well as

SELF-FASHIONING AND VISUALIZATION AMONG THE COTTICA NDYUKA 281

their connections, not always visible, with Surinamese political parties in Marowijne – was not only verbally emphasized but, as we shall see, 'materialized' in the choice of the event's participants. Nonetheless, since the Commission's composition was not exclusively Maroon, Yvonne had to activate other networks of family and neighbours in the attempt to plan the organization of an event that was at once familiar but not exclusive to the Maroon population. Over almost two months of preparation, organization of the event contained a tension between producing something that met the tastes of the local populations and constructing a synthetic composition of this diverse 'representation.'

In the middle of formulating this program, it was Marcel who first had the idea of something specific, an activity that would, in principle, unite Maroons, Amerindians, Javanese and those keenest to take part: a decorated boat parade on the Cottica river in which each village or group could show what 'it wants from its culture.' His idea was to organize something 'local' with the participation of the 'community.' When this plan was discussed with Bas, Bina and Yvonne, it aroused some concern. How would the kabitens and basias be involved in the organization of the boats? How would they fund the preparations? What elements would be prioritized? The issues appeared even more complicated when Yvonne and her friends realized that the parade would include not just the Ndyuka and their villages but the entire 'community' of Marowijne. All groups represented there were expected to be interested in participating. Even so, it suffices to observe that the very choice and naming of the event in the Okanisi language and its localization – the river – contributed to a general disinterest. The river parade, along with its debatable implications, seemed only to make sense from a Maroon viewpoint.

On Boats, Funerals and Fears

The idea of the boat parade was inspired by an activity linked to the funeral rites performed in Ndyuka villages. Among the Ndyuka, *booko dei* or *ayiti dei* and *puu baaka* are ceremonies marking, respectively, the lapse of eight days and the lapse of six to twelve months after the person's death, the latter formally ending the mourning period.[10] Because it involves more time, resources and people, *puu baaka* is undoubtedly a period of intense movement in the villages

---

10   The calendar of funerary rites is subject to various injunctions, related to the politics of the villages, the conditions surrounding the death and the social position of the deceased, without mentioning the economic questions that involve the decisions of the family and the Ndyuka villages (Parris 2011:54).

when goods and food are shared and exchanged. But it is also a moment when kin and affines fulfil their obligations to the deceased and his or her family members. Funerary ceremonies attract Maroon and non-Maroon people to the territory of the villages and involve an enormous cost and organizational investment. Though varying in their scope, format and ritual elements, such ceremonies generally include exchanges, procedures for purifying the body and adding objects that belonged to the deceased to the buried remains, encounters between village authorities and kin, food preparation and commensality, and, rarely on the Cottica, consultation with oracles.

While food is being prepared by the deceased person's family, kin and friends climb into the boats and head off to the forest in search of firewood to cook the food. The departure and return from the forest is accompanied by music, and culminates in a commensal feast. The aim is to provide food and create the conditions for visitors and family to exchange gifts and honour the deceased. I have been unable to locate a specific name for this part of the *puu baaka* in Guianese Maroon ethnography, save for a single reference to the doo udu among the Maroon Aluku, found in Jean Hurault's accounts of funerary practices and commented on by the ethnobotanist Marie Fleury. According to Fleury, the *doo udu* takes place when 'young people go to cut firewood to cook the food for the offerings, as well as feed the large fire set to be lit in the village in the evening and burn all night. Women dressed in their best loincloths danced and sang to the rhythm of the drums, everyone on board canoes that traced arabesques on the river' (Fleury 2014:90). However, my Cottica Ndyuka interlocutors in Moengo referred to this part of the funerary rituals as *faya udu boto* – literally, the 'boat that brings firewood.' This acknowledgement, however, does not seem intended to bestow any special significance to this part of the *puu baaka*. The name establishes a ceremonial dimension to a process that will culminate in commensality and in properly honouring the dead and his or her matriclan. Actually, the relevance of the expression is limited to faya udu and it is not uncommon to hear people in the Cottica, when referring to a *puu baaka* due to take place or that has already been held in a village, use the expression *faya udu wagi* (literally 'car that brings firewood'). This shows that the transportation used to make the exchange of food and gifts possible matters less than keeping the fire and firewood available for cooking. The means to obtain the latter can be adapted to the new times. Since many villages can now be reached by car, and many people not only drive but come from the city in their cars to attend funeral ceremonies, this variation makes sense. The particular situation of the Cottica villages contrasts with the vast majority of the villages located on the Tapanahoni River, accessible only by boat. This ease of access also attracts a more affluent public, more money circulating, widespread use

SELF-FASHIONING AND VISUALIZATION AMONG THE COTTICA NDYUKA 283

of car transportation, and the possibility of inviting musical groups to play, generating more income for the villagers who can sell food and drink to the outside guests.

Firewood can be also brought in small trucks or vans. For villages situated next to navigable river shores, both modalities are possible. I participated in *puu baaka* in two such locations, Akuyutu kampu and Ofia Ollo village, which suggested to me that the boat (boto) was just as readily adaptable as a means of transportation. In the former case, firewood was freighted in trucks or cars and left on the bank of the river, which then had to be crossed in order to reach the village. A group of women, myself included, loaded the first boat with the firewood left on the roadside. In the other boat, loaded with drums, a group of men from the village played and followed the first boat back to the village. In the second example, after being cut and deposited at the village entrance with the help of a vehicle, the firewood was carried by men who loaded another small truck decorated with maipa (leaves from the maripa palm, Attalea maripa) which also carried musicians (donman). The truck filled with music and firewood was accompanied by the villagers, singing and dancing, until it made its delivery at the dede osu (mortuary house) where the deceased's family members were gathered. These examples point to some flexibility in the ceremonial practices making up the *puu baaka*, which may change depending on the Maroon groups and villages involved, the resources available and the preferences of the deceased's family.

However, while some of my Cottica Maroon interlocutors liked attending these funerary celebrations for aesthetic reasons, personal enjoyment, or even as a source of pride, even though they no longer unfold as they did in the past, for others they evoked danger. In Moengo, where conversion to Pentecostal churches has increased in recent years, the attendance of a *puu baaka* is generally followed by discussions and complaints among Christian Cottica Ndyuka, the so-called *keleki sama* (church people), who see the events as morally reprehensible. Some of them, relatives of the Commission members or people contacted by them, immediately recognized the connection with the parade conceived by Marcel and his friends. 'Ndyuka people only take boats to play and dance when [the event] is related somehow to a spiritual or funerary ritual.' In their view, the proposed parade was not an analogy, a way of stylizing faya udu boto, but a dangerous kind of 'disguise' of a ritual dynamic common to funerary ceremonies. It was precisely its inseparable relationship to death, a moment when the spirits of the dead and the dreaded kunus (vengeful spirits that haunt people and their matriclans for generations) were subjected to every kind of magical and spiritual treatment, that raised many concerns. These ceremonies were also seen as a mode of connection with the gaan saman – the ancestors – and their practices, not entirely abandoned by those converted to Christian churches.[11]

Bina was the first to observe that the inspiration for the event planned by Marcel would inevitably provoke all kinds of avoidance. She was heavily pre-occupied with practical issues. How could people perform part of a funerary ceremony without offending older people, or misrepresenting its real meaning? 'Since they don't know what this parade is for, they probably wouldn't be able to participate,' she speculated. As for the Christians, 'they would complain about the event or just wouldn't attend.' These were the issues likely to prevent some of the converted Cottica Ndyuka from participating in or even attending the parade. Bina's concerns were taken into account by Marcel and also her Ndyuka friends. She realized the need to weaken and severe the ties, attenuate or even recreate the connections between the boat parade, with drums and music, and the ceremony of the funerary ritual that had provided the initial inspiration. Both comprised sequences of events in which the Cottica Ndyuka were involved, but they mobilized distinct forces and actions. In faya udu boto, the close kin of the deceased, part of his or her matriclan, constitute the main authorities, alongside kabitens and basias in the villages, in terms of supervising the necessary ritual practices. The entire village, especially close and distant kin, participate in its realization by offering food, money and gifts. In the boat parade, though, the power to direct the event would be formally shared by different components of distinct configurations of the 'local community' and its relations to the Surinamese state. By 'formally' I mean that it was, effectively, the Cottica Ndyuka – accompanied in some situations by a small contingent of the Javanese community in Moengo – who centrally organized the necessary preparations, defined rules for participation, and contacted the villages and local authorities. Thus it was the Ndyuka on the Commission who would be responsible for allaying the fears of many people that the boat parade was simply a recreation of faya udu boto. They knew that the proposal for the parade involved an attempt to differentiate the ritual time in which faya udu took place from the ephemerality of the Carifesta parade. This differentiation between the temporalities of the ritual and the public show seemed to expose another important distinction. The relations that imbued the former with meaning were absent from the latter. For this reason, the production of artefacts, cloths and food, as well as bodies for performances of awasa and music (poku) by

---

11   In the Cottica area, aside from Moravian and Catholic churches and a few Baptist and Adventist churches and schools in the villages, Moengo has experienced the arrival over the last decade of several Volle Envangelie gemeente (Full Gospel movements) from Paramaribo and the United States (Van der Pijl 2010:181).

SELF-FASHIONING AND VISUALIZATION AMONG THE COTTICA NDYUKA   285

village residents, were subject to other forms of engagement, potentializing disputes over its aesthetic acuity.

Bina's hesitation, though, was at least partially based on her own experience. Keenly aware of the dangers of any approximation with death and ancestor spirits, she tried to imagine other paths that the Commission could take to implement Marcel's idea and produce something 'beautiful' (poolo) – an event to celebrate kulturu, but not to remember mortuary ceremonies and the fear they evoked in many. The event would join other festivals, ceremonies, objects and performances that formed part of what she and her friends called 'our knowledge' (wi koni) and that were increasingly being transformed into a sort of 'cultural commodity' – visual artefacts appreciated not just by the Maroon but also by the bakaa (see too Campbell 2012 and this volume). Bina's hope was that the activities would result in a happening enjoyed by everyone, recorded on cameras and mobile phones, transformed into something poolo and good to see. It was important for the event to be recorded and shown to the younger generation and children, and for the recording 'of how life was in the village' to please older people and outsiders too. This intention informed part, albeit not all, of her proposal to alter Marcel's original idea. The boat parade had to involve the display of pangis, apinties drums, food, dance and other elements of the kulturu.[12] It should provide a form of aesthetic appreciation not just to foreign cultural consumers but to Cottica Ndyuka themselves.

For this to happen, it was necessary to counter the immediate association of the boat parade with the funeral ceremonies, thereby appeasing the criticisms of some keleki sama, concerned with the over-proximity to what they called sani (dangerous things) and obia (witchcraft), dangers whose mere mention was reason enough for avoidance. It was Bina who proposed that instead of faya udu boto, the event should be transformed into and be named the Poolo Boto Show – literally, a parade and contest of the most beautiful boats. This not only involved a change of name, it meant the creation of new practices and meanings, an 'invention' of something new (Wagner 1981). The show would not necessarily involve a substantial shift in the contents, substances, performances and artefacts that circulate in the rituals on which it was inspired, but a change in the ways of establishing relationships with them. From an initial emphasis on a controversial and disputed content, the proposed event was transformed into a composition of practices decontextualized from their frame of

---

12   Apinti is a sacred language played on wooden drums built by Maroon people; pangis are
      pieces of cloth traditionally used by Maroon women.

reference. The form, not the content, signalled a way of making kulturu into a visual experience.

Inadvertently, its realization through the event and its transformation into a visual artefact ended up making explicit precisely the meanings that many attributed to the term kulturu and its association with winti – a complex system of gods, spirits, therapeutic practices and religious magic associated with the Afro-Surinamese (Gooding 1981:85). In an everyday sense, the term winti designates the specific way in which each ethnic group expresses its religiosity, and may be an accusatory reference when associated with witchcraft. On the other hand, among the Creole population, kulturu is commonly used as a synonym of winti, designating not only practices and actions, but imparting qualities to a particular object when employed as an adjective (van de Pijl 2010:182). Among my interlocutors in Moengo, and in the context of their preparations for Carifesta, its meaning appeared to contain a certain ambiguity. It was associated with winti and, at the same time, with the multicultural expression that officially characterized the festival. Consequently, the Polo Boto Show was conceived as kulturu in both senses without this duplicity implying any contradiction. Since while, from a Pentecostal point of view, practices called winti constitute the Afro-Surinamese expression of kulturu, all non-Christian magical-religious practices are similar in terms of their proximity to forms of 'mystification' and the belief in the action of a multitude of beings with which humans maintain multiple relations. The Poolo Boto Show is kulturu not because it is distinguished from the faya udu boto, but because it makes use of the same elements and meanings mobilized by the latter; namely, the relations with animated ideas and objects that have the power to transform people.

The organization of the parade as an 'analogy' of the funerary ceremony would face various dangers: the approximation with the bakaa, the reference, albeit tacit, to the ancestors and the dead, and the evocation of life in the villages from the standpoint of the recently converted Ndyuka. Not by chance, any mention of faya udu was erased. The only nominal reference to remain was the boat in the Poolo Boto Show – which we might imagine as a conceptually and materially 'empty' vessel to be filled by women and men involved in the decoration of the boats and bodies. This experience would capture other inventions produced not only by Bina and her friends from the Commission, but by groups of Cottica Ndyuka people living inside and outside the villages. As I show later, they never ceased to generate controversies concerning its 'proximity' to ritual practices, and continued to mobilize new conversations and uses of other kinds of knowledge and artefacts.

Self-Fashioning through Practices of Visualization

Over recent decades there has been a strong attachment to electronic devices as communication tools. Indeed they form part of daily life for Maroon people in the villages – some of which are supplied with satellite dishes – and in urban areas. The interest in images and sounds that document Maroon culture – recorded on digital artefacts like smartphones, cameras, microphones, laptops, tablets, pen drives, stick cards, CDs and DVD s – as well as their uses on social media and radio, traverse complex networks involving the circulation and reproduction of objects, sounds and images (R. Price and S. Price 1999; Bilby 1999, 2000; Migge 2011; van Stirpriaan 2015; van Stirpriaan and Polimé 2009).[13] Urban and young Maroon people's relations to new media and communication technologies are more complex and cannot be treated in depth here. Nonetheless, in order to highlight the importance of electronic devices as a medium to cope with the multiple understandings surrounding the creation of Moengo parade, allow me to briefly invoke some other effects produced by the increasing presence of visual artefacts in the daily lives of Guianese Maroon.

As Bettina Migge observed, 'Suriname has a booming DVD market. Nollywood and US films are dubbed into Ndyuka and sometimes Saamaka and amateurs produce local films' (2015:6, note 6). This production attracted my attention during my first fieldwork trip to Moengo in 2009. Living at Bina's house, I used to spend more time with children and their young friends. After school, when, in the dry season, the mid-afternoon sun is very hot, children spend hours indoors watching TV or DVD movies. It was then that I first noticed the popularity of North American blockbusters like, for instance, Eddie Murphy's Coming to America (1988), dubbed into Okanisi – a homemade and unauthorized dubbing, sold in pirate copies. Since then I have begun to follow and collect this production, as well as got to know a few sellers in Paramaribo and Moengo. With each new trip I could see the rapid growth in popularity and the changes in this new media market. The same kind of homemade dubbing, by then also available in the Sranantongo and Saamaka languages, was not only made for US action and comedy films – with African-American actors and actresses as the main characters – but also Nollywood movies, which were then becoming popular. It is worth noting that, contrary to the former, African films depicting mainly family drama and comedy, but with the ever-present

---

13   This is the case too of Maroons living in French Guiana. Bettina Migge (2011) has studied the effect of multilinguism in the production of radio shows spoken in Maroon Creole in the French territory.

references to witchcraft, ethnic motives and scenarios, were rarely dubbed into Maroon languages.

The arrival of African films on the Surinamese market – which also reflects their popularity among Creole consumers – opened the doors to gospel production made in Nigeria and Ghana. Not only were witchcraft and conversion the main subjects: these African films also offered a new visual alternative to the modern cars, explosions, technology and white characters speaking in Okanisi in the dubbed US movies. Full of healing doctors, deaths, and villages as movie settings, the Nollywood gospel production was consumed as a 'reality close' to the 'primitive life' of Surinamese Maroon, making an important contribution to 'religious audiovisual culture' (Meyer 2010:103). It opened new venues for local production, often associated with church missionary work and commerce. Local gospel films spoken in Okanisi and Saamaka became very popular, not just among Christians. Likewise they created new opportunities for young Maroon artists, producers, photographers and writers.[14] Along with the gospel media initially managed by Afro-Surinamese and foreign Christian groups, however, other visual artefacts and practices controlled by young Maroon have become widespread.

Due to its modern urban landscape, and the fact that the town is now home to dozens of Pentecostal churches, Moengo has regularly been used as a setting for such movies. Many of the filmmakers, actors, actresses, screenplay writers and producers involved are personally related to Bina, Yvonne, Bas, Marcel and their families. They belong to the second generation of Cottica Ndyuka refugees who returned to Moengo and, since 2010, have been directly or indirectly involved in the 'cultural projects' developed by Marcel Pinas and his Tembe Art Studio. They are the children who grew up watching dubbed US movies, but now make their living with the ability to connect to social media, the internet and so on. Individually or in groups of friends and relatives in Paramaribo, they have set up video production firms, some of them specialized in gospel content.[15] These films are spoken entirely in Maroon languages and, in some cases, in Sranantongo or with captions in Dutch. They are aimed at a young urban Maroon audience in Suriname and French Guiana, not completely familiar

---

14   This is the case of the YouTube channel and films produced by the 'The Family Gospel,' such as 'Prins Clyde ft C.K _ Wang uman dje waka gi ing mang': see https://www.youtube.com/watch?v=79TtNuMqUg4. Accessed August 28, 2017.

15   Media groups like Para's Mediagroup and Basta Digital, for instance. The latter gained national recognition with the film 'Kaptin da Palon,' entirely produced in Moengo with many of my young Ndyuka interlocutors. The trailer is available on YouTube: https://www.youtube.com/watch?v=ApsvKTjMmqo.

with the languages spoken by their parents in the villages, but familiar with the media, the internet and digital technology.

This growing production has had important effects on visualization practices and the 'ways of seeing' the Maroon person in diverse spatiotemporal dimensions. Gospel films, for instance, frequently associate a scene performed in a non-converted village with the 'past,' sometimes using special effects. The images frame cultural instantiations in which the present is 'here' and the past 'out there.' Not by chance, when used in pamphlets, films or as a reference point for self-decoration, ethnographic photography magnifies an aestheticized past. By contrasting moralities and places in this way, these gospel and non-gospel films not only 'mediate culture,' as Ginsburg (1995:2810) argued, they create new temporal perspectives. Domestically distributed to Maroon sellers and sold in street markets, stores in Paramaribo and along the entire east coast as far Cayenne, as well as on the internet, these films often depict everyday situations involving young Maroon people in urban contexts. Love, jealousy, school, family conflicts, pregnancy and violence are all frequent themes. The filmmakers' interests are combined with concerns that are not always made explicit: to provide an urban landscape and voice to young Maroon people living in the cities. The use of Maroon language, spoken daily by themselves in lively situations, stands as an important index of differentiation. These movies contrast strongly with western ethnographic films and photography, which, ever since the late nineteenth century, have depicted Maroon people as silent, dressed in traditional clothes, placed alongside wooden houses and objects, and shown against forest backdrops. At the same time, this production is not necessarily intended to make a political or aesthetic statement. Instead it looks to transform the ways in which Maroon consumers relate to the media market.[16]

This brief survey of recent engagements of Maroon people with various forms of media has sought to situate some of their effects on other contemporary visual experiences, including the way in which they affect the production of images of the Maroon person, the still frames of domestic and family life. Photographic images are found in many Maroon houses in Moengo. Some images are printed, displayed on posters and in picture frames carefully decorating the inside of people's homes. Others are shared on social networks or stored on mobile phones, notebooks and computers, shown to relatives and friends. They compose what Van de Port has called a 'personal memory bank' (2006:453) with photography and films of children's graduation ceremonies,

---

16   Faye Ginsburg (1995) has drawn interesting parallels and contrasts between 'indigenous media' and 'ethnographic film,' taking into consideration issues related to the 'local' market and audience.

weddings and other domestic and professional moments. There is no separation, therefore, between planes or spheres of everyday life designated 'sacred' or 'ritual,' and the spaces – the 'house in the village,' the 'house in the city' – in which artefacts, bodily practices and aesthetic preferences are differentiated. For example, a birthday party with balloons, cakes and music popular among Creoles, but held in a Maroon village, may combine elements that index the various worlds in which the Maroon participate differently. The village landscape, the house decoration, the use of the pangi and the uniform of the kabiteni all interact visually and existentially and can thereby form part of the same photographic record. No distinction occurs either among the videos made by Maroons in the villages documenting funerary ceremonies and the induction of new kabiteni, films that are later sold. Unlike the images captured by small digital cameras or smartphones, the camera in these videos seems concerned with recording groups, not individuals. With few cuts, sometimes the films are edited on more than one DVD, adding up to more than three hours of events, recording long sequences of affectionate encounters between friends and kin. The author of the images undoubtedly knows those who are filmed and these, in turn, interact uninhibited in front of the cameras. The fact that the films are transformed into merchandise in the local markets does not remove their status as a domestic artefact: they will be bought by family, neighbours and friends.

Objectified records of Ndyuka social life likewise show relatives and friends wearing pangiss – in photographs produced by outside observers – and circulating in boats, meeting each other and sharing food in the villages. These visual records are made to be shown to different others. They reveal aspects of Ndyuka sociality both to those familiar with it, albeit at varying depths of knowledge, and those who know nothing. At the same time, visual records provide an important resource for the acquisition of certain kinds of knowledge in socialities where it is normally limited to a few. By recording a ceremony in a village – or the display of pangiss at a craftwork fair in Paramaribo, or the funerary ceremony of a close relative held in a village – on digital images stored on a mobile phone, each person thus turns their gaze and participation into an instrument for accessing a body of knowledge whose transmission is mediated by cohabitation, by the relative distance to Christian churches, and by the relationship with their matriclan, gender and generation. Not everyone can share all the stories evoked – especially those associated with the time of the loweman (runaway slaves) in the fositen (in the past, the primordial times when the clans and villages were formed and the people first encountered spirits and other beings) – but many can take part in rituals (funerals and birth rites), meetings and ceremonies that allow people who possess special

SELF-FASHIONING AND VISUALIZATION AMONG THE COTTICA NDYUKA 291

powers (the elders, kabitens, basias) to be present.[17] Thus each movement and image 'frozen' as a visual artefact of knowledge is a record that reiterates the need to observe exclusive access to traditional knowledge and, simultaneously, provokes the creation of a distinct modality of knowing. I shall return to this question later. What I wish to stress here is that what I have called 'objectification' mobilizes a network of new specialists: Maroon people hired to record special events in towns like Paramaribo, Saint Laurent, Cayene and Moengo, but above all family ceremonies – including funerals – held in the villages.

Puu Bakaa and *Ayti Dey* ceremonies have been transformed into visual artefacts by Maroon photographers in the context of the media boom in Suriname. Sometimes hired by bereaved families, they transform these events into DVD s sold in fairs, markets and video stores in Moengo, Paramaribo, and Saint Laurent. The images, which generally show kin meeting up in the villages, are edited with sound tracks and various visual effects. The memory of each relative and family becomes an 'event' sold and purchased by others – in general, Maroons who took part in the event, or family members and acquaintances who were unable to attend. Since, sometimes, the ritual obligations of relatives after a death imbue these 'non-attendances' with all kinds of speculations and moral implications, the visual records extend the absence of some, explaining why others were unable to attend, but also provide the latter with an alternative way of being involved.

For those relatives who have converted to Christianity, this form of participation – mediated by the contact with photographic and video images – allows people to protect themselves from the potential spiritual dangers that surround relatives present at funeral ceremonies, and likewise shield them from negative comments in their church communities. The records reveal who was there and what happened – even though the lenses may not always capture the gossip, comments, slanders, conflicts and quarrels that accompany the re-encounter of relatives – without the risk of exposure to the action of vengeful spirits who wander the villages on such occasions. When seen through the idiom of conversion, the ritual captured by the camera and mobile phone lenses is transformed into a secure and spiritually permitted perspective of the sociality in the villages.

In the case of the ceremonies in the funerary calendar, beside focusing on long sequences of awasa, the performances of aleke bands, and commensality

---

17   The prohibition on the unauthorized transmission of knowledge can have effects on kinship relations, as well as inter and intra-clan relations, and may be subject to spiritual sanctions (Price 1983; Thoden van Velzen & van Wetering 2004).

FIGURE 9.1 Mungotapu Village group at Poolo Boto in Moengo 2013
SOUCRE: OLÍVIA M. G. CUNHA, 2013

kuutus (palavers), these films show new uses of clothes, aesthetic elements and bodies without any direct connections to the ritual. On the contrary, their most direct associations are with the habits of the fotosama (city people) and bakaa. For many, these interactions arouse suspicion, conceived to be dangerous, capable of attracting the force and seductive traps of spirits known as bakus – brought to the villages through contact with baaka. A source of ambivalent feelings and powers, they represent the dangers resulting from easy access to consumer goods. In the past the baaka were also responsible for enslavement and dehumanization. In the present, as the main figures in a constant play of seduction, they are the object of relations that are coveted, denied, concealed and dissimulated (Vernon 1980, 1985).

Records of traditional ceremonies held in the villages, including those that make up the funerary calendar, seem to combine at least two perspectives of death as a unique event: one in which fear of the action of spirits emerges, and another in which the ambiguity of the relation with the bakaa is reactualized. In the former, everything that is unseen, but whose force and power seem irremediable and indisputable, appears to be controlled and hidden. In the latter, the objects associated with the power of seduction of the baaka – the jewellery, electronic goods, mobile phones, cameras, cars, artificial hair and clothes of the fotosama exhibited in the villages – are displayed and desired. Hiding and showing are distinct but asymmetric actions. In other words, certain displayed relations and artefacts are not necessarily authorized, expected or valued, just as the things that are hidden do not include those most feared or prohibited.

But showing and hiding are also related to certain possibilities of learning and creating through visualization.

Pee Kulturu

On a Sunday afternoon, as a crowd began to descend a winding slope stretching from the centre of Moengo to the shores of the Cottica River, men, women and children of all ages began to gather on the river shore. A small group of Javanese instrumentalists and women, who often present gamelan music in Moengo, took part in decorating one of the boats. The other five boats all came from Ndyuka villages on the Cottica and its affluents: Adjuma Kondee, Mungotapu, Benatimofu and Da Akujutu Kampu (where a village and a kampu decorated the same boat), Langa Uku and Ovilla Olo. Each event lasted around three hours, including the parade and the subsequent disembarkation of the people on the boats, a dance presentation, and a procession of food, manioc, herbs and utensils such as baskets, paddles, chests and other artefacts. As they left the boats, men and women danced awasa and performed to the sound of drums. At the end, a commission formed exclusively of Maroon judges chose the boat from Mungotapu village as the competition winner.[18]

Since the beginning, the Cottica Ndyuka who organized the first edition of Poolo Boto Show agreed that the public event was created to be 'enjoyed' primarily as a visual experience. Although groups of Maroon villagers were expected to join the decorated boats with drumming, songs, and dance, the majority of the audience would be present on the shore of the Cottica River in Moengo to see it as their kulturu. As Bina remarked, people could see and make 'beautiful things' out of that experience. They could bring their children and guests, and take photographs and film the events with their smartphones and cameras. She herself participated all the time with and through her mobile. This quasi-detachment – a kind of 'objectification' in which electronic devices are transformed into time machines in which culture is performed as it was in the past – can be reduced to a form of folklorization or production of a 'cultural commodity' for baaka consumers.

More than just an event to be watched enthusiastically by relatives from each village, the Polo Boto Show seemed to elicit interest in a particular kind

---

18 Mungotapu is an important village from the viewpoint of the political networks that reorganized the Marowijne territory in the post-war period. It was there that the main centre of the Maroon guerrilla force materialized and also where congressional representative and leader of ABOP, Ronnie Brunswijk, former leader of Jungle Comando, has kinship ties.

of registration. Photographs or short films were taken incessantly, initially of the boats decorated and waiting for their occupants, and later of the richly attired participants accompanied by the musicians. The mobile phones allowed these records to acquire additional layers of meaning insofar as they were created with objects of personal use. Each image recorded on an electronic device would be – as I was able to observe after the event and in a variety of conversations – added to a diverse set of personal records. Whenever I asked, my interlocutors made no secret of their predilection for certain boats, family members' clothes, decorations, dancing and aesthetic solutions. However, a frequent reference point in my interlocutors' attempts to explain why they had taken particular photos was the 'beauty' of the boat, the pangi or the clothes: they were 'beautiful things' (mooi sani).

In this sense, the production of digital images should not be seen solely or even primarily as a concern to 'record' – whether in the documentary sense, or as the preservation of something that deserves to be remembered – but above all as a form of learning and a means of 'controlled' participation. While, as I remarked in describing Bina's reluctance to use the name Faya Udu Boto for the event, the proximity to funeral rituals, spirits and the memory of the gaan sama is a cause of avoidance among many people, especially recent converts to Christianity, knowledge of the same is not a motive for condemnation. In other words, while some of my Christian interlocutors declined to watch the parade out of fear of what they perceived to be a clear reference to the funeral ceremony, in particular due to the presence of apinties, pangiss and awasa, and to the fact that the event was held on the river, others showed me photographs taken of the event, emphasizing their cautious participation. Using a camera was a form of taking part and showing an interest in kulturu. At the same time, taking a photograph (meke wan fowtow) and showing it to others elicited a series of interesting comments on what traditie and kulturu were.

Among the Christians, the distancing from this field of affections – being vulnerable to the force of kunus, bakuus and other spirits – appeared to imply a certain kind of ontological transformation, becoming a 'modern' person. The production of photographic images seemed to reveal a movement of 'exteriorization,' seeing with the eyes of an 'outsider.' However, this possibility of understanding does not account for the multiple uses of these images and their multitude of creators – not always Christian, but frequently owners of a mobile phone with the capacity to store photographic images to be shared later with family and friends, without mentioning the virtual social networks increasingly accessed by Maroon people in transit between the villages and urban territories. Yvonne, for example, closely examined and interpreted the images of Mungotapu village's participation in the Poolo

FIGURE 9.2 A Poolo Boto being registered by Cottica Ndyuka's cameras in Wanhatti
SOUCRE: OLÍVIA M. G.CUNHA, 2016

Boto Show taken by myself on video and by herself and her colleagues on mobile phones. Looking at the photos with the pleasure of recognizing her friends, neighbours and kin as they took part in different boats, she identified some of the reasons that had led to the village entrants winning the competition: "look at the hair of the women. It's not straightened or full of extensions. Den be meke den uwii [they made their hair]. They don't use false uwii. A no dati na kulturu [They don't use fake hair. It doesn't exist in (our) culture]. At the same time, Yvonne recognized the correspondences and partial continuities between what had taking place in the villages in the past and what could be performed in Moengo in the present. Looking at the images prompted her to reflect on the ways in which things were done 'in the past.' Watching the entry of the boats of women from Ovila Ollo, she contemplated the care shown in the uniform use of the pangis, colours and other details, example of what she called modern fasi, 'the modern way.' Most of the women in the boats, she observed, used false uwii and carried handbags, usually Chinese copies of international fashion labels. Mungotapu villagers, on the contrary, 'did things beautifully': men and women invested in their hair braids and their pangis were painstakingly embroidered. The details of the images produced, then, an effect of temporal depth and distance. The more mooi, the more distant from the present.

Conclusion: Visualization and Interpretation

As I have looked to show, the organization of the boat parade was not just an attempt to encourage Maroon participation through public performances of their kulturu. More importantly, it was a way found by the group of Cottica Ndyuka on the Carifesta Commission to establish relations with non-Maroon wishing to create a public 'cultural event.' During the process of creating the event, it became clear that it would inevitably involve an interpretation of the latter's ways of looking at and recognizing Maroon practices, bodies and kinds of knowledge. But this did not imply the assimilation of a foreign gaze, uncritically reproducing outside views of Maroon people through an ever-present exotic framework. In the past, old people (gaan sama) were an object of the gaze of the bakaa and their camera lenses. What drew bakaa attention were extraordinary situations and elements in which spirits and other powers were invoked. Although the effects of these forces were not visible or felt by the bakaa, they were tenacious and remained powerful over generations of Maroon people from the same matriclan.

By contrast, Poolo Boto Show was a 'form of collective self-production' (Ginsburg 1995: 120) in which their creators were aware of its limits. It combined diverse viewpoints of the relations that encompass not only Maroon and non-Maroon people, but also the former with their ancestors, gods, spirits and spaces of existence. As Santos-Granero has stated vis-à-vis Amazonian Amerindian groups, it resulted in 'a conscious indigenous attempt to incorporate the Other into their sphere of social relations' (2009:479) without losing control over the spiritual effects frequently mobilized by unknown forces brought by bakaa (Vernon 1983; Van Wetering 1992). By incorporating the Other's regimes of visualization, the Cottica Ndyuka involved found a 'sphere' or plane of exchange where they could participate 'as if' – or, to use an Okanisi term, where they be pee (played, acted as, performed something as though it were another thing or a disguise) kulturu. This involved a dynamic process of constant decomposition of other kinds of social relations, insofar as it required gathering corporal expressions, songs, dances, substances, food and drumming from diverse ritual and non-ritual contexts. When put together, these pieces of other social relationships formed a new assemblage. Thus, by combining things and practices no longer used, or that are rarely performed in today's villages, with others that are currently practiced, a scale effect was produced. 'Past' and 'present,' 'here' and 'there' coexisted as an aesthetic and safe experience. It implied interpreting, adding things that young people know, but also other things that are unknown to them – interpreting practices and knowledge that Bina and her friends' generation have 'heard about' but never witnessed, either because

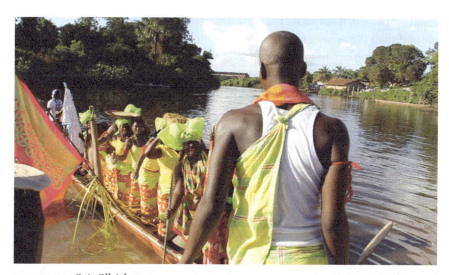

FIGURE 9.3   Ovia Ollo's boto
SOUCRE: OLÍVIA M. G. CUNHA, 2013

they were raised as refugee children far from the villages, or because their families had converted to Christianity.

Marilyn Strathern has observed how effects of scale and movement, produced over the course of experiences of interpretation, affect the knowledge of how and why things happen. 'Interpretation,' the author argues,

> ... implies taking something – an event or location or artefact or whatever – and specifying its singular qualities. It is the resulting singularity of the entity that encourages the divergence in comprehension. For the entity in question is being made apparent both in its particulars and as inevitably summoning a context of a kind, a whole field of (further) particulars and understandings. Think of all the coordinates through which one might address one's interpretation of a photograph, for instance, from its chemical composition to its aesthetic impact. Yet (obvious and mundane observations) to consider the particular quality of the photographic reproduction is to sidestep the subject matter; to focus specifically on the way a face is angled within the frame is to slide past the effect of the smile. The singularity of the selection reveals it as a choice among many. (2002:89)

Strathern's observations appear to acquire another dimension when compared not only to the activity of observing images as a form of commentary on the event, but also to its capacity to create different kinds of relations between people and their life experiences, located in distinct places and times. Taking photos had much more pragmatic and, consequently, different meanings to what I have called a mode of existence or viewpoint absolutely 'external' to the event and everything that it mobilizes symbolically. Like Yvone, the other Commission members, Bina, Marcel and Bas, all took photos to observe aspects of the creation in which they had participated, each in their own distinct way. Bina in particular observed details of awasa songs and asked the older people about meanings with which she was unfamiliar. Based on the photos, new patterns and designs could be incorporated into the painted or embroidered pangis and knick-knacks that she had made, the sale of which supplemented her income as a local school teacher. Bas was concerned to show something of the kulturu to his children, whose mother was a young Javanese woman. He lamented his childhood among other refugees in French Guiana where he had studied alongside other children who had never lived in a village. In their shared creation, Marcel saw echoes of his own creative interventions in Moengo. This time he had composed a collaborative project, since it was his original idea that had inspired a series of alterations and interpretations that had ultimately given life to the Poolo Boto Show. Interested from the outset in the creation of a new aesthetic meaning for the Maroon presence in the region, the Poolo Boto Show functioned for Marcel as a particular kind of obviation. It was at once the invention of something that existed as traditie but known to only a few people. Yvonne asked for a copy of my images and together we headed to Mungotapu to share the performance of the group that had taken part in the boat parade with the elders there. Although involved in its conception, these older people had been unable to watch the parade itself. There we talked for hours with the kabiten and basia, who by then had already learnt about the criticisms from converts concerning the event as a whole, and the dangers that they imagined would accompany any attempt to reproduce part of a funeral ritual on a large scale. Dem pee keleki (they pretend to be from the church), the basia opined. It was kulturu, he observed, that 'had kept them alive until today.'

The relationship that Yvonne and her friends established between faya udu boto and Poolo Boto Show was not one of 'representation,' a quasi-display through which they consciously presented their knowledge to outside gazes. Neither was Poolo Boto conceived as the reproduction of something authentic, and thus non-representational, given that its meaning was a motive for avoidance among everyone. As I observed in describing how the event's proponents offered alternative reasons for its creation, the relations between poolo boto show and faya udu boto are analogical, the former not so much a reproduction as a way of looking at the latter. As a ritual activity with distinct aims

SELF-FASHIONING AND VISUALIZATION AMONG THE COTTICA NDYUKA   299

and effects, faya udu boto was unreproducible. However, it could be emulated analogically, replacing the meanings – frequently pejorative – attributed to the term kulturu by recent converts. This operation, though, resulted in a necessary distancing effect whereby kulturu ideally pertained to other subjects, places and times. In other words, the latter had to be located in the past, associated with life and kin in the villages and thereby distant from urban and Christian modes of living. A kind of ontological transformation had to be promoted in which the subjects who performed the practices imbuing a cultural meaning to the parade distanced themselves temporally from those who observed them.

The production of a visual artefact functioned as though the idea of Cottica Ndyuka transformation to the 'traditional' Maroon ways of life and the simultaneous increase in Christianization was accepted as a given fact in a reality seen from the perspective of the Other. The visualization of actions and practices associated with the past would thus enable people to become 'Maroon' through the incorporation of a mode of visualization (see Santos-Granero 2009). Both modalities of visualization enabled the visual artefact – digital or printed – to singularize details of the event and, in this way, lead those involved in the show to a different interpretation of the entire happening.

As mentioned above, Yvonne, Bina, Marcel and Bas took photos with the aim of observing the effects of their own particular agency in the event that they had jointly created. Bina arrived early and photographed some details with her digital camera. She focused particularly on the lyrics to the awasa songs so that she could ask the elders later about the meanings of certain references, even though she recognized them as a stylized form. She took short sequences of film, observing the performance of the boats from Mungotapu, Ovilla Olo and Damtapu with some admiration. Her attention was focused on the aspects chosen by the creators of these boats in 'recreating' the ritual in their own way. In other words, each had invested in the creation of specific aspects, elements that seemed to participate in the ritual from the point of view of each village, but without the intention to reproduce it as a whole. In this way, each boat produced cuts, combinations of shared memories and creations, avoiding the replication of the entire process that links the procession boats to the villages and these to the dead. In this interpretation the Poolo Boto Show appeared as a combination of events begun in different villages. From this viewpoint, there was a relation between the modes of recreating a parade of boats and the memory of the oldest people. At the same time, seen in conjunction, these different modes of creating analogies between faya udu and poolo boto did not configure a single ritual expression. On the contrary, by transforming into multiple analogies, they created something new.

The separation of the new happening – the public event – from the processes that led to its making and, in turn, from the harmful control of their effects, was sufficient to dampen criticisms concerning the show's similarity to the ritual that had supposedly inspired its creation. Bina went to the river to see and record the event with her small camera. Using these photos, she created new patterns and designs to decorate knick-knacks and pangis with dyes or embroidery. Other details stirred her curiosity, believing them to be more than a mere illustration or even just a creation: they were, de facto, sani and not simply an allegory of something true. Bina thought that people were not limited to 'recreating' in the sense that she herself had said would be necessary. There were signals, details and the introduction of elements motivated by the desire of the boat and group in question to be better than others, or by people's wish to protect themselves from the evil eye – things made by Maroon people in different contexts and, above all, in situations involving competition.

Different effects of fragmentation and separation of the parts and details present in the parade can also be observed in the relation that Alan – a young Ndyuka man who provides computer services to the kantoor in Moengo – and his camera established with the event. Alan makes a living from filming and photographing funerary ceremonies, marriages, birthdays and the induction of authorities in Cottica villages. He possesses an immense archive of iconographic records, but stores them not only for professional reasons. His family also lived through the experience of exile in French Guiana and photography was a way that he found to get closer to the little he knew about his kulturu. Alan photographed and filmed various phases of the preparations for Carifesta – in part for professional motives. Over the course of my field research we frequently found ourselves handling video cameras different from the popular formats used by the Maroon. During the parade, it was just the same, we shared privileged vantage points and angles. Afterwards, Alan tracked me down to see the images I had taken and we agreed to swap our material. Carefully observing the different elements that had caught our gazes and lenses, I perceived how his images oscillated between capturing the poolo boto as an event and a more immersive framing in which his attention focused on the performances of friends and relatives from the Ovilla Olo boat – the village to which his family and matriclan belong. Nonetheless, from the viewpoint of many of my Maroon interlocutors, not necessarily involved in the organization of the show, what I called an immersive framing was essentially the most powerful expression of the particularism of the event in question. It was as though they said: 'every faya udu boto is like that and this (poolo boto) is just a small-scale version.' Alan perceived the relationships, not between groups but between the people present there, as a 'nexus of relationships' (Strathern

2013:48), whether perceived as an event or a ritual. In the former case, it was the Ndyuka residents of Moengo who, transformed through the use of objects, gestures and sounds, figured among the aims of Carifesta. In the latter case, it was the people from Ovilla Olo, kin and neighbours, who appeared related to the village, to the Dju clan and to its spirits, ancestors and gods. Compared to Alan's images, my own sought, erratically, to reconcile what for me were the parts and whole of a single event. It was only later that I grasped how people were transformed in their relations with Maroon and non-Maroon interlocutors. What Poolo Boto seemed to bring forth were relations of different kinds. Making use of Strathern's observations on the use of ritual artefacts and their relations to the person, we could say that it involved the 'person as a nexus of relationships. Not a matter of clothing concealing the body, but of the transformation of a person composed by his or her domestic and private relations into an object for public gaze that then conceals those domestic and private relations' (2013:48). Not coincidentally, effects of fragmentation, scale and depth pervade the comments of other members of the Commission. Bas's attention, for instance, was focused on the bodies, music and dance, and the danger of people confusing recreation with 'those things' (disi sani). In evaluating the images, the boats that were truly mooi were those most removed from what Yvonne and the components of Mungotapu considered 'false,' referring to the hair: the standardization of the pangi patterns, the control of bodies in the awasa performances, the attention paid to the parade time of the boats. There were those boats where the performances appeared less authentic, deep or true. What enchanted her was the production of an aesthetic meaning devoid of the agency of spirits. Marcel, for his part, saw the event as a shared creation, reflecting his own creative interventions in Moengo – an aesthetic creation of the contemporary Maroon experience. Like him, the Commission and the boat members created an artefact made of relations emergent from an idea.

References

Asad, Talal. 1993. Genealogies of Religion: Discipline and Reasons of Power in Christianity and Islam. Baltimore: Johns Hopkins University Press.

Battaglia, Debbora. 1997. 'Ambiguating agency: the case of Malinowski's ghost.' American Anthropologist 99.3: 505–510, 1997.

Battaglia, Debbora. 1995a. 'On practical nostalgia: Self-prospecting among urban Trobrianders.' In Rhetorics of Self-making, 77–96. Edited by Debbora Battaglia. Berkeley: University of California Press.

Battaglia, Debbora. 1995b. 'Problematizing the self: a thematic introduction.' In Rhetorics of Self-making, 1–15. Edited by Debbora Battaglia. Berkeley: University of California Press.

Bilby, K. M. 2010. 'Surviving Secularization: Masking the Spirit in the Jankunu (John Canoe) Festivals of the Caribbean'. New West Indian Guide 84(3–4), 179–223.

Bilby, K. M. 2000. 'Making modernity in the hinterlands: new Maroon musics in the Black Atlantic.' Popular Music 19(03), 265–292.

Bilby, Kenneth. 1999. ' "Roots Explosion": Indigenization and Cosmopolitanism in Contemporary Surinamese Popular Music.' Ethnomusicology 43 (2): 256–96.

Bilby, Kenneth. 1990. 'The Remaking of the Aluku: Culture, Politics, and Maroon Ethnicity in French South America.' PhD Diss., Johns Hopkins University.

Campbell, Corinna Siobhan. 2012. 'Personalizing Tradition: Surinamese Maroon Music and Dance in Contemporary Urban Practice.' PhD Diss., Harvard University.

Clifford, James. 2004. 'Traditional futures.' In Questions of Tradition, 151–168. Edited by Mark Phillips and Gordon Schochet. Toronto: University of Toronto Press.

Connerton, Paul. 1989. How societies remember. Cambridge: Cambridge University Press.

Course, Magnus. 2013. 'The clown within: Becoming white and mapuche ritual clowns.' Comparative Studies in Society and History 55.4: 771–799.

De Coppet, Daniel, ed. 2002. Understanding rituals. New York: Routledge.

Fleury, Marie. 2014. 'La Lévee de deuil (Puu Baaka) chez les Aluku'. Guyane Geographique (3), 86–91.

Ginsburg, Faye. 1995. 'Mediating culture: indigenous media, ethnographic film, and the production of identity.' In Fields of vision: Essays in film studies, visual anthropology, and photography, 256–91. Edited by Leslie Devereaux, and Roger Hillman. Berkeley: University of California Press.

Wooding, Charles Jr. 1981. Evolving Culture: a cross-cultural study of Suriname, West Africa and the Caribbean. Amsterdam: University Press of America.

Goury, Laurence, and Bettina Migge. 2003. Grammaire du nengee: introduction aux langues aluku, ndyuka et pamaka. Paris: IRD Editions.

Handelman, Don. 1990. Models and mirrors: Towards an anthropology of public events. Cambridge: Cambridge University Press.

Huttar, George L., and Mary L. Huttar. 2003. Ndyuka. New York: Routledge.

Kobben, Andre J.F. 1967. 'Unity and disunity-Cottica Djuka as a kinship system.' Bijdragen tot de Taal- Land- en Volkenkunde 123 (1): 10–52.

Meyer, Birgit. 2008. 'Media and the senses in the making of religious experience: an introduction.' Material Religion 4.2: 124–134.

Migge, Bettina, and Isabele Leglise. 2015. 'Language Practices and Linguistic Ideologies in Suriname.' In In and Out of Suriname: Language, Mobility and Identity, 13–57. Edited by Eithne Carlin, Isabelle Léglise, bettina Migge, and Paul Tjon Sie Fat. Leiden: Brill.

SELF-FASHIONING AND VISUALIZATION AMONG THE COTTICA NDYUKA   303

Migge, Bettina. 2011. 'Negotiating social identities on an Eastern Maroon radio show.' Journal of Pragmatics 43(6), 1498–1511.

Moore, Sally Falk, and Barbara G. Myerhoff (eds.) 1977. Secular ritual. Uitgeverij Van Gorcum.

Parris, Jean-Yves. 2013. Interroger les Morts: essai sur la dynamique politique des Noirs marrons ndjuka du Surinam et de la Guyane. Matoury: Ibis Rouge Editions.

Pires, Rogério B. W. 2015. A Mása Gádu konde: Morte, Espíritos e Rituais Funerários em uma Aldeia Saamaka Cristã. PhD diss., PPGAS/ Museu Nacional, Universidade Federal do Rio de Janeiro.

Polimé, Thomas. 1998. 'Dood en begrafenisrituelen bij de Ndjuka.' OSO 17: 71–73.

Price, Richard, and Sally Price. 2015. 'Epilogue: The Aesthetics and Politics of Multilingualism among the Saamaka.' In In and Out of Suriname: Language, Mobility and Identity, 13–57. Edited by Eithne Carlin, Isabelle Léglise, Bettina Migge, and Paul Tjon Sie Fat. Leiden: Brill.

Price, Richard. 2008. Travels with Tooy: History, memory, and the African American imagination. Chicago: University of Chicago Press.

Price, Richard, and Sally Price. 1999. Maroon Arts: Cultural Vitality in the African Diaspora. Boston: Beacon Press.

Price, Richard, and Sally Price. 1994. On the mall: presenting Maroon tradition-bearers at the 1992 FAF. Vol. 4. Bloomington: Indiana University Press.

Price, Richard. 1983. First Time: the historical vision of an Afro-American people. Baltimore and London: John Hopkins Universitry Press.

Robbins, Joel. 2004. 'The Globalization of Pentencostal and Charismatic Christianity.' Annual Review of Anthropology 33, 117–143.

Sahlins, Marshall 1999. 'Two or Three Things that I Know about Culture.' Journal of the Royal Anthropological Institute, NS. 5: 399–421.

Santos-Granero, Fernando, et al. 2009. 'Hybrid bodyscapes: A visual history of Yanesha patterns of cultural change.' Current Anthropology 50.4: 477–512.

Scholtens, Ben. 1994. Bosnegers en overheid in Suriname: De ontwikkeling van de politieke verhouding 1651–1992. Paramaribo: Afdeling Cultuurstudies/Minov.

Strange, Stuart Earle. 2016. 'The dialogical collective: mediumship, pain, and the interactive creation of Ndyuka Maroon subjectivity.' Journal of the Royal Anthropological Institute 22.3: 516–533.

Strathern, Marilyn. 2013. Learning to see in Melanesia: Lectures given in the Department of Social Anthropology, Cambridge University, 1993–2008. Manchester: HAU Society for Ethnographic Theory.

Strathern, Marilyn. 2002. 'On Space and Depth'. In Complexities: social studies of knowledge practices, edited by Annemarie Mol and John Law, 88–115. Durham: Duke University Press.

Strathern, Marilyn. 1981. 'Culture in a Netbag: the Manufacture of a Subdiscipline in Antrhopology.' Man 16 (4), 665–688.

Thoden van Velzen, Bonno, and Van Wetering, Wilhelmina. 2004. In the shadow of the oracle: religion as politics in a Suriname Maroon society. Long Grove: Waveland Press.

Van der Pijl, Yvone. 2007. Levende-doden: Afrikaans-Surinaamse percepties, praktijken en rituelen rondom dood en rouw. Amsterdam: IBS en Rozenberg Publishers.

Van der Pijl, Yvon. 2010. 'Pentecostal-Charismatic Christianity: African-Surinamese Perceptions and Experiences.' Exchange, 39(2), 179–195.

Van der Pijl, Yvon. 2016. 'Death in the family revisited: Ritual expression and controversy in a Creole transnational mortuary sphere.' Ethnography 17.2: 147–167.

Van de Port, Mattijs. 2006. 'Visualizing the sacred: video technology, "televisual" style, and the religious imagination in Bahian Candomblé.' American Ethnologist 33.3: 444–461.

Van Stipriaan, Alex. 'Maroons and the Communications Revolution in Suriname's Interior.' In In and Out of Suriname: Language, Mobility and Identity, 139–163. Edited by Eithne Carlin, Isabelle Léglise, Bettina Migge, and Paul Tjon Sie Fat. Leiden: Brill.

Van Wetering, Wilhelmina. 1992. 'A Demon in Every Transistor'. Etnofoor 5(1/2), 109–127.

Van Wetering, Wilhelmina. 1996. 'Witchcraft among the Tapanahoni Djuka'. In Maroon societies: Rebel slave communities in the Americas, 370–388. Edited by Richard Price. Baltimore: Johns Hopkins University Press.

Van Wetering, Wilhelmina, and Thoden van Velzen, Bonno. 1982. 'Female Religious Responses to Male Prosperity in Turn-of-the-Century Bush Negro Societies.' New West Indian Guide 56.1/2: 43–68.

Vernon, D. 1980. 'Bakuu: possesing spirits of witchcraft on the tapanahony.' New West Indian Guide 54 (1): 1–38.

Vernon, Diane. 1985. Money magic in a modernizing Maroon society: Institute for the study of languages and cultures of Asia and Africa (ILCAA) Tokyo university of foreign studies, Tokyo.

Vernon, Diane. 1992. Les representations du corps chez les noirs marrons Ndjuka du Surinam et de la Guyane française. Paris: Editions de l'ORSTOM.

Viveiros de Castro, Eduardo B. 1998. 'Cosmological deixis and Amerindian perspectivism.' Journal of the Royal Anthropological Institute 469–488.

Wagner, Roy. 1981. The Invention of Culture: Revised and Expanded Edition. Chicago and London: The University of Chicago Press.

Werbner, Pnina. 2014. 'Between Ontological Transformation and the Imagination of Tradition: Girls'. Puberty Rituals in Twenty-first Century Botswana.' Journal of Religion in Africa 44.3–4: 355–385.

PART 4

Creations

∵

CHAPTER 10

Modeling Cultural Adaptability: Maroon Cosmopolitanism and the Banamba Dance Contest

Corinna Campbell

In the liner notes to the 1977 Smithsonian Folkways recording, Music from Saramaka, Richard and Sally Price introduce their 11th track as, "drumming for bandámmba, an old dance that is now only rarely performed."[1] What a surprise, given its purported scarcity at the time, that forty years later bandámmba (hereafter spelled banamba)[2] would be flourishing as one of the most popular Maroon dances in Suriname, French Guyana, and their diasporic communities abroad.

Today, in addition to the ritual and celebratory contexts with which it was initially associated, banamba is abundantly referenced in the lyrics and percussive textures of Maroon and Afro-Surinamese popular music genres, including aleke, kawina, kaseko, and even locally produced dancehall and EDM-inspired music.[3] In music videos and in concerts and clubs, dancers respond to these musical references with the sinuous rolls and articulated isolations of the hips and midsection that are characteristic of the genre. Maroon cultural groups feature banamba in their repertoires, arguably second in popularity only to the awasa dance genre of the Ndyuka Maroons of eastern Suriname.[4] And in Paramaribo, adolescent youth (primarily young women) perform banamba in dance competitions and multi-talent pageants as a way of affirming both their

---

1 R. Price and S. Price 1977, Liner notes p.6.
2 The term bandámmba is used in previous scholarship (including van Kempen, though without the accented "á" (2002)), R. Price and S. Price (1994, 1999), and Herskovits and Herskovits (1936). Although many Maroons—both Saramakan and from the other five subgroups—pronounce the "d" in bandámmba, here I use the spelling that proliferates in popular media, both through the Banamba Contest, on popular music track names, and other projects including DJ Fredje's Banamba Riddim Mix and subsequent remixes. Note that even in cases in which the word is spelled "banamba," sometimes it is pronounced with the "d" sound, including in Wi Sani's accompaniment to the 2008 and 2009 Banamba Contest. In all cases excepting direct quotes, I use a consistent spelling to avoid confusion and because the Banamba Contest (which uses this spelling) is the primary focus of this chapter.
3 Examples include: A Seke Doti (aleke), Naks Kaseko Loco (kaskawi), Wi Sani (kawina), Mataka Boys (kawina), DJ Fredje (EDM/house). See Discography.
4 For more on Maroon cultural groups, see Campbell (2013).

© KONINKLIJKE BRILL NV, LEIDEN, 2019 | DOI:10.1163/9789004388062_012

connection to their Maroon culture and heritage and their femininity. What may have at one point seemed like a genre of peripheral and diminishing status now has become a widely celebrated marker of Saramakan and Maroon identity.

This chapter considers the often-controversial role that competition culture plays in establishing new spaces, meanings, and uses for traditional performance practices such as banamba in urban and cosmopolitan contexts. Culturally themed contests and pageants are seen by some as a survival tactic—as a way of encouraging young people who are fully immersed in globally circulating genres like hip hop or R&B to invest in local traditions. According to others, these contests lead instead to a damaging simplification and decontextualization of traditional practices, eroding the very distinctions they claim to uphold. Still others dismiss these competitions as fluff, a diversion and source of light entertainment of little social consequence, one way or the other.

Using the longstanding Paramaribo-based Banamba Contest as a case study, I illustrate how contests that highlight traditional genres of music and dance are involved in the dual processes of perpetuating tradition and changing it through adaptations to logistical demands, audience expectations, and the competition format. I suggest that a successful contestant must master a skill set that has more to do with performing tradition in the perpetually fragmenting and hybridizing social currents of Paramaribo than with the demonstration of the most thorough understanding or competent performance of a particular genre. Finally, the refutation of the judges' decisions—so dependable as to act as an element of the contest ritual itself—may in fact function as one of the greatest social benefits of these events. Through challenging the judges' appraisals and the competition structure, event participants create a discursive space in which to contemplate the competing demands of the genre and its cosmopolitan mode of presentation.

These competitions, then, exhibit what Katherine Meizel refers to as the "Concurrent erosion and articulation of particular discursive boundaries." Meizel (2011: 15). Through them, authority is undone even as it is made explicit. Rather than being isolated and elevated through competition, traditional music and dance genres are presented alongside and fused with a wide array of performance forms. Instead of resulting in a stalemate of sorts, such processes encourage exploration, debate, and ultimately a better understanding of a genre's expressive potential in a contemporary age. The Banamba Contest and similar projects are by no means the only factors contributing to a revived interest in banamba, but they do provide compelling examples of the kinds of social translation through which age-old traditions come to be experienced as socially relevant.

MODELING CULTURAL ADAPTABILITY 309

Competition Culture in Paramaribo

Ranging from beauty pageants to breakdance battles, formalized competitions comprise a vital component of popular culture in Paramaribo, in particular for young people. These are public events in which teams or individuals perform for the general public as well as designated official judges, vying for the winning title, a trophy and/or prizes that may include a cash reward, promotional opportunities, or gifts from local businesses. By and large, these events escape the notice of international audiences, yet their local importance is readily apparent. Citywide TV, radio, and print advertisements proliferate in the weeks leading up to a competition, and the contests themselves are often documented via live broadcasts, newspaper articles, and commercially produced DVD s. Attendance at such competitions regularly numbers in the hundreds.

Not all such contests bear a particular ethnic affiliation—hip hop dance battles and popular song competitions are among the most successful at garnering an ethnically diverse pool of contestants[5]—yet many groups and organizations have recognized that competitions are effective in encouraging young people to learn about their heritage and take part in traditional practices. Using beauty pageants as an example, Paul Tjon Sie Fat details the political implications of these competitions, particularly in light of the ethnic clientelism that characterizes Suriname's national political structure:

The national and non-ethnic Miss Suriname Contest was discontinued in 1999, apparently due to financial problems, and was replaced by a proliferation of ethnic pageants. Various groups and individuals copy the concept of pageants from other ethnic groups and organize alternative pageants within their own segment as a strategy to acquire legitimacy and status within the apanjaht narrative. Ethnic pride becomes gendered as it is channeled through young urban women who compete in the mastery

---

5 To date, the most popular song contests include the long-standing Suripop Song Competition (see Campbell: 2014) and Surinaamse Televisie Stichting (STVS)'s Youth Voice competition, which concluded in 2015. In both cases, the use of foreign and cosmopolitan forms of performance is useful in helping to galvanize a national(ist) and interethnic community. See Rommen (2007) for a comparable case study using rock music in Trinidad. A third, citywide example is the adjudication of the Wandelmars/Avondvierdaagse—a four day long parade event that sends participants through the city. Each group is appraised at a series of "hotspots" by local judges, who then award prizes in a number of categories, including best cultural group, brass band, etc. Note that, while the above initiatives might achieve moderate success in promoting ethnic diversity, they tend to be staunchly middle- and upper- class affairs.

of "authentic" and essential folklore, and stereotypical racial ideals of beauty. And so by 2006, Suriname had the Misi Sery Contest for Afro-Surinamese women (the successor of the Miss Alida contest held on the evening before Emancipation Day, 1 July), the Miss India and Miss East Indian Beauty Pageants for women of East Indian extraction (the Miss India Pageant is held under the auspices of Miss India Worldwide), the Miss Indra Maju and Miss Djawa Beauty Pageants for Javanese women (organized by the Vereniging Indra Maju and Sana Budaya respectively), the Miss Amazonia Beauty Pageant for Amerindian women, the Sa Ameva Beauty Pageant for Maroon women (usually first week of October to commemorate the 1762 peace treaty with the Maroons). (Fat 2009: 240)[6]

As Fat makes clear, the anxieties about ethnic representation within the national political structure resonate within competition culture as well. Ethnicity-based competitions do not simply reflect a desire to merge cultural particularities with cosmopolitan forms; they are also a way of demonstrating that one ethnic group has the same capacity to do so as any of the other major ethnic groups within the city and country. Thus, while the events focus on the competition of individuals and their supporters, they also engage larger, city-wide and national competitive structures.

Yvon Van der Pijl has noted that, of all the ethnic groups involved in Suriname's competition culture, Maroons in particular have been drawn to tradition contests, which require skills ranging from proper use of Maroon languages to excellence in traditional performance styles (Pijl, 2005). She suggests their heightened interest in competitions of this sort is in itself a way of calling attention to the unique relationship between Maroons and their African cultural roots, which distinguish them not only from other populations within the city but the nation and the African diaspora as well. Such efforts at social and cultural uplift likely have a particular importance for Maroons in Paramaribo, given the discrimination and negative stereotypes they face as an increasingly influential minority presence within the city (Bilby 1999: 266; Jaffe and Sanderse 2010).

The Maroon talent competitions to which Pijl refers are of two general types: 1.) Beauty or multi-talent pageants that feature multiple rounds of competition, each one demonstrating a different skill or mode of presentation, and 2.) Competitions that focus exclusively on a particular genre of music or dance.

---

6 Fat borrows from Edward Dew the concept of apanjaht consociationalism, defined as, "The practice of ethnically based political parties playing upon prejudice, fear, or communal interest to gain support." (Dew 1990:192, quoted in Fat 2009:9).

MODELING CULTURAL ADAPTABILITY

The former, including the Sa Ndyuka Misi, Sa Dumma, Sa Ameva, and Sa Mooi Pangi competitions, present contestants as generalists who are expected to demonstrate their strength in multiple skills. Single-genre talent competitions, which have featured banamba, loketo, awasa dance and aleke singing, frame contestants as specialists. In different ways, both types of competition maintain a focus on tradition and ethnic pride.

Talent competitions and pageants are among the first opportunities for urban Maroons to demonstrate their skills to an audience beyond their immediate community of friends, neighbors, and family members. They serve as a validation and acknowledgement of adolescents—in particular adolescent girls—as cultural agents, equipped with the skills necessary to perform Maroon identity within a cosmopolitan social sphere. Boys and young men can find in popular music (both global and local) ample opportunity for self-expression and the working out of contemporary Maroon identities (see for example, Jaffe and Sanderse 2010, Bilby 1999, 2000), however the performance of popular music continues to be a gendered field, deemed less socially acceptable for women than men. Competitions and pageants constitute one of only a few comparable outlets for self-expression and public acknowledgment that are widely available to girls and young women.[7] In the process of showcasing these girls' talents, as Fat noted, tradition-based competitions further engrain the notion that cultural perpetuation and transmission is a responsibility that falls primarily on women.

Professionalism

Contests serve as a validating mechanism, bestowing upon prizewinners a credential through which they can establish themselves as professionals. Thomas Turino defines musical professionalism as, "the functional and conceptual articulation of music and dance activities with money and markets." He clarifies further, "I use the term professional to refer strictly to income-generating activity, whether or not specialized skill is required, and specialist to refer to special skills and knowledge, whether or not money is involved." (Turino 2000: 354, 52)

Successful competitors (certainly the contest winner, but also notable runners up) gain recognition for having exemplary or exceptional skill, as appraised by a panel of judges. These judges are typically individuals who are

---

7   Participation in parades, local dance troupes, and Church-related organizations and events have the potential to fulfill similar expressive needs. Talent and beauty competitions are distinct in that they focus on the individual, rather than the collective.

easily identified as "professionals" themselves in one capacity or another, who may or may not have specialized knowledge about the style of performance under consideration. As designated winners or finalists, contestants become legible, particularly to those without the ability to evaluate the merits of a performance for themselves, as having attained a level of social approval. They can then be targeted as likely candidates for a range of demonstrational, touristic, or promotional events. As time passes, competitions often reaffirm a former winner's professional status by absorbing her back into contest proceedings. She might serve as a judge, a coach or mentor for a fresh batch of contestants, or a featured performer during the night of competition.[8]

A contestant's viability within the professional realm is confirmed with the bestowal of a title and cash prize. Beyond its function as incentive to attract participants and a way to establish a contest's weight and prestige, the cash prize indicates that a performer's skills are worthy of monetary compensation. Contestants are "priced" in accordance with their rank—the results of the competition establish the economic value of each contestant relative to their fellow competitors within the "market" of eligible participants. The judges are the primary agents in bestowing status upon contestants, yet audience opinion can provide counter-narratives that exert similar influence within a cultural economy. The prestige of a contest win has the additional benefit of helping a young woman better negotiate for financial compensation as a performer in subsequent commissioned appearances.

As Turino makes clear, a professional designation does not guarantee the performer demonstrates exceptional talent or knowledge. This is certainly the case in the Banamba Contest, for example. In recent years, contest organizers have pre-screened contestants to ensure they exhibit a basic proficiency in banamba and to narrow the number of contestants down to a manageable size. Contest founder and director Freddy Huur's approach to talent in these screenings is instructive: "If you see someone who doesn't know banamba but you see that it's possible, then you teach her. But another one you'll see that they really don't know what they're doing ... you tell them, another year—go practice at home and come back."[9] While the Banamba Contest aims to highlight the best dancers in the pool of contestants for a

---

8   For example, in 2009, two former Banamba Contest winners played an active role in the event: 3-time competition winner Ernestine Adjako performed in between semi-finalist and finalist rounds of the competition, and Magali Lieveld, winner of the 2007 Banamba Contest (Lieveld) served as a judge.

9   This and all subsequent quotes from Freddy Huur are from an interview with the author on September 17, 2009 in Paramaribo translated from Sranan Tongo by the author.

MODELING CULTURAL ADAPTABILITY 313

given year, it is clear that contestants can fall well short of a specialist designation. During the competition, the audience members who dance informally in between rounds of competition exhibit abilities on par with or even surpassing the competitors. Contestants are set apart as much by their desire to compete and willingness to embrace this presentational format as they are by ability.

Yet while professional status as Turino describes it is tied explicitly (and exclusively) to financial compensation and a degree of specialization is not to be assumed, I hesitate to see this designation as based purely on the premise of garnering income. Professionalism in Suriname's cultural economy is more frequently referenced in relation to a mode of comportment—an ability to "put on a good show," to adapt to a wide array of performance scenarios, to behave in a way that reflects well on any group a performer may be taken to represent, and to work effectively with the commissioning individual or organization in order to meet their demands while self-advocating for adequate performance conditions and compensation.[10] A contestant's degree of specialized knowledge about a type of music or dance might not play as large a role in a competition's outcome as one might be led to believe, however these are but a few of the skills and competencies a successful contestants might be expected to exhibit.

One example of such additional performance expectations is evident in the commercial DVD of the 2009 Banamba Contest. Before the pool of 20 semi-finalists was narrowed to 10 finalists, a cameraman and a member of the production team ventured backstage to ask contestants some general questions: "How do you feel about your performance?" "Do you think you'll be a finalist?" "If you don't win, will you be angry?" "How do you feel about your scores?" These mini-interviews—conducted in Dutch—were not a judged portion of the program, yet the questions were clearly aimed at rewarding specific character traits and skills, including a positive attitude, an outgoing and self-confident nature, and facility in the Dutch language. Such interactions mirror the interview component of pageant competitions, the implication being that the ideal contestant is one who can effectively function as a spokesperson as well as a dancer.

The Banamba Contest, mentioned above, is among the longest running and most popular of the Maroon pageants and competitions in Paramaribo. Its durability as an institution, coupled with the resurgence of popular interest in banamba dancing, make it a compelling case study with which to explore how

---

10 Campbell 2013: 122–132.

the competition framework interacts with a particular music or dance practice. In order to do so, however, some general information about the genre is instructive.

Banamba

Banamba is a Saramakan Maroon dance style, performed primarily by women. This genre highlights a dancer's ability to isolate and manipulate movements in her waist and hips. Its most characteristic elements include quick, articulated movements of the hips, called koti, and smoother, undulating rolls of the waist and hips, called lolo. The dancer's arms may be placed on her hips, held out to the sides, or above her head, while her legs and upper torso stay relatively still, further drawing attention to her skillful manipulation of her hips and midsection. A talented banamba dancer will execute these movements in a rhythmic fashion, in dialogue with the beat provided and whatever percussive variations accompany her performance—whether drummed, sung, or clapped.[11] Banamba is performed wearing a pangi, a traditional wrap skirt, with another piece of cloth (called an angula) tied around the dancer's waist and knotted in the back to further magnify her hip movements. These must be firmly secured to ensure that the pangi does not fall as the result of vigorous hip movements, or loosen to expose a woman's upper thighs.

Men dance banamba as well, if less often. They do so either soloistically or with a woman, adding their own stomach rolls and stylized pelvic thrusts in playful reference to a flirtatious or sexual encounter, or to express their own sensuality.[12] At times their performances may garner considerable attention and enthusiasm from onlookers, yet women are the true champions of the genre, and banamba's characteristic moves are designed to compliment a woman's figure and to feature styles of movement that are socially coded as feminine. This dance provides a prime opportunity for women of all shapes and sizes to flaunt their physical assets and demonstrate their deft manipulations of their hips and midsection. Onlookers cheer to encourage the performer(s), but are expected to refrain from making physical contact during the dance itself.

---

11   For a brief video example of banamba as performed in the village Goejaba can be seen in the 1979 documentary film, Kobogo. Banamba dancing starts at roughly 1:06.

12   Male attire in these instances might include a cape and loincloth, but in the city or in contexts in which popular music is also being performed, most men wear pants instead of a loincloth. Some affix an angula, as would a woman performer.

MODELING CULTURAL ADAPTABILITY

Traditionally, the dance is accompanied by singing and percussion, either clapped, played by an ensemble of drums,[13] or struck on the side of a box or basket (called a mánda or mánchi) that is prepared as part of a marital gift exchange. While a variety of rhythms are used to accompany banamba dancing, its most common feature is the steady accentuation of a regular pulse. When performed by a drum ensemble, the lead drummer plays the higher pitched pikin doon, whereas for many other genres (including Ndyuka genres awasa and songe) the lower drum (gaan doon) takes the lead role.

In keeping with the spirit of the dance, song lyrics tend to be playful and celebratory, often alluding to the sensual movements and physical attributes of the dancer. Two examples from the repertoire of the cultural (folkloric) group Saisa demonstrate this broad trend. "Booster Banti" takes as its point of reference the tires of a locally popular "Buster" brand of moped, likening their (motorized) spinning to the movements of a dancer's hips:

> Lead Singer (Carlos Pinas):   Di Booster banti de, a ta biya no. Ayy!
> The Booster (moped) tire there, it's [really] spinning. Ayy!
> Koor (chorus):   A ta biya no
> It's [really] spinning!

In a second song, "Doeli," lead singer Silvana Pinas states simply that a woman named Doeli is sewing ("Doeli naai oo Doeli"), the motion of the needle in a sewing machine taken to be the back and forth (or, if in a horizontal position, up and down) motion of a person's hips. The chorus sings back the same words and melody as the lead: "Doeli naai oo Doeli" (Doeli is sewing, Doeli). In both cases, after introducing the main text and subject matter of the song, the lead singer can utilize word substitutions or alter the rhythmic and tonal material from the initial call in order to prevent the song from getting overly monotonous. The only parameter that must stay constant is the amount of time the lead singer has before the chorus enters, maintaining a consistent response phrase for the duration of the song.

These two song texts highlight a few notable trends. Both implicitly focus attention on a dancer's hips. The lines of text are characteristically short, leading

---

13   These drums are referred to most frequently as apinti doon (apinti drum), however apinti refers to a drum language rather than the instrument itself. For these reasons many Maroon drummers prefer that the drums are known either as "doon" (drum), or by their pitch and function within a drum ensemble, which is determined in part relative to the other drums—gaan doon (large/lead drum), pikin doon (little/supporting drum), tun (timekeeper).

to a rapid alternation of lead singer and chorus, and an overall tendency toward rhythmic play as opposed to melodic elaboration. Finally, both draw reference from mechanized products that are not deemed explicitly Saramakan. As such, they effectively illustrate the ways in which imported and cosmopolitan items can serve as subject matter for songs in a more or less traditional performance idiom. These lyrics provide an excellent reminder that, while the Banamba Contest can be seen to strengthen cosmopolitan links, performers readily explore such links outside of a contest format as well, and have done so for quite some time.[14]

Banamba in Public Discourse

Information about the dance's history and its initial performance contexts vary widely. Below are a number of historical and/or contextualizing statements about banamba, collected via interviews with Cyriel Eersteling (a Maroon of Saramakan and Ndyuka descent and prominent political figure), and Banamba Contest founder Freddy Huur, alongside quotations from published works by Michiel van Kempen and Sally and Richard Price.[15] Many of the below statements need not be mutually exclusive. In fact, all the sources were careful to disavow the notion of a singular explanation of the dance's history. Nonetheless, the particular constellations of interpretations they cite, even in an admittedly partial list, create a distinctive impression as to the character of the dance and its social purpose. Taken together, these statements illustrate the variety of ideas about the genre that were circulating in print and among Maroon cultural representatives in Paramaribo from the mid-2000's to the 2010's.

– Banamba is a celebratory dance, meant to welcome men back from a long trip (Kempen, Price and Price), a successful hunt (Eersteling), or (particularly in fesi-ten—the early history of Maroons in Suriname) return from battle (Kempen, Eersteling). Eersteling explains, "The banamba is just to give [the men returning home] a feeling like ... you're a man, you're brave."

---

14   Another example of the wide array of influences utilized in song can be found in R. Price and S. Price 1999: 239, in which they recall, "[One] man's rendition of the rhythms of a Coca-Cola bottling machine he saw in Paramaribo becomes a popular piece for local drummers." Incidentally, earlier in this same book (p. 141) we see the sewing machine serving as inspiration for a woodcarver.

15   This section references the following sources: Huur, personal communication 9-17-09; Eersteling, personal communication 10-10-09. Kempen 2002:145–146; S. Price 1993: 73–75, S. and R. Price 1999: 250.

MODELING CULTURAL ADAPTABILITY 317

- Banamba was danced in the context of marital gift exchanges between a man and woman, associated in particular with the preparation and presentation of a basket or trunk of gifts called a manda or manchi. (Huur and S. Price.) Huur indicates that the manda could be used as a percussive surface to accompany the dancing.
- In many villages that were deeply influenced by Moravian or Roman Catholic missionaries, banamba was deemed too erotic for public consumption. As a result, starting in the 1700s, the dance changed from being a public and communal celebration to a private ceremony with explicit ties to marriage—either a wife's performance for the pleasure of her husband (in particular on their wedding night), or a dance transmitted among female family members (often patrilineal aunts) as a way of instructing a young woman how to satisfy her husband sexually (Eersteling).[16]
- After the Saramaka signed the 1762 peace treaty with the Dutch, banamba was used as a distraction in order to mitigate severe punishments that colonial delegates would mete out against recent runaways on behalf of slave owners. Huur explains, part of the 1762 treaty between Saramakaners and colonial officials, as with treaties with the Ndyuka and Maroon populations in Jamaica, required a Maroon group to refuse to accept additional runaways into their ranks—instead they were required to relinquish these individuals to colonial authorities. When the colonists got a tip that a new runaway was residing in a Maroon camp or village, they would collect said individual, beat him (or her) and then return that person to the city for further punishment. Huur claims that women would perform banamba while a recent runaway was being whipped to distract the person administering the punishment so that it might not be so severe.[17]
- In addition to a secular banamba, the dance can take on a variety of spiritual and ritual functions. Kempen claims that there are separate kinds of banamba that are particular to gods in a Maroon pantheon, including apuku (ampuku)—forest spirits and vodu (papagadu)—reptile spirits. Price and

---

16 The intervention of the Church can be seen to have multiple effects: first, making explicit that a sensual or erotic performance is intended exclusively for the benefit of a woman's husband, above all on their wedding night; second, as Eersteling told it, the dance becomes linked to a woman's coming of age; and finally, the relationship between dance acts and sex acts becoming increasingly explicit.

17 Eduward Fonkel, leader of the cultural group Saisa, posited that banamba had a similar function on the plantations. According to him, women's dancing in this fashion created a diversion that allowed slaves to run away undetected. I found fewer people who would corroborate this explanation, yet it does strike me as significant that the dance's use as a diversionary tactic surfaces in two versions.

Price note that the genre is associated with fertility and can be used for rites concerning twins. It can also serve in connection with the spirits of Maroon ancestors from the 18th century, who are pleased by the performance of musical styles that were popular in their lifetimes.

In surveying these explanations, two things become immediately apparent. The first and most obvious is the breadth and number of explanations regarding the dance's origins and significance. As Eersteling's explanation of the church's involvement illustrates, the ways in which banamba is absorbed into communal life can vary dramatically from one location to the next—in this case, between settlements that were more or less influenced by Moravian and Roman Catholic missionary efforts.[18] However tempting it may be to search for a definitive master narrative, evidence suggests a multiplicity of applications for the dance genre in response to a given location and moment in time, each finding a particular use and meaning, even while utilizing the same musical and kinesthetic elements. Secondly, these variations make clear that performers' understandings of the history of the dance and what it represents can potentially span a huge affective range, from dancing banamba as a way of redirecting the brutal gaze of a colonial emissary, to an intimate and seductive performance a woman would give her husband on their wedding night.

While the Banamba Contest encourages contestants to learn some rudimentary information about the genre in advance of the contest,[19] information about banamba is notably absent from the event itself. Dancers execute the movements but at no point during the public event are they asked about the dance's history or meaning, and no supplementary information is given by event MC's or organizers. In light of the disparate interpretations of the dance, it is easy to understand why. Should the organizers promote one singular interpretation, inevitably the varied and fractured nature of banamba's history and cultural context would surface, thereby risking the alienation of audience members and participants, or posing challenges to organizers' authority. The competition focuses squarely on physical execution of the dance moves, steering well clear of more contentious matters of origin and meaning.

Introducing the Banamba Contest

I said, no—we can't lose this culture. We must hold it and give the children what came before, because [nowadays], everything is westernized. People are doing things with hip-hop and this and that, and people aren't

---

18   Eersteling cites in particular the villages of Jaw Jaw (Roman Catholic), Boto Pasi (Moravian), and Tumaipa, Bente, and Ankununu as villages without a strong Church presence.

19   See Huur's contributions to the above list.

MODELING CULTURAL ADAPTABILITY   319

> looking to our own culture. Then I said no, and we founded the [Banam-
> ba Contest] organization to show that banamba continues to go forward.
>   -Freddy Huur
>   Founder and Director, Banamba Contest and Stichting Banamba

The first Banamba Contest in Paramaribo was held in 1997, and it has grown in size and popularity with each passing year. Freddy Huur approaches this event as a form of cultural advocacy, encouraging young people to become involved in activities that reinforce pride in their heritage and to breathe new life into long-standing Maroon practices. The following sections detail the format and proceedings of the 2009 Banamba Contest. A quintessential cosmopolitan creation (Turino 2000:7–9), its overall framework shares numerous similarities with other talent contests and pageants, yet it also bears the mark of Huur's own creative decision making and the particularities of banamba as a performance genre.

Format

The Banamba Contest begins with opening remarks by the event MCs (usually two individuals), the Surinamese National Anthem, a listing of event sponsors music and dance groups that will be featured throughout the course of the evening as interludes in between rounds of competition. Following these initial comments and activities, the MCs introduce the contestants, typically numbering around 20 participants, and the panel of five judges.

In the first round of competition, each contestant dances for roughly two minutes, receiving her score from each of the five judges immediately after her performance. Contestants' scores are tallied during a brief interlude, after which the finalists are announced. During another interlude, the finalists prepare to perform for a second time. Many but not all choose to change into a new outfit for their second performance. Each finalist then performs to the same song as before, for roughly the same duration. Judges mark their scores but do not share them with the audience or contestants at this time. While a final supporting act performs, judges confer and tally up the total number of points awarded to each finalist. The finalists are called back onstage and the names of the top five scorers are announced. Each of the top five contestants receives a cash prize and a trophy. The evening concludes with informal, celebratory dancing by competitors and audience members.

Each of the aforementioned interludes is filled by local acts. These might include dance crews performing loketo or hip-hop, folkloric music and dance groups, bands playing popular styles including aleke and kawina, or a dance performance by a former contest winner. They serve to connect banamba to other music and dance styles and collectives with which it shares some kind of popular affinity, effectively contextualizing the banamba contest in relation to specific popular trends of the time and the communities and interests represented in the audience.

Assessment

According to Huur, there are two requisite elements that a successful banamba solo must have: first, a dancer must be able to pick out and respond to the banamba musical elements in her accompaniment and, second, she must secure her pangi and angula, ensuring that they do not fall down or expose her indecently while she is dancing. Beyond these basic criteria, it is up to the judges to determine what elements of performance they deem most important and to score the contestants accordingly. A judge might consider such aspects of performance as stage presence, a dancer's ability to isolate her hips and midsection while keeping the rest of her body relatively still, or the degree of variation, control, or technical difficulty incorporated into a contestant's dancing.

The judges appointed by the Banamba Contest committee are treated as experts, yet their authority and qualifications derive from a wide array of experiences and skills. The 2009 judges were characteristic in this regard. The jury was comprised of: A teacher and organizer of the Little Miss Marron pageant, Little Aleke Festival, and the African Queen Contest; a dancer from the cultural (folkloric) group Maswa; a youth parliamentarian for the Sipaliwini District; the winner of the 2007 Banamba Contest; and an acclaimed dancer from Kampalua, a village along the Upper Suriname River, well south of Paramaribo. All but the first were Saramakan. In addition to experiential knowledge of banamba and its cultural context, involvement in competition culture, folkloric ensembles, and political forums all functioned as markers of authority and expertise. Beyond the two criteria that Huur outlined the judging criteria are opaque, however the adjudicators' credentials suggest that the evaluation may reflect adherence to the aesthetic conventions of the competition format as much as the dance it is meant to showcase.

The Jury of Public Opinion

August 20, 2009

The ten finalists of the Banamba Contest 2009 are lined up on stage, anxiously awaiting the announcement of the five contestants with the

MODELING CULTURAL ADAPTABILITY

highest score. The fifth and fourth place awards have been announced to scattered applause. The tension mounts as we approach the declaration of this year's winner. "With a score of 2,200 points this evening ... sister Veronique Apowna!" The echo effect on MC's mic reverberates in the auditorium as the full crowd falls nearly silent, digesting the news. Veronique Apowna, clearly a crowd favorite, pauses and glances at the contestants on either side of her. She scratches her head and takes a tentative step forward in order to receive her third place trophy and certificate. Gradually, the crowd begins to react, a number of women in the audience rising from their plastic chairs approaching the stage, waving their hands in disapproval. Eventually the MC's entreaties for the crowd to calm down are heeded and he resumes reading off the top two prize-winners, but the discontent lingers, still visible and audible as a jubilant Kontesie Kudemusu is announced as the winner, and spilling out into the street as the event concludes and the hundreds of spectators head home.

Every year, as surely as a panel of judges will designate an official winner of the Banamba Contest, the public expresses dissatisfaction with the ranking of contestants. In some years, as was the case in 2009, public disapproval can be so immediate and adamant that it threatens to disrupt the competition proceedings. In other years, as in 2008, it has been more scattered and subdued, but the existence of dissenting opinions remains a constant. Spectators have many recurrent criticisms: the judges don't know what they're doing—they're not Saramakan, or their experience with the dance is limited; they exhibit bias against candidates based on, for instance, age or community affiliations. Critiques extend beyond individual contestants and how they are scored to the contest itself—the musical accompaniment strays too far from banamba rhythms, the pool of competitors is on the whole too inexperienced, the competition format changes the character of the dancing too drastically.

Through the informal talk that takes place during and after competition, spectators can hold in check any claims the Banamba Contest organization or any one contestant can make to cultural authority. Audience opinion has tremendous power to reframe a competition's outcome. (Veronica Apowna provides a great example—although she did not win the top prize in the Banamba Contest, she had generated as much interest as first prize winner Kontesie Kudemusu, and could likely benefit from the same kind of prestige and future performance opportunities that a first place contestant might enjoy.)

Beyond this, however, the viewpoints exchanged among spectators, participants, and interested third parties keep ideas and information about banamba circulating alongside its signature movements. As people share their impressions and opinions of the contest and contestants, they contribute to a critical discourse that draws directly from their accumulated knowledge and experience of the genre. With an ever-increasing number of young women taking part in the contest every year, each one drawing from a network of family and supporters, the Banamba Contest is poised to draw people into these conversations at an impressive rate. Whether in support of a family member or friend or prompted by disagreement with the judges' scores, the Banamba Contest encourages dialogue. It prompts people to share, debate, take stock of what they know, and consider for themselves what they deem the limits and potentials of the genre may be.

Accompaniment: The Role of Wi Sani Kawina Band

As previously discussed, there are a number of different sounds and musical textures that can be used to accompany banamba dancing, from hand clapping or the percussive beating of a manda to an ensemble of several drums and auxiliary percussion—there is not one single sound or, arguably, even one rhythm that is required for banamba dancing, but rather a set of musical features that create the appropriate rhythmic framework and mood. Yet kawina, a genre derived from the Arawak (Amerindian) kauna and widely associated with Suriname's Creole population (See Campbell 2014), is not among the many forms that could potentially register as traditional in relation to banamba.

In 2004, after failed attempts to recruit accomplished Saramakan drummers to accompany the event and inadequate amplification for hand clapping to have the necessary effect, Huur solicited help from the kawina band Wi Sani (lit. "Our Thing"), and they have been supplying the accompaniment for contestants ever since. As a band of enduring popularity hailing from the Saramakan village Gujába, Wi Sani is in some ways ideally suited for this project, despite the apparent contradiction of having a kawina band commissioned to accompany an event that was created ostensibly to celebrate the "real banamba." Regardless of their kawina instrumentation, Huur insists the accompanying music is stylistically distinct from the genre. "There's a drum [rhythm] inside there, that the men play. That's for the banamba rhythm." The ability to listen through the characteristic sounds and patterns of kawina and pick out the rhythms suitable for banamba dancing, while omitting the more full-bodied swaying motions that characterize dancing to kawina, is one of only two basic criteria that Huur maintained were required of a contestant.

Musically, kawina and banamba (as played by a percussion ensemble) have a number of features in common. Both have a steady duple pulse of comparable

MODELING CULTURAL ADAPTABILITY   323

tempo. The highest pitched drum in the ensemble (the koti dron for kawina and pikin doon for banamba) leads the ensemble and has the greatest freedom to improvise, while a lower pitched drum (hari and gaan doon, respectively) maintains the characteristic rhythmic patterns associated with their respective genres. Additionally, both ensembles commonly include in their instrumentation a kwakwa bangi—a wooden stool or bench that is played with two sticks, and both feature call and response vocal parts.

Wi Sani's adaptation of kawina to a banamba feel consists of multiple small adjustments. While beats one and three generally receive the most weight from the koti dron in kawina performance, in the banamba sections Wi Sani places drum hits on every beat, resulting in a 2/4 rather than 4/4 feel and giving the sense that the tempo speeds up. A call and response format is typical of both styles, but for the banamba version lead singer Djo Banai shortens his phrases and, as with the koti dron, aligns the syllables so they emphasize the pulse. Taken together, these seemingly slight adjustments make the music a functional accompaniment for contestants in the Banamba Contest. Wi Sani used variants of the song, "Banamba" off Wi Sani's 2007 album, in both the 2008 and 2009 competitions. The main lyric has lead singer Djo Banai singing, "Di u'o miti baka oo" ("When we meet again"), to which the chorus responds "Hali banamba," ("Dance banamba"). Such a message affirms one of the most agreed upon scenarios under which banamba would be performed—after a man returns home from a long trip. The song goes on to praise a woman's physical features—her beautiful face, long neck, slender waist, etc.

Likely in an effort to eliminate variables or the potential for bias, all contestants in a given year perform to music that, although live, consists of nearly identical lyrics, melodies, and rhythms. Only slight variations exist in the band's accompaniment, including the koti dron's percussive embellishments, Banai's choices from among roughly a half dozen phrases to include in his call, and occasional, short, vocal interjections—either a sound or vocal effect or a simple word like "faya" (fire). Beyond these small changes, the live band is used, by and large, as though it was a recording—they are stopped, cued up, and replayed for each successive candidate.

As a result of the degree of repetition (the same musical contours with only minor changes for roughly 30 individual performances), the music ceases to be a major point of interest and the performance as a whole lacks the interactivity between musicians and dancers that one could normally expect from a live performance of banamba. This helps contestants by giving them a predictable format and facilitating their ability to practice at home, but the repetitive and regulated structure of the music and competition format creates a sense of uniformity among competitors. During the contest, the rapid succession of performances with so much in common could prompt judges and spectators to hone in on finer details, potentially encouraging an enhanced level of connoisseurship, even if the performances tend to fall within a narrower expressive range. On the other hand, with so much predictability built into the competition, it can be difficult for contestants to engage or illustrate their ability to improvise on the spot in response to the musical patterns and ideas that are offered to them. This is one example of a valued skill and a prime source of interest in performance that is diminished within the competitive framework of the Banamba Contest.

The inclusion of Wi Sani's hybridized music in the Banamba Contest marks a clear divergence from generic expectations, potentially risking confusion or misinformation about banamba in the contest setting, or even changing the ways in which the dance is learnt or experienced. In another light, however, Huur and fellow organizers instituted changes that reflect the contexts in which Maroon youth in Paramaribo are most likely to encounter banamba—at a concert or party, on the radio, or on a music video. Wi Sani's adaptation of banamba fits neatly into a longstanding practice of mixture and quotation in Afro-Surinamese music. Among the abundant hybrid genres that thrive within the region are the popular kawina/kaseko combo kaskawi, aleke-kaseko or alekas, or the blending of aleke with Jamaican Nyabinghi drumming with aleke to create what is alternately called reggae-aleke or Nyabinghi aleke.[20] From this perspective, cultivating the ability to filter out the musical characteristics of one dance genre while honing in on another can allow contestants to acclimate to such rampant musical mixing, while also developing the skills necessary to isolate the particular references and make meaningful stylistic distinctions in the course of performance. With such abilities, performers can maintain stylistic distinctions even as genres intermingle.

The musical components of the Banamba Contest can be used to substantiate conflicting arguments concerning cultural adaptability. On the one hand, "listening through" a musical texture to find the rhythmic ideas suitable for banamba dancing is certainly an adaptive process. We can see the broader relevance of these ideas in the proliferation of references to banamba included in popular music in the 2010's. Artists rely on dancers' ability to pick up on the kinesthetically relevant rhythmic ideas in order for these dance songs to have

---

20   See Bilby (1999: 286–287) for a list of genres that bear evidence of similar mixture. This kind stylistic mixing can be propagated even on an individual level. I met a Maroon man in French Guyana who had gained local notoriety by combining his own Rasta aesthetic with awasa, an Okanisi (Ndyuka) traditional dance form and performing at concerts and contests as "The Awasafarian."

MODELING CULTURAL ADAPTABILITY   325

their intended effect. It is largely thanks to the cultivation of these skills that banamba enjoys its current popularity and has been able to infiltrate music videos and a diverse array of concert settings. However, from another angle the musical accompaniment in the Banamba Contest is largely static, resulting in a similarly muted range of dynamism and interactivity among contestants. Repetition and predictability narrow the points of interest within a performance to a few parameters.

Wi Sani's experiments with banamba rhythms have garnered significant attention outside of the Banamba Contest as well. The song the band features in the competition (titled "Banamba") was commercially released in 2007 on their album, Kill Somebody, and quickly became a No. 1 hit on local Maroon radio stations and a perpetual favorite at live shows. "Sen em Dam," an earlier track off their 2006 album, Goontapu, makes use of a similar stylistic shift from kawina to a banamba mid-song, prefacing the switch with a deliberate mention of "banamba mindii" (banamba waist) immediately before introducing banamba rhythms.[21] These fusions of kawina and banamba constitute a paradox—in competition they are intended to highlight banamba as its own distinctive dance genre; in its circulation outside of the contest as a widely performed and distributed popular dance tune, it has affirmed and contributed to a widespread interest in stylistic mixing.

Were anyone to need further proof of the applicability and relevance of being able to listen through a musical texture to find the banamba rhythm and dance, a quick consideration of the riddim compilations by Alfred Bisonia (aka DJ Fredje) would surely put any remaining doubts to rest. This Paramaribo-based DJ and producer has experienced considerable success in creating riddim tracks[22] that blend aspects of Jamaican dancehall and electronic dance music with Maroon musical styles, including aleke, seketi, and banamba.[23] His Banamba Riddim (2016) is in many ways representative. It features a highly produced, looped backing pattern based loosely on banamba rhythms, played

---

21   See "Sen En Dam" from their 2006 recording, Goontapu, and "Banamba" from their 2007 album, Kill Somebody for examples. In the latter, the strongest banamba rhythms come in at 1:45.

22   Ethnomusicologist Michael Veal clarifies, "The term riddim, initially a localizing of the English word rhythm, has taken on a distinctive meaning in Jamaican music over time, used to [...] generic chord progressions and/or bass lines that have formed the basis for subsequent songs." Veal 2007, 48.

23   Fredje's productions are not limited to such explicit references to Maroon musical styles. He has produced similar mixes in a more squarely pop/EDM idiom. These include his Forgiving Riddim (2015), Love Riddim (2014) and Mek Money Riddim (2017). As with banamba, I use the unaccented spelling in accordance with Bisonia's own usage.

by a kaskawi ensemble (a mixture of kawina percussive instruments, with the addition of electric guitar, keyboards, and electric bass), intermixing local musical elements with sounds, effects, and flashy transitions that link it to electronic dance music. This backing track then functions as a riddim—a prerecorded musical template over which vocalists sing. In his remixes, Fredje records and produces a number of popular singers—mostly but not exclusively of Maroon descent—each one giving their own vocal rendering over this simple and repetitive framework.

Fredje's riddim remixes are essentially a compilation of 30-second to minute-long features by different vocalists over a single riddim. They have proven to be an effective way of promoting an array popular and aspiring singers in rapid succession. Singers featured on the same riddim remix often tour together after its release, pooling their musical resources and extending their performances into full sets in a live concert setting. Such projects demonstrate Fredje's own unique take on bringing Maroon musical elements into step with international popular music trends, in particular from the United States and Jamaica.

Just as there is a clear difference between contestants in the Banamba Contest who can pick out the musical elements that are characteristic of banamba dance and others who fail to identify them, some singers on Fredje's Banamba Riddim Remixes deftly identify and manipulate characteristically banamba features, while others perform in a more generic pop idiom.[24] The ability to identify and perform these features can act as a powerful affirmation of Maroon identity, rooted in knowledge of a tradition but owing its impact to the combination and coexistence of local and cosmopolitan ingredients.

Conclusion

Thirty-plus years after Richard and Sally Price described banamba as a dance fading into obscurity by virtue of the infrequency of its performance, it seems that, if anything, it currently suffers from the opposite affliction. Contemporary concern derives from the impression that banamba is losing its identity through its ubiquity as it is quoted and featured in any number of musical mixtures and cosmopolitan reformulations—that, as it adapts to such a wide

---

24   Listen, for instance, to the difference between Denty's "Zamani Sembe" (10:21) and Cotje's "Lalu Mauw Deng" (16:48). Denty's rhythmic style of delivery proves far more conducive to banamba dancing than Denty's longer, more lyrical phrasing.

MODELING CULTURAL ADAPTABILITY

array of applications, it sacrifices many of the aesthetic qualities and points of reference that make it distinctive.

Certainly as a genre, banamba exhibits a large degree of internal variation, both in its musical features (rhythm, instrumentation) and in the history and context of its performance. It was subject to reinterpretation and diverse applications long before its contemporary adaptations to a competition format or electronic dance music and nightclub culture held any sway. As such it resists preservationist critiques that place a high premium on cultural purity or originary states. Perhaps this fluidity has aided in its comeback from near-obscurity in the 1970s to its undeniable popularity 30–40 years later. But at what point and in what ways does a competition format in particular prompt this genre to reshape itself, and what are the knock on effects of these adaptations?

One of the competition's biggest functions is as a potential vehicle to transition a young dancer from social and largely informal performance opportunities into a professional realm. A prize win can operate as a credential that allows a girl or young woman to continue expanding her audience beyond her community to more formal settings and wider audiences, effectively representing a tradition and its practitioners to diverse audiences. Her prestige entitles her to pursue opportunities within Suriname's cultural economy, in which her "expert" credentials often entitle her to financial compensation. A professional designation does not affirm the exceptional nature of her talent as a dancer, but a contest win is a good indication of the contestant's ability to adapt a traditional style of dance to a cosmopolitan mode of presentation in a convincing way.

For as often as staged productions of performance traditions are derided as superficial or inauthentic, few would deny the political importance of ethnic representation on a national level. Paul Tjon Sie Fat has argued compellingly that political and economic interests often underlie what might otherwise be taken as a benign, culturally themed diversion or a bland celebration of multiculturalism (Fat 2009). In order to succeed as a cultural representative in Paramaribo, performers need to exhibit certain skills that go beyond proficiency in a particular music or dance style, for instance the ability to perform with a recording or with whatever musicians might be available, a demonstration of stage presence and poise in self-representation. The adaptations the Banamba Contest demands of participants act as a primer for these secondary abilities.

This flexibility is likely best demonstrated through the use of kawina instruments as accompaniment for banamba dance. The ability to "listen through" kawina affirms a skill set that can assist cultural representatives, as well as those interested in making specific references while dancing to musical mixtures in informal or communal settings. For young people involved in banamba's popular circulation, this is in fact a translatable and immediately applicable skill.

Many if not most of the popular culture references to the genre require choosing to highlight and respond to banamba-compatible elements within a hybrid musical texture. Given the proliferation of banamba references in popular music and media, the capacity to make aural and choreographic differentiations could be a crucial element in maintaining the genre's stylistic integrity.

Finally, a competition format sparks critical discourse. The refutation of the judges' decisions—so dependable as to act as an element of the contest ritual itself—may in fact function as the greatest social benefit of these events. Through challenging the judges' appraisals, event participants create a discursive space in which to contemplate the multiplicity of tradition, conservative versus dynamic interpretations of performance, and the clashes and synergies between the demands of the competition format and the genres' essential social functions.

References

Bilby, K. M. 2001. "Aleke: New Music and New Identities in the Guianas." Latin American Music Review 22(1).

Bilby, Kenneth. 2000. "Making Modernity in the Hinterlands: New Maroon Musics in the Black Atlantic." Popular Music 19(3): 265–292.

Bilby, Kenneth. 1999. " ' Roots Explosion': Indigenization and Cosmopolitanism in Contemporary Surinamese Popular Music." Ethnomusicology 43(2): 256–296.

Campbell, Corinna Siobhan. 2014. "Kawina." and "Suripop." Bloomsbury Encyclopedia of Popular Music of the World, Vols.VIII–XIII, 412–13; 814–6. Edited by David and Horn John Shepard. New York: Bloomsbury Publishing.

Campbell, Corinna Siobhan. 2013. Personalizing Tradition: Surinamese Maroon Music and Dance in Contemporary Urban Practice. PhD Diss., Harvard University.

Dew, Edward. 1990. 'Suriname: Transcending Ethnic Politics the Hard Way'. In: Gary Brana-Shute (ed.), Resistance and Rebellion in Suriname: Old and New. Studies in Third World Societies no. 43, Williamsburg VA.: Department of Anthropology, College of William and Mary.

Fat, Paul B. Tjon Sie. 2009. Chinese New Migrants in Suriname: the Inevitability of Ethnic Performing. Amsterdam: Amsterdam University Press.

Herskovits, Melville Jean, and Frances Shapiro Herskovits. 1936. Suriname Folk-Lore. Vol. 27. New York: Columbia University Press.

Jaffe, Rivke and Jolien Sanderse. "Surinamese Maroons as Reggae Artists: Music, Marginality and Urban Space." Ethnic and Racial Studies 33.9 1561–1579.

Kempen, Michaël Henricus Gertrudis. 2002. Een Geschiedenis van de Surinaamse Literatuur. Uitgeverij Okopipi: 145–146.

MODELING CULTURAL ADAPTABILITY

Meizel, Katherine. 2011. Idolized: Music, Media, and Identity in American Idol. Bloomington: Indiana University Press.

Pijl, Yvonne van der. 2005. "Missverkiezingen en de Articulatie van Etnische Identiteit." OSO 24(1): 115–135.

Price, Richard and Sally Price. 1994. On the Mall: Presenting Maroon Tradition-Bearers at the 1992 FAF. Vol. 4. Indiana University Press.

Price, Sally. 1993. Co-wives and Calabashes. Ann Arbor: University of Michigan Press.

Price, Sally, and Richard Price. 1999. Maroon Arts: Cultural Vitality in the African Diaspora. Boston: Beacon Press.

Rommen, Timothy. 2007. "'Localize It': Rock, Cosmopolitanism, and the Nation in Trinidad." Ethnomusicology 51(3): 371–401.

Sanders, J. and R. Jaffe. 2007. "Jonge Marronmuzikanten: Muziek en Marginaliteit in Paramaribo." OSO 26(1): 43–60.

Thoden van Velzen, B., et al. 2004. In the Shadow of the Oracle: Religion as Politics in a Suriname Maroon Society. Long Grove: Waveland Press.

Turino, Thomas. 2000 Nationalists, Cosmopolitans, and Popular Music in Zimbabwe. Chicago, University of Chicago Press.

Veal, Michael. 2007. Dub: Soundscapes and Shattered Songs in Jamaican Reggae. Wesleyan University Press.

Wilk, Richard. "Learning to be local in Belize: global systems of common difference." In Worlds apart: Modernity through the prism of the local, 110–33. Edited by Daniel Miller. Psycology Press. 1995.

Discography

Bisonia, Alfred "DJ Fredje". "Banamba Riddim Remix Video Clip." 2016. https://www.youtube.com/watch?v=DqRbfYqq63c&t=1022s. Web. Accessed 6/19/17.

Mataka Boys. "Banamba." Mbei Mi Ta Lobi Ju Noo. Vol. 11, 2009.

Naks Kaseko Loco. "Banamba." Sani o P'sa Dja, 2008.

Price, Richard, and Sally Price. "Drumming for Bandámmba." Music from Saramaka: A Dynamic Afro-American Tradition. New York: Folkways Records FE 4225, 1977. Phonograph record with ethnographic notes.

Saisa. "Doeli," "Booster Banti." Album Title Unknown. Paramaribo, SU.

Wi Sani. "Sen En Dam." Goontapu. 2006.

Wi Sani. "Banamba." Kill Somebody. 2007.

Videography

"Banamba Contest 2009," Visicom Production, 2009. Film.

"Miss Banamba Contest 2008 in Grun Djari." Visicom Production, 2008. Film.

"Ko Bo Go." Jan Venema, dir. NOS, 1979. Film.

CHAPTER 11

"Real Bushinengué": Guianese Maroon Music in Transition

Kenneth Bilby and Rivke Jaffe

Introduction

In thinking about the future of contemporary Maroon societies, a question that inevitably arises is: can minority cultures with relatively small populations, such as those of the Maroons, survive and maintain their integrity in this era of globalization, and how? Connected with this question is another: what exactly is "Maroon culture," and can it exist outside of the Surinamese interior from which it emerged? We attempt to provide preliminary answers to these large questions by focusing on Maroon music, tracing musical developments and social identities as Maroons are increasingly integrated into Surinamese and French Guianese urban society and global networks. Specifically, we will consider similarities and differences between Maroon music and musicians in the forest and in the city. We argue that Maroon music today is, in fact, rooted in long-term processes of (proto)globalization and continues to adapt in new urban and transnational settings. The combination of old and new elements, and the articulation of concepts of authenticity and innovation,[1] are central to these musical traditions.

Maroons have often been represented, or even celebrated, as living in isolation from mainstream Surinamese society and the rest of the world. This isolation, and the associated sense that Maroons reflect the most "uncontaminated" presence of Africa in the Caribbean, probably explain part of their attraction for anthropologists and tourists alike. However, from the time the first groups escaped plantation slavery in the 17th century, Maroon isolation was never complete. Interactions between coastal settlements, the plantations and Maroon communities in the rainforest interior, while furtive, continued to take place and intensified following the signing of peace treaties and missionary activities in the mid-18th century. Following the abolition of slavery in

---

1 This chapter is a significantly revised and updated version of Bilby and Jaffe (2009).

© KONINKLIJKE BRILL NV, LEIDEN, 2019 | DOI:10.1163/9789004388062_013

Suriname in 1863, Creole-Maroon contact grew stronger, as gold mining and balata bleeding brought Creoles to the interior and Maroon men migrated to the coast in search of work.

While Maroon urbanization only really took off in the 1990s, then, economic and cultural exchange between the interior and the wider world dates back to much earlier. In fact, the origins of the Maroons lie in the global flows that constituted European colonial expansion into the New World and the transatlantic trade in enslaved Africans. However, the scope and intensity of flows of people, ideas, capital and material culture have changed dramatically from the "proto-globalization" of the 17th century to the contemporary era of globalization. Popular music is both a reflection of and a reaction to social change, including the social changes associated with globalization processes. The social changes Maroons have been experiencing in the late 20th century and early 21st century, ranging from the impacts of gold mining and tourism in the interior, to stigmatization as well as political empowerment in the city, influence musical developments.

Music and Globalization

Globalization has often been depicted as entailing unilateral cultural transfers from "core" countries to geo-economically weaker entities including the Caribbean. For Suriname, the influx of cultural flows from the United States and Europe through old and new media, tourism, and transnational networks is evident. Yet such external influence is by no means new. Processes of cultural domination and the reproduction of European and to a lesser extent North American ideas, values and habits were the norm rather than the exception during centuries of colonialism. But even in a context of cultural hegemony, oppressed groups were able to modify and mitigate dominant cultural forms in creolizing processes of creative resistance. Caribbean people are not passive victims of globalization and cultural domination; they are self-conscious actors who can circumvent, adapt and subvert foreign influences. Cultural forms are often "indigenized" and resignified as they enter new contexts: they gain new meanings interwoven with the symbolic and aesthetic contexts of everyday life. Moreover, Caribbean communities are also capable, individually and collectively, of effecting cultural changes abroad. Both through transnational networks and through mass and new media, the Empire strikes back, culturally. Caribbean musical genres in particular, from salsa to reggae and soca, have become ineradicable elements of the urban cultures of Europe, the US, and beyond.

Popular culture and music in particular are prime sites of "cultural globalization": new musical influences—instruments, rhythms, melodic and harmonic systems—or entire musical genres enter into different cultural landscapes, influencing more traditional practices. At the same time, these "traditional" musical forms can gain a much broader dissemination through migrants and media. In this way, music itself forms a "global flow" that can connect people worldwide through what Barbadian poet Kamau Brathwaite calls "bridges of sound." Similarly, the popular culture associated with musical genres—from slang to video clips to fashion—travels as well. However, music and popular culture also provide a space in which to negotiate and try to influence other social processes, including those associated with globalization. These negotiations and interventions—aimed at changes within Maroon communities, the Surinamese state and broader global change—are evident in Maroon popular culture as well. In this sense, contemporary Maroon music is both the product of and a response to globalization processes.

"Indigenous" Musical Traditions of the Guianese Maroons

The traditional musical cultures of the six Maroon ethnic groups (Saamaka, Ndyuka, Matawai, Aluku, Paramaka, and Kwinti) are very similar in their general outlines, although each displays distinctive characteristics of its own. The Maroons can be divided into two main cultural and linguistic zones: on the one hand, there is the eastern group (Ndyuka, Paramaka, and Aluku), whose traditional villages are dispersed along the Maroni, Tapanahoni, and Cottica Rivers, near the border with French Guiana; on the other hand, there is the central group (Saamaka and Matawai), whose territories are located along the Suriname River and other areas in the central part of Suriname. (The Kwinti fall culturally somewhere in between.) The most significant musical differences between Maroon groups correspond to this schema. The musical traditions of the Ndyuka, Paramaka, and Aluku, which are in many respects nearly identical, are easily distinguished from those of the Saamaka and Matawai.

All Maroons have very rich and diverse traditional musical cultures. African-based drumming and dance play a prominent role in musical life among all groups, although types of drums vary, as do music and dance genres. Songe, susa, and awasa, for instance, are seen as distinctively eastern genres, while sêkêti and bandámmba are identified specifically with the Saamaka.

Some genres, such as kumanti, papa (also known as vodu), or ampuku, have explicitly religious or spiritual associations, being used primarily for obia pee (ceremonies held to invoke specific gods or spirits); others lack this association

FIGURE 11.1 Aluku Maroon women dancing Songe
SOURCE: KENNETH BILBY, 2007

with specific spiritual beings. Among the most important of the latter are a number of "secular" genres sometimes performed during death rites (such as mato, susa, songe, and awasa among the eastern groups, and adunké among the Saamaka). In addition to these, there are a number of genres generally associated with younger members of the community and less formal social dances, such as aleke—although these too can also sometimes be performed during ceremonial events.

Surinamese Maroon musical traditions are generally acknowledged by scholars as being among the most African in the entire western hemisphere. Most traditional Maroon music and dance genres show little or no European influence. Although none of these traditions can be traced back wholly or directly to a single African source, many elements can be related in a more general way to particular ethnolinguistic zones of the African continent. For example, kumanti drumming is clearly cognate with certain drumming traditions that remain important in Akan-speaking areas of West Africa (including parts of Ghana and Côte d'Ivoire), and kumanti songs are in an esoteric language derived in large part from languages belonging to the Akan group. Similarly, papa (or vodu) drumming and chanting are derived in large part from the musical traditions and languages of the West African peoples who are today classified by linguists as speakers of languages in the Fongbe family (e.g., Ewe and Fon). In contrast, the "secular" genre known as susa is clearly related to Central African traditions from the Kongo-Angola region. Yet, all of these Maroon genres also incorporate musical and cultural elements from other parts of Africa. The same is true of the musical instruments on which these genres are typically played. The three drums that make up the ensemble used in a majority of eastern Maroon music and dance genres feature a design and tuning technology that is widespread in coastal West Africa. Other drums used in various other genres, both among eastern and central Maroons, have distinctive designs and tuning mechanisms that betray an origin farther to the south, in what is today southeastern Nigeria and Cameroon (for instance, the Saamaka deindein, or certain variants of the agida drum used in both Ndyuka and Saamaka papa gadu ceremonies).

While the genres and instruments just mentioned have existed since at least the 18th century, there are other Maroon musical traditions that are much younger. The most prominent of these is aleke, which emerged during the 1950s among eastern Maroons. While aleke was born out of a meeting and merging of Maroon and coastal Creole musical traditions and also drew on earlier "mixed" (Creole-influenced) Maroon genres such as loonsei and maselo, it retains a thoroughly "neo-African" sound, such that most non-Maroon listeners do not perceive it as any less "African" than the older genres. In the 1970s, a major innovation took place, when a new type of long drum was created specifically for aleke performances, inspired in part by the Cuban conga drum but incorporating the kind of head and tuning mechanism associated with the traditional drums used in most eastern Maroon musical events. Today a stylistic continuum exists within aleke, ranging from older, more "traditional" variants to newer, more "modern" ones, and various traditional Maroon musical genres, popular urban styles, and mass media all continue to influence this still-evolving "semi-traditional" genre. It is a type of Maroon music found equally in the interior and on the coast (Bilby 2000a, Bilby 2001).

Maroon music, like other Maroon arts, has a long history of dynamism (Price and Price 1980, 1999). Even the most conservative musical traditions, including those closely tied to religious life in villages in the interior, incorporate innovations and undergo subtle changes over time. At the same time, younger, self-consciously "modern" genres such as aleke remain firmly rooted in tradition. For all their openness to change, they continue to be influenced by older styles and to incorporate elements from traditional Maroon music, including the most conservative genres such as kumanti and papa. In aleke music so far, neither tendency has overpowered the other.

FIGURE 11.2 Drummer Miefii Moesé
SOURCE: KENNETH BILBY, 1987

One important characteristic shared by all Maroon groups is that musical life in traditional villages is very closely integrated with social life more generally. In fact, certain crucial events in village life cannot take place without the proper music and dance. In order to summon certain gods or spirits (for example, kumanti gadu, vodu gadu, or ampuku gadu), the correct music must be used. Major council meetings (kuutu) and the arrival of the paramount chief (gaanman) must be announced with a special drum language known as apinti tongo, as must all deaths in the community. The funerary rites that make possible the successful transition of a deceased member of the community from the world of the living to that of the ancestors, which may take a year or more to complete, require the proper music and dance. Clearly, whether musical traditions so intimately tied to local social life can remain viable in the face of rapid change will depend partly on the extent to which changing economic circumstances and social conditions allow continuing social coherence, both in the interior and in urban environments on the coast, as well as across the

336 BILBY AND JAFFE

ocean in the Netherlands, where increasing numbers of young Maroons spend their lives.[2]

From the Interior to the World

As mentioned earlier, migration by Maroons from the interior to coastal areas is nothing new. Nor is the emergence of urbanized Maroon populations an entirely recent phenomenon. For more than three decades, young Maroon migrants have been participating in the popular music scene of Paramaribo, refashioning the musical traditions of their elders, and drawing on a cosmopolitan array of influences to create new urban popular musics of their own. One of the more influential Paramaribo kaseko bands, the Cosmo Stars, was formed by young Saamaka Maroons in 1977. (Kaseko is a uniquely Surinamese style of popular music, based largely on coastal Creole music and dance traditions, that came into its own as Suriname's "national" music around the time of independence in 1975.) Many kaseko bands composed wholly or partly of Maroons were to follow in the footsteps of the Cosmos, and before long these young Maroon musicians were helping to set new trends in Suriname's urban popular music.

During the 1980s, as labor migration to the coast and proletarianization of young Maroons increased, Maroon musicians and musical influences, both Saamaka and Ndyuka, began to move toward the center of the popular music scene in Paramaribo. Not only did young Maroon artists have a significant impact on Creole kaseko bands, but many formed bands of their own. Maroon kaseko bands proliferated, and they joined their Creole peers in experimenting with and absorbing elements from various Latin, Caribbean, North American, and African popular musics, adding their own touches to these. By the early 1990s a host of entirely or predominantly Maroon bands—groups such as Jong Cosje, Rensje and Awojo 2000, Johan Lekker and Dymo Action, Lamora Sound, Yakki Famiri, Papylon Special, High Class, Exco's, and many others— were keeping the recording studios of Paramaribo heavily booked and were experiencing unprecedented popularity.

This period also saw the emergence of Maroon bands across the ocean in the Netherlands. One of the earliest and most successful was the Exmo Stars, formed in the early 1980s. Some of the most innovative and popular Maroon

---

2 For a classic discussion of Guianese Maroon music (and other arts) in traditional contexts, which provides more background information than is possible to present here, see Price and Price (1980).

(or largely Maroon) kaseko groups during the late 1980s and early 1990s—for example, Ghabiang, Livemo Bradi Banti, Ghabiang Boys, and Yakki Famiri—either got their start in Dutch cities or moved to the Netherlands and continued to build their careers there after forming in Suriname.

The Interior War of the late 1980s and early 1990s triggered Maroon migration to the city and out of Suriname on an unprecedented scale, and the social and economic repercussions of these movements continue to be reflected in popular culture. As the Maroon presence in urban areas increased during the 1990s, yet another crop of young Ndyuka and Saamaka bands emerged and enjoyed great popularity, including groups such as Aphiong Boyz, Kriss Kross Deki Strepi, and Big City Maraniau. They and other young Maroon bands continued to incorporate new influences both transnational and local into their music, ranging from Dominican merengue and Jamaican dancehall to kawina, a traditional Surinamese Creole genre that was revived by urban youth and experienced a boom of its own during this period. (Kawina became particularly popular among young Saamakas, developing into something like a Saamaka equivalent of Ndyuka aleke.)

Urbanization of Maroons has continued to increase rapidly from the 1990s on, and this has had a powerful impact on Surinamese Maroon culture and music. The range of cultural and musical influences from "outside," already remarkably wide, has continued to grow and a new generation of young, urban Maroon reggae artistes has risen to prominence along with those young Maroon musicians working in other popular genres. Simultaneously, the opportunities for Maroon music to reach a broader audience within Suriname as well as internationally have grown as new channels of distribution have opened up. The changing content of the music also reflects changes in the social position of Maroons, and may presage the emergence of a stronger pan-Maroon identity as urban Maroons experience collective marginalization and make new political claims to the Surinamese nation.

The Maroon musicians in contemporary Paramaribo are mostly young men, who were either born in the city or moved there at a young age. In their music and broader social practices, they draw flexibly on multiple levels of reference and identification, including their backgrounds in specific Maroon ethnicities (Saamaka, Ndyuka and so on) and a broader pan-Maroon unity that emerges more distinctly in the context of urban life and national politics. Representing themselves as "real fayaman" (a term borrowed from Rastafarian-oriented Jamaican dancehall music), they express a cosmopolitan worldview. On the one hand, they draw on their roots in the forest and further back in a largely imagined Africa. On the other, they make references to Jamaican and African-American counterparts, as well as those suffering in "ghetto" circumstances worldwide, extending a trend begun by urbanizing Maroon popular musicians in the 1980s and 1990s.

Living in the city has made it easier than ever to connect with globally disseminated forms of popular culture. Whereas musical innovations in the more distant past were most often mediated through contact with Creole musicians in the forest or on the coast (Bilby 2000a, 2001), in the last few decades urban Maroons have been able to access a wide range of popular culture genres through increased access to media such as radio, television, records, audio and video cassettes, and more recently, CDs, DVD s and the internet. Hiphop, reggae and dancehall in particular have been popular "urban" genres. Young Maroon musicians in Paramaribo study and adapt these genres' lyrics, beats and instrumental "riddim" tracks, mixing them with older Afro-Surinamese genres such as kawina, kaseko and aleke. They also draw on the imagery of the various lifestyles and identities associated with them, from Jamaica's Rastafari and "rudeboys" to US ghetto life and "gangstas." There are no signs that the pace of change is slowing. The latest global trends continue to attract young Maroon artists. For their part, young producers stay on top of globalizing studio technologies, mixing these with older influences to give birth to uniquely Maroon techno concoctions such as the "Aleke Roots riddim" and the "Banamba riddim remix."

Urban life has also meant increased opportunities for the distribution of Maroon music. Suriname has no effective copyright laws and unofficial copies of CDs, VCDs and DVDs featuring music by Maroon artistes (like audio cassettes before them) became easily available at Paramaribo music stores such as Boembox and the Poku Shop. More recently, the exploding popularity of digital audio and video files (especially in mp3 and mp4 format), readily available via the internet, including popular video-sharing website YouTube, has made it easier than ever to acquire, copy, and disseminate popular music recordings without resort to conventional means of marketing and distribution. This means musicians' profits from sales of recordings (whether albums or singles, physical media or downloadable digital files) are small. Many Maroon bands earn most of their income through performances at parties or events with audiences reflecting Paramaribo's diverse population. The more successful artists perform abroad as well, catering to Maroons and broader audiences in French Guiana, France, and the Netherlands, where music is central to Maroon youth who want to stay in touch with their Surinamese roots (Adekoya-van Geelen 2007). For more than a decade, video clips on YouTube by artists such as King Koyeba, Damaru, I Ta Ves, Melly, Ghetto Crew, Botty, and Tega have received tens or even hundreds of thousands of views each.

FIGURE 11.3 Local Song, a Ndyuka-Aluku Maroon dance band
SOURCE: KENNETH BILBY, 1987

Migration between Suriname and French Guiana has also been important factor in recent musical developments, resulting in cross-influences between Maroon and other musicians on both sides. Large numbers of refugees from the civil war ended up not only in Paramaribo but in French Guiana, in areas such as Saint-Laurent-du-Maroni and Mana, some temporarily and others permanently. Cross-border links expose young Maroons in Paramaribo, even if sometimes indirectly, to many different cosmopolitan currents via the powerful cultural impact of Le Métropole (and its former colonies in Africa and the Caribbean) on France's South American Département d'Outre-Mer. This cross-fertilization has been going on since at least the 1980s and results in further fusions of Surinamese musical styles such as kaseko, kawina, and kaskawi with reggae, zouk and soukous. An active Maroon-based popular music scene persists in French Guiana today, ranging from aleke to reggae and dancehall and beyond, starring artists such as Koloni, Energy Crew, Family Sound, Spoity Boys, Jah Youth, Sco2, Rickman & G-Crew, Positif Vibration, and Success Fighters. These artists' styles are obviously linked with similar developments in Paramaribo and Surinamese points in between, such as Albina and Moengo, and are influenced by connections to both France and the Netherlands. A good example is the young Ndyuka reggae singer Prince Koloni, who has become particularly popular in France, and has performed and recorded there and in the Netherlands, where he lived for a number of years. Though often associated with the French Guianese reggae scene, Koloni was a founding member of, and sometimes still performs with, the very popular Surinamese aleke band Fondering, which hails from a part of the Ndyuka territory in the interior forest near Stoelman's Island, where the border between Suriname and French Guiana is extremely porous. Several years ago, Fondering relocated to the coastal Surinamese border town of Albina, located directly across from Saint-Laurent-du-Maroni on the lower Maroni River, and the band regularly performs and sells its music on both sides of the border.

As suggested above, a particularly conspicuous recent trend, both in Suriname and French Guiana, is the growing popularity of Rastafarian-oriented reggae among young Maroon musicians. Once again, this is not an entirely new phenomenon. Internationally acclaimed Jamaican artists such as Bob Marley, Black Uhuru, and Gregory Isaacs have been popular in both Suriname and French Guiana since the late 1970s, and elements of the Rasta message and style they projected to the world were quickly adopted by many young Maroons, along with the smoking of cannabis (previously unknown in these societies). By the late 1970s, there was already an aleke band named Rasta in the Aluku Maroon territory.

As the 1980s got under way, the colors and graphic symbolism of Rastafari were everywhere to be seen in upriver Maroon territories, and dreadlocks were far from uncommon. Several young Maroon reggae bands sprang up during the 1980s and 1990s, some of them explicitly aligning themselves with the larger Black identity they divined through Rastafarian music and lyrics (Bilby 1990b). The pioneering Aluku reggae band Wailing Roots, which formed in the mid-1980s, even secured international distribution for some of its recordings and toured in Europe and the United States in the early 1990s (Bilby 1991).

But the most recent explosion of reggae music produced by young Maroons appears to differ from these earlier examples both in degree and kind. Not only are their numbers much greater and their audiences larger, but the young Maroon reggae artists of today—or at least some of them—are engaging more seriously with the Rastafarian faith, actively connecting with ever-expanding transnational networks of Rastafari as the movement continues to spread across the globe. Young Maroon Rasta reggae bands and individual artists such as Faya Wowia, Cry Freedom (whose members are affiliated with the Twelve Tribes of Israel), I Ta Ves, Aiatonda, I King I Opo, Prince G, Faya Gan, Intervibration, West Kantoro, I Wise, Blaka Fesi Shaba and many others display a much deeper knowledge of the fundamental tenets of Rastafari than their predecessors. Their increasingly intricate music (which sometimes incorporates traditional Rastafarian Nyabinghi drum rhythms), their lyrics praising Selassie as the godhead, and their sophisticated use of Rasta iconography suggest that they experience

FIGURE 11.4 Rastafari youth in front of traditional Aluku Maroon house
SOURCE: KENNETH BILBY, 1985

the reggae music they create not only as a bridge that connects them to a wider, "modern" Black world of similarly proletarianized young "ghetto"-dwellers and "sufferers" with a broadly shared history but as a personally-felt faith that they continue to adapt in unique ways to their own Maroon cosmologies. And although much of this new Maroon reggae, musically speaking, appears to mirror Jamaican (or international reggae) styles quite closely, with relatively little input from local sources, it is interesting to note that most of the explicitly Rastafarian songs recorded by younger Maroon artists are composed in their own Maroon languages (sometimes combined with the coastal Creole, Sranan), display distinctive vocal qualities and melodic contours clearly related to indigenous Maroon song styles, and touch on local themes.[3]

---

3 Hélène Lee's film, Une Voix sur le Maroni (Paris: France Mexique Cinéma, Radio France Outre-Mer, and Centre National de la Cinématographie, 2001), nicely captures this new wave of Rastafari influence among young Ndyuka aleke and reggae artists while it was still in its early stages.

FIGURE 11.5   Paul Neman, member of Ndyuka-Aluku Maroon dance band
SOURCE: KENNETH BILBY, 1987

It is also important to recognize that young Maroons have engaged with Rastafari not just via mass-media and cyber communication, but through actual movement and contact between people in the physical world. Ongoing migration and increasing mobility have played a significant role in contemporary popular music, as young Maroon migrants or travelers come face to face with consumers and makers of both familiar and new kinds of music in other parts of the world. Contacts with internationally popular Rasta singers who act as vectors of musical cosmopolitanism are not limited to "outside" contexts. In recent years, many Jamaican reggae and dancehall artists, for instance, have visited and performed in Suriname and French Guiana, and some have even toured in some of the traditional Maroon territories. The upriver Aluku village of Papaïchton, for example, has hosted concerts by such famous musical ambassadors as Capleton, Richie Spice, and Lutan Fyah.

Also highly significant is a pattern that has only very recently become common: the collaboration of young Guianese Maroon artists with Jamaican reggae and dancehall stars on joint recording and video projects. Examples of such transnational collaborations readily viewable on YouTube include "Mi

FIGURE 11.6   CD by Aluku Maroon reggae band Positif Vibration
SOURCE: KENNETH BILBY, 2008

Krakti" (2003), bringing together the Ndyuka group Energy Crew with Luciano; "Nature" (2011), featuring the Ndyuka artist Prince Koloni with Tarrus Riley; "OK" (2012), combining the Aluku artist Neïman with Sizzla; and "Turbo Wine" (2013), in which Aluku artist Rickman joins forces with Konshens.[4] We can see from such examples that young Maroon artists are now part of a larger phenomenon that increasingly brings together aspiring reggae artists from across the globe with established Jamaican stars for reputation-enhancing joint projects. These transnational collaborations take place both in local studios while Jamaican artists are on tour in various parts of the world, and in the mecca of Kingston, to which hopefuls from many countries continue to flock in search of the ineffable "vibe" that is thought to be unique to Jamaican studios.

Despite its prominence, the recent wave of Rastafarian reggae among young Maroons in Suriname and French Guiana is but part of the story. The Surinamese popular genre of kaseko, originally identified with the Creole population,

---

4 To view these videos, see the following links: Energy Crew ft Luciano—Mi Krakti: https:// www.youtube.com/watch?v=6dzmj_noqDQ; Prince Koloni ft Tarrus Riley—Nature: https:// www.youtube.com/watch?v=eAncikOXE9k; Neïman ft. Sizzla Kalonji—OK: https://www.youtube.com/watch?v=T6sdoisoHco; Konshens ft Rickman & G-Crew—Turbo Wine: https:// www.youtube.com/watch?v=X1l5XrxUQLQ (all accessed October 11, 2018).

FIGURE 11.7   Poster advertising Jamaican reggae artist Richie Spice's 2009 tour
SOURCE: KENNETH BILBY, 2009

has itself long served as a vehicle for the expression and negotiation of shifting identities for younger Maroons. During the early 1990s, for instance, the new Maroon-driven fusion known as aleke-kaseko (pioneered by the band Yakki Famiri) became one of the leading musical trends in Paramaribo and the Surinamese diaspora. Drawing its rhythmic feel from aleke, a drum-based neo-traditional Ndyuka genre that was, and remains today, a powerful symbol of Maroon identity (Bilby 2001), aleke-kaseko, though popular across ethnic boundaries, clearly spoke in special ways to young urbanizing Maroons (especially Ndyukas) in coastal Suriname and the Netherlands. And contemporary kaseko continues to be open to influences from older Maroon genres. Indeed, these genres themselves continue to thrive, not only in their original settings in the traditional Maroon territories, but in the new context of staged, formally choreographed performances by amateur and semi-professional troupes launched by cultural activists both in coastal towns and in the interior (Campbell 2012).

A good example of the continuing injection of traditional Maroon elements into urban popular music in Suriname is the dance music fad known

"REAL BUSHINENGUÉ": GUIANESE MAROON MUSIC IN TRANSITION   345

as banamba, a kaseko-based innovation that has spread over coastal Suriname and made itself felt in recording sessions and music videos over the last several years. Banamba is inspired in part by the traditional Saamaka dance and song form called bandámmba (a generations-old dance style that, as it happened, shared certain kinetic features with Jamaican dancehall moves that were spreading across the world at the same moment that the banamba fad was taking off). For a time, banamba became a veritable dance craze in Paramaribo, and artists such as Sieka, the Zware Guys, Henkie, and Scrappy W put out hit after hit catering to the banamba crowds. The banamba fad is just one of many examples of the ongoing incorporation of traditional Maroon stylistic elements and references into the latest youth music trends in coastal Suriname and French Guiana.

Another recent example can be seen in a music video made to promote the song, "Je Suis un Boni" (I Am an Aluku), by Rickman & G-Crew, which recently became a local hit in French Guiana. Rickman is an Aluku (Boni) originally from the upriver village of Maripasoula deep in the interior rainforest of French Guiana. After years in the coastal music business, during which he produced songs and videos in a variety of styles (kaseko, reggae, hip hop, etc.), he struck big in 2016 with this song and the associated video, which proudly affirm his identity as an Aluku (and also, more broadly, his identities as a "Businenge" [Maroon] and a diasporic Black person). Of all the Guianese Maroons, the Aluku, because their traditional territory is located in a French overseas department that officially forms part of the European Community, probably experienced the earliest and most intense pressures to assimilate into the larger society surrounding them, and they continue to struggle to maintain the integrity of their culture while experiencing the overwhelming effects of political incorporation into a world power (the French state) and ongoing economic incorporation into the European and global capitalist systems (Bilby 1990a, 2010). The video, shot in the traditional Aluku territory, is rich in symbols and meanings. The music is based on the popular "Aleke Roots riddim," an instrumental track created in a state-of-the-art studio, but the dancing is basically in traditional Aluku awasa style (with the dancers' clothing inspired by traditional Aluku attire of a kind no longer worn in daily life). The lyrics are partly in French, so that they will be accessible to the rest of the Francophone world, and partly in Aluku (with French subtitles), in line with the song's theme of reclamation of local cultural identity (at the same time being largely intelligible to other Guianese Maroons, who speak cognate languages). Rickman ends his song with the spoken Aluku words: "yu mu sabi pe te yu kumoto fi yu sabi pe te yu e go" (you must know where you are from to know where you are going). During the last thirty seconds or so, the video switches to scenes of traditional dancing by members of the current younger (school-age) generation of Alukus to the sounds of "pure" traditional awasa drumming. The video made quite a splash in French Guiana, receiving considerable television and other media coverage.[5]

There is every reason to believe that the dynamic interplay between old Maroon traditions and new introductions that can be seen in examples such as these will continue to guide new trends in the popular music of Suriname and French Guiana in future. Like earlier musical expressions used by young Maroons to negotiate concepts of "modernity" and relationships with wider worlds, the Maroon youth musics of today, no matter how strongly influenced by mass-mediated trends in global pop culture, would seem to maintain a certain balance between the centripetal claims of local social and cultural worlds and the centrifugal forces associated with various kinds of globalization. Perhaps partly because they balance these forces so effectively, they increasingly provide young Maroons with a strategic means to combat the cultural dislocation and alienation and social and economic marginalization they face as they move into new urban environments (Sanderse 2006; Sanderse and Jaffe 2007; Bilby and Jaffe 2009; Jaffe and Sanderse 2010).[6]

Conclusion

Contemporary Maroon music is both the product of and a response to globalization processes. Yet, it is more than this. It represents a contemporary extension of a unique, centuries-old Maroon tradition of music-making. Some observers express concern regarding the damaging of the cultural integrity of Maroon communities in a context of globalization (St-Hilaire 2000)—and with good reason. But the case of the young Maroons also establishes that globalization, as Eriksen (2003, 224) argues, can also involve a democratization of symbolic power, by means of which artists outside the metropole—not just intellectuals residing inside the centers of knowledge and power—are able to define and construe the world. The musical strategies of the Maroons

---

5 To view this video, see: https://www.youtube.com/watch?v=ntJ9jBlvlK8 (accessed October 11, 2018).

6 On the related question of how both local traditional genres and cosmopolitan popular music have helped specific communities of Maroons cope with the devastation caused by the "Interior War" of the late 1980s and early 1990s (the aftereffects of which continue to be felt in towns such as Moengo, where many Ndyuka survivors and their families now live), see Olivia Cunha's film, Poku fu Kenki ("music for change") (Rio de Janeiro: Laboratório de Antropologia e História, Museu Nacional, Universidade Federal do Rio de Janeiro, 2015). The video is available for viewing at: http://www.lah-ufrj.org/poku (accessed October 11, 2018).

in Paramaribo and other coastal towns are also evidence that creolization is an ongoing process. Their use of popular culture weaves together traditional Maroon elements with Surinamese Creole, French Guianese Creole, Dutch, French, Jamaican, North American, African, and other ingredients. These aspects are effectively integrated with the social and physical world in which these young musicians live.

In the self-proclaimed "ghettos" of Paramaribo, young Maroons are able to connect to global soundscapes, where they devise musical strategies to combat their marginality. Much like earlier Maroon popular musicians, who used their new musical creations to assert their "modernity" and symbolically mediate and define their relationship to a larger, cosmopolitan Black world (Bilby 1999b, 2000b; Reijerman 2000), the current younger generation of urbanizing Maroons creatively balance old and new in their efforts not just to survive in an economic sense, but to make meaningful lives in challenging and rapidly changing social and economic environments.

Indeed, this holds not just for young Maroons in coastal Suriname and French Guiana, but for those who have become global travelers, including an increasing number of popular musicians. Certain key moments in these artists' transnational itineraries are now trackable, from anywhere in the world, via the internet. A YouTube video of one such performance by Prince Koloni leaves us with a striking final image. Recorded at the Francofonie Festival at La Rochelle in the south of France in 2011, the video shows a large and enthusiastic audience taking up the chorus of a song, "Real Bushinengué," together with Prince Koloni, who is accompanied by an ethnically mixed, non-Maroon band. In French, Koloni urges the audience to sing along; in Ndyuka, he sings (in this context, largely to himself) of making the journey upriver into the forest, evoking the ancestral flight from slavery, and stressing the need once again today to stand up and fight oppression; and in English, he offers a prayer to "the creator of the universe, Jah Rastafari." Unbeknownst to most of the audience, the sung phrase they faithfully repeat after Koloni is a very specific affirmation of identity, meaning, quite simply, "real Maroon." And this is exactly what Koloni, staging a scene scarcely imaginable only a few decades ago, has proven himself to be.[7]

While the cultural and musical "grey-out" against which folklorist and ethnomusicologist Alan Lomax (1968, 1977) years ago raised an alarm remains a very real possibility for these Maroon peoples, as for many other

---

7   This video may be viewed at: https://www.youtube.com/watch?v=SNoRDu3TSJo (accessed October 11, 2018).

minority populations in the contemporary world, it is far from a foregone conclusion. Prince Koloni and his musical comrades-in-arms remind us that, so long as the forces that bring about and exacerbate social disintegration do not reach overwhelming proportions, there are grounds to believe that young Maroons will continue to find musical ways of resituating themselves in radically reconstituted worlds without abandoning the spirits of their elders.

References

Adekoya-van Geelen, Simone. 2007. "Marroncultuur in een modern jasje: Een studie naar Surinaamse Marronjongeren in Nederland en hun verbintenis met Surinaamse Marronmuziek en -cultuur." MA Thesis, Radboud University.

Bilby, Kenneth. 1990a. "The Remaking of the Aluku: Culture, Politics, and Maroon Ethnicity in French South America." PhD Diss., Johns Hopkins University.

Bilby, Kenneth. 1990b. "War, Peace, and Music: The Guianas." Hemisphere 1 (3): 10–12.

Bilby, Kenneth. 1991. "Maroons and Reggae: The New Music of French Guiana." The Beat 10 (4): 34–38.

Bilby, Kenneth. 1999a. "Maroons and Contemporary Popular Music in Suriname." In Identity, Ethnicity and Culture in the Caribbean, 143–54. Edited by Ralph Premdas, 143–54. St. Augustine, Trinidad and Tobago: University of the West Indies Press.

Bilby, Kenneth. 1999b. "'Roots Explosion': Indigenization and Cosmopolitanism in Contemporary Surinamese Popular Music." Ethnomusicology 43 (2): 256–96.

Bilby, Kenneth. 2000a. "Aleke: Nieuwe muziek en nieuwe identiteiten." OSO: Tijdschrift voor Surinamistiek en het Caraïbisch Gebied 19 (1): 31–47.

Bilby, Kenneth. 2000b. "Making Modernity in the Hinterlands: New Maroon Musics in the Black Atlantic." Popular Music 19 (3): 265–92.

Bilby, Kenneth. 2001. "Aleke: New Music and New Identities in the Guianas." Latin American Music Review 22 (1): 31–47.

Bilby, Kenneth. 2010. Music from Aluku: Maroon Sounds of Struggle, Solace, and Survival (compact disc and booklet) (SFW CD 50412). Washington, DC: Smithsonian Folkways.

Bilby, Kenneth, and Rivke Jaffe. 2009. "Marronmuziek: tussen traditie en mondialisering." In Kunst van Overleven: Marroncultuur uit Suriname, edited by Alex van Stipriaan and Thomas A. Polimé, 166–75. Amsterdam: KIT Publishers.

Campbell, Corinna Siobhan. 2012. "Personalizing Tradition: Surinamese Maroon Music and Dance in Contemporary Urban Practice." PhD Diss., Harvard University.

Eriksen, Thomas Hylland. 2003. "Creolization and Creativity." Global Networks 3 (3): 223–37.

Jaffe, Rivke, and Jolien Sanderse. 2010. "Surinamese Maroons as Reggae Artistes: Music, Marginality and Urban Space." Ethnic and Racial Studies 33 (9): 1561–79.

Lomax, Alan. 1968. Folk Song Style and Culture. Brunswick, NJ: Transaction Books.

Lomax, Alan. 1977. "An Appeal for Cultural Equity: When Cultures Clash." Journal of Communication 27: 125–38.

Price, Richard, and Sally Price. 1999. Maroon Arts: Cultural Vitality in the African Diaspora. Boston: Beacon Press.

Price, Sally, and Richard Price. 1980. Afro-American Arts of the Suriname Rain Forest. Berkeley: University of California Press.

Reijerman, Meike. 2000. "Sranankondre a no paradijs: de constructie van lokaliteit in de populaire muziek van de Saramaka." OSO: Tijdschrift voor Surinamistiek en het Caraïbisch Gebied 19 (1): 59–82.

Sanderse, Jolien. 2006. "Jonge Marrons als wereldburgers: De invloed van (mondiale) muziek op de identificatie en culturele representatie van jonge Marrons in Paramaribo." MA Thesis, Utrecht University.

Sanderse, Jolien, and Rivke Jaffe. 2007. "Jonge Marronmuzikanten: muziek en marginaliteit in Paramaribo." OSO: Tijdschrift voor Surinamistiek en het Caraïbisch Gebied 26 (1): 43–60.

St-Hilaire, Aonghas. 2000. "Global Incorporation and Cultural Survival: The Surinamese Maroons at the Margins of the World-System." Journal of World-Systems Research 6 (1): 102–32.

CHAPTER 12

An Anthropologist's Dilemma: Maroon Tembe in the Twenty-First Century

Sally Price

Then and Now ... for Maroons, for Anthropologists

In the fifty years since RP and I have been learning and writing about the history and culture of the Suriname Maroons, increased contact between the villages of the interior and the towns on the coast—by both Maroons and non-Maroons—has led to the introduction of a monetary economy, transforming key aspects of daily life, from patterns of subsistence to understandings about gender. For example, while all men once hunted in the forest to provide meat within the villages, hunting has now become a specialized activity and the game is sold rather than distributed to kin and neighbors. While women provided the mainstay of the diet from the gardens where they grew everything from rice and okra to corn and bananas, these foodstuffs are now often purchased in stores, both on the coast and in the interior. While women remained mainly in the villages of the interior and depended on men to provide the manufactured goods necessary for life in the interior, most women now have direct experience with life in the towns and cities of coastal Suriname and French Guiana, and in many cases provide their own livelihood. And while tourists were once unheard of in the villages along the river, now they are legion, with numerous tourist camps being run by both Maroons and outsiders on islands near Maroon villages.[1]

Artistic production is another area of life that has been deeply affected. Until the end of the twentieth century, all men were expected to develop woodcarving skills so that they could provide essential items of material culture for life in the forest—houses, canoes, stools, mortars and pestles, winnowing trays, cooking utensils, combs, and much more, usually for their wives. And they took pride in the embellishment of these items, from door lintels and canoe prows to elaborate virtuoso carvings on small items whose function was

---

1 Some of the ethnographic material in this essay has been published elsewhere; see in particular S. Price 2007, 2018.

© KONINKLIJKE BRILL NV, LEIDEN, 2019 | DOI:10.1163/9789004388062_014

AN ANTHROPOLOGIST'S DILEMMA

purely decorative. Today this is no longer true, as woodcarving—known in the various Maroon languages as tembe—has become a specialized activity, with particular men carving more or less full time, producing items for sale to both Maroons and outsiders.

For the increasing number of Maroons living in the French overseas department of Guyane—they now make up some 35% of the total population—the turn to a monetary economy (and all that it brings with it in terms of lifestyle) has been particularly swift and deep. This has been engineered in good part by an aggressive assimilationist program called "francisation" ("frenchification") authored in Paris, which is designed to bring populations from the interior (both Maroons and Amerindians) more in line with European French norms, from language and education to housing and diet. In Guyane the evolution of tembe into a market commodity, aimed primarily at tourists, has inspired young enterprising artists (and the Europeans who help them market their wares) to invent new forms and, more importantly, new discourses concerning both its history and its meaning. In this situation they are joining "ex-primitives" throughout the world who, encouraged by outside promoters of many stripes, are learning to perform their culture—or at least a facsimile of it that plays well in the new setting in which they find themselves.

This paper explores the consequences of these developments for understandings about Maroon culture, and points to the ethical and epistemological dilemmas that they raise—dilemmas that have concerned anthropologists who study (and care about) societies undergoing rapid change at least since the 1980s. An article by Jean Jackson, for example, focused on evolving discourses among the Tukanoan Indians of Colombia, and the way "a given group of people invent, create, package, and sometimes sell their culture" (1989:127). As she pointed out, "speak[ing] of people as political actors who are changing culture, runs the risk of seeming to speak of them in negative terms, the implication being that the culture resulting from these operations is not really authentic" (Ibid.; see also Hanson 1989). Or, as Jocelyn Linneken put it, "The concern, at times phrased as an accusation, is that writing about the contemporary construction or 'invention' of culture undercuts the cultural authority of indigenous peoples by calling into question their authenticity. ... The cultural invention thesis touches a political nerve outside the academy and, indeed, among many anthropologists sympathetic to nationalist causes" (1991:446).

More generally, attention to the situation of peoples who are entering into increased contact with (and adoption of) western lifestyles has moved over the past twenty-five years into the center-stage of anthropological research and writing. References to Mary Louise Pratt, the virtual copyright-holder of the idea of "contact zones" (1992), have become ubiquitous in articles and book chapters on anthropological explorations of culture. And James Clifford's influential essays (1988, 1997, 2013) have been fundamental in directing our attention away from the allegedly isolated villages studied by anthropologists of the first half of the twentieth century, toward a focus on the culturally fluid "in-between" settings, emblemized as transit lounges, shopping malls, and hotel lobbies (see, for example, 1997:1). As I once put this turn in terms of art, "While scholars once strained to discern the stylistic essences of particular arts in particular cultures, they are now directing their gaze more frequently toward the doorways where artistic and aesthetic ideas jostle each other in their passage from one cultural setting to the next" (2001:128). In the same spirit, no one has dared to go near the once-foundational concept of an "ethnographic present" for many decades. And the concern with defining authenticity has given way to its active de-construction. As Richard Handler commented recently, "In modern ideology, authenticity indicates the true essence of a social or material entity, but modern knowledge, with its methods of description and analysis, almost by definition deconstructs (or, in the anthropological variant, relativizes) authenticity in every attempt it makes to discover it" (2014:205).

Given the rapid increase in what we might call inter-cultural contacts around the world, virtually every anthropologist operating in the twenty-first century must at some point decide how to feel about (and how to write about) the way in which cultural practices and understandings of the group under study that were once relatively distinctive have merged with or given way to Western-inspired replacements.

Part of the irony (as well as the logic) of the situation is that, as anthropologists distance themselves theoretically from essentialized constructions of culture, the people they study are often moving in the opposite direction, insisting on (or inventing) cultural continuities with distinctive ancestral pasts and ethnic identities. That is, while contemporary anthropologists deconstruct the culture concept as it was conceived during most of the nineteenth and twentieth centuries, many ex-primitives (and their promoters) are aggressively embracing it and marketing it to an international body of consumers. As John and Jean Comaroff have shown, people throughout the world have been creating "Ethnicity, Inc."'s, calling on consulting firms and other organs of twenty-first century marketing strategies to "move the politics of ethnicity into the marketplace, ... hitching it, overtly, to the world of franchising and finance capital" (2009:7–8).

The market economy into which Maroons have been moving thrives on the adoption of essentialized visions of their way of life. Promoting and selling the products of Maroon origin requires a focus on their makers' fidelity to an exotic past as rainforest dwellers. Again quoting Handler: "Contemporary capitalism,

AN ANTHROPOLOGIST'S DILEMMA   353

with its restless energy and apparently unlimited reach, seems intent on objec-
tifying all aspects of experience and marketing them as authentic products to
be consumed, ... which creates new marketing opportunities for those who sell
it and new desires for purchasers" (ibid.).

Given the discrepancy between the evolution of anthropological understandings on the one hand, and the strengthening of essentialized ethnic and
cultural identities among many of the discipline's subjects on the other, Jean
Jackson's question about whether it is even possible to talk about culture without making enemies (1989) takes on new relevance. Certainly in my own case,
the dilemma complicates my once-comfortable position as a celebrator of Maroon perspectives and attitudes, replacing it with a decidedly more problematic role as chronicler of new, market-driven narratives about Maroon art. In
this paper I explore how the evolution of the relationship between Maroons
and the larger world has ended up raising ethical issues that simply didn't exist
when anthropological studies of their cultures got off the ground in the mid-
twentieth century. First some background.

Maroon Art History

Maroon arts are constantly evolving from one generation to the next, and often even within the space of a few years. (For a discussion of quick-paced developments in women's art, see S. Price 2003.) The twentieth-century art of
tembe that many outsiders have imagined to be a direct legacy of Africa in
fact evolved over time from the relatively crude woodcarving of the early nineteenth century. The vibrant colors for which Eastern Maroons are so famous
for incorporating in their woodcarvings began only after the introduction of
commercial paints in a few conservative colors in the early twentieth century.
And the vividly multichromatic narrow-strip textile art that bear such visual
resemblance to West African kente cloth was developed only after its mainly red, white, and navy predecessors—symmetrical embroidery designs and a
style of patchwork based on small squares and triangles—fell out of fashion at
the beginning of the twentieth century. Finally, it was men who first decorated
calabashes, using woodcarving tools to incise geometric patterns on the outside surface, until women invented an entirely new art in the mid-nineteenth
century, using pieces of broken glass to cut shapes into the interior surfaces,
and then developed the new technique into a remarkable new art based on
free-flowing organic shapes (Figure 12.1).

Maroons tend to view the evolution of their arts as a linear progression, from
simple and technically inept attempts to more sophisticated and technically

FIGURE 12.1 Calabash bowl carved about 1960 by Anaaweli (Aluku)
SOURCE: SALLY PRICE

perfected work. Men talk about late nineteenth-century woodcarving as crude and raw, with a marked improvement once "wood-within-wood" overlapping bands (Figure 12.2) were introduced (soon after 1900), and then further improvements, including the use of ornamental brass tacks in the 1920s, increasing refinements in "tooth-work" as the century progressed, and the use of highly-polished hardwoods, especially in carvings for the tourist trade. Likewise, women in the late twentieth century say that the stunning patchwork textiles of the early twentieth century did not yet reflect the "proper" rules of rigorous bilateral symmetry that came to characterize later compositions. And today, women consider the precision and varied forms of stitching afforded by sewing machines, which they began to use several decades ago, as marked progress in relation to the embroidery designs that women of the twentieth century executed so meticulously by hand with needle and thread. Maroons like to celebrate each new generation's innovations; one man explained the progress in their artistic production by pointing to the changes in automobiles, from the clumsy-looking machines he'd seen in the city in the 1920s compared to the more streamlined vehicles he saw a half century later.

Much of the published literature on Maroon art presents a rather different picture. Observers focusing on what they see as a visual similarity between Maroon art and selected African objects, have often concluded that they must be the product of direct historical continuities (and more generally that Maroon societies are a more or less direct transplant of African societies). Jean Hurault, a geographer who frequented the Aluku Maroons in the 1940s and 50s and wrote several books about these "Africains de Guyane," was correct in placing the origins of woodcarving in the period 1830–1870 (which he labeled "archaic"), and describing a gradual refinement in the art culminating in the "classic" period, lasting until 1920–1925. But at that point he diverges from the Maroon view of steady progress, asserting that the art began a general decline—an impoverishment of artistic sensibilities and creative abilities, with artists becoming prisoners of the geometric grid and obsessed with the idea of symmetry, which led to total artistic decadence (Hurault 1970:87–92).

The claim that Maroon art (and Maroon society more generally) constituted a direct legacy from Africa was developed within a larger context focused on pinning down the nature of the connection between the societies of African descendants in the New World and their ancestral homeland. The work of Melville Herskovits and his students in Afro-American studies was specifically aimed at demonstrating the extent to which elements of African cultures had survived in New World societies. Herskovits's brief visits to the Saamaka Maroons in the 1920s were particularly pivotal in fueling what became a lifelong dedication to demonstrating the pervasiveness of Africanisms of different kinds throughout the hemisphere; contemporaneous depictions of Maroon life by Morton Kahn, John W. Vandercook, and others put a sensationalist spin on the same perspective and helped to promote the image of Maroons as "a little Africa in America" or "an African tribe in the South American jungle" (Herskovits & Herskovits 1934, Kahn 1931, Vandercook 1926a, 1926b). During the 1970s, growing Black activism gave a further boost to this perception, with U.S. African Americans claiming Maroons as "the original brother" (Counter & Evans 1981) and art historian Robert Farris Thompson, depending heavily on visual comparisons, creating a picture in which Maroon art was "unthinkable" except in terms of its African ancestry (1983).

In the face of all this, Richard Price and I took on the challenge of exploring the chronological development of Maroon art, beginning with Saamaka accounts of forms, styles, techniques, and aesthetic principles of earlier generations and supplementing them with intensive work in archives and museum collections around the world (S. & R. Price 1980, 2005). The result was a densely documented picture of Maroon art history in which certain underlying aesthetic principles that had been widespread in West and Central Africa worked in combination with a lively appreciation of novelty, invention, and change to produce arts that were at once indebted to a generalized African past and, at the same time, to the decidedly innovative creativity of each succeeding generation, creating what Amiri Baraka has called (writing about African American music) "the changing same" (Jones 1967). Because this picture, including its opposition to the vision of most of the earlier analysts, began with an exploration

FIGURE 12.2   Table top carved by Marcel (Saamaka)
SOURCE: SALLY PRICE

of the perceptions and memories of Maroons themselves, we were secure in the feeling that we were honoring the interests of the people who had shared their lives with us over the years.

Art as a Symbolic Language

Another dominant element of twentieth-century writings on Maroon art was a focus on symbolism. In the mid-twentieth century, the literature was chock-full of assertions that tembe was the conveyer of a veritable language of symbols. Each named motif, it was claimed, carried a specific meaning, and the various motifs on a given carving worked together to transmit a discursive message. As a Surinamese forestry worker who compiled a dictionary of Maroon symbols put it,

> The motifs can be considered like words. ... By assigning the right meanings to these motifs and reading them correctly, just like letters and words, it is possible to bring out the maker's intent. Exactly the way a comma can

AN ANTHROPOLOGIST'S DILEMMA

change the sense of a sentence, the presence of a particular motif next to another one alters its meaning. (Muntslag 1979:31)

Melville Herskovits, who visited the Saamaka Maroons in the late 1920s, was also taken with the idea of symbolic meaning in tembe. He reported, for example, that the crescent moon motif represented the "male member" and thus carried a sexual message. When Richard Price mentioned this in an interview with Asipei, a Saamaka man in his fifties, Asipei looked a little puzzled, and said he'd never heard that interpretation. The next day he came to our house looking decidedly embarrassed, and said he had a question. With profuse apologies for his ignorance, he wanted to know whether perhaps the penises of white men were shaped like that.

Our own investigations of meaning in Maroon art was based on a concerted effort to privilege the insights and perspectives that we heard from our neighbors in the villages of the interior. Their explanations of what the designs (whether in a woodcarving, an embroidered textile, or an engraved calabash) were intended to convey consistently underscored the aesthetic dimension. And they were unanimous in stating categorically that, aside from a very few marks that could be added to a finished work of art (interlocked v's to evoke sex, or an x to thank the design's admirers and curse its critic), the motifs transmitted no symbolic meanings. Motifs did have names such as "monkey's tail" and "turtle's penis," but these names, they insisted, were simply descriptive labels, part of the enjoyment of assigning names to everything from models of machetes and patterns of cloth to kinds of necklaces and varieties of okra.

Although young Eastern Maroon carvers sometimes say that they learned about the symbols and the slave origins of tembe from their fathers (see, for a sample of their work, Figure 12.3), all the Maroon woodcarvers of their father's generation with whom we've spoken describe claims for symbolic meaning as the mark of a Maroon artist's willingness to mouth any discourse that will increase his success in the market. Many of these older carvers express pride in never having abandoned their integrity through any nonsense about symbols, and some betray bitterness over the success that the discourse brings. They say that woodcarvings can be taken to convey sentiments such as love, but only in the general sense that a heart-shape at the end of a letter does in Western conventions. And they scoff at the idea that the various motifs on a carving can be combined, like words in a sentence, to be read as messages. One Ndyuka carver, Wani Amoedong, has even developed a comical parody of a Maroon artist claiming to "read" a woodcarving in order to please a tourist.

Where, then, did outsiders come up with the idea that Maroon art was a symbolic language? Reports in the literature of encounters in which outsiders

FIGURE 12.3   Tourist art that combines painting with bas-relief
SOURCE: SALLY PRICE

were expressing interest in a Maroon art object, often with an eye to the purchase of a woodcarving, revealed a persistent tendency for the outsiders to start out with preconceived notions about the lives of dark-skinned, barefoot, cicatrized natives (all that to avoid the term "primitive")—including the conviction that they lived in a world not only of superstition and magic, but also of pervasive (and dominantly erotic) symbolism, and to insist on them with their Maroon interlocutors. This same tendency has been amply documented by evidence from every corner of the non-Western world. Having devoted a whole book to the subject (Price 1989[2000]), I won't belabor the point here, except to say that well-meaning visitors, enjoying the power of persuasion that comes from being on the privileged end of a financially unbalanced relationship, were able more often than not to extract the interpretation that comforted their initial assumptions.

In the case of Maroons, however, there was a second factor that fed into the idea that art constituted a system of symbols capable of transmitting

AN ANTHROPOLOGIST'S DILEMMA   359

messages. Men's woodcarving (the only medium to be taken seriously by outsiders, who seemed only dimly aware that women also produced art) has traditionally served as an important instrument in the ongoing maintenance of
sexual relationships. In fact, most carvings have been destined as gifts of affection for wives and lovers, and in this sense they have operated to communicate feelings of love. But the motifs operate in much the same way that, in the
Western world, a bouquet of roses, a diamond ring, or the heart shape penned
at the end of a letter can communicate feelings of love. That is, they are not
the lexemes of a symbolic language that combine to produce the equivalent
of sentences.

Because of the clear lessons of our ethnographic and museological research on Maroon art, Richard Price and I have made a point of counter-
ing (debunking) the symbol-oriented interpretations that have dominated
the popular imagination. As we presented our findings in countless books
and articles and lectures, we felt in ethically comfortable terrain, confident
that we were fulfilling our mission as anthropologists to protect the understandings of people whose culture was being misread and stereotyped by
outsiders.

Incursions, Migrations and Assimilation

I want to turn now to the twenty-first century to explore the way in which
understandings about Maroon visual art have responded to political events
of the past few decades in both Suriname and French Guiana. To summa-
rize the background very briefly: following Suriname's independence from
Holland in 1975, the government began to step up efforts to exploit the riches
of the interior (particularly timber and gold). This led to serious tensions with
the Maroons, whose once-sacrosanct territories were being invaded by timber and mining companies from China, Indonesia, Canada, and elsewhere,
which had been given concessions by the government. In addition, war broke
out between Maroons and the government, which lasted from 1986 until 1992.
Villages were bombed, people were massacred, and life in the interior became
very difficult. (As the Maroons point out, the Dutch colonists granted them
their independence, but now it's their very own "brothers"—people whose
ancestors crossed the Atlantic in the same slave ships as the ancestors of the
Maroons—who are violating their rights to live peacefully in the lands they've
owned for 300 years.) As a result, many Maroons fled across the border to
neighboring French Guiana. Today, fully one third of Maroons are now living
more or less permanently in Guyane.

Here, France's assimilationist politics is creating new opportunities for the production and distribution of Maroon art. ... and new challenges for the anthropologist. In this setting it would be disingenuous to talk about Maroons in general, given the disparity among those who are French citizens or legal residents and those many others who are maintaining a precarious existence, often by the sale of woodcarvings, as undocumented immigrants living in constant fear of deportation back to Suriname, where their villages have been ravaged by the civil war of the 1980s and 90s. Our visits with Maroons in this second category have, over the past thirty-two years, continued to confirm the vision of their art as one of constant innovation, creativity, and play. And the question of symbolic meaning has continued to be vehemently denied by the Ndyukas, Pamakas, and Saamakas who make a living as independent artists, many of them selling their carvings (and sometimes the women's decorative textiles) from rudimentary settlements along the road between Cayenne and St-Laurent or on the Route de Mana. As we've followed the constantly evolving sequence of new materials, forms, and patterns—from painted wrap-skirts and abstract purple-heart sculptures to motorbike passenger seats and openwork calabashes—our original characterization of Maroon art as "the changing same" seems as spot-on as ever.

The setting in which we began to lose the sense of a "changing same"—and where the ethical clarity of the anthropologist's mission began to take on a bit of mud—has been the much more active world of souvenir shops, cultural festivals, art exhibits, public commissions, and government-supported cooperatives. As Guyane has grown from a sleepy little neo-colony with a population in the tens of thousands at mid-twentieth century to the booming home of the European space center and a population fast approaching the 300,000 mark, it has (or rather, France has) implemented measures for the promotion of local art that have had a profound impact on Maroon tembe—or at least that considerable portion of it that passes through these new channels of distribution.

Aluku artists (who are all French citizens, and have representation in the government) and other Maroons who have been able to acquire residence papers (and in some cases even citizenship) have, quite logically, moved their time and energy away from the provision of traditional objects for their wives (who, in any case, had adopted commercial replacements, from washing machines to rice-cookers) and into the more lucrative field of framed paintings and souvenir items, from carved armadillos to painted paddles suitable for hanging, that they can sell for cash. Some of them have been able to land commissions for the decoration of public buildings such as schools and town halls. Exhibition opportunities have also opened up, with cultural undertakings such as the massive Biennale du Marronnage in Matoury providing the venue for

AN ANTHROPOLOGIST'S DILEMMA 361

displays and sales to non-Maroon buyers. Articles on individual artists and Maroon art more generally appear with regularity in local publications such as Une Saison en Guyane or Semaine Guyanaise and on Internet sites such as Blada, giving their work welcome exposure to tourists and residents of Guyane alike. Some Maroon artists (and we're still talking only about those with residence papers) have had opportunities for travel (to places as far flung as France and China) that brings their work to the attention of an international clientele. And many have created their own websites or Facebook pages, which also attract new buyers for their art.

The most important development in this expansion of opportunities is arguably the program of government-recognized and supported cooperatives. These associations have played a key role in defining, promoting, and controlling Maroon artistic opportunities in Guyane, each with a slightly distinctive character. A brief description of two of the most active ones will give some idea of the range of their goals and strategies.

The "Mama Bobi" cultural center, founded in 1990, is based in the westernmost town of St-Laurent-du-Maroni with a second office upriver in the Aluku village of Apatou (now accessible by road from St.-Laurent). Its vocal spokesman is Gérard Guillemot, a Frenchman who arrived in Guyane in the 1970s and who has amassed a personal collection of Maroon artworks (mainly Eastern Maroon paintings on wood) that is rumored to be several times larger than that of any museum. Guillemot (universally known only as "Gé") exerts tight control over the association's activities, claiming political motivations related to an interest in decolonization and Guyane's independence movement. It's clear to anyone who's dealt with him that he's also driven by intimate personal ties with the association's members, most of them relatively young men of the eastern groups—Alukus, Ndyukas, and Pamakas—but also some Saamakas. Mama Bobi supports programs involving environmental concerns and alternative medicine, for example through ties to a drug rehabilitation center and projects centered on the diffusion of traditional knowledge about medicinal plants. In addition to organizing art exhibits and demonstrations of herbal remedies, the cooperative sells art works, postcards, posters, and T-shirts and intervenes in school programs with lessons about selected aspects of Maroon culture. Mama Bobi has received considerable support from the Direction Régionale des Affaires Culturelles (DRAC) and other government agencies.

The "Libi Na Wan" cooperative, founded in 1994, also promotes Maroon artists, especially in connection with its goals of development and job training. Based in the coastal town of Kourou (home to the space center that launches European Ariane rockets), it has close ties (in both personnel and financing) with the Société Immobilière de Kourou (SIMKO), the company responsible for providing housing in this fast-expanding town where class and ethnicity correlate purposefully with the construction style of each separately designed neighborhood. Among its other projects, SIMKO has the concession for constructing standard housing to replace the insalubrious shacks of the Maroon section, built by Maroon men using detritus culled from the construction sites where they worked as laborers during the original construction of the town in the 1960s. Libi Na Wan also collaborates closely with the Architecture School of Grenoble in France, including two professors and a designer who have authored a series of glossy books and catalogues on Maroon culture and art through the school's publishing outlet in Grenoble. Libi Na Wan has received generous financial support from governmental agencies in Guyane, the European Community, the Architecture School of Grenoble, and a number of other sources. Its organizational structure includes several art-producing workshops organized by medium and ethnicity— Ndyuka painting, Saramaka sculpture, and so forth. By 2005, many of its Maroon members had left the association for independent careers and most of the workshops had been discontinued, but the cabinetry workshop was still actively producing upscale furniture with Maroon embellishments for use in environments ranging from restaurants to public buildings. Libi Na Wan's creative design projects have also produced gift boxes, knife handles, beach chairs, and more—the combined product of European-inspired designs and decorative art by Maroon men and women. Members of the association have exhibited their art in a number of locations, including galleries in Paris.

New Forms, New Discourses, New Marketing Tools

Some forms have survived what we might call the "new look" of Maroon art. Most notably, various models of stools, which are as adaptable to Western-style living rooms as to rainforest environments, are still being produced and sold, especially by Saamakas. But the great bulk of items available in the souvenir stores are the products of recent marketing trends. Bas-relief carving, the very essence of Saamaka tembe, has ceded its central place to brightly colored Eastern Maroon paintings on board or canvas, and a new term, ferfi tembe, ("painted tembe") has been coined, reflecting both the aesthetic change from bas-relief to color and a shift from Saamaka carvers to Eastern Maroon painters as the dominant producers for the Maroon art market in Guyane. A second new term, "art tembe," also recently came into vogue, ostensibly to clarify things for francophone people in Guyane who might not have encountered the Maroon word tembe. (These terms then led to another new one, piki faka tembe ["little knife tembe"], to label work in the traditional mode of being carved but not painted.)

But by the early years of the twenty-first century, the rise of colorful painting to the detriment of bas-relief carving was only the beginning of a larger redefinition of Maroon art. When the cooperatives founded in the early 1990s had been operating for about a decade, new discourses, often developed with the help of Europeans, also began to surface. My own introduction to them came some ten years ago when I was browsing through a bookstore in Cayenne and came upon a coloring book for children, twelve pages long, called Colorie Tes Tableaux Tembé! (Amete 2004, Figure 12.4). The author was Franky Amete, an Aluku artist and active member of the Libi Na Wan cooperative. I had earlier attended the opening of an exhibition of his work in a trendy upscale Cayenne bar, where glossy brochures provided by Libi Na Wan offered background information on Maroon art and on the artist's unique contributions to the range of Maroon forms (see S. Price 2007 for illustrations). Amete's art was dominated by the brightly colorful Eastern Maroon paintings that had come to be known as feifi tembe, but he also embodied the spirit of innovation that we had come to expect of Maroon artists, branching out in a novel direction by creating characteristically Maroon designs centered on geometric patterns of interlaced ribbons, but executing them in a more subtle palette, using the warm-hued sands and soils of Guyane instead of commercial paint. (His French wife, Anne, had told him about Navajo sand paintings, and he took it from there.) These artworks were technically refined, quietly sophisticated, and elegantly presented.

Amete's coloring book, however, made no mention of sands and soils. Instead, it offered a discourse that foregrounded the role of color, asserting that the motifs communicated symbolic meanings not only by their form but also by their color. Each page carried a small diagram indicating which colors to use for which motif in order to make the design say, for example, "Take care of yourself," "You and me for eternity," or "Marry me." The coloring book's closing page, entitled "A Secret Code," explained that art tembe can be studied like a language, with colors playing a part in the themes to be expressed. Red, it asserted, represents man and blood, white is woman and beauty, black is earth (soil), blue is the earth (planet), and so on.

But there's more. The coloring book also introduced a claim concerning the early history of Maroon art that I had never before encountered. Page one declared:

> The art of tembé was used as a means of communication among plantation slaves, comparable to secret messages in code. After the slaves escaped their servitude and established themselves on the banks of the

FIGURE 12.4   Cover of Franky Amete, *Colorie tes tableaux tembe*
SOURCE: SALLY PRICE

river … it became the written language of a community that had until then been based on an oral tradition. (Amete 2004:1)

Although Franky Amete was a member of the Libi Na Wan cooperative when he wrote this scenario, the Mama Bobi cooperative was also promoting the same version of the origin of tembe. A long, discursive hand-out composed for the 2004 Biennale du Marronnage, entitled "Tembe: Repères essentiels," took readers back to the slave era in florid prose to evoke the setting:

Knowledge of escape, charged with vigilance, calling each day on a new creativity. And at the beginning, communication.
 The obligation for resistance. The call to solidarity and the recognition of others on the road to Liberty: The mark.
 The thousand marks of human dignity that all resisters in the world one day discover and invent.

AN ANTHROPOLOGIST'S DILEMMA

The marks of secrecy, the marks of combat. This early knowledge of clandestinity. The tracing of movements and struggles of liberation on the walls of the factories, in the dust of the plantations.

In fact, oral tradition tells us that everything began with a few lines furtively scratched in the soil. The mark of the Maroon in full power preparing his flight in complicity. Or already organizing that of others.

The trace, the sign, the mark ...

Signs of reconnaissance. Warnings. Invitations. Coded messages, discrete, secret, and ritualized.

... From the gestures of a guerrilla, the Tembe softened into gestures of tenderness. ... Once peace came and freedom was won, there was leisure time, and the Tembe was transformed into an art form. (Mama Bobi 2004)

This depiction of slave-era origins for tembe was a serious eyebrow-raiser, given the results of our decades-long multi-sited research that placed the beginnings of woodcarving in the early- to mid-nineteenth century.

A few years later, when I was in St. Laurent for a major conference on Maroons organized by Aluku historian Jean Moomou, I noticed another coloring book in the local bookstore. Mon Tembe-Magique (self-published and undated), by an Aluku artist named Jean-Luc Maïs, is designed for children 6-to-10 and adds a novel pedagogical angle to the fun of art. The child answers a simple exercise in arithmetic in order to discover the color needed for each segment of a design; for example "3+2" is marked "red" in the key for the first design, telling the child to use red for those parts of the design that are marked with a 5. Like Franky Amete's coloring book, the one by Maïs includes a page on color symbolism and an introduction to the history of tembe.

The lists of colors in the two books are essentially the same, but claims for their symbolic meanings include some discrepancies. In one white is said to mean women and beauty while in the other it translates as power; in one orange means sun, fire, and gold and in the other it means the harvest; in one gray means night and rain and in the other it means sadness. And a third set of claims for the symbolic meaning of tembe colors—one developed for the logo of the anti-AIDS campaign in Guyane—gives yet another set of interpretations: yellow, for example, here means "evil" (le mal) rather than, as Amete and Maïs would have it, "sun." Finally, are we to read brown as "fertile land," as Maïs tells us, or "invisibility" as the AIDS logo claims? (Brown is not included in Amete's chart.) How can a child, or even an interested adult, learn to read the colors and thus the message being transmitted when there are such divergent claims?

But let's return to Mon Tembe-Magique to see what Maïs has to say about the origin and history of tembe. His more recent version makes much more ambitious claims than either Amete's or the one put out by Mama Bobi. Africans fresh off the boats from Africa (the "beaux-sales"), we're told, invented a writing system for communication on the plantations that they then used to record the story of each slave's escape. This writing system also allowed them to record the genealogy of each family as well as information on "customs, traditions, culture, and other kinds of information that was indispensable for the transmission of their history and identity" (Maïs n.d.:2). With all this very detailed data preserved in tembe, one might wonder what need we have today for research in oral or archival history!

The Gender Dimension

Leaving coloring books aside, I want to return now to the claim that tembe transmits messages from men to women. Here's the dilemma. If, indeed, the motifs carry meanings by which the man who makes the carving sends a message to the woman who receives the carving, one would hope that the woman could make out the message from her lover. That is, a system of communication works only if those who speak or write and those who listen or read—or, in this case, those who carve motifs and those to whom the motifs are addressed—agree on what the forms signify. Because almost all the descriptions of tembe in the literature come from male outsiders talking with male Maroons, the question of how much women can interpret the symbols has rarely come up. But when we do ask women about how they read tembe designs, the response is universally negative. I'll cite three kinds of evidence, all of which go in the same direction.

First, my own efforts over the past half century to get women to "read" trays, combs, stools, and so forth has resulted in the identification of quite a few names for motifs, but no symbolic meanings for them and no messages in the way they were combined. None whatsoever. These encounters included conversations with women close to the artists who were making claims for tembe as a language of symbols–including, for example, the young Ndyuka woman whom I met at the Mama Bobi Cultural Center (during an invited tour 1 May 2005 that was clearly aimed at persuading me of symbolic interpretations in tembe), who told me that she herself couldn't read any woodcarvings.

Secondly, a systematic survey conducted over four-to-five months in 2008 by the cooperative "CRABASI," in Suriname gave a 72-item questionnaire to 54 Maroons (Saamakas, Pamakas, and Alukus). As a supplement to the

AN ANTHROPOLOGIST'S DILEMMA   367

questionnaire, each person was shown ten tembe designs and asked to talk about what they meant. The great majority of the men said that they had no idea and the women "know nothing about woodcarving" (CRABASI 2008:10). The abstract idea of symbolic meaning was understood, and several of the people interviewed excused their ignorance on the matter, suggesting that perhaps educational efforts could be made to teach Maroons about the symbols.

Finally, the fact that Olivia Gomes da Cunha was conducting research with Ndyuka Maroon women as I was thinking through this problem was a resource too good to pass up. I emailed her in the field, sent her some sample tembe designs, and asked her to see what the women she was working with had to say about their symbolism. She kindly agreed and interviewed twelve women, aged 35 to 65, on the subject, and sent me the results:

> None of them know about Tembe or, even, have demonstrated interest on it. I think they thought somehow "funny" that I had addressed questions about Tembe to them! They always say there are other people that know (always men) but they don't. [email of 7 August 2013]

These three independent efforts to plumb women's knowledge of tembe symbols lead us to conclude (1) that the idea of motifs carrying meaning seems perfectly possible to them in the abstract, but (2) if such meanings were to exist, they do not have the key to them and could not read the messages the men might be trying to send them.

This situation is sometimes recognized even by the most ardent promoters of the idea of tembe symbolism. One Libi Na Wan publication, for example, asserts that "The proper, unique meaning of an artwork belongs above all to the artist" (Barthelemy 2009:61). Or, as another commentator put it: "The symbolic content of the designs is frequently such that it is impossible for a Bush Negro, other than the artist, to decipher their meaning" (Dark 1954:48–50).

As for the men, Eastern Maroons tend to be more open than Saamakas to the abstract idea of tembe symbolism, pointing most frequently to a motif called geebi lobi ("graveyard love") and explaining that it means "eternal love." But there's a big difference between on the one hand such a one-to-one relationship between a motif and its meaning, and on the other a claim that full messages are being spelled out through grammatically structured combinations of motifs. Take, for example, a painting by Antoine Lamoraille, one of the founders of the Mama Bobi cultural center (see Mama Bobi 1998:5). I have no problem with the assertion that the motifs carry names such motyo olo, amaka, etc., and perhaps even that they convey meanings. But it is much less evident whether the woman who receives the artwork in question will understand that, as the artist explains, it carries the following message: "Tu as su éviter le piège qui a pris tes frères désormais méfie-toi de l'arbre qui penche." ("You have been able to avoid the trap that caught your brothers; from now on watch out when you see a tree that's bent over.") It seems to me that this brings us into the realm of the famous Zen image that evokes the sound of one hand clapping—a language designed for communication between two people in which only one of them understands the words.

At some moments, even the most enthusiastic supporters of the new ideas concerning symbolism, such as the color chart and the slave-era origins, recognize that they're dealing with an invented tradition. A publication by Libi Na Wan, for example, points out that older artists think of tembe in essentially aesthetic terms, in contrast to young artists who, "motivated by economic and touristic considerations," attribute specific meanings to different colors (Barthelemy 2009:74). The fact remains, however, that in the context of a market economy there is much to recommend a discourse on tembe in which it incorporates symbolic meanings and has the power to transmit messages. Western expectations about "exotic" peoples makes the decision to adopt such a discourse a real no-brainer. Neither the metropolitan advisers who basically direct cooperatives like Mama Bobi and Libi Na Wan nor the artists who produce tembe in the context of present-day Guyane are unaware of the power of such a discourse for their clientele. And of course the more it can be internalized as the truth of the matter, the more powerfully it can be put into play.

Establishing the new version of the history and meaning of tembe as fact happens not only in individual encounters, publications, exhibitions, media outlets and the like, but also, and very crucially, in school programs, where the understandings of the next generation take root. The cooperatives in Guyane are taking full advantage of their access to classrooms, and young children are being instructed in the story that they have chosen to tell.

Inventing Traditions

This phenomenon is, of course, hardly limited to Guyane. We find it everywhere in the world, from Australia and Africa to both North and South America. For example, Sidney Kasfir has documented the way post-colonial cooperatives in Africa have succeeded in putting a new spin on the arts they promote, and the extent to which the new discourses are influenced by regional politics and national agendas. The hundreds of examples that she presents demonstrate "the emergence of new African art onto the world stage, beginning in the 1950s and 1960s, [as] a major act of cultural brokerage by a small number of mainly

AN ANTHROPOLOGIST'S DILEMMA

European supporters" (1999:65). To cite just one example, the organizers of workshops in Namibia, acting in a "protective" role toward Bushman artists lest they be exploited by unscrupulous outsiders, have ended up "constructing and authenticating a Bushman culture for the benefit of rest of the world, [linking] the workshop artists with a Bushman hunting and gathering past, even though none of the artists or their families have ever lived that way, because this gives their art a pedigree which spectators will recognize as authentic" (1999:63; see also Kasfir 2007, in which she describes how the discourse attached to Idoma masks in West Africa and Samburu spears in East Africa are each the result of the invention of a product of global consumption, a response to changes operating in the post-colonial world economy).

Anthropologists have long been aware that a great many of the traditions taken to be ancient in their origins are in fact recent inventions (Wagner 1975, Hobsbawm & Ranger 1983). Present-day Guyane, with the pressure it puts on assimilating segments of the population to adapt to new social, cultural, and economic norms, would seem to provide a particularly fertile environment for Maroon culture to develop in this direction. And given the active role of cooperatives in the promotion of Maroon culture, it seems likely that the newly invented discourse about tembe—its origins in slave rebellion, its power to transmit messages from men to women, and its dependence on the symbolic meaning of different colors—is very much here to stay.

To contextualize the situation of Maroon art in Guyane, I would cite another case of claims for symbolic meaning in African American art, one that centers on quilts made by women in the antebellum United States. This is a story that hit the front page of the New York Times in 2007 in connection with a large commemorative statue of the abolitionist Frederick Douglass that was being erected in Central Park (Cohen 2007). The installation was well under way, at a cost of $15.5 million, when historians pointed out a problem. Next to the figure of Douglass was the granite representation of a quilt whose squares contained symbols that, according to an adjoining plaque, signaled "the location of safe houses and escape routes" along the Underground Railroad, as well as other "information vital to a slave's escape and survival." But as historians were quick to point out, the idea that quilts carried secret messages was, beyond the shadow of a doubt, historically inaccurate—nothing more than "spurious history" that grew out of a popular book entitled "Hidden in Plain View" (Tobin & Dobard 1999). Nevertheless, the idea of quilts carrying messages that helped slaves escape to freedom was attractive enough so that the historians' correction made no difference in the popular imagination. The book, which quickly sold several hundred-thousand copies, was featured on the Oprah Winfrey Show and in the newspaper USA Today. And it was eagerly picked up by elementary school teachers, especially in districts with a heavy African American population, who saw it as an inspirational pedagogical tool for the classroom. Even today, a decade after historians pointed out the error, sales of Hidden in Plain View are up, and amazon.com carries praise from people expressing gratitude to the authors for having revealed this inspirational contribution to African American history. A few years ago it even inspired a best-selling children's book called The Patchwork Path: A Quilt Map to Freedom (Stroud 2007), which, says amazon.com, "tells the story of two of the thousands who escaped a life of slavery and made the dangerous journey to freedom—a story of courage, determination, and hope." A review in the School Library Journal declares that it "works well as a lesson in African-American history."

The appeal that launched this "secret code" claim, like that concerning tembe art, isn't hard to discern. As one op-ed columnist noted,

> Few aspects of the American past have inspired more colorful mythology than the Underground Railroad. It's probably fair to say that most Americans view it as a thrilling tapestry of midnight flights, hairsbreadth escapes, mysterious codes and strange hiding places. So it's not surprising that the intriguing (if only recently invented) tale of escape maps encoded in antebellum quilts ... should also seize the popular imagination. ... Eye-catching quilts and mysterious tunnels satisfy the human penchant for easily digestible history. Myths deliver us the heroes we crave, and submerge the horrific reality of slavery in a gilded haze of uplift. (Bordewich 2007)

Time now to return to the dilemma raised by Jean Jackson: is it possible to write about culture without making enemies, or at least find an ethically comfortable position within the conceptual thorn bush of invented traditions? Like Jackson, I find myself involved in describing "how a given group of people invent, create, package, and sometimes sell their culture [and running] the risk of seeming to speak of them in negative terms, the implication being that the culture resulting from these operations is not really authentic" (1989:127). A few years ago I tried to deal with this dilemma by promoting the idea of "shifting authenticities" to characterize the new developments in Maroon art (Price 2007 [2010]). This rhetorical twist seems to have satisfied one of the participants in the new system, a British textile artist who was producing Maroon-style designs that she had manufactured in Indonesia and sold on-line and in the Guyane airport together with a card that identified the meaning of each motif. But the idea of "shifting authenticities" has hardly had a warming

AN ANTHROPOLOGIST'S DILEMMA 371

effect on my relationships with people in cooperatives like Mama Bobi or Libi Na Wan.

This dilemma (together with its various offshoots) has clearly been some time in the making. Jean Jackson posed her question about making enemies in the 1980s. And Jim Clifford recounts an anecdote from the early 1970s that voices a related concern. In a conversation he had with Raymond Firth at the London School of Economics, Firth "shook his head in a mixture of pretended and real confusion. What happened? Not so long ago we were radicals. We thought of ourselves as critical intellectuals, advocates for the value of indigenous cultures, defenders of our people. Now, all of a sudden, we're handmaidens of empire!" (Clifford 2013:2). Insisting on our understandings of the history and culture of the society we study (no matter how irrefutably established through work with native interlocutors supplemented with research in museums and archives) when a new generation of that society is adopting a different storyline as part of its accommodation to forces operating in the twenty-first century world requires a recognition that we are no longer necessarily "advocates of indigenous cultures, defenders of our people." This means acknowledging that the story we tell is one of several legitimate narratives, clearly useful for some purposes but not others. And it means adopting a good dose of humility in terms of the intellectual positions we decide, in the end, to adopt.

References

Amete, Franky, 2004. Colorie tes tableaux tembe! Cayenne: Plume Verte.

Barthelemy, Karol, 2009. Den taki foe a Tembe. Kourou: Roger Le Guen.

Bordewich, Fergus M., 2007. History's Tangled Threads. New York Times, 2 February, p. A19.

Clifford, James, 1988. The Predicament of Culture. Cambridge MA: Harvard University Press.

Clifford, James, 1997. Routes: Travel and Translation in the Late Twentieth Century. Cambridge MA: Harvard University Press.

Clifford, James, 2013. Returns: Becoming Indigenous in the Twenty-first Century. Cambridge MA: Harvard University Press.

Cohen, Noam, 2007. In Douglass Tribute, Slave Folklore and Fact Collide. New York Times, 23 January, pp. A1, C12.

Counter, S. Allen & David L. Evans, 1981. I Sought my Brother: An Afro-American Reunion. Cambridge MA: MIT Press.

CRABASI, 2008. Surinam Maroon Tembe: A Means of Living. Paramaribo: CRABASI Foundation. [booklet and CD]

Dark, Philip J.C., 1954. Bush Negro Art: An African Art in the Americas. London: Tiranti.

Handler, Richard, 2014. [Review of] Thomas Fillitz & A. Jamie Saris (eds.), Debating Authenticity: Concepts of Modernity in Anthropological Perspective. American Ethnologist 116/1:205–206.

Hanson, Allan, 1989. "The Making of the Maori: Culture Invention and Its Logic." American Anthropologist 91(4):890–902.

Herskovits, Melville J. & Frances S. Herskovits, 1934. Rebel Destiny: Among the Bush Negroes of Dutch Guiana. New York: McGraw-Hill.

Hobsbawm, Eric & Terence Ranger (eds.), 1983. The Invention of Tradition. Cambridge: Cambridge University Press.

Hurault, Jean, 1970. Africains de Guyane: La vie matérielle et l'art des Noirs Réfugiés de Guyane. La Haye: Mouton.

Jackson, Jean, 1989. Is There A Way To Talk About Making Culture Without Making Enemies? Dialectical Anthropology 14(2):127–143.

Jones, Leroi, 1967. Black Music. New York: William Morrow.

Kahn, Morton C., 1931. Djuka: The Bush Negroes of Dutch Guiana. New York: Viking.

Kasfir, Sidney Littlefield, 1999. Contemporary African Art. London: Thames & Hudson.

Kasfir, Sidney Littlefield, 2007. African Art and the Colonial Encounter: Inventing a Global Commodity. Bloomington: Indiana University Press.

Linnekin, Jocelyn, 1991. Cultural Invention and the Dilemma of Authenticity. American Anthropologist 93(2):446–449.

Maïs, Jean-Luc, n.d. Mon Tembe-Magique (L'enfant du fleuve vol. 1). Guyane: Self-published.

Mama Bobi, 1998. Koti a Keti. Saint-Laurent: Marwina Art.

Mama Bobi, 2004. Tembe: Repères essentiels. Ms.

Muntslag, F.H.J., 1979. Paw a paw dindoe: Surinaamse houtsnijkunst. Amsterdam: Prins Bernard Fonds.

Pratt, Mary Louise, 1992. Imperial Eyes: Travel Writing and Transculturation. London: Routledge.

Price, Sally, 1989/2001. Primitive Art in Civilized Places. Chicago: University of Chicago Press.

Price, Sally, 2003. Always Something New: Changing Fashions in a "Traditional Culture." In Eli Bartra (ed.), Crafting Gender: Women and Folk Art in Latin America and the Caribbean, Durham, Duke University Press, pp. 17–34.

Price, Sally, 2007. Into the Mainstream: Shifting Authenticities in Art. American Ethnologist 34:603–620.

Price, Sally, 2018. Maroon art in Guyane: New Forms, New Discourse. In Sarah Wood & Catriona MacLeod (eds.), Locating Guyane. Liverpool: Liverpool University Press pp. 168–82.

AN ANTHROPOLOGIST'S DILEMMA 373

Price, Sally & Richard Price, 1980. Afro-American Arts of the Suriname Rain Forest. Berkeley: University of California Press.

Price, Sally & Richard Price, 2005. Les Arts des Marrons. La Roque-d'Anthéron (France): Vents d'ailleurs.

Stroud, Bettye, 2007. The Patchwork Path: A Quilt Map to Freedom, Somerville MA, Candlewick Press.

Thompson, Robert Farris, 1983. Flash of the Spirit: African and Afro-American Art and Philosophy. New York: Random House.

Tobin, Jacqueline L. & Raymond G. Dobard, 1999. Hidden in Plain View: A Secret Story of Quilts and the Underground Railroad. New York: Doubleday.

Vandercook, John Womack, 1926a. "Tom Tom," New York, Harper & Brothers.

Vandercook, John Womack, 1926b. We find an African Tribe in the South American Jungle, The Mentor 14(3):19–22.

Wagner, Roy, 1975. The Invention of Culture. Chicago: University of Chicago Press.

Index

adultery 153, 259n. 18
aesthetic 117, 128, 254–255, 259, 269, 275–277, 278n. 7, 283, 285, 289–290, 292, 294, 296–298, 301, 320, 324n. 20, 327, 331, 352, 355, 357, 362, 368
Afobaka Dam 4, 39
African 2, 7, 19, 29, 38–40, 50, 54, 57, 60, 60n. 11, 75, 86, 86n. 5, 87n. 6, 110, 117, 256–260, 287–288, 310, 320, 332–334, 336–337, 347, 353–355, 368–369
Agedeonsu 55, 55n. 2, 57, 67, 69–70, 78, See also Gwangwella
AIDS See HIV/AIDS
Akalali 71, 75n. 39, 76n. 40, 76–77
Ampuku 207, 208n. 2, 208–209
Ampuku, spirits 59, 72
ancestors 236, 240–241, 251, 254, 256, 259, 263
Art
    arts 2, 39, 255, 255n. 14, 260, 334, 336n. 2, 352–353, 355, 368
    Maroon art 43, 353–363, 369–370
    Maroon artists 361, 363
    Maroon artworks 361
artists 278, 288, 336, 338–340, 341n. 3, 341–342, 345–347, 351, 355, 360, 366, 368–369
assimilationist politics 360
authority 4, 36, 57, 77, 142, 149–150, 159, 170, 172, 185, 194, 208–210, 218–223, 225, 227, 232, 235, 239–240, 242–243, 245–246, 248, 251–253, 255, 257–258, 260–263, 308, 318, 320–321, 351, See also traditional authorities

bakuu 157, 158n. 14, 166, 228
bauxite 135, 271, 278
body 8, 15–18, 62, 125n. 10, 130, 134–135, 135n. 32, 143, 178–179, 205–206, 208, 210–212, 220, 223–224, 235, 238, 241–243, 247, 252, 257, 258n. 17, 282, 290, 301, 320, 352
Brazilians 42, 183
Brokopondo 243
Bush Negroes 20, 38, 40, 48, See also Bushinengué

Bushinengué 117–118, 125, 135–136, 138, 183, 330, 347, See also Bushnegroes
Busikonde 177, 190n. 8, 190–191, 193, 197–198
Businenge 19, 177n. 1, 183, 234, 255–256, 256n. 16, 259–260, 263, 345
businengue 6

Caribs, Amerindians 54
carte de séjour 160n. 17, 167
Cayenne 31, 36, 42, 44, 135, 135n. 33, 137, 137n. 36, 144, 160n. 18, 162n. 21, 165, 168, 176, 179–180, 188–189, 289, 360, 363
Charbonnière, La 162–163, 190–192, 197, See also social housing, dwellings
Charvein 166, 185, 280
children 147–151, 153n. 11, 153–156, 159–160, 163–164, 167–174
Chinese 37, 42, 208, 277–278, 295
Christianity 22, 97, 130, 150, 269, 271–272, 279, 291, 294, 297
    Christian 4, 41, 84, 98, 149, 172, 234, 237n. 5, 247, 269–270, 273, 283–284, 286, 288, 290, 294, 299
    Christian missionaries 4
    messianic cults 5
church rules 237, 237n. 5
citizenship 14, 118, 139, 169, 184, 191, 261, 360
Civil War 36, 40–41, 44, 108, 153, 156, 159, 179, 185, 189, 256, 261, 279, 339, 360, See also Interior War, Guerilla, Jungle Comando
clothing 35, 117, 120, 139, 153, 235n. 3, 301, 345
code alternation 98–100, 102–103, 110, See also maroon languages
Commewijne x, 61, 61n. 13, 64
conjugality 122
Coppename 2, 24, 90, 104, 183
Cosmopolitics 6–7, 11, 13, 19–20
Cottica IX, 5, 24, 26, 38, 47–49, 57n. 7, 64, 77, 135, 161, 164n. 23, 184–185, 199, 249n. 12, 268, 270–273, 284n. 11, 276–286, 288, 293, 296, 299–300, 332
Creole 9, 27, 32, 37, 43, 47, 49, 73, 99, 110–111, 113–116, 122, 131, 134–135, 137, 139–141, 164n. 23, 167, 178n. 1, 178–180,

277–279, 279n. 8, 286, 287n. 13, 287–288, 322, 331, 334, 336–338, 341, 343, 347
Creoles 41, 49, 72n. 31, 83–84, 88, 89n. 7, 111–114, 180, 183, 197n. 21, 208, 269, 290, 331
Surinamese Creoles 84, 98, 113, 183
creolization 1n. 1, 10, 31, 260, 347

dance 44, 135–136, 158, 271, 275, 279n. 8, 283, 285, 293, 296, 301, 307–311, 311n. 7, 317n. 16, 317n. 17, 313–321, 324n. 20, 324–327, 332–333, 335–336, 344
Death 212, 241, 247
decoration 235n. 3, 286, 289–290, 360, See also Art
democracy 250–251
Deportation 184, See also Undocumented migrants, migration
Diitabiki ix, 9, 38, 55, 55n. 3, 61n. 12, 63n. 18, 72n. 32, 72n. 33
dress 120, 137
drums 136, 282–285, 285n. 12, 293, 315, 315n. 13, 315n. 13, 315n. 13, 315n. 13, 322–323, 332, 334–335, 340, 344
dwellings ix, 4, 8, 150, 173, 177–178, 180, 182–183, 193, 198, See also social housing, Charbonniè re, La

education 40n. 3, 118, 121, 123, 130, 135, 141–142, 147, 351
elders 55, 83, 91, 94, 97, 99–100, 108, 122, 130, 132–133, 136, 150, 158, 215, 218, 240, 242–243, 245–248, 251–252, 262–263, 275, 291, 298–299, 336, 348

family x, 16, 62n. 16, 74, 87, 94, 96–97, 118–119, 122, 124, 127, 129–130, 133, 137, 139–142, 148–155, 159–160, 164–168, 170–172, 174, 184, 188, 194, 196, 204–205, 208, 210–211, 213–214, 217, 219, 222, 226–229, 235–236, 242–243, 244n. 8, 244–245, 249–250, 252, 259n. 18, 268, 271, 275, 281n. 10, 279–283, 287, 289, 291, 294, 300, 311, 317, 322, 334, 366
federation 57, 57n. 7, 59
female 62, 103, 117–120, 122, 124, 127, 130, 131n. 26, 133n. 29, 143, 147, 156, 161, 164, 171, 317
festival 272, 275–279, 286

films 8, 44, 135n. 32, 269, 288n. 14, 287–289, 292, 294
flight 19, 54, 71, 73, 78, 132, 140, 156, 161, 172, 235, 252, 255, 255n. 15, 261, 263–264, 347, 365, See also slavery
freedom 19, 55, 73, 123, 129, 137, 251, 254, 323, 365, 369
French Creoles 172
French Guiana x–1, 5–6, 13, 14n. 5, 19–21, 27, 30, 35, 37, 47, 85, 85n. 4, 89–90, 113–114, 117–118, 122, 147, 157, 159, 160n. 17, 160–161, 170, 177–179, 185, 189, 277, 279–280, 287n. 13, 287–288, 298, 300, 332, 338–340, 342–343, 345–347, 350, 359
funeral rites 41, 125, 149, 236, 242, 253, 281, See also funeral, mortuary rituals, funerary cycle, funerary rules
funerary cycle 235, 248, See also funeral, mortuary rituals, funerary rules, mortuary rituals
funerary rules 234, See also funeral, mortuary rituals, funerary circle, mortuary rituals

gaama 35, 41, 244–246, 252n. 13, 259n. 18, 259–262, See also gaaman
Gaan Tata ix, 55n. 2, 55n. 5, 54–57, 57n. 7, 60–61, 63–64, 76–78
gaanman 108, 136, 138, 220, 335
garimpeiros 26, See also Brazilians, gold mining, goldmining camps
gender 5, 39, 120, 137, 143, 157, 179, 248, 250, 275, 290, 350
globalization 24, 37, 330–332, 346
gods 4–5, 7, 9, 11, 13, 14n. 5, 14–16, 19–21, 23, 54, 58, 61, 67, 72, 78, 206, 269–270, 277, 286, 296, 301, 317, 332, 335
gold mining 37, 117–118, 133, 331
goldmining camps 42
gospel 6, 247, 288–289
guerilla 161, See also Civil War, Interior War, Jungle Comando
guerrilla 261, 293n. 18, 365
Guyanese 137, 139, 167, 183, 208
Gwangwella 55n. 4

Haitians 183, 192
health 148n. 3, 148n. 6, 148–149, 150n. 8, 156, 159, 170, 174n. 27

INDEX 377

HIV/AIDS 37, 150, 160, 162–163
homosexuality 130–131
house 18, 62n. 16, 69, 77, 94, 107, 119, 127,
129, 139, 153, 159–160, 167–168, 171, 175,
177–179, 183, 185–193, 196–197, 207, 213,
217, 229, 235, 237–238, 242, 247–248,
250, 280, 283, 287, 290, 307n. 3, 357, See
also osu
household 142, 152, 279

Indians, War of the 73
Inini Territory 36
Inter-American Court for Human
Rights 35n. 2
Interior War 6, 269, 337, 346n. 6, See also
Civil War, Guerilla, Jungle Comando
intimacy 118, 122, 133, 209

Jews 56
Jungle Comando 293n. 18, See also Civil
War, Guerilla, Interior War

kabiten 69n. 24, 76n. 41, 100, 103, 150–151,
156, 163, 166, 168, 172, 298, See also
kabiteni
kabiteni 242, 244n. 11, 244–246, 248–251,
259n. 18, 259–260, 262–263, 290, See
also kabiten
Kali'na 22, 279
kina 62, 210, 227, See also tjina, taboo
kinship 2, 13, 21, 38, 121, 179, 184, 186, 204, 213,
221–222, 226, 230, 232, 240, 257–258,
291n. 17, 293n. 18
kulturu 270, 285–286, 293–296, 298–300
kumanti 332–335
Kumanti 55, 59, 73, 228
kunu 149, 209–210, 229, 244n. 9, 283, 294
kuutu 14, 92, 103, 171, 220, 226, 235, 242–243,
246, 249n. 12, 248–254, 263, 335, See
also political institutions, Consulte

land 5, 13, 48, 56n. 6, 66, 75–76, 78, 124, 134,
149, 153, 159–160, 185, 187–188, 193,
196–198, 230, 236, 244n. 9, 253, 255,
255n. 15, 258–259, 276, 360, 365
lanti 14, 153, 164, 172, 196, 208, 216, 220, 242,
244n. 8, 244–247, 250
Law 38, 123, 129, 140, 142, 149, 149n. 7, 152,
169–170, 173, 177, 188, 237n. 4, 239,
253–254, 258n. 17, 261, 263

Lawa 2, 20, 36, 40, 42, 55, 56n. 6, 74, 117–118,
121–122, 131, 135–136, 138, 141, 143, 148n. 6,
157–158, 183, 189, 191
loincloth 35, 72, 120, 124, 128n. 19, 128–129,
314n. 12
love 122, 125n. 14, 125–127, 129, 135–136, 138,
141, 152, 156, 163, 171, 173–174, 189, 357,
359, 367
Loweman 66, 69, 71, 73, 78, 290, See also
runaways
Lowesama 54
loweten 9, 59, 128, 140–141
Lycée 185, 188, 190, See also School

Mama Ndyuka x, 56–57, 59, 64, 66n. 21,
66–67, 69n. 24, 69–71, 73
man 7, 69–72, 77, 99, 101, 104–106, 117, 119,
121, 123–124, 125n. 11, 125n. 15, 125–128,
130, 133n. 28, 133–134, 135n. 32, 138–140,
142, 150–153, 156, 158n. 15, 166–167,
170–173, 194, 197n. 20, 205, 207, 208n. 2,
211, 213n. 5, 213–214, 226, 242, 251–252,
252n. 13, 262, 300, 316n. 14, 316–317, 323,
324n. 20, 354, 357, 363, 366
Maripasoula 36, 134, 137, 162n. 21, 345
Maroon bands 336–338, 347
Maroon cultural groups 307, 307n. 4
Maroon languages 83–85, 87–89, 91, 96,
108–109, 177n. 1, 288, 310, 341, 351, See
also code alternation, mixed code
marriage 64n. 19, 118, 121, 125, 129, 136, 141,
150–153, 155–156, 159, 171–173, 175,
300, 317
marronage 59, 117–121, 128, 132
Marronnage 46, 360, 364
matrilineage 15, 17, 149, 209, 211, 213n. 5, 227,
230, 237, 240, 244n. 9, 242–245, 247,
273, 277
mediumship 12, 15, 77, 157, 207–209
men 3, 5–9, 15–16, 18, 35–37, 39, 59, 75, 95,
97, 100, 104, 110, 117n. 1, 117–118, 119n. 4,
119–120, 122–124, 124n. 9, 127–128,
128n. 19, 128n. 21, 130, 133–134, 136,
138–140, 142, 142n. 44, 147–152, 156,
158–159, 160n. 18, 161n. 19, 160–165,
167–168, 170–173, 180, 183, 193, 218,
236–238, 242, 246–252, 262, 271, 278,
283, 286, 293, 295, 311, 314n. 12, 316,
322, 331, 337, 350, 353, 357, 361–362,
366–367, 369

378 INDEX

menstruation 17, 128n. 19
migration. See also undocumented
migrants, deportation
Migration 4, 13, 22, 83, 89, 156, 160, 164, 178,
269–270, 275, 336–337, 342
mining 4–5, 135, 270, 359
missionaries 8, 148n. 6, 270, 317
mixed code 99, 104, See also maroon
languages
Moengo 20, 24, 41, 47, 135, 178, 199, 271,
278n. 7, 276–280, 282–284, 284n. 11,
288n. 15, 286–289, 291, 293, 295, 298,
300, 339, 346n. 6
Money 20, 37, 39, 130, 139, 147, 153, 157, 161,
168, 170–172, 186, 193, 196, 206, 269–270,
282, 284, 311
monogamy 172
Moravian church 234
Moravian missionaries 84
mortuary rituals 234, See also funeral,
funerary rites, funerary cycle, funerary
rules
movies 287–289
Mungotapu 293n. 18, 293–294, 298–299, 301
music 44, 135–136, 158, 247, 271, 275, 277,
279, 282–284, 290, 293, 301, 307n. 2,
307–308, 309n. 5, 309–311, 313–314,
314n. 12, 319, 325n. 22, 322–328, 336n. 2,
330–340, 342, 344–346, 346n. 6, 355
musical genres 331–332, 334
musicians 330, 336–340, 347

nenseki 120, 131, 205, 229

Oath 61
Oath, God of the 55, 218
The Blood Oath 60–61
obia 15, 132, 165, 237, 237n. 6, 285, 332, See
also obiya
obia rules 237
obiaman 165
Obiya 60n. 11, 60–63, 66–67, 69–70, 70n. 26,
73, 208, 225, 227, 230, See also obia
kiibi pikin obiya 70, 70n. 26
Obiyaman 66, 74, 204, 207–208, 211, 213,
225, 229, 231
Papagadu Obiya 69n. 25
oracular medium 204

osu 8, 62n. 16, 107, 127–128, 149, 186–187,
191, 193, 196n. 18, 196–197, 197n.
19, 217, 279, 283, See also house
dede osu 283

pageant competitions 313
pangi IX, 15, 120, 124, 164n. 23, 290, 294, 301,
314, 320
pan-Maroon 6, 14, 178, 337
Papagadu IX, 55, 58, 67, 69, 69n. 25
Papaïchton 189, 197, 342
Paramaribo 6, 8, 20, 26–27, 35, 41, 44, 49,
51, 76–77, 79, 90, 96, 101, 106–108, 135,
135n. 32, 147, 149, 153, 156, 159–161,
161n. 19, 161n. 20, 173, 178n. 1, 178–179,
189, 207–208, 213, 235n. 3, 241–242, 268,
279–280, 284n. 11, 287–291, 307–310,
312n. 9, 312–313, 316, 316n. 14, 319,
324–325, 327, 336–339, 344–345, 347
parenthood 118, 122
performances 43, 179, 224, 228, 255, 272, 274,
284–285, 291, 296, 300, 314, 323, 326,
334, 338, 344
person 1, 4–5, 10, 12–17, 19–20, 22, 62,
93–94, 100, 107–108, 120, 124, 131, 150,
203, 205, 207–209, 211–212, 219–224,
226, 228–229, 231, 236–237, 239, 242,
245, 247, 249, 253–254, 270–271, 277,
281–282, 289–290, 294, 301, 315, 317, 345,
367, See also personhood
personhood 2, 6, 13, 15–16, 20, 204, 209, 232,
See also person
plantations 9, 55–56, 58–63, 71, 73, 78, 119,
132, 140, 179, 197, 254, 276, 317n. 17, 330,
365–366
poku 135, 137, 284, 346n. 6
political organization 258
politics 13–14, 14n. 5, 23, 25, 38, 147,
203–204, 229–232, 235, 246, 251, 253,
255, 258, 261, 281n. 10, 337, 352, 368,
See also politiki
political institutions 14n. 5, 264, See also
kuutu
political organization 258
politiki 14, 204, 237, 263, See also politics
polygamy 118, 121, 123, 127, 140, 152, 172–173,
175, 194
poverty 8, 126, 141, 157

INDEX

pregnancy 126, 148n. 4, 149n. 7, 152, 155, 160, 160n. 16, 170–173, 289

prostitution 162

puu baaka 268, 281–283

radio 113, 136, 287, 287n. 13, 309, 324–325, 338

rape 128, 149, 149n. 7, 152, 166, 259n. 18

Rastafari 338, 340, 341n. 3, 341–342, 347

refugees 62, 78, 161, 179, 179n. 2, 185, 288, 298, 339, See also runaway slaves

reggae 137, 324, 331, 337–340, 341n. 3, 341–343, 345

rules 4, 11, 14, 62, 78, 86, 94, 108, 129, 134, 151, 237n. 5, 237n. 6, 234–240, 245, 252–254, 261–263, 275, 284, 354

runaway slaves 21, 261, 290

Runaways 54, 63, 78

Saint Laurent du Maroni 6, 20, 147n. 2, 147–148, 150n. 8, 159, 162n. 21

Saint-Laurent-du-Maroni 35, 39, 49, 120n. 5, 134n. 30, 134–135, 137, 145, 177–179, 183, 339, See also Soolan

sani 62, 101, 130, 133, 141, 197n. 19, 205–206, 208n. 2, 213n. 5, 215, 217, 285, 294, 300–301

Santigoon 56, 76, 76n. 40

Sara x, 5, 8, 25, 57n. 7

school 96, 101, 124, 135, 155, 158–159, 164, 167, 171, 173, 175, 188–190, 192, 194, 280, 287, 289, 298, 346, 361–362, 368, 370, See also Lycée

self 32, 37, 122, 130, 179, 205, 211–212, 219, 221, 231, 253, 271, 274–277, 289, 296, 311, 313, 327, 331, 334, 347, 365

sex 119, 122–123, 125, 131, 134, 139, 143, 152, 155, 163–164, 196, 237n. 6, 239, 317n. 16, 357

sex distinction 120

sexual identity 118, 132

sexual practices 122, 127, 133, 133n. 28, 137, 162n. 21

sexuality 97, 117–119, 122, 124–125, 127, 130, 133–134, 136–137, 143

slave 2, 9, 54–55, 60, 60n. 11, 62, 84, 115, 229, 261, 304, 317, 357, 359, 364–366, 368–369

slavery 2, 13, 19, 21, 62, 73, 78, 87, 117–118, 132, 251, 255, 330, 347, 370

social housing 180–185, 188–190, 196–198, See also dwellings, Charbonniè re, La

Soolan 177, 179, 188–190, See also Saint-Laurent-du-Maroni

sorcery 133, 157–158, 161n. 19, 165

spirits 4–5, 8–9, 11–12, 15–16, 18–22, 32, 55, 58, 60n. 11, 66–67, 72, 73n. 34, 75, 157, 158n. 14, 166, 175, 204, 206, 210–212, 213n. 5, 213–215, 219–222, 224–225, 226n. 7, 231, 244n. 9, 253, 269–271, 273, 277, 283, 285–286, 290–292, 294, 296, 301, 317, 332, 335, 348

state 4, 9, 13, 14n. 5, 17–18, 24, 36, 99, 158n. 15, 167, 172, 177–180, 184, 193, 196, 210, 225, 234, 239, 253, 258n. 17, 259n. 18, 255–262, 264, 274, 278, 280, 284, 332, 345

nation state 4, 14

Stoelmanseiland 148, 150n. 8, 157, 158n. 15, 158–159

subjectivity 13, 30, 203–205

suicide 140, 172

sweli 61, 132, 134, 218

Sweli 54, 61n. 15, 61–62, 72, 73n. 34, 73–75

Sweli Gadu 54, 61n. 15, 61–62, 72, 73n. 34, 73–75

taboo 11, 18, 133–134, 138, 153, 238–239, See also tijna

Tapanahoni IX, 2, 5, 9, 20, 36, 38, 41, 47, 55, 56n. 6, 56–57, 59, 61, 66n. 20, 72n. 31, 71–74, 76, 135–136, 138, 141, 183, 189, 282, 332

Tata Ogii 57, 71n. 30, 75n. 39, 76n. 40, 71–78

technology 271, 288–289, 334

teenage 152, 163, 172–173

tembe x, 255, 351, 353, 356–357, 360, 362–370

timbe 125, 125n. 13, 127, 132

tjina 237n. 6, 237–239, See also Taboo

traditional art 6

traditional authorities 4, 136, 273, 280

treaty 54, 56, 57n. 7, 59, 64, 64n. 19, 73, 244, 260–261, 310, 317

Tropenmuseum 28, 42–43, 49

undocumented migrants 184, See also migration, deportation

Upper Suriname   234, 239, 241, 243, 252n. 13, 320

urban   4, 6–7, 13–14, 18, 20, 89–90, 96–97, 100–101, 110, 131, 134, 138–139, 143, 148, 150, 158, 164, 164n. 23, 168, 174, 174n. 27, 178n. 1, 177–180, 182, 184–186, 188, 190, 193, 195, 198, 268, 270, 274–276, 279, 287–289, 294, 299, 308–309, 311

Urban   287, 330–331, 334–338, 344, 346

Urbanization   331, 337

video   268–269, 288, 290–291, 295, 300, 307, 314n. 11, 324–325, 332, 338, 342, 343n. 4, 345, 346n. 5, 346n. 6, 346–347, 347n. 7

village   IX, 4–7, 7n. 3, 9, 13, 16, 36, 41, 55, 56n. 6, 59, 60n. 11, 61n. 14, 62n. 16, 62n. 17, 66n. 20, 67n. 23, 69n. 24, 66–70, 70n. 27, 72, 72n. 31, 76n. 40, 74–77, 83–84, 90, 92, 94–99, 101–104, 107, 117, 119, 124, 127, 127n. 18, 129–131, 134, 136–137, 139, 141, 141n. 43, 147n. 1, 147–148, 148n. 4, 150, 152–153, 156–157, 159–160, 161n. 19, 167, 171, 175, 188, 191, 207, 210–211, 211n. 4, 220, 226–230, 234–235, 237n. 5, 237–238, 249n. 12, 240–252, 260, 262, 268, 268n. 1, 273, 275, 279, 281–285, 289–290, 293n. 18, 293–294, 298–300, 314n. 11, 317, 320, 322, 335, 342, 345, 361

village council   245, 248, 250–251

village authorities   208, 273, 282

violence   2, 22, 76–77, 127, 140, 181, 245, 252, 259, 261–264, 275, 289

wage labour   117

wealth   127, 230, 270

Winti   25, 205

wisiman   55

witchcraft   5, 9, 38, 55, 57, 71, 74, 76, 76n. 40, 161n. 19, 205, 226–227, 230, 270n. 3, 285–286, 288

women   5–9, 15–18, 35, 39, 41, 59, 62n. 16, 75, 77, 95, 97, 99–101, 107–108, 110, 117n. 1, 117–118, 119n. 4, 119–120, 122–124, 124n. 9, 127–128, 128n. 19, 128n. 21, 130–131, 133–134, 136–137, 139–140, 141n. 42, 141–142, 142n. 44, 147n. 1, 148n. 4, 147–150, 152–153, 153n. 11, 156–157, 161n. 19, 159–165, 167–168, 170–174, 174n. 27, 180, 184, 186, 192, 214, 216, 219–221, 246, 248, 250, 262, 271, 275, 278, 283, 285n. 12, 285–286, 293, 295, 307, 309, 311, 314, 317, 317n. 17, 321–322, 350, 353–354, 359–360, 362, 365–367, 369

young Maroons   336, 339–340, 342–343, 346–348

youth   162, 307, 320, 324, 337–338, 345–346

Printed in the United States
By Bookmasters